PRAIRIE STATE BOOKS

In conjunction with the Illinois Center for the Book, the University of Illinois Press is reissuing in paperback works of fiction and nonfiction that are, by virtue of authorship and/or subject matter, of particular interest to the general reader in the state of Illinois.

A list of books in the series appears at the end of this volume.

Publication of this book and others in the Prairie State Books program was supported in part by a generous grant from John Nuveen and Company of Chicago.

ACROSS SPOON RIVER

Edgar Lee Masters in 1915 at the time
Spoon River Anthology was published

ACROSS SPOON RIVER

An Autobiography

BY EDGAR LEE MASTERS

With an Introduction by Ronald Primeau

UNIVERSITY OF ILLINOIS PRESS

Urbana and Chicago

Manufactured in the United States of America
P   5   4   3   2   1

This book is printed on acid-free paper.

Library of Congress Cataloging-in-Publication Data

Masters, Edgar Lee, 1868–1950.
    Across Spoon River : an autobiography / by Edgar Lee Masters :
with an introduction by Ronald Primeau.
        p.   cm. – (Prairie State books)
    Reprint, with new introd. Originally published: New York : Farrar
& Rinehart, c1936.
    ISBN 0-252-06051-2 (pb : acid-free paper)
    1. Masters, Edgar Lee, 1868–1950—Biography.   2. Authors,
American—20th century—Biography.   I. Title.   II. Series.
PS3525.A83Z463   1991
811'.52—dc20
[B]   90-11005
                                                                CIP

Introduction

BY RONALD PRIMEAU

Across Spoon River appeared in 1936—over two decades after *Spoon River Anthology*. Masters was sixty-six years old and had been living in New York for thirteen years, a time he called "the most peaceful" in his life. The world-wide reputation of the "Spoon River poet" had cooled down, and for some time critics had been impatient with his uninspired verse and his habit of writing too quickly. In 1935 *Vachel Lindsay: A Poet in America* had been praised as his best book in two decades; four years earlier his *Lincoln: The Man* (1931) had produced great controversy. Recognition of the autobiography was at best mixed. Few reviewers were sensitive to his insights on the difficulties of finding one's voice as a writer in turn-of-the-century America.

Across Spoon River is a fragmentary work with at least a hint of a promised sequel that never appeared. The title is meant to guide us across the Spoon River region Masters used as the microcosmic setting for much of his work. For the student of American literature, the book serves as a reminder that Masters is one of those transitional figures with one foot in the nineteenth century and the other on the path to what we now think of as the modern period. The contemporary feel of *Spoon River Anthology* (1915) makes us forget that Masters was around to compose poems on the deaths of Browning and Whitman.

Masters had a lifelong interest in biography. From his early plays, *Benedict Arnold* (1893) and *Maximilian* (1902), to *Mark Twain: A Portrait* (1938), biographical studies were foremost among his publications. In the thirties in addition to his stud-

vii

ies of Abraham Lincoln, Vachel Lindsay, and Mark Twain, he published works on Walt Whitman and Ralph Waldo Emerson. Just a year before *Across Spoon River,* he presented his theory of biography, "Histories of the American Mind," in *The American Mercury* (July 1935). Popular opinion, Masters contends, is generally shaped by "manias" that cause people to be "wildly for a man or wildly against him, changing in a day from one extreme to another." Thus what he calls a "vast mendacity" is internalized as it "gets into our books" and here the biographer must enter to set the record straight: "Meanwhile someone is keeping a journal, as Emerson did, in which there is a sane record of men and affairs. That becomes a correction in later days." *Across Spoon River* was Masters's "sane record" of his own experiences, the correction he wanted later days to value. He didn't mind at all being thought of as what he called one of those "obstinate and pugnacious spirits who could not bear to see history falsified." He thought the good biographer should get the historical figures out of "the dust bins" and "clean them" in order "to make them rallying points of cultural progress, forces of correction and readjustment and inspirations to a wisdom which reshapes." Such was the renown of his own *Vachel Lindsay.* Then again, he added, "some of the gilt may be taken off figures too much gilded." Such was the controversy of his *Lincoln: The Man.* The struggles, the literary combat required to set the country straight again formed "the idea behind the best biography." So how did Masters do as combatant-demystifier-biographer of Edgar Lee Masters? How does one write autobiography as corrective?

Across Spoon River is precisely that kind of pugnacious corrective—an intensely personal self-portrait, highly opinionated and digressive. Masters begins at his birth in Garnett, Kansas (a year off on the date, not bad by more contemporary standards), and moves up to 1917. For reasons that aren't entirely clear, he chooses to take his autobiography only as far as his forty-ninth year, including his growing up in central Illinois and his move to Chicago, where he established a career in law and became involved in politics. Throughout these years he struggled with society and the workday world in an effort to make himself into a poet.

He divides the chronology into roughly six periods. (1) Everything goes back to the pastoral scenes on the Masters' farm in Menard County, which he loved but where he felt "longings and griefs for something that seemed far off." (2) When he was fifteen, his teacher Mary Fisher introduced him to books and culture. (3) At twenty-three he moved to Chicago, which carried him "out of overintrospection" and brought him "face to face with people." (4) There followed a long period of involvement with William Jennings Bryan and the agrarian movement. This was also a time of "omnivorous" reading, the period when his "Shelleyan studies" moved forward. (5) Then there were the affairs—most notably with "Deirdre"—along with the urge to unite celebrated in "Amphimixis" and the longings he called "the woman hope." (6) Finally there was the serialization of *Spoon River* in *The American Mercury* under a pseudonym, the world-wide notoriety after the book was published, and the next two decades summarized in the Epilogue.

As a boy Masters discovered early that it wouldn't be easy to find his way. He watched with indignation as his father endured widespread philistinism about politics and religion. "The attitudes of some leading citizens toward my father," he recalls, "helped to solidify my opposition to the churches and to the religion they preached." He watched these men of "small natures and inveterate prejudices" and the "village ignorance of everything really good and beautiful" make a deep imprint that didn't fade when he moved to Chicago. He saw his father's liberalism as a "great blessing," teaching him that "joy in life" was still possible in the wake of "dour Puritanism," ignorance, and worship of practicality. These early experiences stimulated his desire to be a poet and prompted his lifelong desire to follow his "solitary independent nature." "I wanted to be by myself," he would often say, and he often was precisely that in his views on politics, religion, literature, and the law.

There is poignance, as well as the well-known stubbornness, in this self-portrait of the early years. At twenty, after working at various dead-end jobs (printer, telephone operator), trying to educate himself, and encountering more or less continuous disapproval because he was expected to be doing work worthier than writing poetry, Masters hoped to attend Knox College. Ashamed that he wasn't ready for college entrance, he spent a year living in Galesburg, reading everything in sight, bursting with excitement about classical literature, and attending lectures on campus. "Everything was magical," he says. But his father prevailed upon him to return home to clerk in his law office. (It's curious also how Masters did the same violence to himself. For example, he loved music but quit lessons because he "didn't like the notes.") Thus began a long series of jobs in which he saw himself as a "wage slave," too tired at night to read and write. In 1903 he became a partner in a criminal law practice. (This is one of the clandestine or circuitous sections of the story: Masters never mentions his partner, Clarence Darrow, by name.) All the while Masters had a burning desire to write a play successful enough to permit him to retire. He would become a full-time writer—only much later, while writing Spoon River poems at Spring Lake, Michigan.

Across Spoon River might startle readers with its bluntness, its indecorously overpersonal and almost coarse unguardedness. We might see self-pity in "no great luck ever saw me," pathos in "my parents didn't care for me," and perhaps a classic struggle with a father who looked upon him often "with silent regret." Some of this is, of course, a part of growing up: Masters the adolescent feeling his parents saw him as "a kind of wonder bred amid their quiet crew and a problem past solving." Or maybe some of it is a part of growing old: "I longed to escape the life of a pack horse." At times he seems misanthropic: "All human disaster comes from the weakness or perfidy of those who are in one's life." Most of the abrasive talk is about the difficulty of making it as a poet and the incompatibility of his two careers.

Masters saw his early upbringing as a hindrance to his development as a writer. Keats, he notes, had "far more inspiring friends and far richer cultural influences." In one of those caustic moments he quips, "My sister was not a Dorothy Wordsworth." "No one came and discovered me," he laments. Or the clincher: "No poet in English or American history ever had a harder life than mine was in the beginning in Lewistown or among a people whose flesh and whose vibrations were better calculated to poison, pervert, and even to kill a sensitive nature." After going to Chicago to escape "village spites, the melancholy of the country and bad will that follows me everywhere," he finds the city is no mecca. Though he was later to change his mind, at first Chicago was "the wrong place for poetry." It was there that Judge Kenesaw M. Landis told him he could learn to "write opinions with one hand and poetry with the other," a plan that had its ups and downs. The problem was colleagues who considered poetry a waste of time or, at best, effeminate. There he felt "the swords of the Lilliputians shot around my steps and tangled them," and he complains often that he could have moved forward with poetry faster and sooner had he been "moving in a circle which understood and loved it." It is clear from *Across Spoon River* that up to 1917 at least Masters seldom felt understood or loved. He saw his "talent for writing wasting away under the attritions of the city." On the whole he thought of himself as a Walter Scott who "wrote under a pseudonym while he was a lawyer and a sheriff." He thus describes himself as two persons: the first "annoyed, fatigued, even degraded by inferior human contacts" and the second "existing aloof and untouched by demoralizations." Even at its best, "life was scrappy and unmanageable."

Long under the influence of his father's liberal politics, Masters was committed to what he called "the Democratic creed of 1896 and 1900" where it was "Americanism and Democracy as against European domination and Toryism." His devotions to Bryan, agrarianism, and populism are well known. He found a common concern with humanity in works by More, Bacon, Milton, Mill, and Shelley. His early years in Chicago, he later recalled, were "as Milton lived, fighting for liberty and justice." In 1900 he published *Maximilian,* a play about imperialist Mexico. At thirty-four he was well known in Chicago as the author of numerous constitutional articles and political essays as well as a pamphlet, *The Constitution and Our Insular Possessions.* Meanwhile he took on law cases in defense of people and causes consistent with beliefs that were out of favor. Disillusion accompanied much of this, though. He had hoped that Bryan would bring the "beginning of a changed America." He had been "full of wonder, hope, and excitement," and when Bryan and the cause lost, it was hard "to take up life again after." By 1910 he felt a skepticism about a "new day of justice in American politics." At times he thought he could see through people "with penetration," while at other times he saw himself as "a dreamer who doesn't see the tangles." Woodrow Wilson, he felt, had "ruined America for years to come." As it had been for so many people, the World War was a turning point—destroying "the era out of which *Spoon River* came." Though in moving to New York Masters retreated as much from politics as from the law, he never abandoned the combative unguarded commitment to what he called "a moral responsibility" for his time.

Although he felt distracted and almost assaulted by the workday routine, Masters saw the value of a poet's interaction with apparent obstacles. "If I had lived a cloistered life I should not have learned much besides books," he says in a moment of rare resignation. In spite of the difficulties, he felt that day to day he was gaining what a writer most needs: "vast understanding of human nature and of the world." He saw writing his autobiography as a chance to "live it all over and sort it out"—an experience "like being resurrected from the dead" that would allow him to make peace with "the sacrifices and the shame endured for poetry."

To work through obstacles, Masters developed some rituals. He read on the sly, poetry stuffed in drawers or tucked behind textbooks and law journals; when he did squeeze out some free time, he would write with "exhaustless energy" and "with such ease" that he didn't realize how creative bursts could "sap the life forces." In "The Genesis of Spoon River" (1933) he speaks of a "flame" igniting after months (really years) of exploring, and he loved the times (though they were rare) when in the "rapture of writing" he found "a balanced level of creative forces." It was a nervous energy, an endless search to "fill a void," long evening writing sessions after consuming much coffee at dinner ("to spur my falling spirits" after a day at the office), only to be revived by cold baths in the morning. He speaks of bursts of inspiration, times when he would write from "a reservoir that seemed exhaustless," when it seemed that "swarms of powers and beings were watching me and protesting yet inspiring me to go on." In the middle of the night he would experience a "hypertensive state of clairvoyance and clairaudience." In these moments he scarcely knew who he was and "the inner core of things became the exterior of things and nothing seemed real." Always he would be brought back by the daily routine, and the material for *Spoon River Anthology* would be set aside to incubate. Later he could go back to use what he calls "my long-gathered material." Always there was the ambivalence about whether intrusions were creative or debilitating. For every decloistering educative life experience there were several "visitations of serpents of fire that flew about my head and at last poisoned every moment."

Masters's account of his personal life is dominated as well by what commentators have seen as womanizing and what he preferred to call "the woman hope." In *Across Spoon River* he says he was "directed toward satisfaction" more or less from the age of seven or eight when an older girl had "explained the technique of love-making." Thus begins the book's lengthy and detailed recalling of amorous adventures. There were Lucy, Zueline, Anne, and long accounts of "Deirdre." "Women in general expect that lighthearted adulteries are carried on behind their backs," he maintained. "They do not care so long as they do not know about them, so long as their own forward positions as wives are not affected." This is not, however, a kiss-and-tell book. The brashness of the stories overshadows philosophical and aesthetic longings traced back to teenage years: an idealism, a longing for oneness embodied in images of female beauty and sexual union. "There grew up in me," he notes, "a passion for intellectual beauty fed by the poems of Shelley, by such poems as 'Epipsychidion.'" This influence is strong in "Amphimixis" (written in 1938 though not published until 1975), a poem that epitomizes the theme of sexual urge prominent in the autobiography as well as in *Invisible Landscapes* (1935) and *The Serpent in the Wilderness* (1938). In *Across Spoon River* sex is a metaphor for everything seeking unity. It is what Cleanthus Trilling from *Spoon River Anthology* had called "the urge to unite," an image for literary influence creating new unities out of separate identities. The process of "amphimixis" is itself sexual union achieved through "urge." He calls it "The Secret Power" or "God—which hour by endless hour/Stirs plasm and awakes it, which conceived/Sex as the way for life to be retrieved/From floating jelly." Masters's assessment in the Epilogue is one of his most lucid self-pronouncements: "I divine the operation of the cosmic mind in the love of men and women, and hence I have identified a beloved woman with the mysteries of creative beauty, with influences and magnetisms, with summons from afar. So identifying her, I have placed all the women in whom I was deeply interested in a role that flesh and blood cannot often fulfill."

Masters's classical training led him frequently to Latin and Greek derivations of words. For example, what he calls "influences and magnetisms" reflect his striving for greatness through the influx of past riches, a flow he entered through his reading. *Across Spoon River* is dominated by lists of what he read and accounts of how he hoped to transform what he "digested" into his own poetry. Just after high school he spent a good deal of time with Anne, the daughter of a clergyman whose two libraries were "thrown open." "I tried to read everything in both libraries," he recalls, "with the result that I soon became badly stuffed, and had to rest to digest the material." From "Learning to Write," an early essay published in 1889, through the autobiography Masters saw reading as a neoclassical imitation for the purpose of liberation, an influx of power and energy from the past that could be transformed through a kind of "amphimixis" into a new creation. He read widely with the enthusiasm and vehemence one has for the forbidden.

Across Spoon River is a fascinating account of the growth of a poet's mind. Shelley, Goethe, and the Greeks were prominent in his reading, as were Whitman, Emerson, and Browning. Masters always had strong opinions: "Wordsworth not Pope, Thackeray rather than Fielding. George Eliot rather than Sterne." He read Milton "again and again" and Blackstone's *Commentaries* because Byron had. Always there was the pleasure of the hard-to-get. While teaching school briefly, Masters hid Homer "behind a large geography" book while students got their lessons. Arriving in Chicago he noted that a head "swarming with Chaucer and Keats and Petrarch" meant nothing to "egotistical experts in their line." There he read Racine and Tolstoy with his Uncle Will and at the age of thirty was especially drawn to Arnold's "Power of righteousness," the beauty of women in Poe, the divinities of Shelley. He read all of Ibsen in 1901 and discovered as well the "refreshing realism" of *Sister Carrie*. He was drawn to Emily Dickinson, Shakespeare, and "all the English poets," insisting that *Domesday Book* (1920) was written before he ever heard of Browning's *The Ring and the Book*. In rapturous torture looking at the sky on the Masters' farm, he celebrated Swedenborg and proclaimed that America needed the magnanimous man rather than the falsification and enervation promoted by Christianity.

The Epilogue resembles a commonplace book in its listing of volumes Masters owned and diary entries reexamined. In all, he sees six periods of influence and overcomings of influence. (1) He discovered the poetry of Robert Burns in school and read the classics with Mary Fisher. (2) At nineteen he read Spencer, Huxley, and Hulme and wanted to be a metaphysician. (3) While living on the Knox College campus in that "magical" year 1889–90, he absorbed the riches of Greek literature. (4) In his "Shelleyan and Platonic" period he embraced agrarianism and argued against imperialism. (5) As a lawyer he read widely and surreptitiously, slowly accumulating work that would become *Spoon River Anthology*. (6) After *Spoon River* there was the wide reading that fed the corrective biographer and combative critic who emerged in the thirties. In all, Masters is Harold Bloom's "strong reader," at once angst-ridden and nourished by the riches of the past. Rejecting many of the influences of his own time, he preferred to leapfrog back to Whitman, to Goethe, to Greece. Perhaps heeding Emerson's warnings about overinfluence and embattled even against the notion of influence itself, he proclaims in the major chord of the autobiography: "I was the chief influence of my own career."

Over fifty years after its first publication, *Across Spoon River* will appeal to the quite different and varied interests of our time. This is not one of the great American autobiographies, nor was it ever intended to be. No one is likely to find the prose very graceful or the story telling captivating. Masters never makes clear why he chose to stop the story in 1917 and then breeze through the next two decades in an Epilogue. However, despite the work's lack of intrinsic aesthetic value and its acknowledged fragmentariness, it addresses with considerable skill several concerns of contemporary critical theory.

Above all the book is a lucid and honest and sometimes painful account of growing up in the late nineteenth century in a small town on the Illinois prairie. While this is not always a pretty picture and is told from only one perspective, the story is a valuable addition to our increasingly multidisciplinary study of Midwestern culture. Also, there is the draw of an often intriguing and sometimes controversial self-portrait by a famous poet, novelist, and commentator on American history and politics. And there is still the persistent allure of learning how *Spoon River Anthology* was conceived and coaxed through its incubation, and more on how that still-astonishing work dazzled the literary world. Menacing questions linger about why Masters would never again come close to the achievement of that one book. (Or would he?) Alongside Masters's essay "The Genesis of Spoon River," this account provides clues for our ambivalent fascination with authorial intention.

Across Spoon River is likely to be read today with considerable interest by reader-response critics and students of "the creative process." These self-portraits of the "omnivorous" and "surreptitious" reader—self-educated in literature as he hid Homer, Goethe, and Shelley behind law books—will take on new significance in reception theory and intertextual criticism. The last third of the book chronicles ELM the developing writer as a strong reader who sought space for his own poems in the evolving or entrenched literary canons. Masters wanted, in fact, to rewrite the canons. He thought scholars, critics, and editors had somehow gotten it all wrong, and nowhere is he more combative than in this book's Epilogue.

Across Spoon River often reads like a self-interview and in its most revealing moments speaks to questions about the psychology of creativity—principally about how Masters courted the muse while researching legal cases. Most of the time he thought the law and literature were like "oil and water" for him, but there is considerable material here also about his work habits, the influence of the environment, and time management. In *The Creative Process* Brewster Ghiselin has described a recursive pattern of "overstriving," conscious release, and incubation in the creative habits of painters, musicians, scientists, and poets. Masters's striving was often tortuous, his conscious release the distractions of work, women, and song, and his incubation the long gestation of that one big anthology that he acknowledges could have been an even bigger bouquet. Ghiselin speaks of the artist's "secret efforts . . . induced and focused by intense conscious effort." The more mundane details of daily routine in the law office match Ghiselin's demythologizing of the creative mystique: "Though the tension of conscious striving tends to overdetermine psychic activity, to narrow it and fix it, such tension gives stimulation and direction to the unconscious activity which goes on after the tension is released. The desired developments are usually delayed for some time, during which presumably something like incubation is going on and attention may be profitably turned to something else. Then without warning the solution or germinal insight may appear" (p. 29). Masters didn't think of the law as stimulating poetry, and he didn't see the often merciless delays as anything but frustration. Nonetheless, the ritualized interactions between what he considered nine-to-five busywork and creativity after hours explain some of the problematic contours of Masters's public life. Did his office appointment book provide creative release or did it merely distract the poet and frustrate what might have been?

Beyond its interest for reception theory and the study of the creative process, *Across Spoon River* is an important and so-far-neglected critical document in its own right. In it, Masters presents a strong minority opinion at a time when American literary canons had been realigned away from Emerson and Whitman and toward Eliot, Pound, and the imagists. He thought it typical that in America writers would be neglected, their "essential selves" overlooked. He took heart in the observation that "Americans do not come to a possession of their gifts" as early as the English do. Masters saw *Across Spoon River* as a corrective to the misguided criticism and politics of his time. He felt that the Eastern establishment had a stranglehold on publishers, reviewers, and academics; that Midwestern writers were afforded only qualified acceptance; that what he called "American Philistinism" (and elsewhere a literary "Cinderella complex") had skewed perspective away from what was solid and worthwhile in the American tradition.

The book holds up as well as an interesting account of his contacts with prominent American writers spanning several decades. His opinions were bold and unequivocal. Lindsay was "America's greatest lyric poet," Dreiser a great man but a "confused handler of words," Sandburg's "Chicago" an "interesting extravagance." Whitman he judged America's Hesiod with "someone yet to arise the Homer."

Masters's response to reviews of his own books and to the general critical climate of his time is equally brash. He would quote warmly reviews that praised his work but felt that critics were mostly "erudite schoolmen" who measured poetry too much on past models. (He didn't mind erudition, though, when John Cowper Powys called him "the reincarnation of Chaucer." His one worry: "how was I to sustain that role which had been thrust upon me?") In 1912 he thought *Poetry* was haughty and amateurish—a view that would change. After *Spoon River* he lived with the fear that critics would be out "sharpening their pencils" for any sequel. At the time of *Spoon River* he felt that criticism was at a "low level" due to the "Knickerbocker Schools" that had taken over after the death of Whitman. He felt that critics had missed the Uranian as well as the Dionysian Venus in his works and weren't much interested in his attempts to "interpret and memorialize Illinois" as in *The Great Valley* (1916). (With candor he adds that he too wished the poems in that volume were better.) Overall, he saw his own poems in the "two strains" of realism and mysticism. *Spoon River* was the product of his penetrating "cyclopean eye" while with his "dreaming eye" he wrote poems like "The Star" and "The Loom."

In "The Poetry Revival of 1914," published in *American Mercury,* July 1932, Masters attacked poets and publishers who produce "correct verse without inspiration." At the same time he praised Stedman's *American Anthology* (1900), which called for poetry "native to the American scene." In "The Genesis of Spoon River" (1933) he complained that "poetry had been taken over" by "fourth raters" and "clerical sonneteers and lyricists." Petit the Poet's wisecrack in *Spoon River* about versifiers who prefer trivial formalities "while Homer and Whitman roared in the pines" set the tone for continued attacks. In an interview in 1938, he told August Derleth that critics were "little men all mixed up with ideologies," and he complained to Robert VanGelder in the *New York Times* (1942) that modern poets had "no principles, no individuality, no moral code, and no roots." Masters felt that his greatest achievement was to live counter to those developments; to live with imagination as his "controlling influence" would be the "deepest secret" of his nature: "I have not lived among facts of economics, among buildings of brick and mortar, among the concrete matters of worldly success." Despite some regrets, a certain amount of self-pity, and perhaps more candor than most readers might want, his mood in the end is conviction.

It is valuable, of course, to read *Across Spoon River* alongside other accounts of the poet's life. Of particular interest are the "insider" versions of his sons Hardin (*Edgar Lee Masters*, 1978) and Hilary (*Last Stands*, 1982) and the biographical poems in *The Wind around the Moon and Other Poems* (1986) by his daughter, Marcia Lee Masters. Each has its own perspective, and, when controversies settle, the self-portrait has its own intrigue. Worthwhile, too, is comparison of *Across Spoon River* and biographical essays Masters published between 1897 and 1935 and the partially autobiographical *The Sangamon*, which he contributed to the Rivers of America series in 1942. In comparison with all these other accounts, the angle in *Across Spoon River* is oblique. As subject and teller of the tale, this ELM emerges on every page as anguished, driven, unlucky, split between the literal and the imaginative. The persona is a courtroom combatant, analyzing and defending himself against the unstated accusation hovering over his poetic career: "Why aren't you better?" He saw his readers as continuous with the "sick and feverish people" who during World War I rushed to get "the truth told before it was too late." He would tell that truth—the truth about how he was pulled away from poetry by the stultifying demands of the daily workplace, about the people around him who weren't challenging or stimulating, about bad fortune and poor environment early in life and about poor family circumstances. This is a chronicle of survival, a statement of how he was nearly "obliterated" and could have been a much better writer with luck. How much of this is accurate and how much is a fictional rendering of felt struggles will never be decided. Clearly, this apologia is not intended to win new friends or reassure old ones.

Though Masters traded the small town for the city for good

when he was twenty-three, in many ways he never left at all. Surely the solitude and longings of the prairie never left him. What he called "soul fatigue" drove him out—the loneliness of the small town, the melancholy introspection of life in the country. Several posthumously published poems show that to the end he continued to be haunted by an image of himself flying a kite on the lonely prairie, with urgent and unfulfilled longings reaching skyward. In these silences he always felt himself "choking" and yet he was ambivalently grateful for the longing to go beyond the complacency he held in such contempt. "All my life I have endured loneliness," he recalls, and yet that loneliness reached for eternity and the mysterious "realms that lie below life's surface." The realization that people in small towns and in cities have the same nature led him to explore the fears, the longings, the ultimate loneliness of the grave in *Spoon River Anthology*. He closes the autobiography on that note of solitude. "I had lost everything except my health and my concentration of mind," he reflects while living alone at the Chelsea hotel. Somehow the circle of imagination connecting this reminiscence and his early years on the prairie would remain unbroken: "All I have to do is close my eyes and I can look at the Mason County hills and see my kite high among the clouds."

BIBLIOGRAPHICAL NOTE

Works by Edgar Lee Masters are mentioned with dates in the text.

Barnstone, Willis. Introduction. *The New Spoon River*. New York: Macmillan, 1924.

Bloom, Harold. *A Map of Misreading*. New York: Oxford, 1975.

Burgess, Charles E. "Edgar Lee Masters: The Lawyer as Writer." In *The Vision of This Land*. Ed. John E. Hallwas and Dennis J. Reader. Essays in Literature. Macomb, Ill.: Western Illinois University, 1976, pp. 55–73.

————. Introduction to *The Sangamon*. Urbana: University of Illinois Press, 1988.

————. "Masters and Some Mentors." *Papers on Language and Literature* 10 (1974), 175–201.

Claytor, Gertrude. "Edgar Lee Masters in the Chelsea Years." *Princeton University Chronicle* 14 (Autumn 1952), 1–29.

Derleth, August. *Three Literary Men: A Memoir of Sinclair Lewis, Sherwood Anderson, and Edgar Lee Masters*. New York: Candlelight Press, 1963, pp. 39–56.

Flanagan, John T. *Edgar Lee Masters: The Spoon River Poet and His Critics*. Metuchen, N.J.: Scarecrow Press, 1974.

Ghiselin, Brewster, ed. *The Creative Process*. New York: New American Library, Mentor, 1952.

Hansen, Harry. *Midwest Portraits*. New York: Harcourt, Brace, 1923.

Hartley, Lois. *Spoon River Revisited*. Ball State Monographs, no. 1. Muncie, Indiana: Ball State Teachers College, 1963.

Masters, Hardin. *Edgar Lee Masters: A Biographical Sketchbook about a Famous Author*. Rutherford, N.J.: Fairleigh Dickinson University Press, 1978.

Masters, Hilary. *Last Stands: Notes from Memory*. Boston: David R. Godine, 1982.

Masters, Marcia Lee. *The Wind around the Moon and Other Poems*. Georgetown, Calif.: Dragon's Teeth Press, 1986.

Primeau, Ronald. *Beyond Spoon River: The Legacy of Edgar Lee Masters*. Austin: University of Texas Press, 1981.

————. "Shelley and Edgar Lee Masters' 'Amphimixis.'" *Old Northwest* 1 (1975), 141–57.

Tietjens, Eunice. *The World at My Shoulder*. New York: Macmillan, 1938.

Wrenn, John H., and Margaret M. Wrenn. *Edgar Lee Masters*. Boston: Twayne, 1983.

ACROSS SPOON RIVER

Chapter I

I WAS BORN AT GARNETT, KANSAS, ON AUGUST 23, 1869, AT the hour of four o'clock in the morning. My father and mother had gone there from Illinois shortly after their marriage, where in fact they lived just long enough to spend their honeymoon. Then they returned to Illinois when I was a year old. My memory of the world begins when I was three years old, or perhaps four years old, and naturally it is all of Illinois. My mother told me that I was a solemn child, and never smiled until I was handed to my grandmother Masters at the front door of the farmhouse upon the arrival of herself and my father from Kansas. My grandmother, a passionate lover of children, and the mother of thirteen of her own, lifted the veil from my face; and as she cooed and laughed my face broke into a smile. I was her first grandchild, and her favorite to the end of her days.

My grandfather Masters's farm was in Menard County, Illinois, five miles or so from Petersburg, the county seat; and about seven from New Salem of Lincoln fame, which by the time my grandfather bought this farm in 1847 was a vanished village. Jack Kelso, the fisherman, may have been still living there at this time; but I am not sure about it. The Masters family was planted in Virginia sometime in the eighteenth century by Knottley Masters, who was born in England or Wales, and being driven from home by a stepmother went to an island off the coast of Wales with his sister, where they lived in poverty like aboriginals. One day a sailing vessel passed the island, the master of which was attracted by the smoke of Knottley's campfire. He landed and took Knottley and the sister on board and sailed away with them to Virginia. I got

this story from Robert S. Masters in 1927, when I visited
Overton County, Tennessee. This man was a great-grandson
of Knottley. He also wrote me about his grandfather Hillory,
or Hilary, Masters, who was born in that part of Virginia
which became in 1790 Wythe County; and this tallied with
what my grandfather had told me as a youth, including what
he said of Hilary's children and career. Hilary was a soldier
in the Revolution. He moved to Overton County in 1804 and
died there.

My grandfather's father, named Thomas, was born in Virginia on August 1, 1787. He went to Tennessee with Hilary
and pursued a life of farming until 1829, and there he acquired several hundred acres of land. This he sold to move to
Illinois, where he lived until his death in 1847, bequeathing
to my grandfather $600 which he used to purchase land in
Menard County.

Through the unearned increment and by stock raising my
grandfather became very well off. At his best he was worth
perhaps $80,000. The War Between the States helped him to a
fortune; and when I came on the scene his house was a place
of peace and abundance. His education, I fancy, was meager;
but he had read to some extent. He loved the poetry of Burns;
and being a devout man, the Bible was his constant study. His
manner of speaking and writing and saying prayers was formed
out of the Bible—the King James version of the Bible. In a
voice of medium depth and with a tone of habitual tenderness
he commanded a patriarchal eloquence. He spoke with fluency
at Concord Church and elsewhere on public occasions, always
moving his pioneer listeners to tears. For he was a man of
profound feeling, to whom man's pilgrimage on earth and
his end in the grave constituted a mysterious tragedy, which
nevertheless had been turned to hope and gifted with immor-
tality by the grace of the blood of Jesus. If anyone would
catch the poetry of his prayers and his little talks at Concord

Church, they may read some of Lincoln's most tender words, such as those he spoke on the occasion of his departure from Springfield. Until I wrote *Children of the Market Place* I did not know that Lincoln's voice was high keyed. I supposed that it was deep like my grandfather's, seeing that their use of words was similar.

My grandfather kept up with the politics of the country by reading many newspapers—these and the Bible were his daily occupation. He was fifty-seven years of age when I was born, and I never knew him to work on the farm beyond such things as plowing a potato patch, or mending a fence, or helping to break a colt. My grandmother mildly hinted that he never had worked to hurt himself. Somehow I grew up to look upon him as a farmer gentleman. His fine gold watch, his carriage, his broadcloth suit, his good linen, and the setting of his home with its comforts and its order seemed to me the accompaniments of a gentleman. Over his table in the living room was a large steel engraving of Washington Irving, seated in his study at Tarrytown; and as he often talked of General Washington, and sang a little song which began

"I suppose you've all heard of Washington the Great,
And likewise the Perry boys sailing on the Lake,"

I somehow identified my grandfather with Washington, and his farm place with Mount Vernon. I seemed to feel that my grandfather belonged to the days of the Revolution.

When the Blackhawk War came on in 1832 my grandfather enlisted in Capt. William Gillham's company from Morgan County, and after the war was appointed a captain of militia by Governor Reynolds. In 1849 he was elected a justice of the peace for Menard County. In 1854 he was elected to the Illinois legislature, where he voted against Lincoln for United States senator because he thought Lincoln's policies would bring on war between the states. He was a peace man, and was anything but proud of his part in defeating Blackhawk. He was a devout, kindly man, full of charities, and very opposed to Calvinism. He was greatly beloved in his neighborhood, and esteemed everywhere for his sterling integrity, his human qualities. Even those who didn't like his ideas on the saloon and drink—he was bitterly against both—had a respect for him. He lived to be nearly ninety-two, dying in 1904.

If anything my grandmother was more vital than he. At any rate she was gayer. She took his word on the Bible and schemes of salvation. Her mind ran to the prudential philosophy, and she was wont to paste in her scrapbook all sorts of hortatory verses and apothegms, such as those of Benjamin Franklin. There was quite a bit of worldliness in her, of the devil perhaps. As a girl she had been a dancer when her grandmother Rebecca Wasson ran a tavern in Morgan County. Her grandfather, John Wasson, was a soldier in the Revolution from North Carolina. Her father was a wandering Irishman, named Lawrence Young, whose story I never knew because she did not know it herself. When I was about fifteen I began to keep a diary, and to record in it somewhat at length the events of the days. In this book I set down the Masters ancestry, as my grandfather gave it to me; but for some reason I was content to carry in mind the few things that my grandmother Masters told me along the way of her people. When I was twenty-eight (and I can be specific about the date from my grandmother's affidavit), I was at the farm with my father, who at the time was the master in chancery of Fulton County. I wanted to get in writing all that my grandmother knew about her people. I questioned her and made notes, and then wrote out an affidavit which my grandmother signed and swore to before my father as a master in chancery. She deposed that her grandmother Rebecca Wasson was first married to John Bryan, a friend of her second husband, John Wasson. The two friends went to the Revolution together, with Rebecca following them across the fields, wetting her feet and skirts in the heavy dew of the morning. At last, as she wailed and the children cried, her husband sent her back. What became of the Bryan children I never knew. John Bryan did not return from the war, but John Wasson did and married Rebecca, who bore several children, among them Margaret Wasson, my grandmother's mother. When thus questioning my grandmother I came to the point where Lawrence Young figured in the story. My grandmother had often told me before this time that her maiden name was Lucinda Wasson. How could that be so if her father's name was Lawrence Young? With some diffidence she now told me. Lawrence Young had abandoned Margaret Wasson, and had never married her. She died shortly after my grandmother was born; and soon Rebecca, who raised my grandmother, came from Tennessee with her sons and daughters to Alton, Illinois, and then to a town near Jacksonville.

I never told my father that his mother was a natural child; and I believe he did not know it. Just a few years ago I was in Petersburg paying a visit to my uncle Will, when something came up in the talk about Grandmother's father and mother. My aunt Norma then asked me if I knew about Grandmother's paternity, speaking with such significance that I saw she had the secret. I answered that I knew it. She then went on to say that Grandfather was tragically torn by the fact, and took up with God in prayer the matter of marrying her. Her great beauty and her goodness finally led him to believe that God approved of the marriage, but he was in great distress of mind. As a little boy I heard of Grandmother's wonderful beauty when she was a young woman and a dancer about Whitehall, Murrayville and Manchester. In her vitality and good humor she bore every evidence of being a love-child. Somewhere, from her grandmother or out of associations in Tennessee, she had acquired a wonderful sense of aesthetics. Her habits of life, her manners were exquisite; and all that I ever learned as a youth of etiquette at the table and among people I learned from her. And yet she was never anything but a pioneer woman. She never saw a city or even a sizable town in all her life, unless she glimpsed Nashville on her way to Illinois when she was less than seven years old. All her life, for she lived to be ninety-five, she took care of her garden and her cows, work that she did not relinquish until she was eighty-seven. She bore many children, and my first memories of her are of a woman full of laughter and funny words and even pranks.

Of such parents was my father born, in 1845. He was one of the handsomest of men, athletic and strong, a fast racer, a good swimmer and handler of horses, and much beloved and admired through all his days. He was his mother's own child, and her favorite. He inherited her great dark eyes, her patrician nose, and her vitality. My grandfather had ideas of education; he wanted all his children to be well schooled. Accordingly he did his best to give my father a collegiate training. He sent him first to the North Sangamon Academy in Menard County, where he had Virgil and geometry; then to Illinois College, then to Ann Arbor, the University of Michigan, where he began the study of law. But my father's vitality was against the imprisonment of the study. He had a quick mind, a swift, logical faculty; but one which could get tangled if he had to reflect, to think. I have seen him puzzled by legal metaphysics, and to give over their solution with quick impatience. Also he was too much interested in people and life to care greatly for books. In spite of his opportunities he was imperfectly educated. Before he knew it, and after trying his hand at becoming a pharmacist, then a grocer—my grandfather having bought a store for him, he turned to the law. Along the way he journeyed to Philadelphia to learn the business of wholesaling in dry goods; in fact, he left the University of Michigan to do this. Then about the time he turned back to the law and was admitted to practice he met my mother, then seventeen years old, who had come to Illinois from New Hampshire.

She was the daughter of a Methodist clergyman named Deming S. Dexter and a woman named Jerusha Humphrey, born in Boston and well educated there. My ancestry on my mother's side is much more traceable than on my father's side. Her father, Deming S. Dexter, belonged to the numerous Dexter family of New England. His father was James Dexter, who was born in Rhode Island in 1784 and in 1812 became a farmer at Newark, Vermont. Deming was the son of James's first marriage, and was born at Newark in 1815. James's first wife died. His second wife, named Betsy Putnam, deserted him. Then he married a sister of his first wife, bringing her from Rhode Island to Newark. This marriage was proving a failure by the time Deming had become a Methodist clergyman. He tried to compose their differences, but without success. When Betsy Putnam left Newark to return to Rhode Island old James said to her, "Good-bye! I hope you will find roast pigs running around with knives and forks stuck in their flanks, and men calling, 'come and eat.'" The old fellow was bitter. He was being left utterly alone, all his children by his several marriages having themselves married and gone their way in the world.

My grandmother on my mother's side married Deming S. Dexter in 1836; and being a well-educated woman she helped him to finish his ministerial studies at Newberry Seminary. Her line of descent is clearer than any other ancestor that I have. She traced her forebears back to Jonas Humphrey, who came from England in 1634, and settled at Dorchester, Massachusetts. Jerusha's great-grandfather, John Humphrey, died while in service as a soldier in the Revolution. Her grandfather, also John, married Mary Putnam, a cousin of General Israel Putnam, and probably related to that Betsy Putnam of Rhode Island who married old James Dexter, and then deserted him.

Jerusha Humphrey boasted a coat of arms which may be described as a book opened, and with the rib placed to view and the covers filled with fleurs-de-lis. It is preserved in a Doomesday Book kept by a brother, John Humphrey, who was born in 1834 and lived and died at Keene, New Hampshire.

Old James Dexter was a man of fiery temper, and his son the Rev. Deming S. Dexter was of like spirit; yet he was known as a pacificator, and when churches were torn with dissension he was often sent to them to bring peace. My mother well inherited her high-keyed and unsubduable nature. Her will was unconquerable, and as my father had the same indomitable disposition, their marriage was the union of conflicting and irresistible forces. She had imbibed a sort of theological doctrine, probably from her father, which was that the will had to be broken. She set out to break my father's will, and utterly failed all her life. But when he was ill and very old she seemed to triumph over him to the extent that he deeded her property and gave her money. But I think this was to express his contrition because he had made her unhappy. Their marriage was the conjunction of two kinds of Methodism: New England's and that of the Middle West, which derived from Tennessee and was distinguished by "gospel love," not by gospel hate.

My father's marriage launched him upon the responsibility of a wife and children and he was not prepared for it, as he possibly might have been. His venturing into Kansas to practice law was ill-advised. He might have started in Petersburg, as he did a few years later, and done well from the start. Kansas at the time was a wild country, full of Indians, and of border ruffians who had come over from the war between North and South. My mother, used to New England and very young, was put to an experience much rougher than she had strength or patience for. She lived in terror. On one occasion my father almost lost his life at the hands of a drunken Indian, and there was danger about at all times. The heat of a Kansas summer, in which I was born without nurses and with poor doctors, tortured her beyond words. She could scarcely talk of those days. And to the last she hated the Middle West and its people.

My father failed in Kansas in the sense that there was nothing there with which he could have succeeded. What do we see in people's lives so salient as the taking of the wrong path or the marrying of the wrong person? These mistakes can be traced into the blood, into the myopia or overfarsightedness of physical and spiritual eyes. So come to pass the sorrows and the long after effects of human lives. However, my father returned to Illinois. He longed, no doubt, for Petersburg; he hungered, I know, for his mother's home and for her never-exhausted cheerfulness and affection. Back at the Masters homestead my father resumed his boyhood life of helping with the farmwork; my mother, annoyed by her dependence, and not in agreeable association with my father's sisters nor with my grandmother, lived unhappy days.

At this time, and for the most part all her life, my mother was a sort of innocent soul, or what might be called "green." When my grandmother in her prankish moods said that she had Indian blood, or Spanish blood, my mother grew genuinely terrified. Raised in New England and fed on wild stories of the untamed West, she was not sure that my grandmother would not suddenly utter the war whoop and go for the hatchet. Seeing my mother with wide eyes of anxiety, the sisters would laugh. Then Grandmother, not wishing to carry the joke any farther, would assure my mother that it was all fun. With the imaginative and highly sensitive nature that my mother had, it is not to be wondered at that she never forgave these antics and never really liked any of the sisters or my grandmother. There was trouble, too, about another matter. My mother's imagination ran riot. She could not see anything and tell about it with factual accuracy; she always embellished the tale. To my grandmother, who saw what she saw with the realism of an Indian or an animal, this was telling "whoppers." In addition to this my mother, still frail from bearing me, and tortured with her nerves then and all her days, did not take to the duties of the house with the industry and aptitude expected of her. In fact my grandmother, who was never ill, who bore children one week and then in two weeks did the family washing, who had no nerves and no fears, who was practical to her fingertips, could not understand my mother and did not approve of her.

I don't know the whole story. My mother told me a good deal, and the substance of it is related here. My grandmother didn't say much to me about my mother. She might say on occasion that my mother had not done right in this or the other circumstance. But what she said never amounted to a relation, a story, a character study.

With one thing and another, it was not possible for my father and mother to live at the homestead. And so my grandfather rented a farm for him on the Shipley Hill, about a mile from his own house. And here my father felt the pinch of hard life. In addition to farming he taught a district school two miles away, to which he walked through the bitter winter. Before setting forth he got his own breakfast and chopped enough wood for the day. My mother was ill, and about to bear another child; and she had not yet learned how to cook and keep a house. On returning from school my father had to take care of his horses; he had to milk the cow and chop wood for the night, and help with the supper, and wash the dishes. He was paying heavily for any inattention to school and any neglect of opportunities. All the while he was thinking of getting into Petersburg where he could practice law. But his father was holding him down, with the advantage that he controlled the purse and could remind him of past failures. Then my sister was born in this log house, and was named

Madeline by Aunt Mary Masters, who in her invalidism of seven years read Shelley and Tennyson, while being patiently nursed by my grandmother.

The Shipley Hill farm was a poor makeshift for a living, I am sure. But my grandfather was determined that my father should be a farmer. He feared that at the county seat my father would run wild with that great vitality which was his, and that evil companions would work his ruin. The village of Atterberry, where the farmers took their products for shipment, was four miles from the Masters house; and near Atterberry was a farm which my grandfather had been looking at. He finally said that he would buy it for my father if he would stay on it and settle down to farming, and my father in his plight promised to do this. The farm was about 160 acres with a common house on it, sheds and a barn; the land was very fertile. So when I was about three years old and my sister was about one we moved to the Atterberry farm. And here my memory begins.

One is likely to confuse what one has been told with what one remembers from his own experience. It seems to me that I remember when the veil was lifted from my face and when my grandmother's dancing eyes and her laugh shone upon me like sunshine. But this is doubtless impossible. However, I have no doubt that I remember the Atterberry farm. I cannot visualize the house. I only see it as standing quite a distance back from the front fence, by which stood a great tree. I remember an occasion when an uncle, Beth Vincent, and Aunt Minerva visited us, and this uncle whittled for me a windmill as we all sat under the tree. I have a kind of memory of a spacious back yard with its paths worn hard and smooth. And I recall vividly an occasion when one of my cousins, a youth about fourteen who was living with us at the time, tried to get me to drink some lye from a saucer. My mother was making soft soap, and this lye, obtained by pouring water in a barrel of wood ashes and letting the water percolate through them, was put in a kettle and boiled with refuse grease thrown into it. The lye looked like dark tea, and I was about to drink it when my mother rushed forth and knocked the saucer from my hand.

At that time the ground was cleared for planting corn by first breaking down the old stalks with a break; then they were raked into long windrows and burned. As if it were yesterday I can see my father walking along the windrows setting them afire while the field here and there glowed with the burning stalks. I was sitting in the corner of the rail fence with my mother and my sister as this work was being done. The country here was as level as a table, rimmed far off with strips of forest. The rail or worm fence divided the land. The raking and burning of stalks was done in late March or early April when the balmy winds began to blow and the frogs were setting up their liquid chorus in the meadow pools.

There were days when my grandfather and grandmother came to see us, driving up in the closed carriage with its rear oval window and blue silk curtain. My grandfather was always dressed in black broadcloth and a silk hat, when going forth to see his friends, and with buckskin gloves to protect his hands against the lines and the handling of the horses. My grandmother on these occasions wore her black silk dress and her bonnet with silk ribbons and a jet ornament. There was great shouting on my part when they arrived; for they were always laughing and calling to me and my sister, and my mother who ran out of the house. And they never failed to bring us something. It might be apples, or peaches, or stick candy, or a wonderful condiment which my grandmother made, called peachleather. And we went frequently to the old homestead, often for Sunday dinner. So gradually the house emerged to my eyes, and became a place of enchanting charm. My own home very early, really from the first, seemed a poor and barren place compared with the house of my grandparents. There were a thousand reasons for this, chief of which might be mentioned the many objects of wonder, the books and curios that my grandparents had gathered and cherished; the grindstone in the yard which could be driven by a pedal; the tools in the carpenter's shop; my grandmother's canaries and redbird; the fascinating pictures on the walls; the wonderful parlor with its piano, and much else. But there was such order, such comfort at that old house. The meals were always on time—and the table was filled with delicious things. My grandmother was always laughing; my grandfather always singing, or saying quaint things; and both of them were so full of affection for me, and so indulgent toward me. Soon this old house became a very heaven to my imagination; while in point of fact it was not much of a house, and not to be compared with some of the other farmhouses around it, a number of which were of brick and much larger.

It was only a story and a half high, and had but nine rooms. But it was built of walnut and hickory timbers set upon a brick foundation. Its weather boarding was of walnut, for in 1850 when the house was built, the woods abounded in walnut trees, which the farmers ruthlessly cut down to make rails for fences, or logs for hogpens, or what not. There was a board fence painted white in front of the house; and a brick walk leading from the gate to the front door. My grandmother had planted red and yellow roses under the windows of the living room; and she had flower beds of tulips and phlox; and she had lilac bushes. The ubiquitous pine trees adorned either side of the walk; and to one side were fine maples under which we used to sit on hot days. Entering the front door one came into a hallway from which ascended a stairway with a walnut banister. To the left of this was the parlor, a room where my aunt's Mathushek piano was. At the windows were lace curtains held back by cords fastened around large glass knobs. The couch was upholstered in horsehair, as were some of the chairs. There were two mahogany tables, one lyre shaped. There was a large ornate lamp with a glazed-glass shade on one of these tables. There were two paintings on the wall, of country scenes, paintings of the sort which are done by copyists and can be bought anywhere for a small price. There was a wood stove of Russian iron, always in a high state of polish; and back of it a wood box papered with wallpaper. Back of the parlor was the spare bedroom, always smelling musty and rarely really aired. In it was a walnut bedstead heavily built up with quilts of my grandmother's making. At one side was a stand holding a bowl and pitcher.

At the end of the hallway was a door leading to the dining room. To the right was the living room where my grandfather and grandmother spent nearly all of their time, and where they slept. There was a lounge in the room where my aunt Mary lay for those long years of illness; and a mahogany bureau. In one corner was an old mahogany chest which Rebecca Wasson had brought from North Carolina to Illinois, and which she had given my grandmother. On this chest was a walnut case for books. The chest had two drawers, one used by my grandfather for his awl, needles, flax and wax for harness mending. The other drawer was my grandmother's where she kept her daguerreotypes, and the watch of a beloved son who was drowned in the Platte River in 1862; besides sticks of cinnamon and trinkets of various sorts. In the east wall of the room was a huge fireplace, in which cordwood could be burned; and the mantel over it had a clock with weights, and a bell which rang loudly when the clock struck. In one corner was my grandmother's trunk; and in a closet near by she kept her shoes and dresses, her hats and apparel.

The dining room was a long room running east and west the full width of the house except for a small dark room at the west end which was used as a spare bedroom. Between the dining room and the separate building containing the kitchen and the hired man's room there was a long porch, with a shelf against the kitchen wall where were hung old gloves, turkey wings, or what not; and on one end of which was a water tank supplied with ice in summer. For my grandfather was one of the few farmers about who had an icehouse. Outside this porch was the workhouse, so called, where saws and augers and other tools were kept on a workbench, or hung over it. This was one of my delights from the time that I could saw a board or bore a hole, when I made windmills for myself.

The upper rooms were sleeping chambers, one of them being occupied by my uncle who was nine years my senior. Back of the chambers was a place under the roof, called the Dark Ages, where old trunks were stored, containing, as it turned out, many books which became my delight as the years passed.

But my favorite room was the living room, where as a child and long after I sat with my grandparents before the fireplace: the big burning logs cast a light about the room and on the ceiling. The heat made sizzling sounds in the frozen apples which had been brought from the cellar and placed there to thaw out. Meanwhile the wind whistled from over the prairies and the snow beat at the windows. Here I listened to my grandmother tell about the buffalo grass that overgrew all the country about when she first saw Menard County, and about the days that they lived in the log house on the lower lot when my father was a baby, and until the *new* house was built, that being this house just described. Later I learned that when the wagons from Morgan County, from which they were moving, came up bearing their possessions, and my grandmother got out of one to see where she had come to and what the country was, she broke into tears. The pioneer women were not always enduring uncomplainingly, nor always hiding their disappointments.

Mrs. Anno, whose husband had sold my grandfather this

farm, came from the log house, and comforted my grandmother by saying that the country was a good one, and that
my grandmother would like it after a time. There were Indians
about, and for several years after 1847. They were beggars for
the most part, going from farmhouse to farmhouse asking for
food. One frightened my grandmother very badly one day.

And then my grandfather with a hearty laugh would tell
tales of Tennessee: about the possum hunts there, and the
feasts which the negroes had when they got a possum; about
the little niggers that danced and tumbled and laughed and
smeared their faces with the possum sop; about the fiddlers;
about the brook which ran across his father's farm into which
he put pebbles to be rolled over by the water until they were
made into round marbles. He told me about the Blackhawk
War, and stories out of the Old Testament. He never touched
upon Jesus or the New Testament wonders; for these constituted the mystical miracle of salvation. But he recounted
with great gusto the fight between David and Goliath, and
put the fear of holy men into me by telling me about Elisha,
the mocking boys and the bears. And as time went on I heard
from him about his days in Morgan County: how he hauled
the brick to build one of the buildings of Illinois College; and
how a lawsuit arose out of the purchase of the farm from
Anno in which my grandfather had Lincoln for his lawyer,
and lost the case.

Now the other room of my delight in this house was the
kitchen, where for many months of the year—in autumn
after the heat of summer, in the cold winter, and in the raw
spring—the long table was kept set, spread with a red table-
cloth and full of delectable food when we sat down to eat.
I loved the fragrance and the taste of the sassafras tea which
my grandmother made. The kitchen stove kept the room
warm; and it was a great delight to run from my cold room
to this kitchen, and there find my grandmother laughing and

frying cakes, or baking corn bread. Back of this kitchen was the hired man's room; and this functionary was always sitting by the stove when the meal was about to be served, or if he was in his room I could run in there to see his treasures, like his harmonica and nickel cigars perfumed with cinnamon.

This was the house and these the rooms that emerged into my imagination and my comprehension of my world. It was full of magic. And when on Sundays we set off from the Atterberry farm to have dinner with my grandparents my heart leaped up, my happiness knew no bounds. All their long lives, Uncle Beth Vincent and Aunt Minerva showered presents on me and my sister; as they had given my uncle Will a great many books wonderfully illustrated, such as *The Babes in the Wood*, Grimm's *Fairy Tales*, besides wonderful tops and toys, field glasses, cabinets of tools, and much else that delights a boy. There were these things for me to see; besides my grandmother's trinkets, her illustrated books, and the like. And then there was the dinner.

That long table was filled with wonderful food: fried chicken and boiled ham, and mashed potatoes and turnips, and watermelon pickles and peach pickles, stuck with cloves; and in season fresh strawberries and cream or blackberries, and sponge or jelly cake. All this was enough to fascinate any boy, particularly if his own home was not run on a scale of such plenty and variety, such order and punctuality.

Outside of such memories the days at the Atterberry farm are all a mist. One thing else stands out, and that is the gradual emergence of my sister into this dream world. From a little child her great brow and her large dark eyes, and her tendency to follow me about and to get into my way, are definite pictures. My grandmother did not quite approve of her, and later said that she was not truthful. "Tell the truth and shame the old Harry," was one of her injunctions. She believed that I always told the truth, and perhaps I did at last, even if not at first in all cases. Sometimes I was in fear and held back something; sometimes I invented tales when my imagination ran riot; sometimes I invented stories, as I did when I put the dog into the icepit, to tease the hired man, and then ran to say that the dog had jumped in of its own accord. Despite all this I had a good name from the first for telling the truth. My sister looked enough like me and acted enough like me to make it annoying; yet she was as different from me as possible. She wanted to do whatever I happened to be doing, and she kept getting in my way. Once at the Atterberry farm I was working with a hoe, and she persisted in getting in front of me so that I could not cut the ground with it. When she wouldn't move out of my way, I let the hoe come down on her head, for which I was severely punished by my mother. I tell this here because it contains a symbol which will more and more unfold. In many ways my sister reminded me of Maggie Tulliver. She had riches and a varied life after she was grown, but a kind of esoteric bad luck followed her. She was never a help to me, but in several crises of life she was in my way or else she brought me misfortune. My sister's relation to me can be etched into full understanding by contrasting her with Wordsworth's sister. With a different nature she might have been a wonderful influence in my life. As it was, she imitated me and used me, but she also departed upon a way wholly foreign to my way; and in so far as she got me into her way she was a disaster. Already the strands of fate can be seen: my affection for my grandmother, my admiration for her ways and her house; the feeling which grew more bitter between my mother and my grandmother, and my mother's jealousy and heart hurts that I was so much won by my grandmother; and my sister with her congenital attitude toward me, and her alignment with my mother whom she resembled spiritually more than she did her father or her Masters forebears.

I seem to remember what I am now about to relate, though

it is likely that I don't remember it at all but have made a memory picture for myself from what I heard so often told. The Atterberry farm just furnished a living, and my father worked industriously enough. He did not have a head for dealing in livestock, and if he bought gold dollars at par he would have to sell them at a discount. It was just as well that he left the farm: he would have gone to the end of his days plowing and sowing, and living from hand to mouth. While he was growing up he had been an admired figure around the country for his lively spirits and his handsome figure. When studying to be a pharmacist, and running a grocery store in Petersburg, and studying law there with a local notable who had been in Congress, he had made a host of friends. There was a group of young men in Petersburg really remarkable for their enterprising character, their breeding, and their happy natures. These were all my father's friends. Nearly all of them were Democrats, as my father and his father were. And one day in 1872 four of these young men drove up to the front gate of the Atterberry farm to ask my father to run for the office of state's attorney. This was like a dispensation from heaven, for it lifted my father from the farm and set him down at the county seat, Petersburg, in the practice of law. Naturally he grabbed at this chance. The county was Democratic. It had voted against Lincoln in 1860; it had voted against him again in 1864. It had opposed the war, and was full of "Copperheads," as men were called who did not like the subjugation of the South. My grandfather, a kind of Tolstoian, a man of peace because of his nature and his religion, had for years before the war opposed the politics that he saw was bringing bloody strife upon the country. When the war came on he simply took no part; but everyone understood that he was against Lincoln's policies, as he had been since 1855. As for my father he was only sixteen when the war commenced, and he ran away to join the Union Army. But my grandfather sent after him and captured him.

Nevertheless, there was enough fire here to account for the smoke that rose up around his candidacy for state's attorney. But opposition to him was without avail. The county was full of Germans who had settled there in 1848 and later, coming from Europe to New Orleans, and then by boat up the Mississippi to St. Louis and Alton, and from there overland to this rich cornland of Menard County. Many of these prosperous Germans were for my father and were always his friends. He was triumphantly elected; and we' moved from the farm to Petersburg.

Chapter II

AT THIS TIME PETERSBURG WAS A TOWN OF ABOUT THREE thousand people. It was surveyed and platted in 1832; but in 1836 Lincoln resurveyed it, being at the time a deputy surveyor of Sangamon County, and then residing at New Salem less than two miles up the Sangamon River from Petersburg. Two men at New Salem, Peter Lukins and George Warburton, who had laid out the town first, played a game of seven-up with the understanding that if Lukins won the game the town should be called Petersburg; if Warburton won the game, it should be called Georgetown. Lukins won the game.

About 1837 Lincoln left New Salem to take up the practice of law at Springfield, the new capital of Illinois; and with one thing and another New Salem began to disintegrate. Many New Salem families moved to Petersburg, sometimes bringing with them their log houses, which were set up again about the square or at one side of it. In 1839, Menard County was formed by slicing off a part of Sangamon County; and in the spring of that year New Market, Miller's Ferry, and Huron, a town also surveyed by Lincoln, contested with Petersburg for the honor of being the capital of the new county. Petersburg won the fight. In 1843, a courthouse was built at a cost of $6,640; to which Lincoln often came to try cases. He did this up to the time that he was elected president. This was the courthouse which I knew as a boy, and in which my father had his office as state's attorney. It was a small two-story brick building with an observatory in the roof. When political rallies were held stands were built against its walls, on which men like Douglas addressed the people. On one occasion when my father was perhaps twelve years old he was taken by my grandfather to meet Douglas; and as my father stood beside the great man he was very proud to see that he was as tall as Douglas.

At the time that we moved to Petersburg the town had two railroads, several coal mines, a woolen mill, several grist mills, some factories, a small brewery, and a winery. People had come there from Maryland, Virginia, Kentucky, Tennessee, New Jersey. And the Germans in town and about the country gave a liberal character to the inhabitants. The Americans were a lively people, full of the joy of living and of great hospitality. The Mexican War had given several majors and the like to the town, and with bankers and merchants, lawyers and politicians, it was a center of many activities. The courthouse mentioned stood in a square of trees where men gathered to talk, or loafers lay and slept.

The town had been built on a circle of hills with the business part lying in a level between their feet and the shores of the twisting Sangamon. Driving out of Petersburg to the east, to the north, to the west, one must climb hills. But going along the New Salem and Springfield road one skirts the river and the wooded slopes above it. From the heights of the New Salem Hill one looks down a valley of luxuriant forestry, with the river winding between its heavy greeneries. From this elevation the Sangamon River is picturesque, yellow and muddy as its waters are when closely seen. From the beginning the people built houses on the crest of this circle of hills; and when we moved there many of these houses of brick and frame seemed to me like great mansions. They looked so to me for many years. At any rate they had a certain distinction; and as time went on some very good houses of attractive architecture looked down upon the courthouse and the square; and the square itself acquired business blocks of marble fronts, and blocks of pressed brick, all unusual for a town of this size. To the west of Petersburg lies the rich and level country of great farms; and to the north the equally fertile lands which stretch to the Masters farm, and beyond it to the Mason County Hills.

The town has been improved a little since I was a boy there, but it has not essentially changed. The old courthouse was supplanted by a new one about 1896; and new hotels have been built, and new houses along the crest of the hills. The old schoolhouse, where I started my schooling, gave way to a modern high school; and the like. But the flagstones about the square, and many of its buildings remain to this day. And when I go back I can revisualize Mentor Graham or William H. Herndon, who used to be familiars there when I was a boy. By that time Mentor Graham was a very old man, irascible and always in litigation; while Herndon in his middle fifties was practically burnt out. I don't remember how either of these men looked. Mentor Graham passes through my memory as an old man stamping around the square; Herndon as a man with a beard, who was often with my father.

We went to live in a common house a few blocks east of the square. A switch of the railroad ran by the fence so close that when the engine paused, I could climb on the fence and shake the hand of the engineer. This is one of my memories. The river was not far away; and one spring it overflowed, and came around our house and as far to the west as the square itself. Men were going about in boats on their business errands, and there was much sickness. A little boy, the son of the jeweler who lived a few doors from us, died of diphtheria. That was my first acquaintance with death, for I had played with this boy. His name was Lee too, and he was about my age. One day the house across the street from us took fire. Flames enveloped the roof and the occupants were throwing ticks and bedding from the windows. Something about fire or water makes ineradicable pictures on the mind.

I don't know how long we lived in this house, but it wasn't long. We moved to a house back on one of the hills, where there was an oak tree. And there my sister and I had a swing, about which we strove as about all other things. By this time another child had come into the family, a boy as beautiful as Shelley, and of wonderful precocity. We had playmates here, one of whom was a girl a good deal older than I who swore like a pirate and was a riotous tomboy. We didn't live in this house very long either. Soon we moved to the brick house, the Methodist parsonage it was, next to the Methodist church, on the slope of what was called the Braham Hill. Braham was the banker, and lived with his large family in a fine house on the top of the hill just above us. His large yard was fenced with a white picket fence, along which innumerable poodles raced and barked as I ascended the hill on occasion.

By this time I was slight but wiry, and very strong in the back and arms. One of the Braham boys, who had a toy steam locomotive and a track to run it on, besides all kinds of toys, since he was pampered by his father, wanted to test my mettle. This boy had taken boxing lessons at the gymnasium on the square, which was run by a man who followed the circus in the summer season. I did my best against the skill with which I was opposed but was worsted. I was now six years old, and began to go to school. I have nothing but loathing for those days. The schoolroom had no proper ventilation, and the air that we breathed was full of offense. The toilets were foul beyond description; the first day at school I learned all the obscene words that were then current. Some of the boys were bellicose and brutal. The first day I had to fight it out with two brothers, both of whom I vanquished. But an Irish boy of huge fists afterwards whipped me soundly. Still I fought. Starting with me were the son of the county judge, the sons of the circuit clerk, the sons of lawyers. Two daughters of the cashier of the bank were in school, but were more advanced. One of them captured my imagination even to a kind of amorous madness. The teacher at once took a great liking for me; and pretty soon I was noted for my spelling ability. She offered a pocketknife as a prize to the best speller in the school; and I was ahead, with a Swedish boy crowding me hard just the same. At this pass I came down with measles complicated with pneumonia. The uncle whom I have mentioned was in town one night from the farm to call on his sweetheart; and coming to our house found me in the throes of croup and about to choke to death. My father and mother were off somewhere to one of the parties that distinguished Petersburg. My grandmother was indignant that I was left to take care of myself in such a crisis. She was frank enough to say on occasion that she thought my father and mother both lazy and selfish. I was ill for many weeks, and in consequence lost the prize at school. When I got up I was a shadow and as weak as one could be and live. My left lung felt as though it has been turned to wood; and when I climbed the hill my breath failed me. The spring came on and I began to get better. And now my grandfather bought my father a house three blocks or so beyond the Braham house and on the level that stretched to the farms west of Petersburg. And so we moved again.

This was a small house and common enough; but there was a large yard and trees and a barn. Later my father built an addition to the house; but it had neither water save from a well nor heat save from stoves. And in winter it was as cold as the arctic. In the morning we children gathered up our clothes and rushed shivering to the stove in the living room to dress. There was no roaring fireplace as there was at the Masters farm to which I came to dress, when I was there, where I saw my grandfather and grandmother in happy talk with each other as the morning sky grayed. And here we children were habitually sick with colds. The Sangamon River valley was thoroughly unsalubrious. It was damp, foggy, and in winter bitterly cold. My sister had diphtheria; and that beautiful little brother took the disease in its most malignant form and died after three weeks of torture.

This happened in middle September at seven-thirty in the evening. Uncle Addison had been in constant attention on Alex, day by day, but medical science knew nothing of moment to do for diphtheria in those days. There was a sort of lamp by which carbolic acid could be sprayed in the throat, and this was used; but rain water would have been as effectual. The weather was close and hot as it can be in river towns in Illinois in that season; and this little boy lay there dying as my mother fanned him, and sang to him. He wanted her to sing, and she sang such things as "Flee as a Bird to Your Mountain." Alex was beloved over town as a child seldom is, for his beauty and precocity. People called day and evening to see how Alex was faring. In Petersburg there were many Jews, all devoted friends of my father's. Among them was Julius Rothschild—a generous, handsome man he was, and he loved Alex with a strange tenderness. Years after when I used to meet him in Chicago in the hard days of his poverty and my struggles he would look at me with widening eyes and mention Alex. Grandfather and Grandmother came in and looked at the dying boy, and went their way. My grandfather entered the room, then turned quickly and passed into the yard. I ran after him. He stooped and plucked a spear of grass, tore it apart with trembling hands. I saw tears drop from his eyes. He only said, "The little boy is gone." He knew the end was nearing. And what was this, what was death? How could it enter at this house and take Alex, so that soon his body would be under the earth? My own feelings were full of wonder, speculation, and pain. Mitch Miller came once to see Alex, but only once. He would not come to the funeral. On that day he wandered about through Fillmore's Woods.

The evening was stifling. The room smelt of carbolic acid. Uncle Addison was about the room with ominous steps and activity. My mother was sitting by the bed fanning the little boy; and my sister and I were standing in the doorway looking

at the tragedy. All at once my mother began to sing, and soon
Alex's eyes grew very wide as though he saw something. That
was death. I put something of this tragedy in the epitaph
"Hamlet Micure" in *Spoon River Anthology*. Immediately the
undertaker had to be called in. My father started for downtown with me racing at his side. He seemed suddenly turned to
stone. Above us the clouds parted where the moon was swimming. I asked my father if Alex had gone through there into
heaven. He did not answer me.

Mr. Miller preached the funeral sermon. In the little Methodist Church all of Petersburg seemed to gather, all the men
about town, Julius Rothschild among the others, and my uncle
Will and my grandparents—all but Mitch. Then there was
nothing left but spades and earth, and turning back to the
desolate little house on the Braham Hill.

After so long a time it is difficult to tell what my feelings
were the next few days. I remember that I was much on my
pony riding about the town, and over the hills, a good deal in
company with a hard boy named Frank Miller, not in any way
related to Mitch. This boy Frank seemed to give me something
that I needed. But he was cruelly indifferent to the death of
Alex, and I had at last to keep him away from me. As for
Mitch, he came about very little if at all. In a year from
this time Mitch, too, was gone, killed while flipping a train.
After Alex's death there was no more reading of *Tom Sawyer*.
Mitch fell in with hard boys, as hard as Frank Miller, and they
led him to his doom.

Meanwhile, what was my father doing? He was in all sorts
of trials, the history of which I knew later. But now he was
the dark, rollicking man who came home to play with us riot-
ously at noon or night, or to drive us about the country, and out
to the Masters farm on Sunday. I knew nothing about his life
at this time. He was away much. And my mother was often
gone all day to see her new-found friends. All along she had

kept a maid whenever she could get one; and at last we had
an Irish girl named Delia Halligan, who was a famous cook,
so that the house ran better than it ever had before. Delia had
been trained in a hotel at Bloomington, and was an expert
maid. She wore starched dresses, and her good manners, temper
and independence kept my mother at her distance. Delia was a
memorable exception to the incompetent maids we had along
the way both in Petersburg and in Lewistown. She would not
permit my mother to take any part in the running of the
kitchen, on threat of leaving her service. All the other maids
were ordered about by my mother according to her whim.
There were a good many negroes in Petersburg, and for a time
we had a colored maid whom my mother scolded and drove
about at will; and finally discharged one day. The poor thing
walked away from the house on the dirt road that led from it
toward the square, weeping bitterly. My mother handed me a
pair of gloves to take to her. I ran and gave them to her. Then
my mother further relented and asked me to run and take some
other gift to her. I did so and Dinah wept more bitterly, saying
that my mother was a good woman.

The history of the maids we had would make a story by
itself. For weeks we would be without help, then someone
would come along. They were a poor lot, and my mother did
not get along with them. When she got tired of keeping the
house without help, she would take in anyone who applied.
Once in Lewistown a woman named Em Chicken, with a little
boy about three years old, was suddenly installed in the kitchen.
Em was a slattern; but we children adored the little boy. He
was dreadfully hungry when he arrived with his mother, and
sat at the table eating beans, and saying to his mother, "More
beans, Em." My sister and I went into hysterics of laughter to
hear this boy call his mother by her first name. It turned out
that the boy was a natural child; as for Em, she was a child of
nature and, to my mother's mind, an immoral woman. Indeed

all our maids except Delia were immoral women. And as my mother would tolerate nothing of the sort they went out on their heads for their sexual irregularities, as well as for their incompetence. Long after I was grown and was in the practice of law in Chicago I saw Delia, who after her husband's death ran a hotel in Springfield. I used to call on her in those days when I was in Springfield attending the Supreme Court.

At this time the country about, and in Iowa and Kansas, was cursed with frightful storms and cyclones. Jacksonville, only forty miles away, was badly blown up one Sunday. The truth is that I lived in terror, as well as loneliness, always troubled in my breast with strange longings which music made unendurable. It happened that these storms generally came on Sunday, so that I looked forward to that day with trembling. Many Sunday afternoons I sat on the front steps of this house looking at the blue and green clouds writhing in the west. We had lightning, too, of frightful intensity, which struck houses in Petersburg, once knocking my father from an iron shelf on which he was sitting in the office of the county clerk. This same bolt also knocked me down as I stood under an oak tree in the yard digging a trench with a new spade. At the same time my cousin Daisy, who lived a few blocks away, was struck and horribly burned. She was the daughter of my aunt Jacynthia, my mother's sister, and of Uncle Addison. Uncle Addison practically dropped his medical practice to care for Daisy for a year thereafter. With one thing and another, including his tender devotion to this daughter, he sank into poverty. No sooner was Daisy healed of her burns than she died of membranous croup; and many years later, at the end of almost humorous wanderings about Illinois and into Kansas, Uncle Addison, reduced to humble piety by his misfortunes, died in Oklahoma, where he was being supported by a good son, himself a physician. I was in terror, as I took to feather beds during these storms, and kept to the middle of the room when the lightning flashed.

These Sunday afternoons were lugubrious beyond description. There was such ominous silence as the writhing clouds approached. And in that silence could be heard an organ in the neighborhood playing "Depths of Mercy," as a melancholy voice sang those terrible words. From the beginning I have been profoundly affected by music. A couplet of Mother Shipton was going the rounds then:

> When to an end the world shall come
> In eighteen hundred and eighty-one.

We hadn't long to wait. There were deaths about us; and altogether we lived in terror. The revivalist was flourishing on this soil; but somehow I never confessed my sins and took conversion and the church. My father as a one-minded man had no religion whatever except that he always believed in a God. In his early youth he had joined the Methodist Church, but by this time he was out of it, and he stayed out of it and of all other churches to the end of his days. My mother by this time was in the Episcopalian Church; and sometimes I went to Sunday school there, or to the nearer Methodist Church; but the revivals never caught me. My grandfather's piety may have seemed sufficient to cover my Adam inheritance. I revered his religion, and found protection and sustenance in it. He seemed to be a good guardian for me against an angry God of cyclones and lightning and diphtheria. My grandmother never mentioned the Savior. She also seemed to rest in hope for what my grandfather was doing to appease the Almighty. I do not say that I was not frightened by the terrors of life and death about me, nor that when the lightning flashed, and the wind blew, I did not beg Jesus to save me from destruction. But when it came to joining the church I drew away; and not being pressed to do so by any one of my relatives, I kept out of the fold. Even my grandfather never asked me to join the church. For in truth he believed that whoever lived a good life was already saved.

Altogether I was not happy in this house that Grandfather gave us, though we lived here in plenty. From the farm Grandfather sent us loads of potatoes and turnips, of apples, of fuel wood, of everything. My father on a salary of $600 a year had very little to spend it for. Our clothing cost us little, and a good deal of that was given us by Grandmother. And my mother had presents of dresses from a rich sister who lived in Leavenworth. Still my father saved no money; he made no investments; and when he sold this house to move away from Petersburg, the money he received for it was the only capital he had in the world—$1,000.

What a happy relief it was to get away from this home life and to go out to my grandmother's! Often on Saturday afternoon I would steal down to the square and hunt about for my grandfather and grandmother. I would see him on the square talking with old friends. I would frequently find my grandmother in one of the stores, and then I would beg her to take me home with her. Nearly always she relented. And then I would run breathless to the house on the hill to get my mother's consent, who gave it reluctantly always, and sometimes not at all. The thrill of the ride out to the farm is unforgettable. To see again the familiar road stretching straight ahead; to see the rims of forestry, and the farmhouses that I knew; to pass into the sweet woods and by the oak tree, which a man named Gordon had barked to make medicine for rheumatism; to pass over the bridge which spanned Concord Creek; to come up the hill, and suddenly to see the beloved barn and house; and to drive into the lot and be greeted by the friendly hired man, or my uncle. And then to go into the barn and climb to the sweet-scented hayloft; to look at the horses in the stalls; to see the new calf or the new colt; to go to the shop where the tools were, or into the smokehouse where I could smell the hams and bacon; to watch the martins in the houses on poles which my grandmother had made for them; to look north again to the Mason County Hills, so far away and so dreamy, and to see nearer the houses of beloved neighbors! My heart was full of happiness on these occasions. Then later to go to the Dark Ages and prowl for books, or to rummage through the bookcase in the living room. And that night to have supper, of such delicious food and so easily and quietly served; and then to sit with my grandfather and grandmother until candles were lighted at eight o'clock, when they retired. And then to go to the beloved kitchen where my uncle and the hired man would be telling stories. This was going out to the farm; it was leaving the house on the Braham Hill.

In these circumstances strands were being woven which persisted to the end of the weave, and twisted themselves into unforeseen patterns of fate. I remember a time when my father wept when I wanted to go to the farm. He was stoical by nature, but when his reserve broke the floods of feeling flowed over him. He knew that our home lacked warmth, for no one felt it more than himself. He, too, was a party to what that home was. He was much away, he was out late at night; on the other hand, he had been reared in a happy and well-conducted household; and if he had been fortuned by a bright and well-ordered hearth of his own he would not have had any excuse for absenting himself from it, and probably he would not have done so. I must say here that his father's piety and strict morality rather turned him against denials and led him to live out the gayer nature which he had inherited from his mother. Being of such great strength, of such enormous vitality, and with such a disposition for companionship, he took to games, sports and dances in his teens; and now at this time when he was something over thirty he was deep in all the revels of Petersburg.

Another strand in my own fate, now being woven, was my sister, whom my mother took to her heart more emphatically than she would otherwise have done, I think, on account of my grandmother's partiality for me, and her mild attitude toward my sister. In my infancy my mother looked upon me with passionate wonder, and with a sort of animal love; and all her life she was attached to me, passing from moods of extravagant affection, however, to moods of critical distaste. As little a thing as that episode of the veil was, when I smiled at my grandmother, she never forgot it. And as that infant smile passed to a constant adoration of my grandmother, a situation arose in which my mother was always in a state of resentment, and I was always the prize which was pulled this way and the other. The fascination that old farmhouse and all it contained had for me, the love I had for the domestic comfort of the house, could only have been counteracted by a home of my own that was equally happy. But my mother did not make such a home, perhaps she was unable to do so. I have come to the conclusion that people do not act as they do because they are evilly disposed, but because they are incapable of acting otherwise than they do, even when they see that to do so would bring them greater happiness in life.

My mother at the time of her marriage was slight and of graceful figure, as I learned from her admiring friends in Petersburg when I was growing up. She was stout, even obese, when I first had eyes to note her, and she remained so until she was in her sixties, when she became thin and frail. As a bride she was very beautiful, and she was beautiful of face in her middle and late twenties. Later in middle life and as she grew older there was majesty and dignity in her countenance. She had a faultless skin, white and smooth, brown hair that had a tendency to run into tendrils; a high intellectual forehead, and eyes that sparkled with humor, and radiated moving tenderness when she was in quiet nerves. Her mouth was shapely and sensitive; her nose good, but tending to be somewhat thick at the tip, though it was long enough. In Petersburg, particularly, she was noted for her wit, her humorous characterizations and comments, and also for her command of satire and retort. She had a singing voice of some quality, and played the part of Little Buttercup in a production of *Pinafore* with admired success. She was very popular in Petersburg, but never so much so in Lewistown. There were times when my heart flooded with love for her, moved by her beauty, the speaking tenderness of her eyes. There were other times when her cutting words, her flaming temper froze my heart and filled me with fierce resistance and resentment and, I regret to say, with unloving feelings.

In those days in Petersburg my father was prosecuting various desperate characters who had grown up there in the disordered and lawless days of the War Between the States, or had drifted into Petersburg from the devastated South. Their crimes were the usual offenses against property: attacks with knives and bricks and pistols; sometimes, burning houses or haystacks or mutilating cows and cattle. When these terrible fellows were released from prison they proceeded to hunt my father to get revenge. When he came home late at night he would be followed by one of them, the most wicked of all, who would skulk along in the darkness as my father kept his hand on the pistol which he carried for self-protection. He was never harmed; though once he felled an ugly German who drew a large knife and started to attack him as they met in one of the drugstores. This condition of terror fell with disquieting force upon my mother, and upon us children. I wonder that she lived to the age that she did. Her heart always beat too fast, I am sure; and though her sense of humor and her aptitude for wit helped to relieve her own melancholy, it was still true that her life was one long agony. Her nature had been darkened by her clergyman father; but it had been sharpened by the intellectual outlook of her mother, who did not take to the theology of her day. And thus my mother, like nearly everyone else, was a divided personality.

One of these criminals mentioned used to rattle the windowpanes at night, and steal about the yard as my mother stood at the window in fear, with us children huddled around her. At another time this fellow tried to break in the house. At another time, one afternoon it was, he burned a cat alive under a tree and within plain view of our house. Police protection was nothing, for we were many blocks from the square, and in a part of town which was still very little built up. My mother lived in constant dread. She had endured the wildness of Kansas after a peaceful life in New Hampshire; and now in Petersburg there was this constant horror. This prowler, who went about town reading the Bible and was a regular attendant of Sunday school, lost his life at the hands of the man who had had him prosecuted for burning haystacks and cutting cows. This happened just the month that we moved away from Petersburg, when in the last stages of the insanity that afflicted him he went berserk one day and proceeded to even up all scores.

Since I had started to school with so many of the sons of the principal citizens I should have had them for close friends for life, except for the fact that we moved away; and then as my life went on in Chicago, I lost these friends as influences growing apace with my own life. Nevertheless, I have seen them frequently along the years; and as we have known each other from so far a time, there is something peculiarly deep and understanding about my feeling for them. One of them, with whom I played every day in these years, might have figured closely in my life. He was the son of the banker who lived in the finest house in town, just across a vacant pasture lot from us. When he grew up he, too, departed for a city and became very rich; and I saw him but twice after we became mature. He had an orchard where we played ball. He had a riding horse; and soon my father bought me a pony. This boy and I rode much about the country together. I frequently went out to the Masters farm, there to accompany my uncle on trips to Atterberry and to the homes of neighbors and to race with the horse he rode. I became a skillful rider, and could stand up on his back while this pony trotted about the lot.

Will and Dave Bennett, the sons of the circuit clerk, were handsome, well-bred boys, and I played with them. But Mitch Miller was my particular chum. The Millers lived just a little way from us. There was a numerous family of them of girls and the one boy Mitch. One girl, Sally, was about the age of my mother, and they were close friends. Mr. Miller was a devoted friend of my father's. Mr. and Mrs. Miller were perhaps ten years older than my father and mother, so that my mother found more congenial association with the daughter Sally.

Mitch was a stocky, strong boy, with brown eyes and brown hair, and sallow complexion like his father. He was pugnacious and handy with his fists, and we two together were always enough for the tough Irish boys who lived on the Moody Hill, and who sometimes came to break up our circuses and games. Mr. Miller was a lover of books, and spent evening after evening reading to Mrs. Miller as we children raced through the rooms playing games, in no wise disturbing their calm nerves. When I brought Grimm's *Fairy Tales* from the farm Mitch devoured the book, and I reread it with him; as later we read *Tom Sawyer* together. We read little after the death of Alex. Somehow that painful event did something to take Mitch away into other associations.

There is in human nature something which struggles to do something for the dead, though there is little to do. We find this disposition portrayed in *Antigone*, where the tragic theme is a dishonor that was heaped upon her brother by letting his body lie above earth, a prey to vultures and dogs. Tender and generous as my grandfather was, I was horror-stricken by the grave that Aunt Mary Masters received on the Shipley Hill, about a quarter of a mile from the Masters farmhouse, where the broken rail fence admitted straying beasts and blacksnakes crawled through the tangled weeds and vines. Long after her death my grandfather bought a lot in Oakland Cemetery near Petersburg and removed the little that remained of her body; but she never had a memorial stone from him. This was the fate of the beautiful young woman who for seven years lay an invalid at the old farmhouse, reading Tennyson and Shelley and sending gifts to us children, a silver goblet to me, a napkin ring to my sister Madeline, whom she had named. At the time that my grandfather bought this lot in the new cemetery, my father bought a small lot too, which figures dramatically in this relation of mine. And the beautiful boy who died at five years of age, who was first buried in a very old cemetery of Petersburg, the first one there in fact, was removed to Oakland. But like Aunt Mary, he never had a memorial stone; though when he died my father and mother were stricken to the earth with agony.

All these years I was going to school, and it was close to a mile from our house to the new school building to which I was transferred from the old wreck near the Baptist Church where I started to learn the primer. Of course I had to walk this distance, and also to take my luncheon with me, since the noon hour was not long enough for me to climb the Braham Hill and return. These days at school were not happy, they did not have a particle of charm; the teachers were without personality. They were mere drudges in a thankless business. A part of one year I went to the district school, called the Shipley School, which gave me happiness, because I was enabled to live with my grandmother and to have the delight of the lunches which she prepared for me. The schoolhouse was about half a mile from the Masters homestead, and was presided over by a woman who later taught me at the public school in Petersburg. Without intention on her part she became an influential factor in my life and development.

The Petersburg school by this time was presided over by a red-faced Irishman who was noted for using a pointer on rebellious students; and he put terror into all of us. For a while I had a man teacher who used a piece of harness tug to punish disorderly boys; and I was as afraid as death of him. But he never whipped me. The woman teacher of the Shipley School, having transferred to the Petersburg school, fell to my lot; she did whip me, and cruelly. I was full of mischief, I laughed and whispered, and sometimes threw chalk. I deserved disciplining, but she went too far. She beat me with a pointer until I was black and blue. My father and mother were so enraged over it that I was taken out of the public school and placed in a private German school run by Henry Fisher, an old scholar. The sons of the circuit clerk; Frank and Nora Blane, son and daughter of one of the principal lawyers in town; the son of the richest farmer near town, Harry Schirding by name; and Rainey Braham, already referred to, were in this school when I entered. And I had a hearty welcome from all of them. Here we were taught arithmetic and the other elementary branches, but also we were taught German. We had to speak the language as much as we could, for the master always talked to us in German; and of course we had to read it. Soon I could read the German primer very well. The master liked me and was proud of me. There was scarcely the semblance of what is called school order in the room. The boys chewed tobacco if they wanted to, or ate chocolate. We whispered to one another, we even talked out loud; and on one occasion I had a fight with Harry Schirding, who, being much larger than I, was about to worst me when the master came down the aisle and parted us. The master was nearsighted, and wore heavy glasses, and used to sit on the platform reading or casually watching us as we studied or laughed and talked. Sometimes he would rush for the platform after a boy named Heine Missman; slugging him in the back, he would exclaim, "Hund!" as all of us laughed aloud. It was a happy school, and I got a fair start in German, which later on led me to German literature. This is what ensued from the whipping given me by the woman teacher.

All this while I was going frequently to the Masters farm. Often I went on Saturday to stay over Sunday, and in the summertime I would be there for weeks, or for just as long as my mother allowed me to stay. By this time I had been through all the old trunks where I found Aldrich's *Story of a Bad Boy*, and strange old textbooks that had belonged to uncles and aunts, and some German books; besides Moore's poems and many volumes of *Godey's Lady's Book*, which my grandmother had had bound. They contained illustrations of American houses and scenes identified with American notables, pictures of the mountains and rivers of America, and many other things. Also, by grudging grace of my uncle I played with his wonderful top, looked through his field glasses at the Mason County Hills and the surrounding country, or played engine with his strong two-wheeled wagon. I brought in wood for my grandmother, or worked for her in her vegetable garden, or in her flower beds. I rode horses about the country, or accompanied my grandfather and grandmother when they set forth in the carriage to see old neighbors. And on Sunday I went with them to Concord Church, four miles distant, where I got my impressions of the pioneers, their religion, and their ways of life.

I was nine years old when my brother died. Late that fall my mother took me and Madeline with her to spend the winter with her sister Mary in Leavenworth. This aunt's husband was very well off, and he had lived in Leavenworth from the time that my father tried to practice law in Garnett. I think this uncle had something to do with my father's going to Kansas.

My mother was grieving over the death of her boy, and this winter in Leavenworth was planned to relieve her sorrow. It was a happy time for us children. Our uncle was generosity itself. He heaped us with gifts. His house was a handsome one full of things interesting to children; and he had a wonderful span of black horses, and a colored coachman named William Singleton.

We rode every day about the town and into the country seated in a shining democrat wagon, while William Singleton drove the spirited horses. We often went to Fort Leavenworth and into the wooded country about. Uncle Harvey was a silent man, scarcely ever speaking, though he smiled benignly upon me and my sister, and treated us with great affection. He sat at the breakfast table eating his food in silence while Aunt Mary talked volubly, and engaged in arguments with my mother on the slightest provocation. As soon as he had drunk his coffee and eaten what was served Uncle Harvey would light a cigar and walk to the door with the fragrant smoke swirling about him. I made up my mind then that I would smoke as soon as I could; and often at the barn I used to take a whiff from the pipe of William Singleton. Aunt Mary always followed Uncle Harvey to the door to kiss him good morning. He suffered this demonstration with a kind of weary smile. She had talked him into a state of collapsed quietism.

We had intended to stay all winter in Leavenworth. But one day Aunt Mary and my mother had a dispute as to the pronunciation of the word "attorney." My mother contended that it was to be pronounced to rhyme with "journey"; Aunt Mary insisted that it was to be pronounced to rhyme with "horny." Neither would surrender the debate, and Uncle Harvey came home one night to find us making ready to go back to Petersburg. My mother and Aunt Mary had certainly inherited the nature of old James Dexter of Newark, Vermont.

Uncle Harvey lavished presents of silver cups, glass savings

banks, and silver napkin rings upon us children, and we returned to Petersburg in the bitter weather of middle winter.
At the station my father met us, and we drove through the cold
in the bus up the Braham Hill to our house, where my father
had built a big fire in the stove in the living room. But it had
died down while he was gone to the train to meet us, and we
shivered about the mild stove and then hurried to our cold
beds. At once I missed the comforts of Uncle Harvey's house,
provided, as it was, with a furnace which kept every room at
summer heat.

On this trip I had written down whatever I saw. The dark
way to the Mississippi River which we crossed at a town called
Louisiana; the red lights shining from the bridge down into
the terrifying stream; the crowds at the station in Kansas
City when we arrived; a description of Uncle Harvey's house,
and of William Singleton, and of Fort Leavenworth, and of
the oak woods through which we often drove. The Missouri
River was only a block from Uncle Harvey's house, and often
I walked there to look at its turbid depths rolling their way
filled with ice cakes all that winter.

Aunt Mary had lost her only son by drowning in this river
just a year or so before this. I frequently stood on the bank and
looked at the spot where he slipped from a cake of ice he was
trying to ride. My aunt had taken up with spiritualism and
was holding communication with her boy's spirit. My mother
and she talk spiritualism all that time we were there; and we
children stood about wide-eyed and terrified. At night we hid
our heads under the covers for fear of seeing the ghost of this
boy in the room.

As soon as I could get out to the farm I made my grandfather listen to the history that I had written. He did so with
many exclamations; suddenly these ceased, and I looked up and
saw that he was asleep. This was my first piece of writing, and
it had the reception I have mentioned. About this time my

grandfather had made a trip to Overton County, Tennessee, which he had not seen since 1829, nearly fifty years. He found that every trace of his father's house was gone; and he spoke about the changes with melancholy accents. My grandfather, who laid out his money to his children, either for their education or for their happiness, had sent my aunt Anna to the exposition of 1876 at Philadelphia. By this time Aunt Minerva was living there. By the fireplace at night my grandfather and my aunt Anna talked of Tennessee and Philadelphia. And in these days a clergyman named Oliver Wilson, my grandfather's nephew, was making long visits at the Masters farm. My aunt played on the Mathushek to his singing, and took lessons from him for the recitation of "The Raven." This aunt, in spite of all the advantages that my grandfather gave her, had a hard and tragic life. A plausible man came along. He was interested in Sunday school work and for this reason my grandfather had unlimited confidence in him. After the marriage, my grandfather went into business with him in Petersburg, for which he gave this man $10,000, or rather supplied that amount as a patrimony to my aunt. He lost everything on the Board of Trade in Chicago. My aunt knew nothing about it until she arrived in Oregon, whither he had moved her to try a new country for riches. When she knew what had happened her health gave way and she died.

I stored many memories at this time of my life. My father had moved his office from the courthouse to a new building on the west side of the square, with windows which looked out on the courthouse yard. Here I sat when the Fourth of July was celebrated, and when the Burr Robbins circus came to town and paraded the square with the elephants, the gaudy circus wagons, and the clowns. The circus tents were always pitched on a flat near the Sangamon River. I was never quite sure of money with which to see all the wonders of the circus; but one time Mr. Miller made popcorn balls for me and Mitch, which we sold on the square and got money enough to do the circus thoroughly. In fact, Mitch had no money at all.

These were the days, too, when I saw Mentor Graham going about the square. I did not know that he was fun for all the town on account of his litigious experiences; though once I saw my father play a practical joke on him to the great amusement of the crowd. Nor did it mean anything to me that this was the old fellow who had taught Abraham Lincoln grammar forty years earlier. And there was William H. Herndon who was trying cases with my father in a special legal partnership. Often I rolled on the grass in the courthouse yard as these two talked. It turned out from a long later revelation from my father that Herndon was telling him intimate things about Lincoln.

At the Menard County Fair I often saw William G. Green, who had lived at New Salem when Lincoln was there. He was at this time a man over sixty, with snow-white hair and sloe-black eyes, and known familiarly as "Uncle Slicky Bill." He had won that sobriquet through some of his crafty dealings with the Indians, which had laid the foundation of his fortune, reputed to be about a million dollars. One time I saw him standing by the railing which enclosed the race track at the fairgrounds. The picture of him became ineradicable, so much so that I see it now as freshly as ever. He was dressed in black broadcloth, he wore a silk hat, called a stovepipe; his hair was white as snow. He stood there studying the horses about to race. He and my grandfather were fast friends, often visiting back and forth in my days on the farm. They lived about twenty miles away from each other.

My father loved a horse, and loved racing; and he loved sports of all kinds and took a great interest in the fairs. His good looks, his gay spirits, his physical strength and prowess, his eloquence at the bar, made him a man to be hailed wherever he went in that country. "Hardy," he was affectionately called.

In these days a foot-racer named Ed Moulton came to Petersburg and raced at the fair. Around there he was reputed to be the fastest foot-racer for two hundred yards in the world; he was known to the sports world all over America then and for long after. My father took up with this Ed Moulton and backed him; while Mrs. Moulton was often at our house for meals. She seemed to me wondrously beautiful, and I listened rapturously to her stories of Pennsylvania, where she said she was born, of "Pennsylvania Dutch." True to my strange nature, I conceived a poignant feeling for this woman, not knowing that it was fundamentally romantic. When she left Petersburg I wept bitterly, much to my mother's disgust.

My father had been re-elected state's attorney; and if there was any reason why he could not have gone forward to any honor that the people of Petersburg had to give him, I know nothing about it. I do know that he had not a wandering nature, like Uncle Addison. But for some reason he decided to leave Petersburg. It was an ill-advised step. While Menard was of small population, he could have continued to live there and have followed the life of an advocate, who traveled the circuit of the surrounding counties to try cases, as well as from Lewistown, on which his eyes were set as a future place of residence and law practice. Besides, his roots were so well down in Menard County; everyone knew him there, he was popular with the people; his father had lived there, an esteemed man, for many years, and he himself had grown up with the men who were at this time controlling the affairs of Petersburg and the county. By temperament and by breeding, by political adherence, and by everything else that makes men of similar mind and gives them understanding of one another, this was his place and these were his people. Whereas he was going forth to a very different country and people. It is likely that he did not know this fully; but it was the fact.

Fulton County, of which Lewistown was the county seat,

was much older than Menard County. At one time it had been the county in which Chicago was located. Lewistown was incorporated in 1823, and was the county seat to which people from Chicago came to transact public business, to get marriage licenses, pay taxes, and the like. The Rosses were one of the pioneer families of Fulton County, and Lewistown was named after Lewis Ross, who was born in the same year as my grandfather. I think he was in the legislature with my grandfather; at any rate, they were friends of long standing by this time.

Lewis Ross had been a colonel in the Mexican War, but as a Democrat he had the same attitude toward the War Between the States that my grandfather had. These two men visited back and forth during the years, something I did not know until I was nearly grown. The distance between their houses was about forty-five miles; and they drove it in their carriages, staying for a day or so after arriving. Colonel Ross had a numerous family of sons and daughters. One son John was for a time quite devoted to my aunt Minerva, and often came to the Masters house to see her. All these things put together brought the two families into some intimacy. But there was something else.

When my father was at Ann Arbor in the middle 1860's one of Colonel Ross's sons was attending the university also. This son committed suicide, and my father was one of the students who brought the body back to Lewistown. Thus he saw the place for the first time; whether he ever saw it again until he was making ready to move there, I do not know. I think he believed that Colonel Ross would do something for him professionally and politically; and that with a man of such distinction and wealth as a patron he would start off prosperously. The Ross house in Lewistown was a brick mansion of some distinction, with a large yard around it; and Colonel Ross was reputed to be worth about half a million. He had been a lawyer too, and one of the leading ones in that part of the state; but though but sixty-eight years of age, he was long retired from practice.

We children were thrilled at the talk of the contemplated move from Petersburg. For myself, I looked forward happily to the wonders of Lewistown, of which my father told us: of the riches and the house of Colonel Ross; of the courthouse older and larger than the one at Petersburg; of the mills and industries that there were in Lewistown, of the beautiful country about it, and the great Thompson Lake near it, and many other things. I did not foresee that I would have to go through the difficult process of making friends anew, of establishing myself with strange companions, and proving my mettle over again, something I had not had to do very much in Petersburg, after all. One thing that I looked forward to was the high school in Lewistown. Petersburg had none at that time, while the high school at Lewistown had some reputation, and was under the principalship of a Princeton graduate. So all in all I was happy to leave Petersburg, not thinking that I would thus be separated from my grandparents and from the life that had given me so much happiness. I did not comprehend all in all what the change meant, and naturally I couldn't do so. If my father had been able to calculate all the difficulties that awaited him he never would have broken his settled life and left it behind him. Also my grandfather was against this venture, and my grandmother too. I can't remember now what my mother's attitude was. I know that after we arrived in Lewistown she pined for Petersburg and her friends there.

In the early winter of 1880 my father resigned his office as state's attorney and went on to Lewistown and took up the practice of law. We were to come on later. By this time there was another son, who was named Thomas after my great-grandfather Masters; and we were living in the house on the Braham Hill much as we had before. My mother, who had the greatest trouble in getting and keeping a maid, had taken into the house an orphan named Mary, who had been partly raised by a Petersburg family. She had come to my mother complaining that she had been badly abused in this other household; and my mother, who all her life was taking orphans and oppressed souls to her bosom, took this Mary as a maid. And she was going to Lewistown with us.

In time my father sold the house which his father had given him. My mother would not sign the deed until he promised her that he would give her enough of the purchase money to travel back to Marlboro, New Hampshire, to visit her mother whom she had not seen since she came west in 1867. That being settled the deed passed, and very soon the purchaser, his wife and his children were coming and entering; while carpenters in behalf of the new owner were taking measurements with reference to changes in the house, and the building of a porch. This man had bought one of the grist mills in Petersburg, as well as our house, and was handling everything with a large hand, as though he had plenty of money.

Our life now was spent amid the confusion of packing. The meals were served hurriedly and without order, prepared by Mary, who was not very competent, and my mother, who had one eye on Nigger Dick to see that he put the right things in the right box. My grandparents came in to see us at times and to look sadly upon what was going on. They felt that my father should go on with his profession in Petersburg. By this time my chum Mitch was dead, while the death of our brother and the temporary unfriendliness of the banker's son, marked these days with the characters of a closing period of life.

For some reason my sister went out to the farm in June. She was never attached to it as I was; but my grandfather was fond of her. He used to saddle one of the gentle horses, and lifting my sister into the saddle, would lead the horse around the lot for the good part of an hour. It was still the era of cyclones, and one night in the latter part of this June a cyclone swept down upon the farmhouse, and the buildings around it, wreaking curious destruction. It happened about eight o'clock in the evening.

My uncle happened to be in Petersburg that night, or he would have lost his life. After paying a call upon his lady friend he came to our dismantled house and stayed for the night. Petersburg was not touched by this cyclone, and was not even aware that there was one near. But the next morning rumors came to us; and my uncle bestrode his horse and galloped out to the farm. I followed him soon on my pony, making the distance of five and a half miles in half an hour, or so.

And what a spectacle greeted my eyes! The fences were torn away; the walls of the barn lay flat, with the hay bulging from the dislocated roof. The corn crib and sheds were demolished. The kitchen was swept clear away. The main house was wrenched from its foundation, and the walls at the corners torn apart. A great apple tree was lying on the roof, the roots sticking in a great mass of earth which had been lifted as the tree was snatched up by the storm. In the yard under one of the maple trees stood my grandmother cooking on an old stove which had been set up in this emergency. She was laughing and talking, and when she saw me she frowned and said that I should not have come. I had gone to a store and bought an apron for her for a present. This I now gave her, and she relented with a laugh, but went on to say that she had more aprons than she needed. And so, with other things ended, the farm was gone, at least until the buildings could be restored. But would the carpenter shop be made like the old one? Would the new kitchen be as full of charm as the old one?

This cyclone announced itself with a sound such as can be made by blowing one's breath over the mouth of a jug. My grandfather and grandmother were in bed, and my sister was lying on the lounge in the room. Suddenly things began to crash. The clock fell striking from the mantel. The lightning was terrific, and rain poured into the room through the parted corners and the broken roof. All this was followed by terrible darkness as the cyclone swept on its way toward the Houghton woods. My grandmother got up and finally found a candle. Her first thought was of her son Will, whose room was upstairs. When she got to the hallway she found it filled with debris, and got upstairs with difficulty only to find the door of her son's room jammed so that it could not be opened. The apple tree on the roof had mashed down the timbers so that the whole room was twisted out of shape. And thinking that her son had been killed she descended the stairs, croaking and crying, to take care of my sister. She heard now the voice of the hired man. He was praying as loud as he could. The kitchen walls had been thrown down around his bed, but he was not hurt. And no one was even scratched. The horses in the barn stood at their stalls with the timbers lying about them. The cows in the sheds escaped injury. But strange things were done to the chickens. They were stripped of their feathers, and these feathers were blown with such velocity that the quills stuck deeply into the boards of the house, as if shot there by a bow. Rails from the fences were picked up and carried into the fields and there driven so far into the ground that only a team of horses could have pulled them out. One rail was sent through the west wall of the house as if it had been a javelin thrown from a catapult.

Thus there was confusion all about in the labor of restoring living conditions. My grandmother did not want me; she had work enough on her hands. And the presence of my sister excluded me from staying. So I went back to town on my pony.

This year the Fourth of July fell on Sunday and the celebration was being held on Saturday, the third. On Friday we started for Lewistown. Our possessions had been loaded in a freight car to be taken to Lewistown by way of Peoria, as there was no direct line from Petersburg. So we took the morn-

ing train, after being bidden farewell by many people. In a
minute we passed the house we had first lived in in Petersburg.
At my right I could see the brewery and the Sangamon River;
at my left the schoolhouse where I had been whipped with the
pointer; then soon the hill up which I had gone so often when
riding to the Masters farm. We passed within sight of the Atterberry farm, and then through the village where I gazed
upon the country store where my uncle and I had so often
come when out riding. Next was Oakford, almost as familiar
to me as Atterberry. Then the country was not so well known.
I had never seen Salt Creek, though I had heard of it always.
My grandmother sang some verses about it. Now we crossed it.
Then we got into sandy Mason County, all strange to me. I
was sad now. I could see that I was really going away. But
my father was in high spirits, and my mother, though partly
infected with them, was in meditation, holding in her arms my
brother Thomas then three years old.

At Havana we went to the hotel, one of the largest I had
ever seen; and at mealtime into the dining room, where waitresses scurried about taking care of the guests. There was the
Illinois River about a block away. I walked to look at it, and
saw steamboats for the first time in my life; I had seen none
in Leavenworth. We stayed overnight in Havana. Next morning, amid the firing of cannon and firecrackers, we took the
stage for Lewistown, crossing the long bridge over the Illinois
River, then driving by the side of Spoon River, and so on until
we reached the uplands on which Lewistown was situated.

For more than five miles the road from Havana to Lewistown runs through the Spoon River bottoms, one of the most
forbidding pieces of country that I know anything about.
Jungle weeds crowd the banks of the river, overshadowed by
huge cottonwood trees. The land about is fertile, but is much
flooded, or was then. The farmhouses for the most part were
ramshackle, some of them mere log houses. As it turned out,

the people who lived here were wretchedly poor and drunken, some of them vicious and criminal. My mother found all this out to her great disgust. And as we drove along she took in the scene amid exclamations of distaste. It was July and very hot. The black flies bit the stage horses, and smells of dank weeds, dead fish, and the green scum of drying pools smote our nostrils. At Duncan's Mills, a place of one store and a post office, we crossed Spoon River on a covered wooden bridge, and ascending a long hill a mile beyond reached the uplands that surround Lewistown. Here the country is truly beautiful. The farms are well kept, and were at the time; the houses, freshly painted, were surrounded by yards with lilac bushes and roses. There were rims of forest about. A mile away I saw the spire of the church amid trees. The horses trotted along, and after crossing the Burlington tracks we drove north in Main Street to the hotel, which was larger than anything in Petersburg. The cannon boomed around us, and drunken men whooped and guns were fired. It was Independence Day, but not for us, not for me. A curious crowd of boys and men drew around the stage to see the newcomers, and passing among them we entered the Standard House. A new day set in, far more new than I imagined or my father had any idea of.

Chapter III

LEWISTOWN WAS MY HOME FOR ELEVEN YEARS FROM THIS time. My father and mother lived there for twenty-six years, until they moved to Springfield and thus came again into the Petersburg neighborhood and into closer association again with the people whom he had never quite lost along the years. In some particulars it was as unfortunate for him to leave Lewistown after so long a residence there as it was to forsake Petersburg. In reality, as I have already said, he was not a roving spirit. This return to the Petersburg country was not the result of that longing which idealizes a place of happy days spent in one's formative years; but rather it came about through circumstances which disturbed his equilibrium, and when he was not in good health, though not old. He was just past sixty.

Eleven years spent between the ages of eleven and twenty-two are as long as twenty years in a later period of life. And when I think of all that happened during that time, of the friends I made, of my schooldays, which became more real than those of Petersburg, of my graduation from the high school, of my reading days, and my work on a country newspaper in Lewistown, no period of my life seems so long. I plunged at once into life at Lewistown, making new friends among the boys of the town.

My father rented a house, just a block from the public square, which belonged to a druggist in town. The summer was excessively hot for us, as the house stood right in the sun without a tree. The yard was full of weeds where the crickets sang and the grasshoppers whirred. I remember all this as a kind of sunny desolation. We were lonely too; for my mother went to Marlboro, New Hampshire, to visit her mother, and Mary, the maid, ran the house and ran it badly. She was then about twenty and was much besought by the bad blades of the town. Hence often she was out till late at night; and my father being uptown, or out of town, we were left to shift for ourselves. In the middle of the summer I went to visit my grandparents, taking with me a new-found boy friend. By this time the devastations of the cyclone were somewhat cleared away and the new kitchen was built. This boy friend saw Petersburg and thought it finer and more wonderful than Lewistown. But my mind was divided now, what with the historical old courthouse in Lewistown and the large Beadles Opera House, the furniture factory, and many other things.

Before my mother returned from New Hampshire in the late summer or fall we had moved to another house, one of the many owned by Colonel Ross. It was an old house, as much of Lewistown was old, and smelt musty. The entrance door abutted the brick sidewalk. The roof was rotting from the heavy shade of huge soft maples. The rooms were small; in a word, we were not in comfort. Always I dreamed of the Masters farmhouse, of my grandmother's music box and birds, of the fascinating carpenter shop, and of my uncle Will's priceless tops and wagons. About this time we began to know Colonel Ross and his family, and to go there to dinner occasionally. It was like being received at a country estate in Virginia. I felt that Colonel Ross and my father were very good friends, and that he had an old-time respect for my grandparents. I sat on the lawn with them and listened to their interesting talk. Colonel Ross had a daughter, just a little younger than my mother, who became her friend and remained so through many years. Altogether our relation with the Rosses was happy. But I suspect that Colonel Ross did not do anything professionally for my father. There was nothing he could do, likely, except to recommend him to clients. For himself, he was able to manage his own affairs from the legal standpoint; and thus in this very summer we began to feel the pinch of difficult circumstances.

At this time Lewistown had at least ten lawyers, and one firm in particular which commanded a considerable prestige. The competition for business was intense, and my father had nothing to recommend him in particular, except a certain name as an advocate earned at Petersburg. He was now but thirty-five years old, and as it took him several years to become competent as a business counsel, or a solicitor versed in real estate law, he was ill fitted at the start in Lewistown to do anything but criminal practice. Although my father had tried to be a soldier for the North, a cloud had followed him from Petersburg; and at once in Lewistown he was reputed to have been a "Copperhead." This made trouble for him, and prevented him from getting business. Though Colonel Ross had opposed the war, and yet had thrived, and though Lewistown had many Virginians and men of Southern sympathies, the town was really controlled by Calvinists; while the Grand Army of the Republic made it difficult for the Democrats to win the offices, though at this time they were numerically more powerful. In spite of this Republicans slipped frequently into office in the county. Canton, eleven miles away, and a larger town than Lewistown, was run by Republicans under the generalship of an editor there.

It was not long before the money was gone which my father had received for the Petersburg house, and he applied to his father for help, without success. Thus he found himself caught, and had to put forth all his strength to survive. This he did with magnificent fighting spirit; but for about five years we were in straitened circumstances. I was filled with shame because of our deprivations and my father's struggle to make ends meet.

That fall I started to school. The building had been erected in 1866, and was three stories high and of good architecture.

It was heated by furnace and was light and sanitary. The high school room was called the Chapel, where the man from Princeton presided; and this room was equipped with geological and botanical specimens, cases of butterflies and the like. It had a library, including an encyclopedia. It had recitation rooms off it; for there were two assistants to the principal. To be in the Chapel was to enter the high school, and I did not do this for about a year. I took part in the ball games, had fights with the boys, played marbles, had my enemies and my friends; and as of old was strong in the back and arms. I had to demonstrate this on occasion by wrestling larger boys, some of whom were bullies and wanted to fight with fists when I had thrown them. That attack of measles and pneumonia, which I had when six years old, had left my lung weak, as it was described. And during the winter of wet feet and cold rooms at home I had desperately bad colds. These started always with a sore throat, then with sneezing, then with croup; then they settled down into a painful cough which racked my chest as I spat thick phlegm for weeks afterward. I was as pale as a morning moon, and as thin as a wafer. My father, preoccupied with his fight to get a foothold, and my mother, always in distress herself from nervous dyspepsia and worried about a thousand things, could do little for me. At the end of these winters I was always spent, and so I got into the way of going to my grandmother's when spring came, to stay until the end of the summer, working for her in the open air, and riding about the country on horses with Uncle Will. This I did until I was eighteen. But I was twenty-one before I rallied completely out of this trouble with my left lung. So far as I know I had no tubercular infection. I had inherited remarkable vitality, and was as full of restless energy as it was possible for a youth to be; and that energy has remained with me through life. My grandmother used to say that I was never still. She often complained of my unquiet desires and activities when she was trying to rest, and I wanted to be off with her picking strawberries, or catching chickens, or bringing in the cows when the time had not come for those things. I loved to work, and was always busy at something.

One of my diversions on the farm was flying kites. I learned how to make them from laths and the tough paper of which flour sacks were made. And I kept increasing them in size until they were as tall as I, or taller, with great long tails made of rags, to which was tied a small bush for a ballast. Going to the sixty-acre pasture to the west of the farmhouse and yard I would send these kites into the air as high as I had string with which to send them. Then I would lie amid the grass for hours, watching my kite as it wavered with the breezes and seemed to keep companionship with the clouds. To the north were the Mason County Hills, merely a low ridge along the Sangamon River, but they seemed hills to me, and were full of strange fascination, since I heard much of the people who lived near there, the Germans who had a church and a settlement there. It was called Dutchland by my grandfather and the people in general of that neighborhood.

I had good marks in school from the first. Charles Benton was my first teacher in Lewistown, a man perhaps in his late twenties. He was studying then to be a lawyer; when he became one much later than this, he moved away to Kansas and prospered. The Princeton man in the Chapel soon came to know me. He was an effeminate type with a fine silken beard, and a light voice. He wore women's shoes. Yet he had intelligence and character enough to run the whole school successfully, and to win the respect of everyone. When I was graduated up to the Chapel he was very attentive to me, and kept me in a glow by the complimentary things he reported of my progress to my father. The Chapel had large windows in front and in the rear. The rear windows looked to the north over the level lands surrounding Lewistown. To the south the valley of the Spoon River was five miles away, and was reached by a steep descent nearly that far off. To the east the plateau sloped to Thompson's Lake, an estuary of the Illinois River. But to the north the country was level; to the west it was broken into hills after the upland of Lewistown was left behind. Here at the north end of the chapel were the encyclopedias. And I soon spent all the time there that I was permitted to do, reading incessantly of great men, of Americans like Washington and Franklin, and gazing dreamily at the beautiful country to the north.

It was not more than a year or two after I entered the Chapel that the Princeton man departed. Without mentioning all his successors, I pass to the principal whose ill-starred career had much to do with my own life. His name was Harrison, he had been a clergyman, and he was about sixty-five when he took charge of the school, but old for his age. In addition he was partly paralyzed. His eccentricities were quickly noted by the students, and disorder followed; in fact, it was not long before there was not even the semblance of discipline, and the school would have gone completely to pieces except for the influence of the assistant principal, a woman of unusual character.

This woman, whose name was Mary Fisher, taught rhetoric and literature, American and Engish, besides botany and history, and many of us among the more ardent spirits of the school took fire under her inspiration. She had been born in an Illinois town not far from Lewistown, though in another county. Her father was a butcher by occupation, and her advantages had been limited in the humble home of her girlhood; but by great industry, fired by a consuming ambition, she had become a well-read woman, and was proceeding at this time to acquire French and German. She had traveled a little in the East during summer vacations, and there had met Louisa Alcott, of whom she told us much, to our wondering delight. But above all she was fascinating to me, and to some others who had nascent ideas of the literary life, when she confided to us that she was going to write books. And as it turned out within a few years she became the author of a book on French critics, and one on American literature, and some novels; one of which, *The Journal of a Recluse*, received some critical praise and had a succès d'estime.

Miss Fisher was exceedingly attentive to me by way of advancing me in my studies; but her pride and hope was a youth of about my age who was saying that he was going to be a writer; and Miss Fisher chose him for her prophetic praise. He probably showed more promise than I did. He had more self-assurance, and a readier command of conversation, and at that time was doubtless better read than I. His father was a man of means, and his household contained a decent library and was supplied with the principal magazines by yearly subscription. We had no magazines, and few books.

Miss Fisher had rooms in an old hotel called the Fulton House, not far from where I lived; and night by night the four or five of us who had taken a fresh start in life under Miss Fisher's ministration repaired to her rooms where she talked to us of Emerson, Dickens, Scott and Thackeray, of Byron and Shakespeare, of Eugene Field who was a name to conjure with at the time. She loaned us paper-bound copies of *Oliver Twist* and *David Copperfield;* and thus it came to pass that I read those novels when I was about fifteen, but with some difficulty. It was only my will to read them that took me through. She also introduced us to the lectures of Ingersoll on the *Mistakes of Moses,* and the others; and thus all of us turned atheists, including her pride, who added to atheism a Byronic despair. All this was a new life to me; for at home there were no books but Bryant's *A New Library of Poetry and Song,* a copy of Burns, *The Arabian Nights,* which I didn't enjoy, and my Grimm from the Masters farm, which I read over and over; a few paper-bound plays of Shakespeare, and a copy of Crabbe's poems, which I never looked into. I didn't read Crabbe until after I had published *Spoon River Anthology,* and there was critical comment that it resembled Crabbe's work.

We moved several times before my father bought a house. From the house which my father rented from Colonel Ross we moved to a house to the east part of town, across the tracks of the Burlington Railroad. I disliked this house and its neighborhood with all my heart. It was not in the least like a home. Once when I returned from the Masters farm after one of my delightful visits there, where I rode horses and flew kites, I went upstairs into the heat and the loneliness of a scantily furnished room and sobbed bitterly, much to my mother's unhappiness. She hated the Masters farm, and by vehement sarcasm tried to make me hate it too; but in this she was never successful. While we were living in this house James Dexter, my mother's brother from Marlboro, New Hampshire, came to visit us accompanied by Aunt Fannie, my mother's sister who lived in Pana, Illinois. This Aunt Fannie had received my mother as a guest when she first came to Illinois, and in her house she first met my father as a suitor. Uncle James was a drawling, good-natured man; and Aunt Fannie was humorous and taught me many riddle rhymes; but I missed in them the traits which drew me so amazingly to my uncle Will and my grandmother and grandfather Masters.

We didn't live more than a year in this house by the railroad. We moved to a small house across the street from the woolen mill, a very considerable establishment which was manufacturing blankets and woolen cloth. A number of boys who went to school part of the time worked in this mill; I tried to get a job there too, but failed. Still I was much in the mill watching my boy chums manage the different machines; or I was in the alley where I could look into the engine room and talk with the engineer.

Here I fell in with a new crowd of boys. I was brought into closer association with Miss Fisher's favorite youth, who lived

in a good house about a block from the mill; and I began to
see how well his house was run. In the fall his father bought
maple wood in large quantities, and had it sawed for winter
use. My father bought a load of wood at a time, and it was
poor stuff. His father had hard coal base-burners, and we had
wood stoves, or soft coal stoves. He had apples in the cellar, and
celery laid away from a garden which this youth partly cared
for, assisted by a gardener in town. We had apples by the small
bag, and no celery. He had a fine lawn and a lawn mower. Our
yard grew up with weeds, and was mowed sometimes by Benny
Wilcox, who used a scythe. His father and mother celebrated
the feast days like Thanksgiving, Christmas and New Year's.
My father and mother paid little or no attention to such festival
occasions. Sometimes my mother would bake a chicken for
Thanksgiving, but it was with such effort and such distress of
mind and body that the joy of the day faded.

Still I was happy enough while we lived in this house by
the woolen mill. I made friends with Job and Henry Hughes
who worked in the mill; and with Mickey McFall, the son of
the blacksmith, whose shop was on Main Street two blocks
away from our house; and with Ed. Edgar, the grandson of
Carpenter Osborne, who lived across the street from us; and
above all, with Hare Hummer the son of the well-to-do dealer
in logs and ties. Hare played the banjo and the accordion with
wonderful skill, and sang many songs. We used to sit on the
steps of the mill under the moon and listen to Hare play and
sing, or to Henry Hughes who had a fund of funny stories.
Our game was Red Line, which we played about the mill night
after night. Hare was a hunter, his father had presented him
with a small shotgun and a rifle. Once we made up a party and
went camping by Thompson's Lake. The party consisted of
the Hughes boys, a son of Dolph, the cobbler, Miss Fisher's
pride, and a youth named Chalmer Hupp, whose father was a
prosperous blacksmith. Chalmer had a roadster named Fred;

and often I went to the Hupp farm riding behind Chalmer. I don't know about the home circumstances of the Hughes boys; but all the others had homes much better than mine. Chalmer had a cellar of apples, and sat at an abundant table thrice a day. Already I was beginning to earn money when I had the chance. Not far from our house was a large black-berry patch owned by a man named Sharpe. He paid boys one cent a quart for picking berries, and I worked for him to get spending money, for books sometimes, even at this period.

I had a very unfortunate experience just now, and it grew out of a sort of fateful train of circumstances. A man named Waggoner, who had several times been sheriff of Fulton County, tried for another term of that office about a year after we moved to Lewistown. The cry was raised against him that he had grown rich out of the office, and that he had had it long enough. My father, always ready for a contest, joined with the majority of the principal politicians in Lewistown against Waggoner, and was accused of interloping activity. He was a newcomer and had no business to take part. Such were the remarks of Waggoner and his sons, one a lawyer who was fighting my father and preventing him from getting law business, and another a son about eighteen at this time, a vicious character. He had stabbed a boy almost to death a few years before we came to Lewistown; and he carried a slingshot with which to crack anyone on the head who stood in his way.

There was a tough boy of about my age, named Meyers, who was the son of a butcher who had recently died from the kick of a horse which he was beating in a drunken frenzy. This Meyers boy hated me with terrible venom. I had wrestled with him and thrown him, and he wanted to even up the score by a fight with fists. His opportunity came when Mickey McFall and I were giving a minstrel show in the loft of his father's blacksmith shop. I was manager, interlocutor, and other principal things in this show; and it was attended by the

Waggoner youth, this Meyers boy and many others, who seemed bent on creating such disorder that the show could not proceed. The Meyers boy was the principal offender in this rowdyism, egged on slyly by the Waggoner youth. Meyers rose, once when I told him that he could either be quiet or go out, and said that he would "fix" me after the show.

I had a lamp with which to burn cork for the blackening of my face, a tray and some other articles. When the show was over I washed my face and prepared to go home. Just then Mickey McFall came to me and said that Meyers and Waggoner and a whole crowd of boys were waiting for me; and that I had better steal out the back way. I refused to do this, saying that I could handle Meyers. And so carrying my lamp and tray I went to the sidewalk where I saw Waggoner moving about in the rear of the crowd with sinister slyness; while Meyers had his coat off and his sleeves rolled up ready to fight. Mickey McFall was a powerful boy, whose arms were large and hard as iron from swinging the sledge hammer for his father. Meyers came forward on seeing me, and Mickey walked to him and threw him to one side as if he were a child, though Meyers was strong and was larger than I. With this Waggoner emerged from the shadows of the crowd saying that he was going to see fair play; Mickey bearded him, and Waggoner saw that he would have to use his slingshot to master Mickey. Meanwhile Meyers was circling toward me; when he got within striking distance, I smashed him in the face and rushed him furiously toward a telephone pole standing by the walk. I kept striking and delivering blows without any return of consequence; and then suddenly I was hit in the temple and reeled blindly around and around until I fell in a heap, completely done for. Mickey then jumped in and took from Meyers a piece of lead with which he had struck me. He accused Waggoner of engineering the whole thing. And I lay there with a great purple lump on my temple as big as a large plum. I went home and told my father what had happened. He was furious. The next day when he met young Waggoner on the street he kicked and cuffed him thoroughly. Then the youth's brothers talked of using pistols; and so it went. Out of it all the Waggoner family became my father's bitter enemies and stood in his way politically, and as much as they could professionally, to the end of his residence in Lewistown.

After we had lived by the woolen mill for a year or two my father began to be more prosperous. We had been in Lewistown about three years when he bought a house on Main Street, three blocks from the square. He had successfully conducted some law business for a well-to-do farmer, and had received this house as a fee, agreeing to pay about $1,000 in addition. It was an old house, lately occupied by a man who had lingered for years with paresis, whose wife was of none-too-good repute in town. The rooms were full of stale, sickly scents, as of foul breath breathed into the walls. The paper reeked with terrible odors. The floors were old and broken; the back sheds looked like haunted places. The yard was large and contained many old apple trees covered with water sprouts. At the east end of the yard was a broken-down barn. In front and around the yard, there was a blind-board fence which was broken in places, with boards missing, and sagging here and there. There was no sidewalk along the front, but only a beaten path, which was shaded by many huge soft maples. Mark Twain's birthplace and his house in Hannibal were humble, but with a charm. Walt Whitman's birthplace at West Hills was comfortable and even beautiful. This house of ours had nothing but ugliness, decay, and disorder. Altogether it was a ghostly ruin.

My mother was heartsick about it. We children did not understand her dislikes in the least. We did not know what she meant when she talked of the clear beautiful brooks of New Hampshire and Vermont, of the pine forests, of the clean rivers with rocky shores, of the white New England houses, set in well-kept lawns full of flowers. In Lewistown there were families named Phelps and Proctor who were New England people and had New England houses. By looking at these we understood dimly what our mother meant about the houses of the New England villages. She talked to us of these things in vain.

My mother set to work to make over the house as best she could and to get it cleaned. She set my father to work to this end, one time at doing some lathing. Like his father before him, he had no mechanical aptitude at all, so that the driving of a nail taxed his talent. But by and by fresh plaster was put on the walls, both to make them more presentable and to kill the terrible odor of the old paper and plaster. Also she built a grate in the front room, which sent forth a cheerful light and warmth.

Miss Fisher came frequently now to see us, and to talk before the fire of books and authors. She liked my mother, saying that originality was her gift, of which she herself did not possess as much as she wished. They talked books. My mother, though of imperfect and broken education, had been an omnivorous reader of Wilkie Collins, Trollope, Dickens, and Thackeray. She had a wonderful wit and an unusual gift of humorous narrative, and she kept Miss Fisher in a roar of laughter, matching Miss Fisher's learning with original argument.

By this time the eccentric principal of the school was losing control of it; and Miss Fisher had become discouraged and disgusted both with the principal and with the hard task of doing anything under his bad discipline. She left that spring never to return, having been my teacher just a year. She taught next in Springfield, Missouri, then here and there; while she kept up a steady correspondence with me about books and life. On her annual trips to Europe she wrote me frequently;

and so it continued until I went to Chicago in 1892. I saw her for the last time in St. Louis where she had become a friend of William Marion Reedy and was contributing criticism and the like to his *Mirror*. By this time she had become a proficient linguist in French and German, and very scholarly all around in criticism and philosophy. When *Spoon River Anthology* came along she wrote me a mild congratulation, from which I saw that the book did not please her. She was a type of the Midwest who tried to rise out of it; and depictions concerning it did not interest her.

In these days great disaster struck our household. We were living in the Main Street house in rather indigent circumstances. The fight against my father waxed amain, and sometimes we were without coal, and often without adequate food. He was full of dark pugnacity, as he went about silently with great glowing eyes full of pain and confusion. I was having bad colds as usual, and my mother, full of fighting spirit and having grown to hate Lewistown with consuming hatred, was wont to blame my father bitterly for the pass to which we had come. On his part, he never lost heart completely; he never gave up the fight. But a dreadful accident befell him. Like my boy chums I had bought two pigs to fatten for slaughter, and was keeping them in a pen which I had built around the old barn. The time came to kill them. My father sent me to the butchershop to ask Efe Saul to come down and butcher and dress them. Efe treated the request with great contempt, being in drink at the time, and none too cordial anyway on account of a small unpaid bill at the shop. He handed me a butcher knife and told me to kill them myself, or have my father do it, after which he would come down and haul them away and dress them. My father took the knife, leaped into the pen and killed the pigs.

In sticking them he nicked the large finger of his left hand with the knife, something that he did not notice when he washed his hands at the sink. But that night he was in great pain; and the next day there were red streaks up his arm. In short, he had blood poisoning, and for weeks lay between life and death. My grandmother came over from the farm and nursed him, and perhaps brought money, for he was earning nothing in these circumstances. He lost flesh until he became a skeleton. And finally one day Dr. Hull, the good physician, to whose skillful care I owe so much, came and found no pulse. So I ran for whisky, which I obtained with great difficulty in prohibition Lewistown. He drank the whisky and passed the crisis. When he got up again he went to the Masters farm for a rest. For many months he went about a mere bag of skin and bones carrying his left hand on a pillow, and trying what cases he could get to try in a weakened state which would have driven many men to bed to stay. These were hard days, full of sorrow for all of us. After about seven years of struggle to get business the chance came for my father to step up. It was a murder case, which stirred all that part of Illinois, that gave him a reputation and put him in line for profitable law business.

A man named Ferris had been divorced and gone to Kansas, where he lived for several years before he returned to near Lewistown, and killed the man, McGee, who had married his former wife. By this former wife Ferris had had two children, the older of whom had been writing him to Kansas that their stepfather was beating them. Ferris returned to Illinois to stop this treatment of his children. He came to Canton, partook of liquor, put a pistol in his pocket to protect himself against McGee, and walked to the farmhouse. McGee had said that he would kill Ferris on sight. When Ferris entered the house, after knocking, McGee seized a chair and calling Ferris a vile name approached to strike him. Ferris then shot McGee. Then, according to Mrs. McGee's first story before the coroner, Ferris raped her. The country was wild with excitement. Ferris was brought to the jail in Lewistown. A mob gathered to lynch him, but lost heart; and finally Ferris was spirited away to the jail at Peoria. The Lewistown papers, one in particular conducted by a fanatical prohibitionist, whipped the mob spirit against Ferris to white heat.

On the trial in Peoria—my father had the venue changed to that place—it necessarily developed that Ferris had the right to see his children, even if he was not in a state of life where they could be brought to him by a governess. To go to the house of the man who had married his former wife was not the most decorous thing to do; yet that he had the right to see his children was indisputable. The carrying of the pistol was explained by Ferris's fear of McGee. Mrs. McGee herself testified that McGee started to attack Ferris with a chair, saying that he would kill him. It came out at last that the intercourse between Ferris and Mrs. McGee was by mutual consent. Thus my father drew all the bad stings of the circumstances, in spite of the Lewistown newspapers; and Ferris finally went to prison for twenty-five years.

When this trial was about to be called my father was lying in bed with influenza, in a high fever and saturated with perspiration. Dr. Hull came to see him and told him that it would be certain death to go out into the winter cold, and ride to Peoria to try this arduous case. Ignoring this warning my father went and tried the case, which took several days. This was the turning point in his career. After this he had plenty of business, and even the pick of the business. He was always expert in criminal cases; but the Ferris case caused him to be employed in all the important will cases, and civil suits of various kinds, even in the surrounding counties, the county seats of which he visited at term time, just as Lincoln had done fifty years before.

To return to the school: By the fall of 1885 Principal Harrison had lost complete control, and every day was a circus, a riot of disorder. Boys arose from their seats and fought in the aisles. Chalk whizzed about the room, sometimes striking the principal. Erasers were hurled across the room. The principal expelled scholars; they laughed at him and kept their seats. One day he seized a pointer and started to discipline one of the large boys. This boy with his great strength grabbed the principal and hurled him off, following this up with blows. The principal was humiliated before the whole school, which took it all in with a certain youthful cruelty. My sense of humor was constantly excited by the daily spectacle, and I was as mischievous and insubordinate as anyone. However, the time was past to really progress in the school, and so I determined to learn the printer's trade, following the example of Franklin. I went to the *News* office and applied to the editor for a job as devil, and was hired at $1 a week, being then in my sixteenth year. I did this, but did not yet leave school.

I had to open the office and sweep it, and start the fires in the stoves so that the room would be warm when the printers arrived. It was all fascinating: the smell of the ink and the paper, the look of the type cases, the wonder of the presses. I had to be on duty at seven o'clock, which meant that I had to arise at about six and get something of a breakfast. My mother was never up early, so that I built the fires and got something to eat before setting off. Very soon my father discovered what I was up to, and tried to stop it. He commanded me to attend to my school. But I replied that I would do so and work at this job too and so I went on. I could set type until twenty minutes of nine, and then go to school. School let out at three-thirty, so that I could work at the *News* office until six. At once I began to write little pieces, which the indulgent editor allowed to be printed. By this time I was reading under the tutelage of Miss Fisher's letters; and with one chance and another I was being educated. The first verses I ever published were during the first year of this apprenticeship as a printer. The second printer and I set them in type one night and ran them off clandestinely toward midnight on the job press.

My schooling was thus intermittent, it was casual and interrupted at the very time of life when it should have been continuous and systematic. For these reasons and others I never became a good grammarian, thoroughly versed in syntax and in the knowledge of the rules which govern adverbs, adjectives, participles, and the like. I succeeded better with algebra, and later with geometry. We had a study called "word analysis" in which I excelled, as I did in literature. When I was taking stock of what I had learned in order to see whether I could graduate from the high school I was forced to do some piecing. I could then see that I had not finished the courses along the way as I should have done.

My job with the *News* was such that I could leave it and come back to it, practically as I chose. I became a swift compositor in a little time, but I never learned much of what was then called job work, that is, work featured with various type in bills, letterheads, and the like. But in the straightaway business of composition for the newspaper I was soon able to set as much type as the foreman or his helper.

When school was out this year I went to the Masters farm, as usual; and again worked for my grandmother at gardening, and plowed potatoes under the watchful eyes of my grandfather, who didn't want to see them plowed up by my getting out of the row. I had another summer of kites and horseback riding, and another summer of hunting squirrels with my uncle Will in the woods about. On one occasion we went camping at Miller's Ford on the Sangamon in the hottest weather imaginable. A terrible storm came upon us as we lay in improvised tents by the river under the huge elms and cottonwoods. We were drenched with rain as the tents were blown to the tops of the trees. We returned in the morning to the farmhouse to be greeted with a cry of delight by my grandmother, who had feared that some terrible accident had befallen us during the night. I had some ingenuity in making things, windmills, kites, as I have already mentioned, and in doing carpentry for my grandmother, such as making coops and bird boxes. One summer, perhaps it was this summer, I connected the farmhouse and the tenant house with a telephone. I took cigar boxes apart, and then glued them together tightly, and thus made receivers, which were connected with wire such as the harvesting machines used. This wire was stretched on hickory poles which my uncle and I cut in the woods. At night the tenant farmer sang for us at his end of the line. We sat in the farmhouse kitchen and heard him perfectly; and at times we could send messages with audible distinctness over this line of a quarter of a mile.

I was so full of energy that to keep still was impossible. I was ambitious to do everything that a man could do. In harvest time I carried water to the workers and rode the horses back to the barn. This year, or a year or two after this, I became a harvest hand, and followed the harvester, and later the thresher, around the neighborhood. I cut bundles and sometimes pitched them, and drove a team which gathered up the bundles for the thresher; and in great pride sat at the table at noon consuming the heavy food with the harvest hands. I was as busy and as happy as I could be. During the summer festivals were given at Rock Creek, sometimes at Concord, and my uncle and his wife and I drove to these affairs along the scented lanes of Sandridge, and returned home under the light of the full moon.

That fall I went back to school, but I kept my job on the *News*. The eccentric principal held on through the influence of a brother-in-law, a lawyer in town; but the lack of discipline became worse than ever. Finally the school became such a pandemonium that I refused to continue. I devoted all my time to typesetting. As other students also left school, the situation became serious; the directors woke to the gravity of affairs, and the principal was dismissed and disappeared. Then came on the scene a young man who was graduated from the University of Michigan. He at once put the school in order, organized a Latin class and gave energy to the classes in geometry and the sciences. With all this happening I was sent back to school, and might have begun Latin at this time, except for a kind of stubborn disinclination, connected with my distaste for the study of grammar, and for the Latin grammar in particular.

About this time Edwin Parsons Reese came into my life. He was born in Ohio and with his father and mother and numerous brothers and sisters had moved to Lewistown. He conceived an instant admiration for me; and his good nature and companionable qualities won my friendship. I had a certain distinction at school for lively humor and ebullient energy; and I had won a prize for the best essay one year, but it turned out that the only other contestant had not treated the assigned subject with a seriousness deserving attention. So that my triumph was not very creditable in a competitive sense, while the essay itself was of no merit, even for a youth. Reese's father, though a very poor man, managed by great industry to support his family. It was not long before he bought a house and some land at the east side of Lewistown; and Reese and I began to exchange services. One Saturday I would help him in his garden, and the next he would help me in mine. For my mother was forever setting out blackberry plants and the like, and raising a garden.

Reese had a good mind, he was a conscientious student, and so when I returned to school I had him for a classmate and a help with studies. The new principal was organizing a class to be graduated that year, and Reese suddenly revealed himself to me as being one of the chosen students. I had not thought of such a thing. Reese was also going ahead with Latin, but I could not do that, or at least I did not. I had a good deal to make up, what with my absences from school, and my side interests in books, which had drawn me away from regular studies. But I settled down to hard work now to make the grade. Among other friends at school was Jack, a comedian character, who played, made faces and said odd things. When Jack found out that I was trying to be graduated his manner changed toward me, his heart seemed hurt. It was impossible for him to finish the necessary studies for graduation, and he seemed to consider my aspiration as a kind of treason to our friendship. We were not intimates after he made this discovery, and on the night when Reese and I stood on the stage of Beadles Opera House and recited our orations, mine being on Robert Burns and Reese's on Civil Service Reform, Jack looked at us from the audience with mournful eyes. All this while I was doing some typesetting and some writing for the *News*.

By this time a young man, the son of a physician of means in the south part of the county, had bought a half interest in the *News*. I have drawn a portrait of this man in a poem called "Cato Braden" and need not enlarge upon him here. He was my friend from the first, and paid me what he could for what I did. I was using what money I made to buy books, from John Alden in Boston, such as a complete Shakespeare, Emerson's *Essays*, Bacon's *Essays*, Marcus Aurelius, and books which contained translations in fragments of Euripides, or Hesiod, together with biographical and critical summations of these writers. John Alden was truly a great benefactor to youths, situated as I was, who were glad of the chance to buy a complete Shakespeare for thirty-nine cents.

Along the way I had earned money at odd jobs of real labor with which to buy books. My father was very much against this. He disliked the spectacle of seeing me carry coal for a justice of the peace in town, and when I got the agency of a Peoria paper and began to deliver it about the streets he was much annoyed. He was making a fairly comfortable income now, and there was no need of this work of mine, except on the score of buying books, which he did not approve. I had my schoolwork, and that was enough. And inasmuch as he did not find anything of moment in Virgil at the University of Michigan, he thought that I would waste my time in a study of the *Aeneid*. Still I went on.

My grandmother was so pleased with my graduation that she journeyed over from the farm to be present at the exercise. She was then seventy-two, and she sat in the audience with her eyes riveted upon me the whole hour of that ordeal. She was very proud, so that I was more than welcomed at the farm, where I went soon after graduation day. This was to be my last summer vacation there. Afterward I was there for a few days, but no more for long weeks of work and play. About the house and the carpenter shop were a thousand evidences of days that were ended. Some of my kites were in the loft of the carpenter shop. My name was carved on the jambs of the door. There were the remnants of chicken coops that I had made for my grandmother, and the outlines of flower beds which I had spaded and bricked in for her.

But I found my uncle Will changed. He felt that my graduation had taken me away from him. He himself had attended the Wesleyan University at Bloomington, where he studied bookkeeping and commercial law. This thing of graduating, and orating on Robert Burns, was a different matter! That summer I wrote verses about the Indians in Houghton's woods which I showed to my uncle, saying that I had copied them out of a book. He merely grunted, and perhaps suspected that I was palming my own work off on him. We did not have many enjoyable rides together. And for my part in the flush of adolescence, in the sudden desire to put away childish things I rather turned against the farm. Altogether this vacation was not a repetition of past delights. I have always seen when an experience was ended, a neighborhood or a house exhausted, or an association drifting toward sterility, or a love becoming dangerous or impossible, and have turned away, even when my heart was wrenched.

But now in the midst of this summer at the farm my father called me home. By this time Lewistown had a telephone to Canton and Peoria, which worked very badly. Messages from Peoria had to be repeated at Canton eleven miles away; and sometimes a voice from Canton was not very distinct. The station in Lewistown was in the upper story of a drugstore, where the druggist was manufacturing Cherry Pectoral and a remedy for sweaty feet called Pesodorne. The work was in charge of his son, a dull, heavy youth who had an impediment of speech. I came into contact with all of this when I took the job as operator of the telephone at $2 a week. My father had summoned me home to do this. He thought that I should be doing something to earn money now, and that I was idling my time away at the farm.

So I said good-bye to my grandparents and set forth for Lewistown, going this time not by way of Atterberry, but from Petersburg through Mason City. This change of route was in keeping with a changed day. Often my grandfather drove me to Atterberry to get the train to Havana. Always his eyes filled with tears as he said in his patriarchal way, "Farewell, son." Now I went to Petersburg, taken there by my uncle, at this time not thirty years of age, rather hard, and no longer pleased with me as a chum. Our days of hunting squirrels together were over. And this summer we had had a dangerous fight in which I assailed him with a neckyoke after he had exasperated me by shooting grains of corn in my face as we sat in the kitchen.

My grandmother gave me $15 when I departed, out of money which she had made from selling eggs. When I got to Mason City I had an hour to wait for the train on to Havana, and I spent it walking about and looking into the store windows. In one of them I saw a book bound in red with golden scrolls and decorations, and the words "Shelley's Poems." At school I had read "The Skylark," nothing else, as I remember it; but the beauty of the book and my memory of "The Skylark" drew me inside to buy this book. I took the necessary $2 from the money my grandmother had given me, and walked out with the book, into what proved to be a new world.

By this time I had gone through Burns over and over, through Bryant's *A New Library of Poetry and Song,* and through Poe, both his poems and his stories. Often Reese came to see me at night both before and after our graduation, and sat with me as we read Poe's tales of horror in the little study that I had when my mother built over the Main Street house. But now Shelley took me aloft on wings of flame. This passion for humanity, this adoration for the beautiful, this celebration of the Awful Shadow of an Unseen Power, this exquisite music in words, this ethereal imagery! I was carried out of myself. I began to see that I, too, had a passion for humanity, and that my father's democracy and integrity were the roots out of which this devotion to Shelley's poetry took immediate nourishment. And to what ends Shelley led me! To more metaphysics, to Plato, to the Greek writers. Poe and Burns fled back out of my interest.

However, I had to mind the telephone now; I had to sit and listen to the idiotic and stammering talk of the druggist's son, as he wrapped Pesodorne and Cherry Pectoral; and when I was not at the telephone I wrapped bottles, too, as part of the employment at $2 a week. At the same time I was writing for the *News*, or setting type there; and altogether I was as busy as possible.

It is not important that I should observe a factual chronology in recording the years between the time I left the high school and the time I went to Knox College at Galesburg. I shall try, however, to give account of what I was doing in this interval, even if I do not tell it in the order of years when it happened. For one thing I did not act as telephone operator very long; and soon I was helping my father in his law office. I wrote letters for him, I searched records at the clerk's office for him, and did other services, some of which were of a lawyerlike character, in which he instructed me. It was his fond hope that I should be a lawyer. My literary ambitions disturbed him. He thought that the writing of books was for men of genius, and that I had no genius. And he was concerned lest I become of age and go into life without a reliable means of support, and run into poverty. He knew that authorship and poverty went together; and he was not loath to remind me of the fact. In the office, especially when I really began to read law under his tutorship, I often had behind a lawbook some work of poetry or fiction or philosophy; so that if he entered the office suddenly he would not catch me with Locke or Shelley. This surreptitious reading on my part was like the use I made of the encyclopedias in school, when I was often consulting them not about my studies, but about some investigation of my own, chiefly about authors.

It was in these years following my graduation from the high school that many of my habits of life changed. I ceased to fellow with my Huckleberry Finn, Hare Hummer. No longer did I hunt ducks with him around Fourth Bridge, and at Thompson's Lake. I had managed, in the days of that companionship, to get a gun by trading off a watch which my father had given me. It was an army musket which had been bored out. It was very long and heavy and made my shoulder ache to carry it. With this I did a good deal of hunting with Hare. I also went skating in the winter with him; and in the summer he and the rest of us made dams at Spudaway Creek so that the collected water furnished a sort of dip for us. When roller skating came along my grandfather bought me a fine pair of skates, and soon I was racing; and for two miles was the fastest at the rink which had been made in the theater of the Beadles Block.

With studious days these diversions fell away, and Hare, though still about the square, drifted out of my association, though not out of my affection. Soon he went away to school to study music, and later in life became a phenomenal performer on the banjo, and later still a figure on the vaudeville stage.

My father's office was on the second floor of the Beadles Block, just across from the courthouse yard and with two sides of the square visible. In fact, the square had but three sides; for at the east was an open space of at least a block which was in front of the Presbyterian Church. Thus at the window where I sat in study I could glance up and see what was going on about town as men went here and there on their business, and as the farmers came into town, tied their horses to the rack and started forth to see merchants, lawyers, or what not. This spectacle so affected me at times with its vast futility that I had to go forth and find companions to shake off the depressing feeling. I described this in my novel *Skeeters Kirby* as coming over me on hearing of the death of the character Winifred. Winifred's death was fictional, but the feeling described was profoundly true. I was accumulating a soul fatigue which would in a few years drive me to the city. There was a loneliness in this town and the surrounding country which could not be borne many years longer. It was this loneliness and an introspection produced by the country that gave me melancholy.

The churches added to this. There were revivals every winter at which the lugubrious hymns of the hymnal of the time were sung. Along the years in Lewistown I went to Sunday school a little; but I made myself obnoxious by arguing with the teacher concerning miracles. Mary Fisher, who had started many of us to reading, had inoculated us with freethinking, by directing us to the study of Emerson, and to the reading of Ingersoll's lectures which were enormously popular in those days in that part of Illinois. Sometimes the local newspaper contained controversial articles on the subject of science and religion, in which some clergymen debated with the local scientist; and there were several of these in town or near by. For myself I read the Bible through and through; and by the time I was fourteen or so I was skeptical of it as a revelation. The attitude of some leading citizens toward my father helped to solidify my opposition to the churches and to the religion they preached. These were the banker, the merchant, and their retainers, all men of small natures and inveterate prejudices and village ignorance of everything really good and beautiful. These men made it as hard as possible for my father in politics and in his profession; and all the while he was doing nothing wrong. He believed in the saloon and said so openly. When he wanted a drink he went in at the front door, not the back door as others did who tried to cultivate the banker and the others named. In the boredom of the town he played poker sometimes for a small limit with his boon companions. He loved a horse and went to the county fairs to see the races. He was involved in legal controversies which stirred the community, and he fought in proportion as he was opposed. He lived openly in every way, without any hypocrisy, without any hiding of what he believed and liked. But his humor, his good will, his genial nature, his captivating personality did not win over these bitter Calvinists. They fought him to the end. They compassed his defeat for county judge when we had lived in Lewistown but a few years. What they did took bread from my mouth, and from the rest of the family; and these churchmen knew that they were doing this. Still they went on, until my father vanquished them and won the county to his side.

This situation bore upon my attitude toward the church. I

could not abide the men who controlled it; and as I had thrown out the Bible as revelation, and the miracles as non-sense, my religious position was definite at an early time. Very soon I made friends with a man named Homer Roberts, a schoolteacher, and a student of Huxley and Spencer; also with a Dr. Strode, who was something of a scientist; and then with Judge Winter, an old lawyer in town who was a freethinker and had a considerable library.

It was a tragedy that my father became caught in the circumstances and among the small-minded people that he did, but it could scarcely have happened otherwise. Born in the country and with no desire for city life, and no knowledge of any city; a man not fond of books or of the intellectual life, save as it bore upon his profession, a Democrat by nature and conviction, a liver and a mingler among people, the life of Petersburg or of Lewistown was his fated lot. And yet his distinguished appearance, his gifts as an advocate, his cosmo-politan freedoms and tastes made him seem a misfit in the life he lived among the people whom I have described. Still he had hundreds of devoted friends who were loyal to him through everything; and after he had been ten years in Fulton County he was the most popular man in it and the leading lawyer at the bar. He was professionally and politically ambitious, and fought for himself, and for us. Along the way he received such honors as being made a presidential elector in 1892, a delegate to the National Convention in 1896, and he was ap-pointed master in chancery in 1894, and was a school trustee for twenty years, and a member of the County board of Super-visors. He was mayor of Lewistown for four terms. Yet his political ambition was unrealized.

My father's liberalism was rock-ribbed, and about every-thing. I feel that he was a great blessing to me for his attitude toward the conduct of life. He believed in drink in modera-tion, and made no bones of the fact; he believed in the joy of life, and there in the dour Puritanism of Lewistown he took his medicine without a whimper at the hands of the deacons, the churchpeople. They made it hard for him, almost beyond description. Drink was as bad for some of the rough people in Lewistown and from the Spoon River bottoms as it ever was for the Indians in the Far West. Yet what was to be done with the liquor problem? When there were no saloons in Lewistown, beer and whisky could be brought in from Havana and Peoria. Lewistown, being without police protection for lack of money, when there were no license fees from saloons was at the mercy of rowdies who had bought drink in those other places. So that saloonless Lewistown was not in fact saloonless. My father believed in a few saloons for Lewistown conducted according to law. When he was elected mayor he brought about the licensing of four saloons. He appointed a strong German town marshal with strict instructions to keep order on the streets, to arrest at once the first brawler. He ordered that the saloons might open at a certain hour in the morning, and that they should close at eleven at night, and should not be open on Sunday. He decreed that the first saloonkeeper who violated these regulations should lose his license. These decrees were strictly enforced. Lewistown had $2,000 a year from the license fees, with which sidewalks were built, and the town kept in cleanliness and order. His first administration was so successful that he was triumphantly re-elected, in spite of the churches and the prohibitionists. His majorities kept increasing as he came up for another term. But the office really burdened and annoyed him, and the incessant attacks upon him by the preachers and revivalists, and by the prohibition editor, offended him and disturbed my mother. Though there was a total absence of cases where minors were sold drink, or habituals given access to the saloons, or murders or bad altercations as the result of drink, these righteous forces kept praying for my father or calling down upon him the wrath of Jehovah. He grew very tired of this. At the end of his fourth term I happened to be in Lewistown. His loyal following were urging him to stand a fifth time for mayor. He asked me if he should do so, and I told him to let someone else bear the burden. So he declined another nomination. A lawyer in town was put forward, and was ignominiously defeated. Lewistown started again to be without police and to buy drink from Havana and Peoria.

National prohibition filled my father with deep resentment. He had admired Bryan greatly in 1896 and later; but when Bryan took up with prohibition my father dropped him completely. About 1918 when my father was living in Springfield he was asked to run for Congress on the Wet ticket. He was then seventy-three, but full of vigor. He went forth and made the best campaign he could, but was defeated. My mother, who was a prohibitionist, was infinitely displeased, even disgusted.

Returning to the subject of the churches, my father ignored them. He scarcely entered one; on the other hand, he maintained a dignified silence to all attacks upon him. At the last, however, just before he moved to Springfield he was greatly incensed by something that a man was saying about him on the streets. It was too personal to be passed over. He sought this man out and gave him a thorough whipping. He was then sixty-one and handicapped by a lame hand, having lost a finger long before. But his right hand was sound and effective.

While I lived in Lewistown I stood resolutely with my father against this Lilliputian world and frequently excoriated it in the *News,* to which I had free access; for the editor there loathed these Calvinists and Republicans, and sided heartily with my father on political and town issues. When I went to Chicago Reese took my place on the *News.* He admired my father extravagantly, and he had a command of invective that was better adapted to the town and the cause than I had.

Looking from the window of my father's office out upon the square, and noting any new figure that passed, there was a first time when I saw a young man named Will Winter, the son of Judge Winter already mentioned. Gradually I began to know about him: that he was being educated at the University of Montreal by the Scripps family who were connected with great newspapers. He was always away from fall until summer, when I would see him as he passed along the street. He never lingered or called upon anyone. His house was at the edge of town; it was an old house set on a hill amid trees, in a large yard of some acres. Here, as it turned out, he spent his time reading, without companions, and quite alone. I heard that he knew Latin and Greek and French, and that he read Euripides and Sophocles with perfect ease. That was wonderful to me. I wanted to be friends with Will, and in time it came to pass. We became chums, and thus Hare Hummer for this reason, as well as others, passed out of my life for the most part.

Will's father had a considerable library, in which books like Addison's works and Steele's, and Dryden's and Pope's largely figured, together with philosophical works like Locke's and Hume's. The old gentleman was a freethinker, and the son Will was at this time a man twenty-two or so; so that here again my attitude toward the church, which had its emotional support in a championship of my father whom I could not bear to see dishonored or harassed, received intellectual support from these two who were men of some learning. I had bought with money earned by some of the odd work I did a copy of Locke's *The Conduct of the Understanding;* and now Will's father urged me to read Locke's *Essay Concerning the Human Understanding,* and I did so. I followed this up with Hume on *Miracles,* with many novels by Scott, whom Judge Winter read habitually; and with many other things. Judge Winter was a Republican and for many reasons did not like my father. Yet he took me under his friendly devotion. When we first moved to Lewistown the judge of the Circuit Court was a man of really brilliant mind, who later became a member of the Supreme Court of the state. Though he had urged my father to move to Lewistown, he treated him with great unfriendliness, with sly, scheming enmity after my father was moved and was thus caught in the circumstances of a new abode. This judge being sent to the Supreme Court was succeeded on the circuit bench by a relative of Judge Winter's, who at once fell in with the church crowd of Lewistown; and my father fared little better at his hands. Thus in going my way I became friends and found sympathetic understanding among people who were alien to my father. My father did not like this. He did not like Anne, of whom I shall presently tell. He did not like Dr. Strode, at least in these days, or Homer Roberts. And I fancy that they did not like my father, and kept still about him in our intercourse out of respect to my feelings. Certainly they kept still about him.

So I was going along feeding my hungry mind. I read Huxley and Spencer with Homer Roberts, particularly *First Principles,* and the *Data of Ethics.* I read Swinburne with him. Often I went to Bernadotte on the Spoon River, where Dr. Strode lived at this time, and rode with him about the picturesque hilly country of that part of Fulton County as he visited his patients. He was something of a botanist, and had made a collection of the mussel shells of the river; and he was in correspondence with Yeomans, who was then editing the *Popular Science Monthly,* on matters of conchology and the flora of that part of Illinois. Dr. Strode's friendship was of inestimable advantage to me. At his invitation and that of Homer Roberts I joined the Fulton County Scientific Association, which was made up of the teachers and students of literature and science of the various towns about. And soon I read a paper on Whitman before one of its monthly meetings, to considerable acclaim. Even by this time I was known as a writer of verse, for I was publishing verses in a Quincy newspaper and in one at Bushnell, and in the Chicago *Inter Ocean.* As I was friends with these people and others who were not friends of my father, though not his enemies, and as I was engaged in studies and interests which my father disapproved, I found myself much out of his sympathy, and even looked upon with a sharp eye.

But it was Anne who drew all his bronze opposition to my ways; and between these two I was shaped and changed.

I can end this chapter by saying that all this time from my twelfth year until my nineteenth was largely wasted, and misused energy—all except for the books I found mostly for myself, and except for the interesting and helpful friends I made. My father did not know what to do with me, and he did practically nothing for me. The precious and abounding vitality, and intellectual hunger of those years needed to be turned to a regular course of study and cultural development in some good school, or under some competent tutor. I made my own way, finding the path after many misjudgments of the directions, and after many obstacles of circumstances, of my own making, and that of my parents. As I look back at it now it seems to me that my parents did not really care for me, or have any proper interest in me.

Chapter IV

I HAVE MENTIONED THE PRECOCIOUS PASSION WHICH I CON-
ceived for an older girl in the Petersburg school when I was
about six. Later when I was seven or eight a girl of ten or so
explained the technique of love-making to me, and my emotions became directed toward satisfaction more or less from
that time forward. When I was about ten a cousin of sixteen
came to Petersburg to spend the winter with us. Seeing that I
was partly initiated into the mysteries, she encouraged amorous
intimacies on my part as she held me in her lap. When, however, I proposed something more real she told my mother, who
whipped me cruelly. On the other hand, while seeking these
girls, I shrank away, my feelings of adoration faded when I
had won them to an embrace or a kiss. In Petersburg was a
brown-eyed little girl named Lucy who won my heart to such
an extent that I could not sleep; I went about exclaiming, "O
Lucy, I love you so." My mother heard me and was greatly
amused. But one day Lucy came to our house to play; and we
went to the barn to see my pony. There Lucy proposed that I
give her a kiss. I was immeasurably shocked, so much so that
Lucy was ended. On the contrary, I would fondle the cousin
referred to by the hour, and even try to win her over completely; and there were two other girls whom I endeavored to
win, much to my discomfiture when my mother found out
what I had done. Wherever my idealism was involved I kept its
object high and afar; where my passion was the only thing with
which I was concerned I was bold enough. And then there
grew up in me a passion for intellectual beauty fed by the
poems of Shelley, by such poems as "Epipsychidion." In these
days of my adolescence with Dr. Strode and the studies I have

mentioned I longed for a woman who was beautiful of person and gifted in mind. I expected to find such a woman finally, and I dreamed of her. That was the love I sought. Somehow I believed that Shelley had found such a mate in Mary Godwin, in the face of his poems revealing that he had not found such a mate, and that this dream of the highly organized masculine nature is a false lure.

To show the nature I was when I met Anne at about eighteen years of age I must go back to the time I was eleven, and we had just moved to Lewistown. At once I met a girl of about my own age named Zueline. That name was of itself magic; it somehow associated itself with the houris of *Lalla Rookh*. And in fact she was somewhat of a Persian face and beauty. She had bright brown eyes, silken brown hair, exquisite features. We met somewhere at a party, and she took to me with the same ardent emotions that I felt toward her. At once we became child-sweethearts, which had for expression all possible chivalrous attentions on my part, like pumping water for her, waiting upon her, carrying her skates, and the like. I worshiped her. It seemed a blasphemy to me to want to kiss her, and I never did. I held her in a mad, sacred reverence. This madness went on for a good part of a year at school, and in play and at parties; and then my mother and her mother became alarmed. They conferred together and decided to part us, and they did part us. My suffering was beyond all words. When I tried to see Zueline she now avoided me under the instructions of her mother; when I met her finally so that she could not escape me she told me that she did not want to see me any more. Something like cold poison went through me, something like sudden and violent hate. A great agony stormed my breast, and twisted through the great nerves of my solar plexus. Then it was that spiritual antibodies built themselves in my emotional blood and circulation. It was like having measles which could not again be contracted. It was more than that: it was an acid which had entered my spiritual veins with which I could subdue subsequent affections of the heart.

In the days after I was graduated from the high school, and when I was writing for the *News* and publishing verses in the newspapers, it came to me that I should have a heart interest, as Shelley and others had had for inspiration to love poems and for intellectual stimulus. About eight years had elapsed since the days of Zueline; and in the meantime I had managed very well on the matter of natural gratification through the compliance of servingmaids about town and in my mother's service without any disaster either of body or of mind, so far as I can see even to this day.

Somewhere I heard about Anne, the daughter of the Presbyterian clergyman. She was not often seen, because she was frail, and spent her days reading, and studying Greek under the instruction of her father, a Princeton man. I wanted to meet this girl. She seemed the very soul I was looking for. The fact that her father was opposed to my father, and in league with the bankers and the merchants who supported his church in all the puritanical crusades and fights in town, did not come to my mind as important considerations. Anne, just my own age, was an unusual mind, of phenomenal verbal and other memory. I heard about her as the prodigy of memory and reading; she heard about me as the contributor to the *News,* and as a writer of verse and an omnivorous reader. I don't know when or where it was that we met. But it came to pass. She was much better read than I, and she took a hand to help me along. Her father was something of a scholar, who had a good many books, of a very different character from those of Will's father. The clergyman had books of philosophy and metaphysics, but they were Plato, Berkeley, and Sir William Hamilton; he had poetry but it was Wordsworth, not Pope; he had novels, but it was Thackeray rather than Fielding, and George Eliot rather than Sterne. Whatever he had was thrown open to me, and I tried to read everything in both libraries, with the result that I soon became badly stuffed, and had to rest to digest the material. It was Poe's stories which had led me to metaphysics; it was Shelley who kept me away from Poe, and even from Dryden. Anne was not beautiful. She had fine eyes and features; but her back was a little twisted, and a little humped, and she carried her head on one side because of the shape of her spine. She had a way of looking down as she walked, which seemed like modesty or diffidence. She walked the streets not looking up, not speaking to many people. With a foolishness scarcely to be condemned enough I made myself fall in love with her, thinking that it was the thing to do. I succeeded well enough at this preposterous business, and had suffering in plenty as the result.

Anne and I began on the plane of books and studies; but it was not long before we began to kindle toward each other. I was slow to take fire because of the experience at the age of eleven; and Anne did not take fire so far as I know until I did. Anyway it came to pass after much reading together and many tramps into the surrounding country during the spring days. Often we had with us a girl named Alfreda, the daughter of one of the deacons of the Presbyterian church, and six years younger than Anne. We would go forth into the wooded hills north of town always provided with some book by Anne; and as she and I read resting on the bank of Big Creek, Alfreda would stray off to gather wildflowers. When it was dark, or by the rise of the moon, we would return to town, to Anne's house, and there make supper for ourselves, and feast and talk. Anne drank quantities of coffee, and it was very harmful to her; for when she was a child she had suffered from scarlet fever, which had left her heart with damaged valves. However, when she had drunk two or three cups of coffee her mind flowed; and then she would recite long ballads from Percy's *Reliques*, or long passages from Shakespeare, or deliver monologues in language that sounded like pages from Dickens or George Eliot.

She knew that I was not religious; she knew my attitude toward the Bible. Sometimes we argued these subjects, but had to give over such contests, because neither could overcome the other, and we frequently became ironical and bad tempered. She had a sharp tongue among her other gifts. And at this time she wrote good verses; while mine were less meritorious because I did not observe the standard measures, as she did, such as the ballade forms. I could see that she disapproved of my father and his course; and that she gave admiration to the prohibition editor and his causes. She even said that he had ability, whereas in truth he had nothing but violent prejudices and intemperate words. But as he was a member of her father's church she reposed a blind faith in him which did no credit to her judgment and integrity. This is a brief enumeration of the threads which went into the weave of our relationship, and made its final pattern.

Meanwhile Reese was assisting his father, who worked in the lumberyard in town. As of old we helped each other make garden, and we read together. He, too, got acquainted with Will, and sometimes we were at the latter's place under the trees. But at this time Reese was doing little with books, save to read a history of the Civil War. He did not wander into the many fields that I did in these years, following an ever-widening taste.

My home life now was not agreeable. My mother did not like Anne's mother; my father did not like Anne's father, or his church. He looked at me at times as if to say that my association with Anne was a sort of treason to him. And in a way I felt this to be the case. Openly he remonstrated with me for spending so much time with Anne. My sister, who at sixteen had remarkable beauty, disliked Anne keenly. My sister was annoyed by Anne's superior reading, her wonderful vocabulary, and by her pointed sarcasms. They exchanged retorts whenever they met, and for that reason and my mother's attitude I could not have Anne at our house. My sister did not go through the high school; neither did she do much at this time to improve her mind. She had great vitality, and was not afflicted with colds as I was, but on the contrary was generally in health. She had had diphtheria in Petersburg, with a consequent injury to her heart. But this did not make itself evident until she was in middle age.

She associated with a young crowd who had no use for me, or for my studious ways. Among them was that Waggoner youth who had been adjutant to the Meyers youth in that fight in which I was injured. However, the bitterness of that affair was passing by now, or had passed so far as I was concerned. I do not think of the circumstances of my life at this time with anything but aversion. We were living fairly well, however. The house was better furnished than ever; and my little study was provided with a stove and a library table which I had had made for myself by the furniture factory. To this room I could retreat with Reese or Will, neither of whom my sister liked. She affected a gayer and more worldly type of young man. Having learned to play the guitar she entertained her callers with strumming "Sebastopol" and Spanish pieces upon it. I had brought from the Masters farm, in addition to the books already mentioned, a copy of Boyd's *Milton's Paradise Lost* with copious notes explanatory of the mythology and Biblical allusions. This I read again and again. My sister's guitar was brought from the Masters parlor bedroom where she found it under the bed, where it had been since my Aunt Minerva was married twenty-five years before or more. It was a very fine guitar, just as everything was excellent which my grandfather gave his children; but my sister managed to persuade my grandmother to let her take it. When Aunt Minerva found out that she had it she suddenly developed a fresh interest in the guitar, and took it away. Then Grandfather bought my sister a guitar;

but it was not so good an instrument as Aunt Minerva's, and cost nothing like so much.

My father was about forty years of age when he came to death's door with blood poisoning. That illness ended at last with the amputation of the infected finger on his left hand; the operation was performed by Dr. Hull, as I stood by and helped to hold my father as he went under the anesthetic. At this time he was a mere skeleton, a desperate-looking creature with great dark eyes and hollow cheeks.

Before this illness he had been very slender. When he was well again he began to put on flesh until he weighed about 190, and that weight he kept until he reached seventy-five years of age. This increased girth added to his good looks. With his black curly hair, his glowing dark eyes, his olive complexion, he was an arresting figure. With all the rest of it he had a quick masterful way of speaking, and he kept after me with a keen scrutiny so far as my studies were concerned. That is to say, he did not like my miscellaneous reading; he destined me for the law and while teaching me various practical things in the office, such as the abstracting of records, and the like, he kept urging me to read the elementary books of the law. Somewhere I saw that Byron had read Blackstone; and I thought I might do so, if Byron did, as a matter of general culture. So I took to Blackstone, and enjoyed the *Commentaries* immensely. I then bought an abridged Blackstone, and finally committed to memory all the definitions found in the full text.

My father was a fierce intercessor; he could not stand to see anyone wronged, any underman dealt with cruelly. At the time he left Lewistown for Springfield his practice was worth about $5,000 a year, and he had accumulated something like $25,000 in property. If he had attended to advantageous investments, if he had let those who were down and out take care of themselves or go to other lawyers, he might have been quite well off by this time. He spent his incredible energy in cases like the

Ferris case, where he got no fee at all. Indeed the note that he took for his fee in that case proved the occasion of a disaster. He went in a buggy to the south part of the county to collect this note. The horse became unmanageable and he jumped from the buggy, and broke his ankle, and was laid up for some weeks while it mended. He never collected the note. I must tell of one other case which shows his mettle and the circumstances in which I was developing.

The annual issue in Lewistown was saloons or no saloons. And about 1888 when I was setting type and writing for the *News,* and otherwise full of activities and studies, the saloons were voted out. A terrible man named John Logan was appointed town marshal by the prohibition mayor, with instructions to keep order on the streets and to hunt down the drinkers. Logan looked like a huge ingot of copper. He was red-faced, powerful, weighing perhaps 200 pounds without an ounce of fat. He was provided with a gun and a cane made of steel and knobbed with a ball of lead almost as large as an egg. So accoutered he walked about the square herding loafers off the sidewalks, and quieting boisterous voices. Eleven miles away from Lewistown was Havana with its German population, which had never voted the saloons out; as to that, they ran openly in the days of prohibition, from 1920 to the end of the prohibition folly. It was easy therefore to get drink at Havana, and that's all Lewistown's saloonless state came to. One day a man named Weldy, a fellow peaceable enough, returned from Havana and walked on one of the side streets toward his home carrying a jug of whisky. He was a little intoxicated, but was not disorderly. Logan spied him and crossed the street, commanding him to go home. Weldy replied that he was going home, whereupon Logan struck him over the head with the lead-knobbed cane, knocking Weldy flat. Then he began to beat Weldy with the cane. Weldy finally got to his feet and drew a small twenty-two caliber revolver and fired it. The sound of the explosion was so slight that Logan did not hear it; nevertheless, the bullet penetrated his abdomen, and he soon sank to the sidewalk while beating Weldy with the cane. Then there were cries. The city hall bell began to ring. I was at the type case, and hurried with the others to the shades of the city hall where Logan lay with the purple mist of *rigor mortis* already mantling his iron face and jaws. Thus came the end of Logan, who had killed two men in brawls and who, having joined the church, had become an avenging angel of the law.

A mob gathered to lynch Weldy, and it looked as though he would soon dangle at the end of a rope. That was the demand of the prohibition paper in Lewistown. My father would not suffer this to be. He took hold of Weldy's case; and though the circuit judge was that relative of Judge Winter's, he managed to plead Weldy guilty and get a life sentence for him. The state's attorney was a reasonable man who admitted that Weldy was grossly abused. He was willing to receive a plea of guilty and to recommend a life sentence. The judge was satisfied with that arrangement, and it was done. This is the technique of such settlements. No lawyer worthy of a license to practice law ever pleads his client guilty without having an understanding with both the judge and the prosecutor.

But my father's interest in Weldy was not exhausted. When Governor Altgeld was at the head of Illinois my father went to see him with affidavits and petitions from citizens, and with recommendations for a pardon from the prosecutor and the judge. Altgeld listened to a statement of the circumstances, and without looking at the papers granted an immediate pardon to Weldy, saying that Weldy had a right to kill Logan for such uncalled-for brutality. Weldy came back to Lewistown and remained a peaceable and industrious man to the end.

All this may have been very well for my father who was

working out his own fate by these championships. But they brought him no money, and no reputation among the conservative people; though his name went far among the counties around for his skill and his energy and courage. I could multiply the instances of his lawyership; but it is enough to say that he had so much won the confidence of courts and lawyers for his integrity that what he said to a court or a jury had a kind of sworn testimony effect, something to be depended upon fully.

At the east side of Lewistown, across the railroad tracks, stood a large two story and a half brick building, situated in a large space of ground with some pine trees along the walk that reached to the door. Long before we came to Lewistown, somewhere in the days of the War Between the States, this building was used as a Methodist college, but for many years now it had been occupied as a residence by the man who raised the vegetables and the small fruit for the community. Finally this man had moved to the west side of town where he could get more ground; and thus the old college building became vacant, and remained so for some time. Now when I was about eighteen or nineteen an Englishman turned up in Lewistown, of whom it was said that he had been graduated from Oxford or Cambridge. He was an elderly man with sclerotic eyes, and a tinged mustache from much smoking of a meerschaum pipe. He took over this old college building and started an academy where young men could be prepared for college. He did not have much of a staff; but he did bring to his assistance a recent graduate of Drake University, Iowa, a man named Karr of handsome appearance and fresh scholarship. This academy was running along without attracting any attention from me; but finally I entered it under the following circumstances:

Aunt Minerva as the wife of the Reverend Vincent, of some theological note, and as the sister-in-law of Bishop Vincent, of Chautauqua fame, was an admired figure in the Masters annals. All the years of my childhood and youth these two had been devoted to me and to my sister. They had always remembered us on Christmas with useful and beautiful books and other gifts. And as my father and mother never paid any attention to Christmas the day would have been barren except for the generosity of Aunt Minerva and Uncle Beth. Occasionally when Aunt Minerva paid a visit to the Masters farm to see her father and mother she came to Lewistown to see my father, to whom she was deeply attached. She did this, though my mother did not like Aunt Minerva; and sometimes my father saved her the inconvenience, and even the distaste, of coming to our house by going to the farm to see her. Aunt Minerva rather pardoned my father's liberal politics, something that the Reverend Vincent did not do. He was a prohibitionist with false and exaggerated notions of my father's mode of life. Altogether there were difficulties of association that always had to be accommodated. Aunt Minerva had been graduated from what was called the Female Seminary at Jacksonville, Illinois, but she continued to cultivate herself to the end of her days, which lasted until she was eighty-five. She read all sorts of books in and out of the Chautauqua course, and at Chautauqua, New York, she associated with the lecturers and with the notables, among others the Thomas A. Edison family, who had a summer home there. She was devoted to Browning's poetry, to the novels of Gissing and Meredith. I never saw any diminution in her orthodoxy, because among other reasons she never discussed the subject, but I could see that she was more liberal than her husband, Uncle Beth, and looked with a tolerant eye upon nearly everything of an intellectual interest. One time I was at the Masters farm when both were there, and I was speaking of my enthrallment with Goethe's *Faust*, which I had been reading in Anna Swanwick's translation, a book that I had bought at the bookstore in Lewistown. Speaking of *Faust* in their presence, my uncle's face took on a severe

look, his mouth tightened as he asked me what after all did
Faust teach that was good and improving. My aunt smiled
with her eyes, as I tried to answer this sudden poser. Aunt
Minerva knew of my struggles to advance my knowledge of
literature, also I showed her some of the verses I had published
in the *News* and in newspapers about Lewistown, but without
winning from her any praise. Indeed, they were not worth it.
But in this way and many others she had learned of my reading
and writing, my earning money to buy books, and my many
activities. She had a son who was being prepared for college, for
Yale as I recall it. For out of my uncle's small salary this
cousin was to have every advantage that a university could
give him. Whereas it looked now as if I would continue to
battle along by myself with miscellaneous reading in a county
seat of Illinois.

One summer, I think it was the summer I became nineteen,
my father went to Akron, Ohio, to visit Aunt Minerva; my
uncle had a church there at the time. My father was now in
quite comfortable circumstances, being about forty-three, of
more commanding appearance and address than ever. He was
in magnificent health and strength, having overcome all the
effects of the blood poisoning. He was a leader in the politics of
the Congressional district and the boss of the Democratic
party in Fulton County. Altogether he was much of a man in
his place in life. He was so powerful, direct of speech, and of
such impressive common sense, of such pat take-offs when he
wanted to touch me up that I was diffident in his presence. We
were not comrades, as we became a few years after this time.
He was inclined to smile at my absorption in books, he hinted
that my writing could come to nothing, while he was sure that
I would make a fine lawyer. In fact he was saying to me now
that I could be a much better lawyer than he was, something
I did not believe at all. I regarded him highly as a lawyer and
already I knew from my sad attempts at reciting or speaking

in the high school that I could never stand before a court or a jury and sweep them away with passionate argument as he could do, and as I had often seen him do when I attended court to hear the sensational cases of the day. The courtroom was my drama and my movie theater.

When he returned from Akron I noticed that he regarded me with changed eyes. It transpired that his visit was not all that it might have been. I fancy that my uncle did not have much time for him, and that even Aunt Minerva did not stop her daily program of study and church work to entertain him. At least this is what my mother was saying, adding that it was quite useless to try to be friends with people who were so self-centered. I think my father regretted that he had unburdened himself; and it is quite likely that he was oversensitive, and expected a reception such as he always received when he went to the farm to see his mother. There it was cakes and fried chicken, long talks in the kitchen at evening or at any time of the day. My father as a liver put more value upon this sort of communion than upon books and church work.

The very day that my father returned from Akron he said that he wanted to see me; and we walked uptown together and leaned against the Standard House as he unfolded to me what was in his mind. He said that Aunt Minerva had talked to him about me, saying that I should be well educated, that I had the aptitude for learning and that it should be gratified. He said that he had decided to send me to college, and that I should enter the academy recently started by the Englishman and prepare myself in Latin and mathematics. I was almost beside myself with delight. One of the conditions that he made was that I should leave off writing and miscellaneous reading and bend all my energies on my studies at the academy.

So it was that I entered the academy at Lewistown. My teacher was Karr, then a man of about twenty-seven or so, and fresh from his studies at Drake University. I began Latin under him, renewed my geometry, which I had had at high school, and took a course in formal logic. But I did not confine my labors to these things. At the same time I was reading Spencer's *Synthetic Philosophy* with Homer Roberts. Will, who was writing a drama on the story of Clytemnestra, gave me the advantage of what he had learned at Montreal of the Greek writers, and of Horace and Virgil. Then in my association with Anne I went on with the Elizabethan writers, Marlowe and Webster and others. We were keeping up our friendship, and eluding the discipline that had been put on me, by writing notes when we could not meet to walk to the woods, or when I could not safely go to her house. My father's face was set against this romance, as it had become. The idea of marrying Anne never entered my mind. I didn't have the money to marry her; even at this age I had a disinclination to marry anyone. Still we were keeping up this association; and the unfriendliness of our families toward each other was a constant disturbance to our peace. Anne often began a note with a Greek sentence; and I made up my mind that I must learn Greek. Her father had taught me Latin for a time before the days of the academy, but no Greek.

With all the rest that I was doing now I was helping my father sometimes in the law office. I was also writing for the *News,* and publishing poems about the country under pseudonyms, and sometimes in the "Sharps and Flats" column of Eugene Field. As for that, however, I had about made up my mind to be a short-story writer, and at this time or a little later I published some short stories in the *Waverley Magazine* in Boston and the *Saturday Evening Call* of Peoria, mostly under pseudonyms. Any that appeared under my own name were published after I left the academy.

With one thing and another my friendship with Anne began to take wounds and to languish. It had lasted for about two years, and during that time we had gone about at night into the woods, or wherever our fancy took us. We had sat in secluded spots at the edge of town under old trees, or sometimes on the back steps of one of the churches, where we indulged in amorous intimacies natural to lovers. But Anne never yielded, though I tried to make her. Nothing could have been more trying, more exhausting. It was a torture to be so attached to her, to admire her so greatly yet never to make her completely my own. By this time I was in love with Anne, having made myself in love with her. My mornings after these experiences were hours of lassitude and dullness, which the sharp practical eye of my father detected at once. He would say, "Out in the woods again!" with sardonic inflection. Once he said, "You'll quit this or go to hell. I'm not going to send you to college if you keep this up."

However, I didn't leave Anne, nor did I quit my miscellaneous studies. When the Scientific Association met, sometimes in the courtroom, sometimes in other towns of the country, Anne and I attended the meetings together. I heard papers read on the shells of Spoon River, the Indian artifacts of the county, the flora of the prairies, or on some new phase of psychology, or on one occasion on the philosophy of Kant by a scholarly old man living at the village of Table Grove. Anne read papers, also before the association, always to the astonishment of the gathering. I derived great benefit from the association of this body of thoughtful men and women. Sometimes when the society met in the south part of the county I stayed at the house of Dr. Strode at Bernadotte, a picturesque hamlet on the Spoon River with a fine old water mill. All this was highly informative as well as delightful. But my father resented this idling, as he called it; and all the while I was in peril that he would punish me by refusing to send me to college. Besides, by this time there was gossip in town about Anne and me. We had been seen in secluded places together, and the one inference was drawn, though there was no truth in it. Her father being the minister, and her mother as the minister's wife a leader in the moral life of the community, the situation was full of embarrassment for them. But so far as I know they did not interdict my association with Anne; in fact, her mother one day at her house talked to me at length in a moving and motherly way about the difficulties involved, and all with no hint but what it would be best sometime somehow for Anne and me to be married, though that was so long away that the whole matter was badly perplexed.

However, the time was now near at hand when we had to part. Anne had a sharp tongue, a fine command of irony, and sometimes she used it on me. When she did I grew very angry, and thus by degrees, though she was naturally wreaking a woman's resentment for the truly absurd situation into which we had come through youthful thoughtlessness and the circumstances, that old acid which I had got into my blood through the romance of eleven years old, began to increase in my spiritual veins. Sometimes I repaid Anne's irony with direct sarcasm, and like a youth struck back too hard. In a word we began to have little quarrels, which sometimes were composed by Alfreda, who now at sixteen or so was wonderfully beautiful; while Anne had lost by familiarity every feature of attraction that she had ever had. I do not know certainly when Anne and I really drew apart, or rather just when it was that I asserted my strength and brought the end. All the while I could feel my father's eyes, I could see his ironical smile, and sometimes I had to hear something brief and cutting said. Obviously I was at an age when I could have repudiated my father's discipline and married Anne. I didn't want to do this. I was tired of Anne. I wanted to go to college and write poetry. For that matter, I have many times in my life crushed down my heart for the sake of poetry.

After a visit to the south part of the county, where I attended a meeting of the Scientific Association, Anne and I had a bad lovers' quarrel and said cruel things to each other; and I might as well take that occurrence as the time when the end came. For in any case it summed up all that had been growing of dissension and misunderstanding.

We came back to Lewistown together and took a walk about town. Something came up and we began to shoot words at one another. Anne never betrayed then or at any time that she was hurt. She had superb presence and self-control. She could laugh even when bleeding to death; now she did not wince. She laughed at me. She laughed at my paper on Whitman, she laughed at my verses, at my pieces in the *News*. She played bright, poisonous lightning around me; and all the acid in me poured out of increased beats of the heart. I determined then and there to obey my father, to buckle down to harder study of Latin and geometry, and to rove no more with Anne.

The next day I was at the window of my father's office in study, and ready to do whatever he required of me. Anne passed on the street below and looked up. I bowed, but did not go down to see her. The next day I had a note from Anne. I did not answer. When I had leisure I went down to Will's to hear about Clytemnestra. There I chanced to meet Alfreda, who was paying a call on Will's sister. At other times I was at the lumberyard talking to Reese, who was planning to go to Knox College with me. His father, though making but $50 a month, was going to send him, if possible. With these friends I allayed the poignancy of the days. My father soon observed that I did not go walking with Anne; and so he made no remonstrance when I took a Saturday off to go to Bernadotte to spend Sunday with Dr. Strode. But my memory of that summer is of myself at the office window, and of Anne passing below to the post office and looking up. Once we had a brief talk on the corner, and as luck would have it my father passed and looked with withering eyes upon me. Naturally he did not like

to have me marry a woman who had no understanding or admiration of him and no belief in anything he stood for, socially
or politically. He disliked Anne completely and her father and
mother as well. In this talk on the corner I told Anne that I
was preparing for college, and had much to do. Her ironic reply
was, "Yes, very much." When I added that my people wanted
me to attend strictly to study, she made some remark about
Mark Twain's good little boy, saying that I should be careful
or I would be struck by lightning. I made no retort to these
ironies, but turned back to the office.

Yes, our happy days were over, days of reading together, of
writing poems together, of walking the woods of Big Creek, of
coming home hand in hand under the full moon with our
hearts overflowing with that ecstasy which only youth can
experience. Anne had read the Elizabethan dramatists so
thoroughly, she had browsed so deeply in English poetry that
a poetical vocabulary was as natural to her as the daily speech
of the people in town was natural to them. She could sit down
and in a few minutes compose a ballad beginning with the conventional words,

"O lithe and lissome maidens all."

And once while our friendship was at its height she came to
me saying that she had had a wonderful dream in which their
maid had married the butcher boy, an employee of Charley
Ehrenhardt who ran the meat market. The tenor of this dream
was that the butcher boy went away commanding the maid to
keep flying a white flag to signify her fidelity; after a long
absence he returned and saw the flag, entered the house to take
the maid in his arms, and then to marry her. Anne wrote this
in one of the stanza forms which can be found in Percy's
Reliques; and in competition I told the same story in a measure
of my own. We sent these compositions to Eugene Field, who
at the time was conducting his celebrated "Sharps and Flats"
column. He published Anne's poem, but not mine; but he

changed the last stanza of Anne's poem. He made it to read
that the butcher boy returned and saw a white cloth flying;
all this though the maid had married another in his absence.
He rushed forward and kissed the white cloth as the maid came
from the kitchen and said, "That's not the flag, that's where we
dry the baby's things."

Anne was so mortified over this, since Field had kept her
name to the poem as its author, that for several days she kept
away from the square and hid herself at home.

At twenty Anne had found herself. I think she had genius,
and that she would have made something of a name for herself
if given time and strength. Some years after this, when she
was still considerably under thirty, she published a poem in the
Century magazine, which was incorporated by Stedman in his
American Anthology, published in 1900. By that time Anne
was dead.

In these days of my parting from Anne I sometimes saw
Alfreda. I had grown very fond of her during our strolls to
Big Creek, when Anne was my chief interest. There was a sort
of logic, a sort of reactive result that carried me into Alfreda's
arms when breaking with Anne. Though she was Anne's closest
friend, yet I could detect in her manner something which said
that Anne was in the wrong, that Anne had said cruel things
to me, and was at fault for the dissension that had come between us. If I chanced to meet Alfreda when I was on my way
down to Will's we walked together. At other times we left
Will's together and walked up the hill into town, separating
before we came to the main streets, where she proceeded on
home and I turned to go to the law office. There was drama in
these stolen interviews. I saw myself as the misunderstood fellow, who had done nothing wrong, but whom a prejudiced
community saw as a kind of Lothario. When therefore Alfreda
stole away from her house and met me at the edge of town
where I took her in my arms, and she looked into my eyes and

told me that I had done nothing wrong and that she believed in me thoroughly, all my sense of drama and romance was fully satisfied. It was not long before I began to feel the same madness for her that I had felt for Zueline, something that had never really entered my heart for Anne. For Alfreda was truly beautiful. She had fine-spun brown hair with a tinge of gold in it; her eyes were that tiger gray which has always fascinated me, her figure was delicately voluptuous in this her budding period of sixteen years. We were passionately drawn to each other. But the circumstances prevented us from being friends for long. Her father was a deacon in the church of which Anne's father was the minister; and I heard that Anne's father went to Alfreda's father and asked him to prevent Alfreda from seeing me. However this may be, Alfreda's father felt that loyalty to his pastor required that he should forbid his daughter from holding communication with me. I was talked about in the town as a Lothario, when in truth my relations with Anne had been altogether innocent. But it was true that according to the customs of that time and place and all the circumstances I owed marriage to Anne; and that I could not give her. I had no means wherewith to marry her, and I had come to the pass where I felt alien to her nature, and her mind with its convictions so different from my own. Anne was a mind, and by its fascination had blinded me to her physical imperfections, and to all her faults. Alfreda was beautiful of person. If she had possessed Anne's mind I might have thus at this early time met my ideal.

This summer of 1889 went by as I read and studied and endured all the embarrassment which followed from parting with Anne. In the middle of the summer I was seized with a strange state of mind and body. I became very weak, for one thing; for another, the outer world took on the aspect of a dream, of utter unreality. When I read anything I could follow the words, but not the meaning. I walked as in a trance. Music, which always affected me profoundly, became unendurable. I could not bear to hear my sister play her guitar, or use the piano when she practiced Mendelssohn. I was tortured with fears that somehow I had wronged Anne; and then I would quiet my remorse by thinking of the bitter words she had poured upon me at times. My father became alarmed at my condition and called in Dr. Hull, who examined me and looked grave as he said that I would have to give up the idea of going to college. I would have to get into the open air and do some kind of manual work to get my nervous strength back.

At this time we had in the barn a huge blind horse which I had named Rosinante. My father had received this horse as a fee in some case that he had tried, together with an old set of harness, consisting mostly of string and ropes, and an old single wagon. Now my father proposed that I take Rosinante, and this wagon, and go over the county and collect some fees that were owing him from delinquent clients. I asked Reese if he would go with me, and he consented. So off we set one beautiful summer day for Table Grove, for Vermont, for Bernadotte, where I saw Dr. Strode who laughed himself sick to see Rosinante and the wagon, and us two driving about the country. We went to villages up and down the Spoon River, and then returned to Lewistown in about two weeks. Wonderful to say, I was well again; and so pronounced by Dr. Hull. I began to get ready for Knox College.

I had written to Dr. Bateman, the president of Knox, explaining my position: how I was graduated from the high school, and had had but a little instruction in Latin; but that long ago I had studied German, and that I wanted to resume it. He answered that I could take such studies as I wished and that a welcome awaited me. Reese had won the consent and support of his father to go to Knox; and so on an early morning we took the train for Galesburg fifty miles away. I scarcely slept the night before, so great was my excitement about the new life ahead, in a large town where there was a theater and a public library. I rose very early and made coffee for myself, and a time or two called to the rest of the family to come down, that I was soon to depart. They remained in sleep. And soon the drayman came for my trunk. Reese was on the dray with his trunk, very happy that we were setting forth into this new world. My trunk was loaded on the dray. I turned back into the house and called good-bye. My sister appeared at the head of the stair to return my farewell. I leaped onto the dray and was rapidly driven to the train. At seven o'clock the train moved away from the station, and was soon passing the country to the north of town upon which I had looked many days in the high school while studying the encyclopedia. Another period of my life was ended.

Chapter V

THE TRAIN ARRIVED AT GALESBURG IN ABOUT TWO HOURS, and at the station were a number of freshmen and sophomores, some in military caps and gray suits, for there was a cadet corps at Knox College under the instruction of a lieutenant of the United States Army. These youths were scurrying here and there greeting students who were getting off the trains, and who needed direction to boarding places, and information about getting themselves placed. Soon in company with a cicerone Reese and I walked into town past the college campus with its old buildings, just across the square from the court-house, and near the seminary where the women students lived and pursued some of their studies, such as music and painting. With all of this I was greatly enthralled. I felt that I had really left behind me the unhappy days which I had spent in Lewis-town toward the last. I meant now to make the most of the chances at Knox. In the August preceding this September, on my birthday in fact, my father had given me $100, and I was determined to see how far I could make this money go, in order to be as little a burden as possible on him. We soon found a room at $2 a week, and board at $2.50 a week, and then there was the matter of being placed in classes.

To my mortification I found that I could not even enter the freshman class. All my reading in English literature, in phi-losophy, availed me nothing. I had too little Latin to enter college, and no Greek at all. I discovered that there was no youth in the college who had gone as far and as widely into literature and philosophy, except perhaps a young man from Fairview, a town also in Fulton County. By this time I had read a good deal of the Greek classics in translations, I had read

Faust, and I had been through English literature pretty thoroughly, but having nothing but a beginner's knowledge of Latin, and no start at all in Greek, I had to enter the preparatory school. As this was the case I decided to resume the study of German, with which I had done nothing since the days of Petersburg, and to go on with Latin and to begin Greek. In order to make the most of the time I resolved to read as much as possible out of the college library and the public library where there were about 14,000 volumes.

There was a wonderful magic about these days from the first. We roomed just across the street from the campus. At about nine o'clock the chapel bell rang, and at first I went to chapel. I wanted to hear the professor of Greek lecture on Germany where he had taken a degree; or another professor talk on Kant, or Browning. It was all quite wonderful to a youth from the country. Then the room was full of eager faces, pretty young women, and handsome boys and it seemed to me that a wonderful feeling of good will prevailed among the students. I was spoken to cordially by strangers, and seemed to be exempt from that fierce competition and envy which I had always encountered at school in Lewistown. Soon I felt that I was a welcome addition to Knox. My reading feats, my writing for newspapers and magazines soon became known, and I was treated on the basis of a youth with some accomplishment to his credit. At night and on Saturday afternoon Reese and I walked about town or out to Lake George at the edge of town. And it wasn't very long before we knew everyone and everyone knew us. Reese became a cadet and took military training but I settled down to hard study, and to reading out of the library. I found the books that I had never been able to get in Lewistown.

In the late fall I had a letter from Anne, saying that she was going to pass through Galesburg on her way to Kansas City to spend the winter. She wanted me to meet her and so I went to the train and we took a walk through town. We were proceeding west in Main Street as the descending sun shone straight into her eyes. Suddenly she asked me if I had changed toward her, if it was really true that I no longer cared for her. The sun in her eyes separated all the little filaments of coloring in their iris, opening up rifts through which one could look, so to speak, into her very secrets. "Look at me," she commanded after she had asked the troubling question. And I looked at her, and lied, saying that I was not changed. A smile played across her lips, an intellectual strength looked out of her eyes as she said: "There is no use to lie to me. I can see by your eyes what you feel. Very well! I can be as hard as you are. I can cut my heart right out and cast it here on the street." She made a gesture of excising her heart. Then she laughed. "Now we can be good friends," she said. "Come on." And we pursued our walk.

Her train left for the west at about midnight; and after dinner and a talk at the hotel I took her to the station. In the aisle of the sleeper she paused, looking long at me. Then she thrust forth her hand to say farewell, and I left her, walking back to my room in a daze. That night I tossed from side to side sleepless for hours. I could not forget the look of her eyes. After she arrived in the western city we exchanged some letters, which finally bore upon the propriety of re-exchanging all our letters and destroying them. And this was done. But meanwhile I began to hear from Alfreda in Lewistown.

I had not forgotten the alphabet and a considerable vocabulary of German; and I went ahead with that study under a woman teacher who had lived in Germany. Soon I was translating poems of Heine and Goethe, and some of the Grimm stories, which I wrote out at length. I was soon reading and translating the orations of Cicero. But Greek fascinated me beyond anything I had ever studied. The very look of the alphabet gave me a thrill; and I found the language easier than Latin, because of the articles and the demonstrative pronouns. Dissatisfaction with the Greek teacher arose; and another class was formed by secession, and I was among these. We went over to a young professor, Alphonso G. Newcomer by name, who was from the University of Michigan. He was a poet and a very good one; and a widely read man. Besides, he was devoted to Greek literature. We became friends, and my Greek studies proved the happiest of all.

The fall term passed and I returned to Lewistown for the holidays. My family sat down and bent attention upon me as I told of the wonders of the past three months. Given even in those days to character depiction I told about some of the strange boys, the comical professors and the like that I had met. My father looked at me with wide noncommittal eyes. But I took him thus to say that it was hardly worth while to send me away to gather humorous material about the rooster of the college janitor, and about the boys who played pranks on one another. As to my studies, I felt that they seemed futile to my mother. My sister looked as if she thought she should be in Knox, not I, though she had not even gone through high school, and was now quite besought by suitors for whom she played the guitar.

As soon as possible I looked up Alfreda. Anne was still in Kansas City. I could not go to Alfreda's, but she managed to have me meet her at Will's house, where Will's sister was sympathetic with our desire to see each other. Alfreda's fresh beauty had mastered my heart; and she gave me her affection through understanding of my nature, and sympathy with the trouble and bad repute I had gone through on account of Anne. We managed to have several meetings without being caught. One night we lay on the porch of her house for an hour or more. If her father had come forth and found us there, it would have meant a quick dismissal for me and discipline for Alfreda. Somehow through these meetings, through our letters, all things put together, Alfreda and I took it for granted that we were in love and that we had to plan accordingly. If that was an engagement, we were engaged. Thus matters stood with Alfreda on this vacation.

Perhaps a year before this I had met a woman living in Havana, who was about five years my senior. She was a writer for Chicago publications, and had published a good deal here and there. She was something of a musician and sang in a Punchinello voice. She was born malformed with her eyes twisted, her forehead half crushed in, her nose bent to one side. She was really half blind, and all her reading, which was much, was done by someone hired to read to her. Like Anne she had a marvelous memory, for her defective sight made it necessary for her to fix in mind what she heard read. Altogether she was a charming and interesting woman, and had taken a lively interest in my studies and writing. She lived with her father and mother in one of the large houses of Havana; and they maintained a considerable hospitality. It was a great delight to be there, as the house ran in excellent order; and there was music. One of the daughters of the household played Liszt with a good deal of skill and expression. I shall call this woman Louise.

During this winter vacation I went to Havana for a few days' visit at the house of Louise. Knowing my admiration for Shelley, Louise had a fine picture of Shelley for me as a Christmas present. We read Shelley and Byron together. She listened to the report of my days at Galesburg. She knew about my long association with Anne, and we talked of the circumstances which had brought that friendship to a close. She was firmly of the opinion that Anne was not for me, and that I was wise to take myself in hand to separate myself from her. As Louise was older than I her judgment on this matter convinced me of the wisdom of what I had done. However, Louise was deeply affected by the circumstances of that last day in Galesburg, that parting from Anne on the train.

There was much in the circumstances of these days to depress my spirits, and the truth is that I was definitely at the melancholy age. My landlady at Galesburg strummed music on the piano which reminded me of far-off, unhappy things. Shelley filled me with painful longings to achieve his music, and excited my imagination with unearthly imagery. All this before I went to Lewistown for the Christmas vacation and after I had resumed school.

I returned to Galesburg after two weeks' vacation, saddened with thoughts of the past and with reflections that my youth was passing, or even had passed, and that I had done nothing and had more to do than I could ever accomplish. Look at Milton's sonnets written when he was twenty-three— I was now but twenty, to be sure; but Shelley was definitely on his way at eighteen! I pondered the words of my father when he said that the poets I admired were geniuses, and that I had no genius. And wasn't it true, and even proven by my record to this time? With all this I longed too much for Alfreda, and thought too much of the happy days I had spent with Anne. I had seen Alfreda a few times on this vacation, perhaps twice at the house of Will's sister, who was willing to encourage our romance. We had taken some walks together; but it was all surreptitious. And Alfreda was very young, and I was without money, and burdened with ambitions and studies. My difficulties weighed upon me ceaselessly, while Reese went his way lighthearted, drilling with the Knox cadets and taking part in society debates. He could not understand my sufferings, even though he looked upon me with sympathy.

I determined somehow to rise above the circumstances of my youth, and to perfect my education and culture, which had started under such adverse conditions. These months at Knox College I went forward with an industry and a concentration which threatened to reduce me to neurasthenia, such as had nearly overtaken me the summer before. As I took scarcely any exercise, and was reading or studying eight to ten hours a day, I was afflicted with dyspepsia, which tortured me a good deal. And then in the middle of the winter I was attacked by the prevalent influenza which confined me for several weeks.

There was at Knox a youth who was unique in all my observation of human beings. He came from Canton and was the son of a lawyer associated with my father at the Fulton County bar. This youth spent his whole time playing practical jokes. He wandered about town at all hours of the night indulging in pranks. He invented nicknames for everyone: Reese became Socrates; I became the atheist, or sometimes Sophocles. At the party given for the new students in the fall I had met a demure, pretty girl named Grace, for whom I had a kind of admiration. Sometimes I called upon her at the seminary. This youth of practical jokes wrote Grace a note imitating my handwriting, in which he said that I was dying and wanted to marry her before I departed this earth. He went to a dignified and popular minister in town and persuaded him that I wanted to embrace the Christian faith and be baptized before I died. One day when I was half delirious from fever this minister called at my room, and soon knelt down by the bed and prayed for me. He was shocked when I told him finally that I had not sent for him. When I tottered out to the campus for the first time I met Grace, who refused to speak to me. When later I pressed her for an explanation of her coldness she brought up the matter of the "silly note" I had written her. For that matter, I played some jokes myself and wrote humorous verses which were published in the college magazine, verses on the new passenger engine of the Burlington railroad, called the hog-engine. This was about the time that Kipling had sent forth some verses which attempted to show what Homer would do in a description of the engine.

I made some good friends at Knox, casual but none the less substantial. One was Oscar Lanstrum, who afterwards became a physician in Chicago, and later still a notable figure in Montana politics. Another was J. Mack Tanner, whose father was elected governor of Illinois in 1896; another was George Sucher, who was out of Knox when I was there, and a practicing lawyer, but we became friends. Perhaps the man I saw most was the youth from Fairview who had seen a little fast life, and was somewhat sophisticated. He was the only man at Knox who was as widely read as myself. And perhaps he had read more than I. He was a very good Latinist, and knew Horace of whom I was quite ignorant at the time. Outside of his interest in belles-lettres he affected Matthew Arnold; and he and I talked *Culture and Anarchy, Literature and Dogma, God and the Bible,* all of which I read at his suggestion. We walked about the streets of Galesburg debating religious and other questions; or he came to my room. I don't know why with such a beginning we did not become friends for life. But we didn't. His father sent him to the University of Michigan after this year at Knox, when he was a sophomore, and there he idled his time away. When I got to Chicago he was there acting as a collector in a law office. As long as I knew him he never became a lawyer, but went about collecting bad accounts. I saw him a few times, and then we separated.

Everything was magical about this fresh-water college and this little city of Galesburg. The main building of the college filled me with dreams of the past. On its steps Lincoln and Douglas had stood debating the Dred Scott decision in 1858. The gray seminary often took my wandering steps past its many windows behind which the miraculous girls were hidden, engaged in painting and music. The piano sounded from a dozen places with the music of Liszt and Chopin, as I strolled along and looked up, hoping possibly to catch a glance of

Grace. I was permitted to call upon her but once a week, and had to leave at nine o'clock.

During the year I heard a lecture on *Macbeth* by a Professor Snyder which fascinated me utterly. Francis Wilson came along playing *Erminie,* and I heard him sing *"What the Dickie Birds Say."* More than thirty years later I met him at the Players one evening during the time that he was reviving *Erminie* in New York. He asked me to autograph his copy of *Spoon River Anthology;* and I told him that he had captivated my imagination so much in that long ago that I had never got over it.

I enjoyed some of the lectures at the chapel exercises: Professor Willard's talks on Germany and Heidelberg, Professor Hurd's talks on Horace and Lucretius; Professor Simonds' talks on literature, and Professor Newcomer's talks on skepticism and faith. The latter was only four or five years older than myself, and going through some of the same formative ideas that I was; but only to think of it: he had a degree from the University of Michigan and was launched upon the waters of widening culture and speculation! I enjoyed even that lecture by Dr. Bateman on Lincoln, whom he had seen daily at Springfield in the years 1858-1860. In short, my days were full of delight.

In the German class I met with a youth from Omaha, of German parentage, who had been brought up to speak the language. He and I read the first part of *Faust* together. My landlady's mother often came from Chicago for a visit. She was German, and we talked in German together. She told me much of Chicago which up to this time I had never seen. My father had often gone there and returned with wonderful stories about the vastness of the city. He had gone to New Orleans once on business, and to Texas, but I was never taken. I spent all my years going to the Masters farm, or staying in Lewistown.

What with reading constantly from the libraries, and my studies in college, I was not doing much writing. I composed a few sonnets, some of which were published the next year in the Knox College Annual, called *The Gale;* on the occasion of Browning's death in December of 1889 I contributed some memorial verses to the *Inter Ocean,* and later a poem entitled "The Shell." Otherwise I was not productive. As soon as I could read Greek at all I took up the New Testament, and for several weeks made critical notes on the evidence of the Gospels for the credibility of the miracles. This with translations of Cicero's orations and the rest of my activities already mentioned absorbed my full time. I was busy and happy, despite a wanton melancholy, and despite some grieving about Anne when I wondered if I had been altogether fair with her. As to Alfreda I had a high beat of the heart. We exchanged letters occasionally, in which she told me the news of Lewistown, and pledged her devotion. I did not hear from my father very often; nor much from any of my family. I had become to them a kind of wonder bred amid their quiet crew, and a problem past solving.

By Spring our class in Greek was well enough along to read the *Anabasis.* Professor Newcomer made it a wonderful study. He gave us the background and the topography of the recital, so that we read not merely by way of deciphering the text, but with an understanding of the story. I have never had a more delightful experience with a book than with the *Anabasis* in Greek. As the year ended I was reading Homer in Greek; and finally took up Bryant's translation which I absorbed under the trees of the campus.

Ah, yes, reading Homer on the campus! It was June, and June in Illinois can be as beautiful as anywhere. I sat under the trees reading about the King of Men, and about the swift-footed Achilles, with a delight that cannot be expressed. Though school was over some of the students still lingered about. Halliday and Donizetta, two charming girls of about eighteen, were playing tennis, and passed along as I lay under a tree absorbed in Homer. As I think about these girls and other girls whom I saw along the way I am filled with a kind of regret that I did not have the understanding and the skill of approach which came later, to act as adjutant to my youth. What other romances I might have had! And what in life is so sweet? Nothing is, save creative work, the writing of poetry.

When was I going to return to Lewistown? I thought I would not return at all, not even to see Alfreda. I planned to stay in Galesburg and earn money for the next year of school, while pursuing my studies under the trees of the campus. In Galesburg at this time was a vitriolic old editor named Gershom Martin, who ran a weekly paper of the Democratic faith. I went to him and engaged myself to set type and write articles. Just then he was off to Monmouth to attend a Congressional convention, and in consequence I took full charge of the paper. I had scarcely set to work when my father appeared on the scene, on the way to Monmouth as a delegate to the same convention. When he found me working for Gershom Martin he was indignant. He said that this work led nowhere, that Martin would not pay me, that he never paid anyone. He commanded me to return to Lewistown at once and take care of the law office, and read Blackstone's *Commentaries*. I refused to do this; but I was soon caught in circumstances which altered my resolution.

In about a week Martin returned, saying that he did not need me any longer, and that he would send the money coming to me. There I was with no work and no money. I could find nothing to do in Galesburg. And what with wanting to see Alfreda and with dreams of reading Virgil in Latin with Reese, and thus preparing to enter as a freshman in Knox the following fall, I returned to Lewistown. I don't remember where I got the necessary $1 for the fare. It was not from Martin; he never paid me. At any rate I got back home, and began to see Alfreda, and to read under the maple trees around our yard. Will had come back from Montreal, and I read Greek with him. In addition I was deep in *Don Quixote,* in Rousseau, in Flaubert, in Gautier, whom the Fairview youth admired extravagantly. I was very happy, and did not fathom the dark purposes of my father, who watched me from the front room when he came home at noon from court or the law office, and meditated taking me in hand, as it soon appeared. I had a definite plan in mind: to return to Knox and enter college. If I worked at something this summer to get money upon which to go back to school I couldn't make up the studies required for entering as a freshman in the fall. And if I didn't work at something I would have no money, unless my father helped me. And already I was having my doubts that he would do so. Besides I was filled with shame that I was nearing twenty-one and was not ready for college. Most of the seniors at Knox were not more than twenty-one, and some were younger. As always in my life my head was down, and I was thrusting my way forward. No great luck ever saw me and took me up.

Chapter VI

AND SO I WAS BACK IN LEWISTOWN, SITTING IN THE SHADE of the maples around my father's house, reading the *Aeneid* with Reese for an assistant and a fond companion. I didn't mind the dullness of Lewistown in these circumstances. For a time Anne was not back from Kansas City; and when she did return we met, and were as friendly toward one another as the strained relations permitted. Her father met me one day and walked about the outer streets of town with me giving me very kindly advice on the matter of my literary ambitions. I believe he was not convinced that I could realize them; nevertheless, he was friendly toward my aspirations. Alfreda was in town growing more beautiful with the summer days, and I saw her, but not freely.

One day as I was under the trees reading Virgil or Cervantes my father appeared at the French door, which opened from the living room of the house, and said that he wanted to see me at the office after dinner, that is, after the noonday meal. And so I went as summoned, not knowing what was in store for me.

It turned out that the general agent of a book by John McGovern of Chicago was in town trying to get local agents to canvass the country about Lewistown for this book and to sell it. It was a book made up of eloquent prose, of poems of a sort, of illustrations; and came in a cheap and an expensive binding. It was called *The Golden Censer*. As I was always cheated in the trades I made as a boy, and had no head for bargaining, I knew very well that I should be a ghastly failure as a book agent. I told my father that I could not succeed at this business, that I wanted to stay at home and study, while making a little money working for the *News*, as I had done previously. He replied that I had to do something, and that he would not permit me to loaf and read as I had been doing. Pretty soon, as we were talking, the general agent came in. Oil fairly dripped from his mouth as he talked. He looked upon me as a likely agent, that I could see. But he was badly fooled. My father bought the agent's equipment, which cost something like $5, and I set forth full of disgust and reluctance to sell this worthless book. I had to commit to memory the salesman's talk by which it was to be presented to people. This I did on afternoons following at the general agent's boarding place in Lewistown, and then I went on the train to a town near Lewistown and walked about from house to house reciting the eulogium that I had committed to memory, as I offered the book to the villagers. I didn't sell a single book in this town—I believe it was a place called Ipava. Then I went on to the next town with the same result. I got to Table Grove next, where in the happy days of the Scientific Association I had been entertained as one of the speakers and as a local notable. Here I kept away from those I knew, and drove into the country to see the farmers. I sold no book, and came back to the village. At the edge of town I saw a woman hanging out her washing, and went in the yard and began my lingo. She dried her hands and asked me to come into her parlor, so that she could hear better what I had to say. There I went through the piece as she sat spellbound, uttering exclamations of delight, and saying at last that the book was just what she wanted to give her husband for a birthday present. So I sold her a copy of the expensive edition. My courage was thus plucked up somewhat, and I went on and canvassed the town with all my energy, but without selling another copy. Thus I had been soliciting for four or five days and had sold one book. I became indignant, I felt dishonored and foolish. I decided that I would try no further, be the consequences what they might. I threw up the whole business and returned to Lewistown.

My father looked at me with disappointment, with ironical smiles, remarking, "I guess it is over the hill to the poorhouse for you." I said to myself, "Very well, to the poorhouse it will be; for I will not work at something that I cannot do." I spent my time during this summer helping my father in the law office and writing for the *News*.

My sister Madeline was now a young lady, and of remarkable beauty. She had been taking lessons on the piano while I was in Knox under one of the better instructors of the locality. She still played the guitar with some skill. I had bought a cheap violin and learned to play it after a fashion. And we two used to play together at the homes of our friends, and by way of serenading people about town. I never learned to read music, as I was too impatient to get to the actual playing of the instrument to take time for mastering the notes. Neither did I ever learn to use the bow, although I practiced on the violin for several years after this time. I took my violin with me when I departed for Chicago to live, and played it at the several boardinghouses where I abided, but it was always an unmanageable technique for me, just as the waltz was. I couldn't learn to waltz to save my life. Something in my mental make-up tangled and kept my feet out of the rhythm. It was only when the tango and one-step came in that my whole body responded freely and with grace. In Petersburg when I was eight or nine years old my grandmother paid for music lessons for me, thinking, as others did, that I had musical talent. I rebelled at the notes, and gave up the lessons.

My sister was in unpleasant circumstances in regard to suitors of the right quality. There was perhaps but one man in Lewistown who was a suitable beau, and he was a hard man of limited personality. He was calling upon her this summer and later, and they read together. Before this she had engaged herself to a colorless fellow who was a clerk in a store at Pana, where my sister had visited Aunt Fannie. She soon saw the absurdity of such an alliance and broke it. And then one of the sons of Colonel Ross came along, and she engaged herself to him. He was more than twenty-five years her senior, and had been through many amours and engagements. My father did not like this situation. He was in fact a chum of the man, and knew his ways of life and his character. While my father did not say much in remonstrance of the attention which this suitor was paying my sister he was visibly disturbed by it, and looked down his nose when my mother talked of the man's wealth and social position. In truth he had a small fortune of $40,000 or so; but my father saw, I think, that the man did not mean marriage, and that even if he did the prospect was unhappy for my sister.

It was evident to me that my mother and sister were talking about this affair frequently. They were now as close together as two schoolgirls. My studies and ambitions, my very different associates from those my sister had, the fact that I disliked this would-be brother-in-law, shut me out from their communications. All of a sudden it transpired that my sister had broken her engagement with this man, and my mother came forward saying that my sister must be sent east, to New Hampshire, to give her a change. So her wardrobe was replenished and she went to Keene, New Hampshire, there to visit in the household of Uncle John Humphrey, the brother of Grandmother Dexter. Altogether I had spent $200 at Knox, and it took nearly that much to send my sister east to relieve the embarrassment of a broken engagement. My father's income was now about $4,000 a year, and it seemed to me that he could equalize what he had done for me at Knox by giving my sister this trip and also by letting me return to Knox the ensuing fall. I seemed to see evidence of family machination against my aspirations. One day at the gate, as I was departing

for uptown, my mother talked to me about Knox and about my
sister's equal rights to her and my father's bounty. What she
said was pleasant and smiling enough, but it had a deadly
sting in it. So the summer passed along in association with Will,
who was returning that fall to Montreal by grace of the
Scripps family, and with Reese who was going back to Knox
to finish the course. I was as unhappy as it was possible for
me to be.

When fall approached I was told to get a license to teach
a school; either that or to go to work in the law office, and
prepare for entrance to the bar. I decided to teach school. But
before that and as a last resort I wrote to my grandfather asking him to lend me $100. He replied that all his money was
tied up in cattle; but he hinted that he had educated his own
children and could do no more. So with every escape cut off
I took a school in the northern part of the county, and set
forth as lonely a soul as ever lived.

There was a station called Bybee where the train stopped
on flag, as there was nothing there but an abandoned depot.
The schoolhouse was perhaps two miles west from this depot;
and about a mile to the north of it was the farmhouse where I
was destined to board with a farmer and his wife. The country
about was dreary and silent, level and uninteresting; and here
for $35 a month I was entering upon a profitless experience.
The farmer's wife prepared luncheons for me of fried ham and
boiled eggs, of sodden cake and bread spread with strawberry
jam which gave me excruciating indigestion. I had to sleep in a
sort of loft where there was no heat, and where through rifts
in the shingles snow sifted on my face during the night. The
weather was cold that autumn, and there was bitter winter by
mid-November. During the school hours I read Homer while
the students were getting their lessons, keeping my book behind
a large geography. I had no interesting pupils. My life at the
farmhouse was incredibly dull. When I got home there was

nothing to do but sit in the kitchen, the only warm room in the house, and talk with this farmer, who was suspicious and bad-natured. His wife was equally disagreeable. She was the daughter of the chief school director, and I had been maneuvered into coming into their house as a boarder as a part of the perquisites of her father's position.

Our house in Lewistown had much improved since my sister had become a young lady. It was better furnished, there was a piano, and through my studies there were many more books. While I was there near Bybee as unhappy as possible I began to get letters from home. My sister had returned from New Hampshire bringing with her a cousin of my mother's who was about the age of my sister. These two young women were having a gala time. They were taking trips to nearby towns to dances; they were having beaux, and getting up parties. The cousin was a good deal of a musician and she was playing for callers and for the family. And my sister was taking music lessons from one of the most expensive teachers about. All this I heard through letters; and I felt that I was shut out from everything agreeable, seeing that I had no associates and no life except the worst drudgery and boredom. Finally when I could manage it I went to Lewistown for over Sunday and met this cousin, who played parts of *Faust* in the most spirited way, as well as many other compositions, such as those of Chopin and Beethoven. She was not a professional, but a very excellent amateur performer. I warmed to her at once, for she was quite good-looking, and her skill as a pianist won me. But she was a cold nature, and the fact that I wrote verses turned her against me. My sister had to have dresses and cloaks and hats to set forth her beauty, which was marked; and thus with her music lessons and her travels to parties and dances my father was spending considerable money on her. Many men arrived at the age I had now reached have made their own way and done it handsomely. I could not do it. I was too burdened with my program of studies to earn anything; and if I had been more fortunate, I should have been helped at this time. However, the teaching of school was so unpleasant and so profitless that I decided to give it up after the first three months. After I paid my board to the farmer's wife I had about twenty dollars a month, and at this rate I could not save enough in ten months to give me a year at college. I decided therefore to go back to Lewistown and enter my father's law office, and participate in the happy life of music and parties that was going on at home. When the term ended I refused the request of the directors to teach the next three months, and went back to Lewistown and started to study law in earnest.

It wasn't long, however, before our cousin returned to New Hampshire, and scarcely before I knew what was happening my mother had arranged for my sister to go to Knox College to study drawing and French. The idea was that she would thus escape the approaches of the suitor to whom she had been engaged, and who was trying to renew his engagement to her. Thus suddenly everything was changed. The cousin was gone and there was no more music. My sister was at Knox College; and I was all day in the law office reading *Chitty on Pleading* and *Greenleaf on Evidence*. Anne was back from the West, but our communications were like October, balmy but cool. Alfreda was a good deal away, and when she was in town we saw each other with difficulty. By this time it was known that I had an interest in Alfreda, and we could not be seen together without exciting talk. Will at last had left the Montreal University, but without finishing. His father had forced him into the study of law, though he had far less aptitude for it than I. In fact his mind was logically twisted, and he extracted strange deductions from his law studies. However, we saw much of each other, and compared notes every day. He was now my only companion; for Reese had returned to Knox. His father was ambitious that he should finish the course there. And recurring again to my father's attitude, I don't know what inspired it exactly. It could not have been my marks, for in spite of my constant reading at Knox I got a hundred in all my studies.

About this time Dr. Strode of Bernadotte had married again, taking for a wife my friend Julia, who had been raised on a farm near Lewistown. She had been in the high school when I was, and had been inspired by Miss Fisher, as I and others were. Julia was writing stories now, and studying the occult to which she had come from Emerson. As she and the doctor were both my friends, their house became a haven to me in these hard days when I was leaving my beloved studies for the law. And so sometimes on Saturday I went to Bernadotte for over Sunday. As to Louise in Havana, that was an interrupted friendship, and as it turned out, an ended one. My sister, who followed in my path, even to some extent on the matter of books, also took up with some of my friends, frequently with misfortune to me. She cultivated Louise with the result that they had a misunderstanding at last; so that I was forced as a matter of family loyalty to side with my sister and forsake a friendship which had been both profitable and delightful.

I was still writing verses and publishing them in the Chicago newspapers, something that did me no good in a community where poetry was considered an effeminate interest, and not prospering to the real and useful affairs of life, and particularly not advantageous to the study of law. But all the while I was pursuing my law studies with the same concentration and industry which I had given to Greek and to literature. My disappointments had filled me with malicious energy which I poured out on the pages of Blackstone. At night Will and I met in his father's office or in the office of mine where we examined each other on the subjects of contracts, the principles of the common law, and of equity jurisprudence. Finally May came and we went to Springfield together to take the bar examination before the judges of the Appellate Court. My father was along to attend a session of the Appellate Court, and to see me go through the ordeal and come forth a licensed practitioner. He was now forty-five and in the very flush of his vigorous manhood and attractive personality, with a reputation all through that part of the state for his power with a jury and his feats of advocacy. His gift of gathering apt stories and of telling them made him a welcome figure everywhere; and at the hotel the attention which was paid him by lawyers, politicians and judges filled me with pride. We were there together for several days where he treated me like a man at last, inviting me, and Will when he was along, to have beers and to sit with the men who were talking politics and law cases. When the examination was over and I had passed my father happened to encounter me at the door as I was entering the hotel, and with an ironical smile and a little laugh he said, "What do you say now? Do you think you can't be a lawyer? Why, you passed first in all that class of sixty." As the marks were not given out I asked him how he could know that. He replied that he had it from one of the examining judges. I was conscious of having missed but one question, and that was so simple that I was mortified that I could have wrongly answered it.

Just now my father wanted to be circuit judge, and was bending his energies to that end. Fulton County had given him its delegation. There were several counties in the circuit, and each county had a candidate. One of these came over into Fulton County and began to cultivate in his own interest the Calvinistic and church enmity to my father. The result was that one of his bitterest foes got a proxy on the Fulton County delegation. It was the lawyer brother of that youth who had backed the Meyers boy when he slugged me with lead. At a critical time in balloting at the convention, which was held in

Quincy, this marplot started a quarrel which meant my
father's defeat. Seeing that he could not now be nominated,
my father then threw the delegation of Fulton County to a
friend, who got the nomination. He was successful at the polls
that June of 1891, and was the first judge of the court who
could be called at all friendly to my father.

My sister returned from Knox with a little knowledge of
French, and with two drawings which she had made in the
art class, one of the Apollo Belvedere and one of Agamemnon.
She and my mother then started to study French with Will,
and our household filled my father with dismay. There was I
reading Greek when I could, and writing verses. Julia frequently came to run the ouija board, around which my mother,
my sister and I were grouped half hypnotized. My father was
infinitely annoyed at this; for what was not matter of fact
had his contempt. There were my mother and my sister reading *Télémaque* and speaking French; while my father, smart-
ing under the unlucky defeat that had come to him, went about
dark-eyed, as though he did not know which way to turn.
If it hadn't been for the diversity of experience which he had
in traveling the circuit, and his lust of life, he could not have
gone on. For now Lewistown was anything but a happy place
for him. There was a problem, too, as to what to do with me.
I wanted to get into newspaper work, and not pursue the law;
and he was growing tired of me, I think, and would have welcomed anything that got me started in something self-support-
ing.

These were the days when Minneapolis and St. Paul were
mounting in population and drawing attention to their business chances. My father suggested that I go there and enter
upon the practice of law. The second printer at the *News*,
who had set up and printed my first verses, was there in a job
office; and a former law partner of my father's, who had been
in St. Paul for several years, was reputed to be well established

there in politics. So I was given a round-trip ticket to St. Paul on an excursion when the rates were reduced to a trifle, and in July I went to Minneapolis.

I rented a room not far from where the printer lived, and I saw him every night. During the day I was often in St. Paul seeing this old partner of my father, who did everything he could to place me. Before leaving Lewistown I had gone to the farm to say farewell to my grandparents, as I considered that now I was entering upon a life which truly ended all my days of youth. Aunt Minerva happened to be there. She gave me a letter to a man in St. Paul who owned one of the daily papers there, and in his college days had been a mate of my uncle who was drowned on his way to California. As soon as I could get to St. Paul I went to see this newspaper owner to get a newspaper position. After many calls I encountered him one day and told him who I was. I was chagrined to find that his relations with my uncle were not very much treasured, as Aunt Minerva had supposed they were; as to giving me a place on the paper, that was out of the question. Meanwhile my lawyer friend had induced a firm in St. Paul to give me desk room, but with no salary attached. I had no money, none at all; and had to be thinking at once of the means of sustenance. Then this lawyer went to a law publishing house in St. Paul, who happened to need someone to do syllabizing. I went there and was given work to do to prove my capacity for the position. There was a comfortable salary in store for this work, and I sat down with all possible care to show my fitness. I took the work back to St. Paul and in a few days was told that I had done well on two of the cases given me for syllabizing, but had failed on the third one. They admitted that I could soon do the work satisfactorily, but they had to have someone who could do it at once. So I lost this chance. Meanwhile my money was shrunk to nothing. I owed room rent and I was desperate.

My printer friend told me one evening that a printer was

needed at one of the large job offices. The next morning I
applied for the job, and after joining the printers' union, which
was a prerequisite to being employed, I set to work amid type
cases wholly strange to me to compose some tables, a difficult
kind of typesetting in any case; and after a labored morning, in
which I was spurred on by the foreman, I got started and so
worked four days. Thus I had a few dollars, and saw some
plays by Sardou, and heard some concerts, and went out to the
Falls of Minnehaha and other places of interest about the twin
cities. However, I could not see my way to staying in Minneapolis. Already my mind was on Chicago, where if I entered
the law it would be to practice under a system with which I
was somewhat familiar. And if I started on a newspaper it
could be upon the *Inter Ocean* for which I had written verses
for years, and the editor of which had on occasion written me
friendly letters. Using my return ticket I wended my way back
to Lewistown, with the idea of replenishing my money somehow so that I could go to Chicago.

I arrived in August. Court was in session and the new judge,
who was on the bench by grace of my father's good will, welcomed me with cordiality. He was willing to appoint me master
in chancery, which paid something like $2,000 a year, as soon
as the then incumbent could be let out gracefully. On this
score my fortunes were looking up. My father proposed a law
partnership, and we formed one in which my share of the
receipts was $5 a week, and what I could make at times by
abstracting records in cases he had. In St. Paul I had seen the
city arrangements of law offices, so I prevailed upon my father
to rent other rooms and have a private office built in them for
consultation. This was done, he added many books to his law
library, and we started to build up the business. Soon I was
appointed by the judge to defend a man, which then was the
role that a young lawyer first filled. I did my best, I even addressed the jury; but in such a state of terror that I feared my

heart would stop. Seeing before me the ease and power with which my father argued cases, I felt that I could never do it, that I never could succeed at anything except as a consultant, even if that.

Will was doing no better, if as well. He and I were studying logic together and reading the plays of Sophocles. He was teaching French to my mother and sister. I was going to Bernadotte until the doctor and Julia moved to Lewistown, which was in the following winter. Julia and Anne were friends and Julia's house was a meeting place for congenial souls such as Homer Roberts, the doctor's close friend, and for members of the Scientific Association, and for others of literary tastes. Often I was there myself, sometimes encountering Anne. The summer came on, and Alfreda, who had been away for many months, returned to town with many new dresses and pretty hats. She was a full-fledged young lady now, and more beautiful than ever. Our friendship dated back several years and was associated with feelings of devotion on her part in that she had run counter to the wishes of her father in seeing me at all, and on my part in a steady loyalty to her charm. Will's sister was willing that we should meet at her house; but Alfreda was cool to the idea and did not often meet me there.

And now a strange thing came forth. Alfreda's father ran one of the dry goods stores in town, and he had in his employ a clerk who was noted for his shabby dissipations. For years he had been a skirt chaser. His personal appearance was forbidding, with his moss-covered teeth, his tired, bleared eyes, his absurd pompadour hair, his shabby linen covered up by broad neckties. What I saw was that Alfreda was escorted everywhere by this ribbon clerk; and the word went around that they were engaged. I thought I had done nothing to deserve this treatment at the hands of Alfreda's father. All that I had done to advance myself in life, all my studies, my recent lawyership, my writing which had given me a local fame, availed nothing in my devotion to Alfreda. Her father belonged to the church set which defeated my father for the judgeship. All this filled me with indignation, and I decided to go to Chicago, to get away from the village spites, the melancholy of the country, and from the bad will that followed me everywhere.

In most families the time comes when children are like grown birds in the nest. They are in the way. To sit three times a day at the table with a father and mother, to live in the house with them under circumstances where they know everything a son does or even thinks, is not conducive to the amenities of life. My mother was progressing in French and she made no bones of telling me that Greek was useless, and that I could not master it anyway. She and my sister were in secret sympathy with each other; and our arguments about anything and everything were a matter of daily occurrence. The point that seemed necessary to prove by both of them was that they knew more than I did, and had read more than I. My mother was writing stories, and my sister was writing stories; in fact, my mother wrote very well, considering her late interest in literature. We couldn't read our productions to each other without making some comment upon them. These comments led to arguments; and my father sat by wondering how he had ever got into such a mess. Often he seized his hat and rushed uptown to the office to get away from us. One Saturday in July something came up in regard to a literary matter, and my mother grew very angry, and proceeded to castigate me with her tongue, as only she knew how to do. I left the house and went to the office, where I told my father that I was going to Chicago to live. He replied that if I would be more careful I could get along with Mother. I would have to imitate his patience. He said that he wanted me with him, that he needed me in the office; that soon I would be the master in chancery at $2,000 a year; whereas in Chicago I would starve. But anger hardened my resolution. I set my face against his importunities.

I went to the office of the *News* and asked the editor for a pass to Chicago. The next Wednesday it arrived. I had to travel by way of the Red Express which passed through Havana, eleven miles south of Lewistown.

I was to leave Lewistown that evening at about six by the little narrow gauge railroad for Havana; and in the afternoon I packed my satchel and walked out of the house to the office where I settled with my father for what was coming to me. He again importuned me not to go, and warned me against the Chicago climate and the hard conditions of life there. If someone had proved to me that I would be dead in six months if I went, my resolution to go would not have been shaken. My father gave me $15, all that he owed me; and after settling bills at the bookstore and at the laundry, I had about $12. Then I went to Julia's for supper. Anne was there to help prepare it, and she stirred about with a kind of pathetic industry which moved me, as she talked volubly in her bookish language, and made the occasion as happy as possible. But it wasn't happy. Julia thought that I had not been well treated, and she said as much. When I came to leave these two went to the gate with me, and stood with tears in their eyes as I trudged along with my suitcase toward the station around the corner. They knew that this was the end of my days in Lewistown.

I walked meditatively to the Narrow Gauge station. There I found my father on the platform—and no one else of my family to say farewell to me. I don't remember where my sister was; but my brother, then about thirteen, had no interest in me; and my mother was glad enough, I suspect, that I was leaving home. My father was in a sober and shadowy mood, something that pained me greatly. He had done all he could to keep me from leaving Lewistown; he feared the days ahead that I would soon be living. He doubted my ability to make my way. But for all his concern for me he neglected to do for me what a devoted father might have done. He might have gone to Chicago with me and gone about with me to see his numerous political and lawyer friends, and helped me to get established decently in that city. Perhaps he didn't think of doing this. I know I didn't ask him to do it. I was in a stern mood, determined to get away, and survive or go down as the case might be. As the approaching train turned the curve at the edge of town he took my hand, looking down, not looking at me; and immediately I stepped on the platform of the car and entered it not looking back. As we passed out of town, where the track ran beside one of the streets, and on to the bridge which crossed the Burlington road I merely stared absent-mindedly at the houses. I could have seen our house at the left as we went along. But I did not look in that direction. I was in an introverted mood. And very soon the train was twisting through the cottonwood jungles of the Spoon River bottoms as the pygmy locomotive with its great whistle made the hollows echo. The station in Havana was on the west side of the river; and in half an hour, there amid the jungle of the Illinois River where the terminus was located, I stepped from the train carrying that heavy canvas suitcase, which contained my clothing, a lot of manuscripts, a copy of Anthon's *Homer*, an Italian grammar, and a copy of *Mademoiselle de Maupin*. Also I had in my pocket two letters of introduction, given to me by my father: one to the general solicitor of the Alton Railroad, whom my father had known intimately for twenty years and had been associated with in important law cases; the other to the general solicitor of the Northwestern Railroad, who had once lived in Lewistown and had figured with my father in the Democratic politics of the state, and in particular in the nomination of John P. Altgeld for governor that very summer. In the same pocket I was treasuring a letter written me that month of July by William H. Busbey, managing editor of the *Inter Ocean* of Chicago, in which he had said that there was no place open on the paper for me, but that he would keep my name in mind as that of the

author of many verses published in the *Inter Ocean*, which he
had admired. All the while then I planned to escape the law
business, which I did not like, and get into newspaper work.
I knew no one in Chicago but my uncle Henry, who was in
fact no longer my uncle, as my aunt had died several years
before this time, and he had married again, and somewhat
beneath him, according to his daughters. I had written to
Uncle Henry that I was coming to Chicago, and he had replied
to come and to stay with him at 2128 Michigan Avenue, where
he was running a boardinghouse. I anticipated that I should
have board at a nominal rate, at least until I got a foothold.
But why should that have been after all in this world of business? And in truth it did not happen, much to my chagrin.
And so carrying my satchel I trudged to the bridge that spanned
the Illinois River, and set foot upon Havana at nightfall.

Chapter VII

THE HEAT IN HAVANA WAS UNSPEAKABLE. THE FISH FLIES swarmed about the street lights as I walked along changing that heavy satchel from hand to hand to relieve my fatigue. The sweat poured down my face; my tall stiff collar, as shiny as celluloid from the hands of Yee Bow at Lewistown, wilted. My white vest crumpled; but on I walked gazing across the Illinois River into the jungles fed by the fat mud of the shore, which stank of dead fish and decaying weeds. I could have gone to the Taylor House, where I knew the amiable clerk and had had some happy days with my father or when I went to Havana on business for him. And there were those acquaintances in Havana, but our friendship had declined as I have already told. However, I did not want to see anyone. I wanted to get to Chicago as soon as possible; and I was hoping that it would be many days before I saw this country again.

There was a lonely agent at the station of the Red Express. He was walking back and forth behind the grating of the ticket window, whistling at times in a nervous way. We were the only two persons there for hours, and perhaps until about traintime. I knew the exact minute when the Express was scheduled to arrive, yet I asked him its time, and then took up the long wait of about five hours for the train. I began to go out on the platform and to return to the waiting room. Finally the agent spoke to me, perhaps asking me where I was going. Gradually he began to tell me something about himself and his state of mind. He confessed to anxiety and depression. Under my questioning he told me that he had a girl who was driving him to distraction by her mystifying ways. No one came in to interrupt us, and a long conversation ensued, in which I gave him advice out of *Mademoiselle de Maupin, Anna Karenina* and other books I had read. He looked at me in wonder, not realizing that out of my own experience I knew nothing about the perplexity he was in or how to counsel him about it. But that long talk with this man whose name I never knew filled me with reflections all the night and stayed with me the next day as a strange mood, as if I had dreamed what was said between us.

The agent was still talking about his girl when the Red Express rolled in. In the sudden whirl of the exciting moment I parted from him, and never saw him again. I took a seat in the chair-car, as I had no money for a sleeper. Anyway I wanted to see the country from the window; I did not want to sleep. I wanted to think. Above all I had made up my mind to see the first traces of Chicago, to see how and where it began. So all night long I sat looking out at the prairie, an expanse of blurs and darkness, and at the stars which looked like splotches of running grease in the hot sky. When the sun came up like a fireman who has slept, all refreshed for more stoking, we were still many miles from Chicago. There were hours ahead of enduring the stifling atmosphere of the car impregnated with the hot breaths of sleeping men, women and children slumped down in the seats.

Going to Minneapolis I had traveled along the Mississippi River, and suddenly came into the middle of the town. I was wondering what Chicago would look like, how it would begin. It turned out that it didn't exactly begin. It was difficult to tell when we left the prairie, where the Illinois and Michigan Canal ceased, where it was that we first bumped over the tracks of the outlying belt lines, where there was still farming country and widely separated houses. Then came the truck gardens of the city with houses closer together along half-made streets which stretched into vanishing distances of flat country. Then there were the new subdivisions springing up all around, with newly built and half-finished apartment buildings and houses, all in anticipation of the World's Fair, along plowed strips soon to be streets or boulevards, and already half curbed, where newly planted trees were making a desperate effort to grow. Factories, lumberyards, coalyards, grain elevators, tugs, sailing vessels, steamboats on the river and the canal swam into view as we rattled over the switch tracks; and all around was the increasing density of the illimitable city, formed of miles of frame houses, lying cooked by the July sun and smothered in smoke and gas and smell, and in exhalations from the breweries, and in reeks from the stockyards. This was not Minneapolis with its flouring mills and its comparative quiet by the shores of the Mississippi. Now there were noises from a thousand engines, the crash of switching trains, the yells of laborers, and now and then the dull thunder of dynamite; for already the Drainage Canal was being dug to connect Chicago with the Gulf, and thus purify the drinking water of the city. Chicago thus began for me as a mist rising from the sea, in a sense without a beginning. Already Havana and my talk with the station agent seemed far away.

In these last few minutes of the journey two card sharpers, who had boarded the train at Joliet, tried to engage me in a game of poker. They were obviously confidence men who took me for the greenhorn that I was, and probably overestimated the amount of money I had. I have never had the slightest inclination toward gambling and little toward games; and these two fellows saw at once that they could do nothing with me. Just as the train began to slow its speed they dropped off the car and sped through the switch tracks. And then the train drew under the dark shed of the Polk Street station, and there was Uncle Henry, who had come to meet me. From photographs and from memory of him I should have known him, but he was visibly older. He was now about sixty, and somewhat shaky for that age. He was a silent man, a sad-looking man. He smiled a weary cordiality upon me, and off we started to take the Cottage Grove Avenue cable to 22nd Street and Michigan Avenue, dodging through insistent cabmen and porters who wanted to take my satchel.

I took my first glances of Chicago now, noting the countless saloons, and near at hand a whole street which looked suspiciously wanton, like streets I had seen in Peoria, and which turned out to be one of the brothel sections of Chicago. North along Dearborn Street, as we hurried on, I could see the city of the Loop district, not then called the Loop. The Monadnock Block, the Owings Building and some other sixteen-story structures were then standing in that street. Crossing State Street at Polk we were in the midst of saloons, dives, flophouses, cheap hotels, sordid places of assignation. The streets swarmed with people of every clime: Chinese, Poles, negroes, and at doorways the ubiquitous Jew was selling clothes. The great trucks made the cobblestones rattle. The air was suffocating with smoke and gas. And the heat! It seemed to me I had never before experienced anything like it.

My white vest soon looked as though it had been dragged through the dirt. I was thirsty, I ached from sitting all night in the train, I was sleepy from the long wide-awake hours of the night. At Wabash Avenue we boarded the cable, and swept down that feculent thoroughfare, turning at 22nd Street until we came to patrician Michigan Avenue where the jingle of harness and the Glockenspiel of the docked horses trotting upon the pavement gave a very different impression of what Chicago was after all. Here stood the new Lexington Hotel, finer by far than anything I had ever seen. It was soon to play a part in my fate. Two blocks south in plain view was the dignified elegance of the Metropole with the spire of a great church sticking above it. Uncle Henry's house was one of the three stories and basement brick houses which lined Michigan Avenue. Its front door was reached by long steps and a landing at the top; and up these we walked to what was waiting for me in the shape of many strange characters.

I did not know that Uncle Henry's new wife had brought her mother and her sister to live with them. But so it was, and there they all stood taking me in. These women looked exactly alike. They looked the same age. They looked like the Graeae of Greek mythology, those old women gray from their birth, who had only one eye and one tooth in common, which they borrowed from one another. However, I was greeted by them with effusive affection, and conducted at once to the basement dining room after I had washed the cinders from my eyes. Breakfast was being served.

Back in Havana the station agent was commencing another day of perplexed thought about his girl. Here was I facing the group of unfamiliar types, standing there with my white vest and long hair, as I received the satirical smiles of a huge man, who turned out to be a racetrack gambler, and of his wife, a large dark woman of opulent breasts and many diamonds. The others were Madam Y, a French nurse, off duty for the time, and generally off duty as it turned out. Another was a girl with bandaged wrists, but recently returned from Mount Clemens where she had taken the waters for her rheumatism. A few days after this this girl drove me away from her saying that if I was wise I would let her alone. Another at the table was Billy Finnegan, an accountant at the Chicago Edison Company, which just this year had come under the presidency of Samuel Insull, a protégé of Thomas Edison, and whom Robert Lincoln, the son of Abraham Lincoln, had chosen as the best man in the country to advance the interests of electricity in Chicago.

All these stared at me, filling me with a kind of terror. They smiled and then hid their smiles. They began to talk suddenly with that loudness which betrays an effort to conceal what the talkers have just been saying, or are now thinking. Pretty soon another habitué came in to breakfast. It was Clarice, the aunt's niece. And thus Uncle Henry, who for so many years led a highly respectable and quiet life downstate as a businessman, and as the husband of my mother's sister, a woman of Puritan principles and ascetic life——this Uncle Henry was here burdened with these four women. And Clarice was the most forbidding of all. She had red sultry eyes, and rutilant hair, and thick feverish lips. She stared at me with unconcealed amusement. I was the nephew from the country!

At once I wanted to see the city and to call upon Mr. Busbey, and the two railroad lawyers. Especially did I want to place myself in some earning position when I learned what my room and board were about to cost me. That was $7 a week, a full price for that time; and at that rate I had less than two weeks' board in my pocket. Uncle Henry took my satchel up several stairs to the room that was given me. It was in the rear of the house and looked out into the alley back of the saloons and stores in 22nd Street, where that very night I lay awake listening to the rattle of pianos and the shouts of drunkards and the squall of whores. Though I was addressed at once by the Graeae as "dearie," and pressed at table to have more omelette, I was suspicious of them. I began to think that there was no hospitality here to relieve me of thoughtfulness immediately about my finances.

Meanwhile Uncle Henry was very kind to me. He brought me some iced grape juice soon after breakfast, for the heat was mounting. Before he could take me downtown, however, he had to do his morning's work. He turbaned his bald head with a towel and began to sweep rooms—this uncle whose riches we had heard of as children, and who had been at the head of a prosperous business downstate. He went up and down the four flights of stairs, changing sheets and turning mattresses. All the while his wife stood around, saying that he was the best man in the world, and giving him kisses every now and then, as she told me that there was nothing he did not know how to do. The other Graeae also showered endearments upon him. Uncle Henry looked sheepish, he glanced furtively at me. Perhaps he was thinking that I knew all about his past respectable life as the husband of my mother's sister in that small city where he was one of the leading men. Here he was the keeper of a third-rate boardinghouse, surrounded by dubious figures and making ready to get rich the next spring when the World's Fair opened. While this was going on all the others had disappeared: the gambler and his wife, Madam Y, Billy Finnegan who had hurried off to work, and Clarice who was a woman of leisure.

At last Uncle Henry was ready to set off, and we boarded the car, going down Wabash Avenue to Madison Street. The *Inter Ocean* building was on the corner of that street and Dearborn, a towered structure, very impressive to my eyes. Uncle Henry waited for me in the hallway, as I went upstairs and sent in my card to Mr. Busbey. Immediately he popped out from an inner office and invited me in. He was white-haired, white-bearded, with coal-black eyes which looked me through with smiling interest and genuine cordiality. He was in the midst of much nervous and hurried business, but he took time to talk to me at some length.

After he had spoken about my verses with much sincere praise, saying that I looked very young, too young to be the author of so many serious poems, his eyes deepened with evident concern as I told him I wanted a reportorial job. He was silent as he stared at me. Then he said: "Look at me. I am the managing editor here and what does it come to? Go into the law and be independent. I won't give you a job. Wait a minute." He turned to his desk and wrote a letter. "Go and see this young man. I kept him out of this slavery, and made him practice law. If he says he isn't glad that I did, come back, and I'll give you a job."

So I departed bearing a letter to Maltravers, whose name I already knew from seeing it over verses by him in the *Inter Ocean*. I could not understand why Busbey did not hire me, since I wanted the job so badly. He knew me as a writer; he knew that I had had a sort of experience in newspaper work by my connection with the Lewistown *News*. How could so many young men get started on newspapers, young men like Ade and Dreiser, and why did I not make the grade? There has always been something in my fate to work my rejection when I needed so badly to be accepted. And it is not due to my diffidence, my pride, or to any lack of enterprise in presenting myself for acceptance. There I was ready to work and capable of working. I might have risen on that job to literary achievement as other men have done. On the other hand, I might have sunk to the level of a drudge, though I think that is hardly likely. Anyway my hope of newspaper work was now dwindling.

I joined Uncle Henry and we walked in that terrible heat about the district since called the Loop, as Uncle Henry mopped his forehead and grew scant of breath. Except for a few buildings, Chicago was then just as it was rebuilt after the fire; whole streets of four- or five-story buildings in the manner of London or Paris, and in that style of architecture generally speaking. The exceptions were the few so-called skyscrapers: the Home Insurance Building of about twelve stories, the Tacoma of a like height, the Unity and Ashland Block of sixteen stories. But there was also the Masonic Temple of twenty-one stories, at the time the tallest building in the world, from the top of which, according to an old Polonius in Lewistown, one could see Council Bluffs, Iowa, 230 miles distant. I had to try that out, and Uncle Henry took me to the Masonic Temple. We passed the courthouse, a pastiche of every kind of decadent architecture. We went to call upon the lawyer for the Northwestern Railroad. But he was not in. And later on many weary days I tried to find this great personage, and never did so. A year after this time I went to his funeral as the escort of Mrs. Porter, one of my numerous landladies. She was an old friend of the lawyer's wife in the faraway days of their life at Lewistown. After all this we went back to Uncle Henry's boardinghouse for luncheon, where at the table there were the gambler's wife, Madam Y, and Clarice, besides the Graeae and Uncle Henry.

The days went by as I tramped the streets and familiarized myself with Chicago. All the while day by day I was trying to see Maltravers, but he was away on a vacation. I was trying to find these two lawyers. Sometimes I resolved to go to Busbey and to tell him that I must have work and to give me some place on the *Inter Ocean*. My heart failed me, considering that he had given me such generous time when I had called and had then so definitely made up his mind about me. In going about I entered the gorgeous saloons to see the pictures, and the gilded gambling halls to watch the players. I haunted the Art Institute, and walked by the Lake. But always I had to return to the boardinghouse where my silence showed that I had not had any success; and sometimes the Graeae asked me outright what had happened, if I had seen the lawyers or Mr. Busbey. Then at night I sat on the stoop of the boardinghouse with the Graeae and the others, listening to the Pullman car stories of Billy Finnegan, or to the sneers of Clarice about the bandaged wrists of the girl with rheumatism, or to a feline exchange between Clarice and Madam Y. Before us passed the endless procession of millionaires riding behind docked horses, out to refresh themselves against the heat of the day.

Two blocks east of Uncle Henry's house was Prairie Avenue, where Field, Armour, Pullman, and other magnates lived. Two blocks west was the sporting district, where Minnie Everleigh and her mopsies had their sumptuous abode. Around the corner on Cottage Grove Avenue were some concert halls, where

the habitués sat at tables and drank beer and where the chorus
queens on the stage sang "Little Rubie," to which the rhyme
was "so would you be." Billy Finnegan saw that I needed
cheering up and took me one evening to one of these halls. At a
table sat Clarice waiting for company. When we set off Madam
Y protested mildly, asking Billy not to get me into bad company, by which she meant to save me from a woman. For already Madam Y had knocked at my room and entered when she
thought the late hour saved her from notice. It was not the
case; for the witch eyes of Clarice had seen her. A few days
before this amorous alliance had commenced Madam Y had
caught me reading *Mademoiselle de Maupin,* and had sighed
forth a rebuke that one whose face was so innocent should be
reading such a book. It was that night that she stood in her
nightgown at my door knocking to come in.

After this Madam Y took me in hand to instruct me in the
ways of the city. We took long walks together up and down
Michigan Avenue, where she pointed out to me the Romanesque
and Renaissance residences of the Cranes, the Yerkeses, the
Armour sons, the lumber kings, the brewers and truckers, the
rich gamblers and lawyers. She took me past the Calumet Club,
the most swagger club of Chicago at the time, and told me of
the Moore brothers, who later acquired the Rock Island Railroad, and of Arthur Caton, the horse fancier, of Marshall
Field. She knew what purported to be intimate stories of all
these notables; and by a strange turn of fate which took me
outside my predestined path I joined this club about two years
later, and met all of these plutocrats.

After some time I found Maltravers, who knew my name
at once, for our verses had been published on the same Sunday
page for several years. He welcomed me with wonderful
warmth, and sat and talked with me for a long while, afterward taking me to luncheon. He was a short man with a completely bald head and a sparse mustache. He had butternut

teeth which showed forth fully when he smiled; and in his dress affected a certain poetical pose. But there never was a betterhearted man than Maltravers, nor one who would put himself more wholeheartedly at the service of a friend, and do it effectually into the bargain. He warned me against newspaper work, saying that he had had an experience in it; and that Busbey was right in keeping young men out of it, as he had done in his own case. He confided to me that in the law business he and his partner made about $250 a month each, and did it easily; and that he had time for hunting, fishing, and for writing all the verses that came to him. He advised me to go into the law, and to spend my leisure time writing, and not to go into newspaper work where I would have no leisure time, and where what I would be writing would tend to deteriorate my style. All this acted very persuasively upon me, at least my resolution to enter newspaper work got a quieting blow from this advice. The next Sunday I was at the house of Maltravers far out near Humboldt Park. We had dinner and walked all afternoon, talking poetry at times when he was not giving me a complete history of his life. An intimacy thus began at once between us. He was a member of the Press Club, and very soon I began to go there to have luncheon with him, or to meet him to play pool.

But at last I was out of money. The Graeae still called me "dearie," but they eyed me suspiciously, for I might decamp. I went forth and pawned my watch. I could have written home for money, but that would have evoked the retort: "If you want money come home. Be the master in chancery." The new judge there was willing to appoint me, and one of the last things my father had said to me was that I should not go to Chicago and starve when I could be master in chancery at Lewistown at $2,000 a year.

One morning I read an advertisement calling for printers. I went to the shop, located amid the railroad tracks at 18th

Street west of State, a thoroughly foul neighborhood, and applied for the job. I had to join the union to get it, since my union card issued to me in Minneapolis did not suffice. I set to work amid indescribable heat and stench. Growing thirsty I went to the water bucket only to find the water filled with soft splinters and flocculent stuff. It was also as warm as rain, and I could not drink it. I started to go out for a beer, and was called back by the foreman. I worked that day and never went back. Months later I drew the $1.50 which was coming to me.

I was broke and terrified, and did not know what to do. The Graeae slipped about half watchful of what I was doing. Madam Y was after me at night. Clarice laughed at me and raised her eyes as she mentioned Madam Y with an implicating inflection. One Saturday night Billy Finnegan got very drunk, and in the night called to me for help. At the time Madam Y was in my room, and she had to scurry down the hall as I went to help Finnegan. The next morning he was dreadfully sick; and on Monday I had to take a note for him to the Edison Company saying that he was ill and could not report. And still by day I was going about trying to see the Alton lawyer. One day I found him in. He had a cone-shaped head and rat-tailed hair which fell over into his eyes. He wore his glasses on the end of his nose. His eyes, gray and bright, stared at me like those of a mink. I looked at him recalling what my father had said about him, about their long friendship, and about the time when my father as state's attorney of Menard County had got the county board to appropriate money to hire him in a difficult murder prosecution to assist my father. As soon as I sat down he asked mildly, "How is your father?" in a sort of indifferent monotone. When he found what I wanted he proceeded to scold me. "Lawyers are not made in Chicago," he said. "They are made in the country. Go back there, and learn to be a lawyer; then come here if you want to. My son is coming out of Annapolis soon. He will get the only place there is here with the railroad." He turned and wrote a letter and handed it to me. "Go and see Judge Harmison. He is close to the Bar Association. I am not and don't know of any place for you."

So off I posted to see Judge Harmison, who was office attorney for one of the banks, as it seemed on the surface. In point of fact he was the poor slave of the most notorious usurer in Chicago, who was constantly in sensational litigation and often was attacked by victims, who even sought to take his life. Of all this I knew nothing; but it is hardly likely that the Alton attorney did not know all about Harmison's employer; he certainly knew that Harmison was an elderly man of professional decline, and without influence. Judge Harmison took my letter, read it, put it in a pigeonhole, and began to regale me with bucolic stories. He had no job for me and did not know of any. And thus after seeking the Alton lawyer for days this was the total result when I at last found him. I was pretty depressed. I could not stand the looks, the sly questions of the Graeae, and I hadn't a cent.

One evening I was sitting on the stoop looking at the procession of docked horses, and Billy Finnegan began to give me encouragement. "Pluck up, kid," he said. "By the way, I believe there's a job down at the Edison Company. We had a collector there who used to try justice cases and chase bad bills. You can try justice cases, can't you?" I replied that I could. "Well, that's all right then. This fellow stole a thousand dollars and ran away with a woman. Go down in the morning and see Frank Gorton. He's the treasurer. A nice fellow, not like Insull, the president."

The next morning, attired as I had been in the village, I went to see Gorton. I entered his office with a beating heart. There was no outer office and no secretary. One opened the door and there would be Gorton in view at his desk. Conscious of my white vest and flowing tie I stood there observing his

creased trousers of gray check, and the red initials on his handmade shirt, as he sat coatless in the heat. He didn't look up
from his desk at first, and there I stood waiting. He was a
handsome man of about forty-five. Finally he turned his eyes
upon me, large, rather benignant blue eyes they were. But he
said gruffly, "What do you want?" When I told him he repeated what Finnegan had told me, adding that if I stole anything I would go to jail. I became instantly very angry and
turned on my heel to leave the room, remarking that if he
thought that I was that kind of a man I didn't want the God-
damned job, and he could go to hell with it. He broke into a
hearty laugh. "By God, I believe you'll do," he exclaimed.
"Got any letters of recommendation?" I mentioned that I knew
the Alton solicitor, who turned out to be Gorton's daily associate at the Iroquois Club. "Get a letter from him and the job
is yours." I hurried away to see the Alton solicitor—he had
gone to New York for ten days.

In desperation I went to Judge Harmison to get the letter
that had been written to him by the Alton solicitor. Harmison
fumbled for a long while in the pigeonholes of his desk as my
heart beat with fear that he had lost or thrown the letter away.
But finally he found it, and I hurried back with it to Gorton,
who read it with the remark: "You must be all right. Go down
to the indemnity company and be bonded and go to work—
$50 a month." And so I entered upon a galling service.

It was an inhospitable set at the Edison Company. There
were electrical engineers, all high-salaried men, who put on
many airs. They lunched at Kinsley's and liked expensive places,
while I had to steal around to a lunch counter, and take eggs
and buns. There were the superintendents of construction
who were a tough crowd, drawing handsome salaries because
of their special education for the work. Here was I with my
head full of Greek, with my memory swarming with Chaucer
and Keats and Petrarch, and I meant nothing to these egotistical

experts in their line. There were the accountants who were cynical and surly; and the cashier who took a dislike to me at once, and made it as hard for me as possible. Finnegan was my only friend among the employees until I battled my way along and made them respect me, ridiculous as I was with my white vest and long hair. Insull stared at me through his hypnotic glasses, but rarely spoke to me. I fancy he wondered where I came from, unless Gorton happened to tell him. As yet I did not know the streets thoroughly, and when I went out to collect a bill I had to inquire my way to the address. For this ignorance of the city I won the nickname of Charley Ross at the hands of a sinister fellow who was a bookkeeper. And at last I had to stop him by laying him out. In all this I was playing the part that I have always played: Whatever I have achieved has been by way of sheer strength with my head lowered, and my bulk pushing ahead against resistance.

What I had to do was to walk from one end of Chicago to the other in the business district, and often beyond it, from 8:30 in the morning to 5:30 at night, going into tough saloons, into hard-fisted offices, into gambling halls, into brothels to collect bills. I was cursed for the sins of the Edison Company, and railed at as the emissary of a thieving corporation, whose meters were crooked. My other duty was to try cases in the sinister justice courts, where the meter readings as evidence were neither understood nor accepted as credible; and where I was sometimes defeated because the books of the company were not received in evidence. This was always the case where I had to rely upon the meter readings alone.

But in a few weeks I knew every part of Chicago. Night after night I returned through the heat of that summer, and in the bitter cold of the following winter, with my pockets full of checks and money, only to be asked by the eccentric cashier why I had not collected some other bill. As a relief to this slavery I often went to see Maltravers who began to take me to the Press Club where I would sit beside someone like Opie Read, and thus have my pride salved for its wounds of the day. For with my economic problem thus measurably settled, I started out to enjoy the roaring city. It was not long before Maltravers had introduced me to nearly every Weinstube and restaurant in Chicago, and I was frequently at his house near Humboldt Park. Whenever there was a bear dinner at the Press Club, or a haunch of venison served, I was invited by Maltravers to be present; and with a guest card given me at once I sometimes dropped in to see Opie Read, surrounded by a group of admirers as he told stories of Arkansas and Kentucky. At that time he had but recently retired from the editorship of the *Arkansaw Traveller*.

Maltravers admired my verses far beyond their deserts, and he did something to circulate my name around the Press Club, but I was already a faint identity to such men as Opie Read and George Horton, and some others. There was John McGovern, known as the Carlyle of Chicago, according to the fashion there to label writers. It happened that in the spring before I had published two sonnets on Columbus in a World's Fair magazine which McGovern was editing. He greeted me gladly at the club, calling me by my given name at once; and thus it was that I had the solace of these associations when I stole away from collecting bills, and dropped in at the club to find forgetfulness for the irritations of my job. I should mention also Colonel Will Vischer, a strange man who resembled Cyrano de Bergerac, and was as waspish as that visionary. He wrote a few striking poems, and played negro characters in Opie Read's plays with considerable success. Nor should Stanley Waterloo be forgotten, a man of learning and a good deal of solidity of mind who almost rose to general fame through his "The Story of Ab." I knew these men at the press Club, but I failed to meet Eugene Field who at the time was the most famous literary man of Chicago. While living in Lewistown, as I have said, I had contributed verses several times to his "Sharps and Flats" column. But Maltravers, who knew Field, was never able to arrange a meeting for me. Field did not come much to the club, and it was not always an easy matter to find him at the office of the newspaper where he worked.

Altogether I was in a much better frame of mind than I had been in Lewistown. I had escaped the loneliness of that pastoral scene, and the hurts to which I was subjected by the village prejudices and quarrels. And these new-found friends began to broaden my life. But at this time I was not reading much. My work stimulated my physical life to such an extent that my mental activities were coarsened through the fatigues of the day. At the same time I was in better health than I had ever been, owing to this daily walking and to beef sandwiches and beer, which I got at saloons by way of economizing on luncheons. Instead of having colds as I did in Lewistown, and dying from lung trouble contracted in the bitter blasts from Lake Michigan, as my father feared I would do, I became freer from colds than I had ever been. What is stranger I grew in stature as well as bulk; but for that matter, I did not reach my full height until my late twenties.

One time while I was at Uncle Henry's my mother came to see me. Her nature was such that she would never confess to a fault or a mistake, or acknowledge that she was in the wrong. But sometimes she would act out her penitence. When she did this I was grieved to the heart, for I did not like to see her insuperable will give way. My father called upon me once at the office of the Edison Company, finding me upstairs where the cashier's office was. He stood with me only for a few minutes, for every minute of my time was watched by my superiors. He looked upon me and about me with silent regret. And then one day I was called upon by a tall young man, with sort of an elemental faun-like nature. He was handsome and of patrician face, of deferential manner. He had heard from my sister about my studies and my writing and was in awe of such accomplishments. He was going to marry my sister, and had come to present himself for my approval and to get acquainted with me. His name was Carl Stone.

Zetta, a niece of the editor of the Lewistown *News,* had come to pay him and his wife a visit. The editor's wife was also the niece of Carl's guardian in chancery, a lawyer in Chicago, who also was a trustee of the very large Stone estate in which Carl was interested. Carl, who was engaged to Zetta, had followed her to Lewistown. When he met my sister he changed his mind and became engaged to my sister. Life is full of these strange chances, with all their wide and lengthy consequences. And this particular trick of the wheel of fortune made many changes on the green board where the bets were placed.

Carl's father was one of the pioneers of Chicago, one of the New Yorkers who had settled in Chicago in the late eighteen-thirties. By this time he had been dead fifteen years, and had left a fortune of about $300,000 which had quintupled owing to the increase in real estate value. Carl's mother, then about fifty years of age, had been "the queen of Chicago," that is, she had ruled Chicago society, as Mrs. Astor had ruled New York society; but by this time her power had waned. Younger and richer women had taken the scepter away from her. Her old mansion in Prairie Avenue, dating back to the prefire days, was almost an humble affair compared with the castles on the Lake Shore Drive, on Michigan Avenue, and elsewhere. Yet this aristocratic house was filled with art treasures which had been gathered up in Europe along the years. Madam Stone was among the first of Chicago women, if not the first, to know Paris and the other European capitals. She had been friends with George Eliot and with Ibsen, she was a great reader; and when she heard of my literary aspirations I was invited to dinner. I sat in her beautiful dining room amid more silver and

China and cut glass than I had ever seen before, served by butlers, and treated with great respect and cordiality by the great lady. All this came of Zetta going to Lewistown to visit the wife of the editor of the *News*. The wedding between my sister and Carl was soon to take place, and they were going to Italy for a wedding trip. Life was now moving rapidly for all of us.

I have said that no luck ever fell my way. I should say that when luck flashed before me I walked away, following my solitary, independent nature. Mrs. Stone would have been my literary patroness if I had known how to win her and keep her. I didn't try to do this. I passed on, getting deeper and deeper into Chicago life. Not until more than fifteen years after this time did I realize what a delightful and helpful friend she could have been to me.

Chapter VIII

I STAYED AT UNCLE HENRY'S ONLY A FEW MONTHS. IT WAS about November when I made my escape from his door as the Graeae and Clarice followed me there to say good-bye. I owed a few dollars for board which I was then unable to pay, and their loving farewells were implicit with a reminder to that effect. On a salary of $50 a month I was having hard work to get along. I was paying Uncle Henry $7 a week for two meals a day and for a wretched room just large enough to hold a cot. My lunches, economize upon them as I would, and a good deal of the time I had a beer and sandwich at five cents, came to a few dollars a week. Then I had a laundry bill, and a small cigar bill. The fall came on and I had to have heavier clothing; and finally an ulster to protect me as I walked about in all kinds of weather collecting bills for the Edison Company. In short, I was always broke, and I was frequently pawning the watch that my grandmother gave me, and always with remorse, as I thought of what she would say if she knew about it. I was lonely and unhappy and full of anxieties for the future. But at no time did I think of returning to Lewistown. I set my chin and went ahead. But now all my delightful studies were in abeyance. I read a little with Madam Y, and sat on the stoop of evenings with Clarice, and went at night to some concert halls with Billy Finnegan. At the corner was a cigar store kept by a man with whom I talked of evenings. But altogether life was hard, my work was fatiguing and monotonous, and made me feel degraded.

Clarice was a fiery-tempered demirep, and at times she followed Billy Finnegan about showering every contemptuous name upon him that she could think of, and that was enough.

He took this with shamed submissiveness, as if he were at fault for something. I imagine that she was disappointed with his amorous capacity, for it was evident enough that these two met in his room, or in hers on occasion, generally when he was drinking. And at least every two weeks when he got his pay at the Edison Company he went on a drunk. When Clarice and Billy quarreled, or when Clarice assailed Madam Y, Uncle Henry's house was no better than a stew. I must add to this the sinister atmosphere that the Graeae cast over the dark hallways and the close rooms, all furnished with musty hangings at the double doors, and with frayed chairs and couches. Somehow I imagined these hard-looking women standing behind corners of doors, or in dark coigns with axes ready to strike down someone they wanted to rob. They reminded me of the Bender women of Kansas of whom there was bloody memory at this time for their dreadful murders. I am depicting now the way these women affected my pastoral imagination. But in fact these sly sycophants, moving about the house with feline softness and pouring oily words on each other, would occasionally betray the fact that they had claws beneath their silken pads. They, too, quarreled with each other, and then they said poisonous words, speaking in menacing undertones.

Another thing that made Uncle Henry's house intolerable to me was Madam Y. Though she was only about thirty-five, she seemed an old woman to me; and her inordinate amorous demands palled upon me. She was making threats at last; then she took to drink; as I had observed her before this she had not drunk at all. As I was avoiding her she substituted with a quack doctor, who began to get the money that she had saved. And then Clarice was taunting her for her affair with me and with this doctor. Uncle Henry, naturally a silent man, went about amid this vulgar scene silent and apathetic, as if he had come to this kind of life and there was nothing to do about it. My mother's sister, his first wife, had been a high-minded and intelligent woman. It was her religious preoccupations that made her contentious. She had talked Uncle Henry into this dumbness, and I fancy that this second marriage of his was a swing away as far as possible in the other direction from the life he had had with my aunt. Surely he was having a change at this time. To an extent he did not know the kind of people he had about him, for he had spent all his life in a small city down in the state. And these gamblers, drunkards and demireps who infested his house were beyond his analysis.

Obviously I was not the beloved nephew that I had fancied I was. My memory of Uncle Henry brought over from the time when I was nine years old, and with my mother had visited at his house, was all dispelled. Even Uncle Henry dunned me for my board, for as I was paid every two weeks it happened sometimes that I had to pay for two weeks after they had elapsed, and could not pay at the end of the intervening week. I felt sure that the Graeae set him after me. All things put together I was thinking of another place to board, and a cheaper place at that.

By this time Will had come from Lewistown to Chicago to try his fortune at the law. His sister was with him, who had been a member of my class in the high school. They were living in a boardinghouse in 37th Street, a house that had been moved back to make place for a flat building. One reached the door by going through an areaway. The prospect of being with Will and his sister, not to mention the peace of boarding in a family that had recently lived in Lewistown and whom I had known there, filled me with happiness. And though Mrs. Duncan, the lady of the house, did not really feel that she could take me, she yielded at last. She was doing all the housework, helped by her husband who as yet had only a makeshift job; and Will and his sister were almost all she could take care of. However, she wanted me there, and so I went.

Will's sister was taking a course in a medical college, and

Will was supposedly trying to get into a law office. The attempt to do so, the endless walking about following up chances, the rebuffs, the cold stares of lawyers from whom he expected a hearty welcome on the strength of his family connections, his father's place as a lawyer, filled him with loathing and self-contempt. At this time, therefore, he was spending nearly all his time at Mrs. Duncan's reading Greek; while I was up very early and off in all kinds of weather to walk all day collecting bills for the Edison Company. I was the pride of Mrs. Duncan for my punctual habits and industry, while she made no concealment of her opinion that Will was a shirker. Mrs. Duncan went about tired and breathless cooking for us, and for her own family of three persons, and I could see that she could not last very long at the task.

At night when I came home Will would be waiting for me; and after dinner we would talk about the Greek drama and about Racine and other writers. In Lewistown I had paid a good deal of attention to Tolstoy, led to do so by the articles in *Harper's* magazine by Howells. I had read *Anna Karenina, The Kreutzer Sonata,* and other books by this greatest of the Russians; and a little later this was to help me cement some interesting friendships. But Will was indifferent to Tolstoy. After talking a while Will and I would go out for beer, both for ourselves and for his sister. One of us would take a bedroom water pitcher, which held two quarts or so, and bring the beer back in it. Thus we deceived Mrs. Duncan, who was an ardent prohibitionist. By this trick we sat unmolested drinking beer and smoking our pipes, and life took on charming Bohemian qualities. Living in 137, 37th Street Rear was better than hearing the lonely murmur of the bell in the Presbyterian steeple when the wind swayed it, or relieving the monotony of Lewistown by dropping in at the newsstand of Plummer Wright, who toward the last of my life there was not friendly to me, thinking that I had fooled him when I had ordered *The*

Idols of Socrates, when I really asked for *The Idylls of Theoc-
ritus,* and he had misunderstood me.

The winters in Lewistown were bleak enough, God knows;
but this fall and winter in Chicago were cold and snowy beyond anything I had ever known. I had to spend two weeks'
wages to buy an ulster heavy enough with which to face the
blasts from Lake Michigan, as I went out collecting bills. In
February my sister was married to Carl Stone, and I got a leave
of absence to go to Lewistown to be present at the ceremony.
Gorton's wife was in Chicago society, and lived in Prairie
Avenue. So he stared at me as I asked him for permission to
go to Lewistown, and told him my mission. Who is this collector that his sister is being married to the son of Chicago's
society queen? The wedding was as grand an affair as the circumstances permitted. The ceremony was performed by
Uncle Beth who came on from Colorado. A caterer from Galesburg served a breakfast-luncheon. The wedding march was
played by one of my sister's Knox College friends. A private
car took the bridal party back to Chicago; and I returned to
my collectorship a day or two later, back to Mrs. Duncan's
boardinghouse at 137, 37th Street Rear.

There was no woman for me at Mrs. Duncan's, for Will's
sister was a nunlike character. She was a good deal over six feet
in height, and she had an impediment in her speech. Perhaps at
this time I was visiting brothels occasionally, furtively and in
terror; but at any rate I had no girl. In Lewistown I had met
Grace, who was related to a prominent family there, who was
visiting in the home of a leading citizen, whose daughter was
her friend. Grace had taken my heart. She reminded me of
Tennyson's "Maud," and I had sat in her presence spellbound
and worshipful. Somehow I heard that Grace was now in Chicago, and I summoned up all my courage to see her. So I wrote
her a note, addressed to the mansion of her rich uncle who lived
on one of the best streets of the South Side.

Here I was with an address such as 137, 37th Street Rear.
"Rear" had to be added into the address, for the number belonged to the front door of the new apartment building which
had crowded back the frame house where I lived with Mrs.
Duncan. In writing to Grace I gave that number, and not the
Edison Company. I may have been ashamed that I was working
there. Shortly a note came from Grace. My heart beat as I got
it, both with delight and with fear. I opened the note half
expecting that Grace had written me a cold refusal. Instead it
was polite enough, all in her beautiful handwriting and on
exquisite stationery. And I was welcomed to call. I dressed as
well as I could and made my appearance. To call upon a girl in
those days meant for the man and the girl to sit on opposite
sides of the room and to struggle for something to say. Grace
was gay and at her ease; but I was frightfully nervous and
tongue-tied. Later I took her to see a play at Hooley's Theatre,
as it was then called, providing a carriage for the purpose of
covering the several miles from her uncle's house. It did not
seem fitting that Grace should ride in a streetcar. Also I did
something as alien to my real character as anything imaginable.
I bought a cheap imitation of a diamond to wear in my scarf.
I wanted intensely to make Grace admire and respect me,
though I lived at 137, 37th Street Rear. When I became prosperous enough to buy a diamond I never did so, for by that
time I disliked jewelry, and my manner of dress was as democratic as possible.

The next summer, during the World's Fair, when I had
learned a good deal about Chicago, and considered myself
pretty much a man of the world, I hated myself for the absurd
tactics to which I had resorted to win Grace; and in the
exchange of some notes some ironic thing I wrote affronted her,
and she lapsed into silence for good. I wrote her thus out of
pride, as much as to say that I would not trouble myself to
please her. I was thus canceling the self-depreciation I had for

that false diamond. All the while Grace seemed too fair and high for my aspirations. For that matter I could not marry anyway on account of my small earnings; and gradually my resolution was strengthening not to marry at all.

It was not long before Will returned to Lewistown disgusted with Chicago, and beaten in the game of trying to place himself. This was the occasion of Mrs. Duncan's decision to quit keeping boarders; so I was compelled to move. Chicago at this time was alive with people from all the surrounding states who had come to the city to make money during the World's Fair soon to open. Among thousands of others Mrs. Porter from Lewistown had set up a boardinghouse at 3165 Groveland Avenue, a very good street on the South Side, one block from the Lake, and one block from the car-line street called Cottage Grove Avenue, and near 31st Street. She was quite an elderly woman, frail and thin almost to emaciation; but full of a sort of ethereal vitality. She knew me in Lewistown; and when I appeared at her door asking for board she was delighted. In truth she needed a man in her household as a friend and a consultant on the various vexations that attended her business. And so in a few days I was installed in Mrs. Porter's house, and Mrs. Duncan and the group there faded back in the fast receding background.

At Mrs. Porter's the service I was performing at the Edison Company was galling me almost beyond endurance. After walking miles through the snow all day long I was so tired at night that as soon as I had had dinner I feel asleep. I could not keep my mind on a printed page for a minute. Hence all my delightful studies were a thing of the past. I had become a wage slave. All this time I had not written home for any help, though at times I was hard pressed for money. I was not extravagant, but somehow money slipped out of my hands faster than I could earn it. I should have managed to live on $50 a month without pawning my watch; but I was always behind. At the Edison Company there was another collector, an elderly man over sixty who wore a silk hat and a fur-lined overcoat, and sported on his scarf a large diamond. This man, Grout, had been rich, so he told me. He confided to me as we became companions that he had owned a part of the ground where the Auditorium Hotel stood, and that a part of his income was still from a leasehold agreement of a part of that ground. This job of collecting was just something to do, and to make a little spending money. One day he asked me in so many words how much I was getting from the Edison Company. When I told him he went on to say that it was not fair, that he was getting $75 a month, but not to say that he had revealed the fact; but to go to the front and ask for $75 too. From the first I had been trying cases in the justice courts for the company, in addition to collecting bills. And Grout went on to remark that I was young and could get over much more ground than he could, and was worth more to the service. And so I was. But the sharpmen who ran the company were willing to use my greenness, and my industry, my modest submission, all the while that they were drawing large salaries and growing rich on dividends. For already the financial wizardry of Insull was beginning to manifest itself in extended business for the company; and Robert Lincoln was well pleased with the choice he had made in taking Insull to pull the company into prosperity.

Often Grout and I left the Edison building together at the close of the day, and took our way through the snow and the zero weather of that terrible winter. We would drop into a saloon for beer or whisky; and sometimes proceed to other saloons as we walked toward Wabash Avenue. Sometimes as we got to 22nd Street we would get off the car and go to some brothel to see the girls, where Grout, broken old Silenus that he was, would buy beer and hold some prostitute on his lap, as I sat laughing quietly to myself. We never went "upstairs" as it was called. Somewhere on the South Side he got off the car and parted from me for the night. Then I would go to the loneliness of Mrs. Porter's boardinghouse, where she would be chirping like a canary about the weather or the events of the day.

The other boarders here were two Irish girls, an elderly man, the father of Beckwith, the painter, one of the decorators of the buildings at the Fair. This elderly Beckwith had a very young wife. There was also a dark tall man, a medical student, who looked like an Italian bandit. He was attentive to one of the Irish girls. I think this man had a touch of insanity, for later on he accused Mrs. Porter, this wisp of a woman then over seventy years of age, of carrying on an affair with a young doctor in the house. Mrs. Porter appealed to me to protect her, and I did so, and carried to him the word of ejectment by which he was removed from the house. Then the Irish girls left; and it was not long before I moved on. In the meantime the Italian bandit, noticing my fatigue at night and my nervous state, asked to examine my heart. I allowed him to do so and was paid for my compliance by having him tell me that I had mitral insufficiency. I was scared at first; but later I doubted his diagnosis. And he was utterly wrong, and I think through a kind of demoniac malice. Often after that, for life insurance and on annual inventories of my state of health, my heart was pronounced strong and entirely normal.

There was another man in the house who was an artist. One night he drew a picture of me as I lay on the bed asleep. He made me look exactly as Keats looked lying dead on his pillow there in that house near the Piazza di Spagna. I had great self-pity, I am sorry to admit. There was still another young man at this place, the son of a rich woman living in Michigan Avenue, who affected society. She did not care for this son, and had sent him forth to work and live where he would. He was full of complaint about this. We shared a little room together for a while, and talked over our troubles at night. Very soon

I lost this man and for years did not see him. He went to the Philippines as a soldier, and coming back to Chicago called upon me and described to me a charge through the swamps near Manila when a soldier at his side was killed. I used this material for the epitaph "Harry Wilmans" in *Spoon River Anthology*.

In addition to great fatigue at night when I returned from the day's tramping about I was filled with rebellion and indignation, and wounded feelings. I wanted to write, I wanted to read and study and reflect. I did not want to beard tough men at the Edison Company, and encounter insulting bullies in gambling halls, and supercilious secretaries in business offices where I had to go to collect bills. My real life and nature were suppressed and submerged in this occupation; yet I saw no way to extricate myself. I read some books at odd hours, but not many. I wrote some verses, very lugubrious they were too, on Sundays and holidays, and published some of them in the *Inter Ocean* under pseudonyms. Maltravers's mother, a poet of skill, and at this time engaged in translating the *Aeneid*, picked me out as the author of these verses, looking through the pseudonyms, and thought them good, but too melancholy. One night I came home in deeper discontent than usual and wrote off at once the verses "Helen of Troy," which I published under my own name. This was while I was still living at Mrs. Porter's. I carried forward these verses into *Songs and Satires* published in 1916, and into my *Selected Poems*, brought out in 1925, all despite the fact that one of my best literary friends pronounced that poem the very worst ever written to the love mate of Paris.

My work at the Edison Company was becoming intolerable. I was proud and sensitive and I had to stand the orders of rough men full of pride and insolence. I had to fight my way to respectful treatment with men who were only a little higher in the service than myself. One day I went to see Maltravers just to tell him the torture that I was in. At once he remarked that he had an opening in mind that he would arrange for me to get. An old friend of his with whom he had formerly been associated for years in one of the large law offices in town was about to set up an office of his own. And putting on his hat Maltravers conducted me to see this man who bore an astonishing name. We found him, and of a truth he was a queer man to behold. He was extraordinarily thin, his nose tipped to one side, one of his eyes was cocked. His voice was amusingly falsetto. But he had a very friendly manner and quite won me on that score. He seemed to like me at once; and when he asked me about my accomplishments in the work of drafting declarations and other pleadings, he was satisfied with my answers. He confessed on his part that he had no skill in such legal work. In a word, we struck a bargain with each other: I was to be paid $50 a month for what I did for him, and to have the privilege of making what I could by any law business I could pick up. It turned out to be a complicating arrangement, just as my father said that it would when I wrote him about it. However, I went to the Edison Company and resigned my job, receiving many compliments for my days of service and good wishes too from the comptroller of the company. On May the first this lawyer and I sat in a new office in the Ashland Block. It was just ten months after I had arrived in Chicago. My name was on the door as Edgar Lee Masters, something that my associate insisted upon. Before this I had signed myself as E. L. Masters, or as Lee Masters, rarely with my full name.

And now life was all changed for me. My associate's father-in-law was an old citizen who had been a soldier in the War Between the States. He had been in the Fire Department of Chicago years before this, and had almost wrecked his health by his exertions and exposures during the Fire of 1871. He knew all the politicians and firemen and men about Chicago for forty years back, and he was able to send our office a great deal of business. I liked this old Irishman from the first, and he was a friend of mine to his death in 1904. He was a bluff, courageous, hearty, outspoken man. On my part I got a little business from the Edison Company, and from the employees there; and with one thing and another I was suddenly more prosperous than I had ever been, not to speak of the independent and rather dignified life that I was in. As for my associate he had a pocketful of money all the time. A friend of his had been elected state's attorney the fall before, and he was sending our office business, in which I did not participate except by my associate's generosity, which was often exercised.

The World's Fair opened the day we started the law office, and my associate and I at once began to frequent its wonders. It was a gala summer for me. That winter he had been to Biloxi for a throat and nose affection. There he had met the members of a charming Southern family; and one of the daughters of this family in company with a young woman from Minnesota came to Chicago in the middle summer to see the Fair; and on more days and evenings than I can count we were all together sightseeing or feasting on the magical ground of that great exhibition. Nearly every evening we dined at Old Vienna on the Midway. My associate had many German friends in his part of the city. He also loved German songs, and the music of the orchestra at Old Vienna set him into raptures, as it did all of us.

My associate was married and was not romantically interested in the Biloxi girl; but Gertrude, the Minnesota girl, very soon worked her strange hypnotism over me. She came of a rich family and had jewels and beautiful dresses. She had traveled around the world, something that was not so common then. She knew Paris and even Constantinople, and in fact she looked foreign, something like a Persian beauty with her tan-colored skin and her tiger eyes. The Hindus, Turks, Russians always stared at her on the Midway. And her features

were regular, her nose shapely, something that I have always
admired in women. She treated me as an interesting boy,
though we were in fact about the same age. I didn't know it
then, but she was greatly drawn toward me; and if I had not
been so proud, so diffident and sensitive, Gertrude would have
been mine, I am sure. But what did I do? My imagination carried me away. I dramatized her as Faustine and as Félise and
wrote her verses in the manner of Swinburne. Gertrude smiled,
while my associate who was not practiced enough in the art
of love to know Gertrude any more than I was, addressed her
oracularly as a "woman of the World." I fancy that at that
time Gertrude had much to learn. But such were the fancies
of two young men, one fresh from the fields, the other utterly
dominated by ideas of chastity, and without any experience
with women. So it was that I saw myself slipping into love with
Gertrude, and I grew terrified. I began to pour acid into my
fiery veins; I began to draw upon the old wound of eleven years
of age to get myself into a critical, and ironical state of mind.
Gertrude saw this. And it wasn't long before James J. Corbett,
recently famous for defeating John L. Sullivan, strolled through
Old Vienna one night, and seeing us all at the table paused.
My associate had a way of presenting himself as if everyone
would know who he was. That had come from his connection
with the prominent law firm, the head of which was an orator
and a celebrity in town. So he arose and announced himself to
Corbett, who said "Oh yes!" as if the name was known from
one end of the earth to the other. Corbett was introduced to
Gertrude and I saw at a glance that she was fascinated and
impressed. Very soon now he was with her at her boarding
place, and strolling with her on the Midway. He knew what to
do; and Gertrude was lost to me. Afterwards, she wrote me
letters. She came to Chicago the next year as a member of a
theatrical company, and I went to see her act, and to adore her

from afar. Later she married a New York man and I heard of her no more.

Ah, but what delight we had had before the day of separation! Over and over again Gertrude had me repeat my "Helen of Troy" to her, and some humorous verses that I wrote about the Fair. She would look at me and say, "You are an interesting boy." The words did not sound patronizing, for there was admiration in her voice. We drove about Chicago at night under the full moon, and sat at the tables of Old Vienna drinking wine as she told me of Constantinople and other European cities. To this day I reprove myself for not making love to her, for not taking her hand fondly, for not encircling her voluptuous waist. I wanted to do this. I was afraid she would rebuff me, being too green to know that these are natural things to do between admiring hearts. Yet it may have been as well; for if Gertrude and I had consummated our love, or mine if it was I alone who loved, I certainly should have contracted a painful madness. I was too young for her, though our years were the same. I was poor in purse; and perhaps this is the reason I did not play a more ardent part with her. Late that summer a man from Memphis named Howard Hawthorne McGee came to the Fair. He met Gertrude and lost his heart to her completely, so much so that he became an abysmal hypochondriac. He, too, was a writer of verse and celebrated Gertrude over and over again.

Well, I took no wound from Gertrude and went my way full of exuberant disdain, while I wrote more verses in which she was celebrated as a Lamia. Yet if Gertrude had gone just a little more than halfway with me she would have taken me into her coils completely. That she did not do so may be proof that she did not want me. As always from the age of six I was carried along by an ecstasy about women, and filled with wonder and reverence for them as embodiments of mysterious beauty. The pursuit of the eternal feminine was deeply fated in my nature and yet neither then nor later did I say with Faust, "Verweile doch, du bist so schön." The search was destined never to end. I can see now that I was nettled by the experience with Gertrude, for it is proved by the fact that I turned to the young woman whom my associate had been conducting about the Fair and making a dinner companion of, and after a fashion made love to her. After she went South to her home we corresponded, but there was no life in my addresses and at last the feeble flame died away. She had none of the voluptuous sorcery of Gertrude. She was neutral and mild and tame to one's hand.

By midsummer my sister and Carl returned from their wedding journey. They had gone away saying that they would remain in Europe for a year. Carl had no business to return to, and my sister had announced that she would give a year to art in Rome and Paris, pursuing the course she had begun at Knox in drawing and painting, and which had produced her chalk sketches of Agamemnon and the Apollo Belvedere. What happened to cool her ambition I do not know. During the course of her life this ambition revived at times, and had a sporadic expression, latterly in sculpture. But she never devoted herself wholeheartedly to any art, neither music nor painting nor drawing. So now these two were at the Fair with me, and saw the Palace of Art. Carl was the most devoted slave I ever saw. He wheeled my sister by the day around the Fair, and lifted her about as if she were fragile porcelain.

This was one of the most glorious summers of my life, if not the most glorious of all. It brought almost uninterrupted days of blue skies and bright sunshine; but to these I gave the imagination and the vitality of youth beginning to be rugged and tireless after many years of indifferent health. About August the Fair was taking on the phase of a period that was passing. In Chicago we heard of the panic, and Congress was in special session reforming the currency. My money affairs were not affected, but I felt the first cold airs of a changing temperature about me. All along I had roamed the Palace of Art time after time, looking at the pictures and works of art, and making notes for poems, and even writing some poems, one about Andromeda. On a day toward the last of the Fair I saw the pictures again, taking the whole day to do so. And again I stood by the court of Honor, and thrilled with the statue of the Republic, and then wrote a poem called "The White City." I was full of passion for Democracy and for the glory and freedom of the Republic, and my radicalism filled my law associate with resentful arguments in favor of the Republican party which had been consecrated in his mind by the career of Lincoln. At that time I had an admiration for Lincoln, even believing the falsehood that the War Between the States was inevitable and the result of an irrepressible conflict, though my grandfather, who knew Lincoln there in the Petersburg-New Salem country, had given me the materials for a very different judgment of Lincoln. But at this time I followed on after the mythmaking that was being carried on in histories, biographies and poems. The Gettysburg Address was a miracle worker not to be stayed.

It seemed to me that there were wild wails in the air when the White City burned one night just as the gates were closed for good. It was late fall and cold; and in the parks the leaves were drifting down. A kind of autumn was in my feelings, for at last the carnival time was over; and a new and rather unhappy period was setting in. A Jew named Barney was a client of my associate's, and soon he appeared at the office saying that he had bought the lumber of the wrecked Fair, but could not get possession of it against someone who was also asserting title to it. J. Irving Pearce, who ran the Sherman House, somehow had a hand of control over this lumber, and as he was a friend of my father's, Barney wanted my father sent for to negotiate with Pearce and to bring a replevin suit, if necessary, to get this lumber. My father came up from Lewistown, and failing to win Pearce to an accommodation, brought a replevin suit for Barney, whose trick was to get the lumber on a worthless replevin bond and then to sell it and let the trial of the title to the lumber go neglected. This he did. Not only that, he didn't pay my father's fee. And the only compensation for this work that anyone had was some years later when Barney presented me with an evening suit. My sister was then beginning to take me to the opera and she wanted me to be dressed according to the custom.

With the close of the Fair the many boardinghouse keepers had to shut their doors. The numerous World's Fair hotels either burned or stood deserted, and parts of Chicago somewhat resembled an abandoned boom town in Oklahoma. Mrs. Porter had not prospered, and she made ready to quit taking boarders almost as soon as the Fair closed. And so again I had to move on. I had made friends there with a man named Burton, called Doc Burton, as he was taking the medical course at Hahnemann. He was about my age, and though he was rattle-headed, and wild and drunken at times, he was amiable and goodhearted. He came in one day saying that he had found a fine boardinghouse just a block north in Groveland Avenue, just north of the corner of 31st Street. It was run by a Mrs. Fanning, and to Mrs. Fanning's we moved, taking a large room together. By this time I had sent to Lewistown for my violin, which was a fairly good instrument costing originally $50, and was then twenty years in use. I wished to resume my efforts to master the instrument. Sometimes there at Mrs. Fanning's I scraped the few dance pieces that I had learned.

Every one of these boarding places was full of curious people, and Mrs. Fanning's was no exception. Her husband was a small, rather old broken-down man, almost simple-minded, whom she was evidently supporting, for which he was doing the marketing and working about the house, as Uncle Henry did. She had a son named Harry, who was on the stage when he could get a part. She spent much of the money she earned to buy Harry silk hats, topcoats, dinner coats, patent leather shoes, and other things which he needed in the parts that he played. Harry had many photographs of himself attired in these togs. He was what one would call a handsome, or even a pretty, man. And he knew this and was full of admiration for himself. He was a harmless, agreeable fellow, and we got along well together. I am sure that he was an Urning, but I did not know about such specimens of men at that time, save as degraded perverts who haunted hotels or county fairs where there were boys at hand to be picked up. Also at Mrs. Fanning's was a Jewess named Bertha, who during the summer had been and was still in the Ali Baba company as a dancer in tights. She was exceedingly pretty, and I started to win Bertha. She yielded to clipping and cosseting freely enough, but she held back with all the will of her racial blood against a final surrender. One day she told me that she would be glad to take the final step if I would marry her. I had no idea of doing that, and so we drifted apart. There were two women medical students at Mrs. Fanning's. One was from Ohio, from a family fairly well off; the other was native to Chicago, but without a family. They were perhaps in the late twenties or early thirties. True to my intercessor spirit, which the study of Shelley had magnified, I took up with the friendless woman, not romantically, though she had some charm. We were friends and had many talks on medical and psychological subjects. Doc Burton knew these women before we moved to Mrs. Fanning's, and I think they were all in the same class together. When graduation day came at Hahnemann I returned home one night to be told by Mrs. Fanning that the Ohio woman had been given a watch and other presents for her graduation, by her father, who had come on to see his daughter receive her diploma; and was in the house. My Cinderella was in tears, so Mrs. Fanning said, she was in her room unnoticed and unhonored, though she was highest in the class. I had five dollars in my pocket, and only five dollars. So I went forth to a flower store and spent it all for roses for Cinderella, and then returned and summoning Cinderella to her door handed her the roses for her graduation. She wept silently and thanked me in words that did not too much express her gratitude. After her graduation she went away, and I never saw her again. In a few months she married an official of the Rock Island Railroad and became mistress of a fine establishment with every comfort at her command. Somehow I felt that she might have sent me an announcement of her marriage, and that after her life became settled so comfortably she might have invited me to dinner. For I was lonely enough at times. But I never had a line from her.

Groveland Avenue was a street of good houses, and of some class at this time. Two judges of the Superior Court lived there, and one of the most prominent lawyers of Chicago, besides a rich art and picture dealer, and politicians of influence. But I did not know any of these people in my obscure way of life, in my preoccupied days of rising early to hurry to the law office, and of returning late too tired to care much for making new friends. Cottage Grove Avenue one block west was quite a different matter. It was a business street; and here at the corner of 31st Street and from thence north and south was full of saloons, assignation rooms, poolrooms and cheap restaurants. The neighborhood was sordid, noisy, crowded, goatish and dusty. Prostitutes soliciting walked under the dim lights at night, and the sound of tin-pan pianos rattled from back rooms of saloons where women sat to get trade. On 31st Street was the American Theatre, which had been a place of fairly respectable entertainment during the World's Fair. Now it was in the hands of hard-faced coryphees, who wandered from the stage to the tables in the theatre in order to sell themselves to drunken wanderers of the night. Doc Burton had more time than I had; he also was far more reckless than I; and frequently he was forth after he finished his studies looking for women. On Saturday night he prowled with a vengeance. And one night at about two o'clock he came in, and finding me asleep put the crook of his cane around my neck and pulled me from the bed to the floor. He was in a great state of excitement and happiness. He had met at the corner a woman, who turned out to be from near Lewistown. She knew my family, and that was what surprised and delighted him. He had already engaged himself to marry her; and in a few months he did so, and then Doc Burton passed from my life.

On my part I had no romance and I had no girl. Sometimes in desperation I went to a saloonkeeper to inquire about girls; and occasionally in this way I found one in a room somewhere near. I approached these experiences with a heart which almost beat out of my breast. For I was as afraid as death of women of this stamp, and yet I did not know what else to do. Many evenings I went to see my sister and Carl. By this time they had a daughter of surpassing loveliness. She was named Elizabeth after her grandmother Stone, and later I became her godfather when she was baptized by Uncle Beth at Chautauqua.

My sister lived in an apartment house in Michigan Avenue, one of the most expensive in Chicago at the time. She had the numerous relatives of her husband for immediate friends, and they were affectionate toward her in obedience to a family loyalty which distinguished them. As yet my sister was not greatly acquainted in Chicago, though her mother-in-law had placed all her notable friends on my sister's calling list. But childbearing and getting settled in her new home took much of her strength. She was now emerging into the rich beauty of maturity which made her a person of such arresting appearance. She had inherited the fine eyes of her father, and his brow as well, high and broad much beyond the average lot of women. Then she talked exceedingly well, with wit and charm. It gave me great happiness to see her mother-in-law, who was then so much of a figure in Chicago, take to her with such genuine warmth and admiration. She was much at the mansion of this grand lady with its many rich possessions, and was entertained there, first when she returned from Europe, and then frequently on formal occasions. Sometimes I was privileged as a poor relative of my sister to look in this mansion with its marbles and bronzes and pictures, and to peer into the music room with its pipe organ, or into the dining room with its silver and china, and its great buffet. On many nights when I didn't want to practice on the violin or to read I went to see my sister and Carl, and to play with my lovely little niece.

Just now my law practice was not so prosperous as it had been during the World's Fair. On such cases as I had I worked with incredible industry, but the fees were small. And sometimes I was almost as short of funds as I had been when with the Edison Company, and was pawning my watch. The depression of the period was now making itself felt in Chicago, as well as over the country, and banks were beginning to close their doors. I did my best to get law business, but I did not know how to do it; and for that matter I never learned the trick. Naturally in this state of affairs I was out for any professional employment that was honorable, or even permissible by the rules. Down Cottage Grove Avenue was a barber who shaved me and with whom I thus became on friendly terms. And one day he came into my office with some letters which he had taken from his wife. They purported to be written by a wealthy man in that part of town; and the barber said that he had evidence other than the letters that this man had debauched his wife. He wanted me to bring a suit for alienation of affections, and I did it. There was something in the press about this suit, but nothing of moment. And almost at once I was confronted by a physically powerful lawyer who had been attached to the state's attorney's office, demanding that the suit be dismissed, and that the letters be surrendered to him. He was thus acting for the wealthy home wrecker. Then the barber himself descended upon me, accusing me of betraying him. I looked at him thinking that he had lost his mind, which wasn't true, as he had no mind to lose. He too demanded the letters and I gave them to him. In those days suits of this kind were common. I had seen several of them tried in Lewistown; and according to the code which prevailed, as I knew it, there was nothing wrong about them. But suddenly I saw that such cases should not be brought except in the most genuine circumstances of palpable injury, and I was ashamed that I had had anything to do with the barber.

Later when I was in full practice I was offered $10,000 to take such a case, and refused on principle to do so. The case of the barber was my sole case of the kind. In the summer following the World's Fair I had little to do, and was reading again and writing poems secretly. The great A. R. U. strike was beginning to mutter, and Chicago was torturing me in that indescribable way which it did more and more, and in subtler and more various forms as the years went on. My sister, Carl and my niece were paying a long visit in Lewistown, where my father had grown quite prosperous and had built over his house with additions, with new mantels and hardwood floors and with a bathroom. Maltravers had by this time met my father, and had given him great admiration. And when I proposed to Maltravers that we escape Chicago and the strike by going to Lewistown he was delighted, and off we went. Maltravers was something of a notable in Chicago by now, with one published book of poems to his credit and with some acceptance in the magazines. His appearance in Lewistown was that of a visiting celebrity, and an old acquaintance of mine at Galesburg, then connected with one of the papers there, wrote startling headlines for a half-serious and half-humorous article concerning the distinction that had come to Lewistown. Maltravers made friends of all the Lewistown people, and we were invited to dinner by old chums of mine. We sat on the lawn under the great maples where my niece rolled on the grass attended by her nurse and where my father told funny stories of his experiences at the bar. We all went to Bernadotte and took a ride on the Spoon River in a little steamer which was owned by a friend of my father's. Maltravers, my father and I were entertained at Havana by Colonel Langford, the fish commissioner under Governor Altgeld. He had a steamer at his command, and we went up the Illinois River to Copperas Creek Dam, entertained by an orchestra which Colonel Langford had secured for the trip, and feasting on excellent food and drinking good beer all the way there and back. Then I took Maltravers to see my grandfather and grandmother, and my uncle Will and his wife, and their daughter Edith. This was not my first visit to the old farm since my removal to Chicago, but it was the happiest one, perhaps. My grandfather was now eighty-two and my grandmother eighty; but they were the same as they had ever been. My grandmother still milked her cows, she still churned, and cared for the house, she still sat at the head of the bountiful table and laughed and told stories. And we rested under the old maple trees, where Maltravers gave rapt attention to my grandfather as he told about the time that Lincoln had stood under the very shadows of these trees and tried a case before him as a justice of the peace; while my grandmother acting as the chorus to the dramatic recital interpolated that she had driven the men to the yard and the trees because she would not have her floor covered with tobacco juice. Maltravers had brought along his violin. He played much better than I, though by no means with skill. And my niece accompanied him on the piano. The peace, the order, the plenty, the old-fashioned charm of this old home on the farm won Maltravers completely. He confessed that he well understood how it was that it had fascinated my youth and possessed my affectionate memory.

One day we went to Shipley's Pond where the doves were flying; and there my uncle and Maltravers slaughtered dozens of these innocent birds as I looked on. Maltravers went about the neighborhood to some extent, to the Sangamon River by the Mason County Hills five miles north, and to Concord Church and to New Hope meetinghouse. He wanted to see these landmarks of my boyhood. And also he explored the carpenter shop finding remnants of my handiwork, a kite that I had made and which my grandmother had preserved, and a chicken coop in the yard which I had made for her, and the flower bed in the front yard. He possessed himself of all the evidences of my youth which were about, including the jambs of doors where I had carved my name, and the marks of my height at various times which had been made on them. After all this we returned to Lewistown.

My sister had beauty but she did not have that magnetism which attracts men. In Lewistown she had made friends with the worldly fellows, the rather hard, experienced young men. She did this in Chicago. She never had much use for men who read books, or wrote them, or cultivated the intellectual life. In Lewistown the men who lived this life were socially rather impossible, true enough; while her beauty, her pride, her keen wit, and her unconcealed disdain for anything which was not in good form as she knew it kept these men away from her in fear and resentment. So it was that she had little interest in Maltravers. He was not up to her idea of what was good form. She did not much respect his verses, and as for himself he was just a comical man with a bald head and butternut teeth. Carl was just her husband, for whom she had a certain affection, and to whom her fidelity was pledged, and was to be kept because she had deep moral scruples against all wandering fancies.

Chicago on our return was a desolation. The Federal troops had broken Debs and his strike, and there was bitterness in the air, and poverty and misery about. I appeared at the law office to find my associate in a frame of mind none too agreeable on account of my long absence. But also he was hurt that it had not been he instead of Maltravers who had paid this visit to Lewistown, and to the old Masters farm, about which he had heard so much from me. And it was hardly fair that he had not done so, for he had been generosity itself toward me. But the truth was that he bored me to death with his falsetto voice, his interminable bragging about himself, and his envy of me on the score of my superior lawyership. Now I was back to business again, and our association was losing every agreeable feature that it had ever had.

Chapter IX

AND NOW MRS. FANNING WAS ABOUT TO GIVE UP KEEPING A boardinghouse. She was in rather bad health, and her actor son was making some progress on the stage, and was thus able to compensate her long sacrifice in his behalf, and to give her relief from her former hard life. Alone this time I started out to find another boarding place, and finally settled in Indiana Avenue, nearly a mile west of Groveland Avenue. The place was kept by Mrs. Thomas, a tall, sad-looking woman, a typical Indiana type from whence she had come to Chicago during the World's Fair to get rich like the others. Very soon I was shown a photograph of her home in a small city in Indiana, the home she had lost through the drunkenness of her husband, who had wandered off somewhere and was lost to her. She had lived in great comfort before this husband was downed by drink, and now her life was nothing but labor and humiliation. She looked at me at first, and always for that matter, as if there was something ridiculous about me. An ironical, nervous smile twitched on her lips when she talked to me in a faint voice that I could hardly hear. The photograph of her Indiana home showed a large frame house set in a spacious yard with great trees, and with iron dogs and deer by a fountain as decorations. It was not wonderful that she was subdued and taciturn in this dark house in Indiana Avenue, with no yard, and where the noise of the streetcars thundered into the room and shook the walls till they trembled.

The household consisted of a son who was always trying to get work, and of a daughter who was a stenographer in an office downtown. This daughter was amazingly thin and hollow of chest, but she had bright brown eyes which looked at one through glittering nose glasses. She was a laughing girl of about twenty-five or so, and of the sort no man would ever notice. I liked her, for she was amusing to talk to, and she knew the world of business from her work in a ticket broker's office, those institutions which flourished then in Chicago where one could get a ticket to any point for much less than it could be bought at the railroad office. Already the railroads were fighting the sharp men who were depriving them thus of profits, and a little later the courts and the legislature put them out of business. Lena, the landlady's daughter, had stories to tell me every night of what had happened during the day at the office: There had been a quarrel with a customer, or her employer had put over some wonderful piece of shrewdness. At this time I was writing some humorous verses, and some serious ones too. Once I published some in a Chicago paper. Lena came home bringing the poem in print for me to see, and laughing derisively that she had caught me in my folly, before that unsuspected by her. She had the very attitude toward poetry that I had to encounter so much in those days: it was a sentimental and unworthy interest.

That first night at dinner I met a woman doctor named Rachel Yarros, who studied me out of her aquiline slanted eyes, but did not say much. She was a Russian Jewess, and soon it turned out that she was married to Victor Yarros, at the time in Boston, but soon to join her in Chicago. Before long l discovered how well informed she was both in medicine and in literature, Russian, English, French and American. I could talk Tolstoy with her endlessly, though she thought little of Tolstoy as a thinker, but much of him as an artist. She was deeply read in Spencer's philosophy, and as I had gone rather well into him at Lewistown we had Spencer for a subject to talk about in the evenings, and about the doctrine of equal liberty and philosophical anarchy. We were in sympathy about the pardon of the so-called anarchists by Governor Altgeld, and about the labor question, and about freedom, and about poetry so far as she was interested in it, which, as I remember it, was not extensive. She saw my sex problem and upbraided me for what she called varietism; but on the other hand, she was favorable to free relationships, and against conventional marriage. Before her husband came on from Boston I escorted her about to meetings, political and other; and when he came we all went together. Yarros was a few years older than I, but he was vastly ahead of me as a bookman. He read French, German, Russian and English equally well and there was no book, especially in economics or philosophy, which he did not, as it seemed, know. He was a man of infinite dialectic, fluent and profuse, and with his definite convictions clarified many of my ideas. We talked Kant and Schopenhauer; and he told me about the conditions in Russia, from which and from the police he had escaped after they had raided a meeting of young men where Spencer's *System of Synthetic Philosophy* was being read and discussed. Thus I began to read Kant again and other philosophers. But also in these days I wrote a blank verse play on Benedict Arnold which Maltravers admired so much that he interested an actor in looking at it. But nothing came of it.

Lena grew greatly interested in me, so much so that I was both regretful and alarmed, and duly cautious. She had a friend named Helen, whose childlike beauty and modest manner excited my masculine protectiveness. When Helen stayed late after calling upon Lena I would escort her home. On parting she yielded innocently to my caresses which were ardent enough. I desired her greatly, and even after my manner of dreaming impossible dreams I imagined myself as Helen's husband, guarding her helplessness and her beauty and making sacrifices to do so. But meanwhile Lena was so surely mine if I stretched forth my hand to take her that I was thrown back into every prudent reflection. She was not in the least desirable; and I could see that once I possessed her I would have a serious problem on my hands. I should have to marry her to save her from destruction. Dr. Yarros saw this and warned me. But Lena's mother, who was not blind to her daughter's feelings, I am sure, and not oblivious of our long hours together in the little library, went about as if she did not care what happened. All this while the resolution persisted in me never to marry.

It was not long before the Yarroses got acquainted with a family on the North Side in which there were musicians, and radicals on every subject. The father was a broker, but a great reader and a philosophical anarchist. The mother was an accomplished Wagnerian performer; one of the daughters was a musician, and had composed a song cycle based on the Shakespearean sonnets; the other daughter, younger and not married like the other, was a reader and a radical and very beautiful in a large-eyed ethereal way.

I was taken to meet this group, and they welcomed me with open arms. They had been told of my studies, my Shelleyan ideas, my writing. Honoria, the younger daughter, greeted me with both her hands, and often since I have felt that she was the wife that was intended for me by the fate of affinityship in feeling and thinking. When I went there we all talked free love, sex and every imaginable thing. And though I had almost committed to memory the Notes to *Queen Mab* I could not restrain a certain feeling of alarm when I heard Honoria, as we sat together, say that she did not believe in marriage, and that a man and woman who truly loved each other should live together. I told this to my sister, who told her mother-in-law; back came the word to me from that conventional lady of quality that Honoria's mother had divorced her husband to marry the man who was now Honoria's stepfather. My sister, as conventional as any woman could be, was after me to beware of Honoria, saying that if I married her she would tire of monogamy and desert me. For good or evil my sister was always near me to discover what I was doing and to bring her own judgment to bear upon it. As she stood in front of me at the Atterberry farm when I had the hoe, so did she track my steps to the last of her life. It was affection for me, or a dominating will that meant to control me. If the latter it was inherited from my mother, who fought all her life to subordinate my father, and failing to do so, was full of irritated disappointment. Yet I deserved some kind of interference with my course for telling my sister what Honoria had said.

Altogether life was now full of interest every day, as well as work; and I was living to the full, whereas I should have rusted in Lewistown. Karr, who had taught me logic and Latin in the academy at Lewistown, was practicing law in South Chicago as an attaché of a real estate office there. He was trying justice cases for the Poles and Czechs who worked in the steel mills there, and making what seemed to me a great deal of money. Unfortunately he was not saving it. He used to come to my office on occasion, and we would go forth to feast or to play, and to talk about the differences we observed between the city and the country. Karr was a sensitive man; his fine face and features showed his delicate organization. And his life at South Chicago was abrading his nerves, and coarsening his texture. It was natural for him and for me to go down into our more rugged selves for the purpose of bringing up silica wherewith to make a carapace against the hard knocks that came to us. In the youthful cynicism of manufacturing protective shells we made many profound observations upon the game of life. Once Karr said to me, "The city will harden your heart or break it." I handed this remark on to Maltravers, who used it as the refrain of one of his poems; for he too had exposed his tender tissues to the blows of the city, and was already boasting that he had endured everything, and was now beyond hurt. Maltravers was about eight years older than I; and several years older than Karr. Karr did not last very long in Chicago.

He went back to the country rather broken by the city and the way of life into which he inevitably fell there in the rough contacts of the people who manned the steel mills, and those who exploited them. But Maltravers, who drank but little, only a glass of wine at Max Romer's at times when he feasted on roast beef or wild duck, never lost his nerve, be the misfortunes what they might be; and he had the nimblest way of lighting on his feet when about to take a fall of nearly anyone that I have known. It was to him that I addressed the sonnet "Life's Soldier" in *A Book of Verses,* my first book to be printed.

Partly through natural inclination, and partly to accelerate the toughening processes of my resistance to the cruelties of the city, I attended every boxing match that I could, often helped to tickets by Malachy Hogan, a saloonkeeper and referee, and one of the gayest and most generous Irish lads I have ever known. I celebrated him in the poem "Malachy Degan" in *The Great Valley.* Thus it was that I saw Fitzsimmons, Dan Creedon, Terry McGovern, Jim Hall, Choyinski, Young Griffo, and many others face their rivals in the ring. I took my father once to see a fight, thinking that his masculine heartiness would rejoice in this sport; but he turned away from it. As I felt myself growing more and more like him, and as I wanted to cultivate all the strength and manliness that were in me, I was disappointed that this interest of mine did not signify to his mind that I was making progress in these directions, and was outliving the fragility of feeling and the Shelleyan tendencies which he had lamented in me when I was with him in the country. I went to these fights in Robey, Indiana, during the Fair, after the Fair at the Exposition Building on the Lake Front, which stood for several years after I was in Chicago; then to Tattersall's, and sometimes to barns on the dark cold North Side far out, and in the wintertime.

Maltravers took me a time or two to the Press Club, where

it was, in fact, that I saw Fitzsimmons box Choyinski. On another occasion at the Press Club I saw Fitzsimmons take on Ed Dunkhorst, known commonly as the Human Freight Car. Dunkhorst was as large as Carnera of this day, or larger. He weighed about 260 pounds; but Fitzsimmons almost killed him, Fitzsimmons who generally fought at about 160 pounds. While the World's Fair was going on my Irish associate and I went to Robey to see a fight between Dan Creedon and Buffalo Costello. This fight lasted for hours, with Creedon advancing ineffectually and Buffalo Costello retreating out of Creedon's way. A rowdy crowd was outside the octagonal building which had been built by the fight promoter Dominick O'Malley from New Orleans for these exhibitions during the Fair. This disgruntled crowd, kept from entering to see the fight, because they had no money for tickets, started at last to take revenge. The building was as combustible as a matchbox, and these reckless devils, yelling and cursing outside, finally decided to set the building on fire. There thousands of us sat watching Dan Creedon and Buffalo Costello circle the ring, while One-Eyed Connolly, then a played-out fighter sat close to the ring saying over and over in a husky whisky voice, "I challenge the winner." Suddenly looking at one of the entrance doors I saw that the building was on fire. Speaking cautiously to my Irish associate we two got up and carefully tiptoed to an entrance door. Just then there was the cry of "fire" and the vast thousands started in a panic to make their escape. Just as I reached the door I looked back and saw the two pugilists still circling the roped square. They paid no attention to the fire. As we emerged into the open that crowd of ruffians started to throw bricks. I pulled my overcoat collar around my head and hurried to the suburban train waiting to take us back to Chicago. I escaped unhurt. I put this episode into a sonnet entitled "After the Fight in Rome," which was published in *A Book of Verses*.

All the while my days were busy beyond description. I

seemed always to be engaged in some case that required the heaviest labor and yielded the scantiest fees. Though out of its chronological order I shall tell about the Recek case, which off and on took several years of my time. The Receks were childless, elderly people of Polish blood. The old man had worked for years in a foundry, resulting in hands so stiff and crippled that he could not bend his fingers. The old woman at the same time had been taking in washing. They saved their hard earnings and invested them in a lot on the West Side, which was worth about $2,000. Chicago was infested with real estate sharks, who knew every cheating trick that crooked minds could contrive. The Receks advertised their lot for sale; and a shark named Ullman answered the advertisement. Neither of the Receks could read English, and Ullman had them completely at his mercy. He got them to trade their unencumbered lot for a flat building, which was so heavily mortgaged that the equity which the Receks took was worth almost nothing. Ullman had the Receks deed their lot not to him, but to a confederate named Moore, who immediately conveyed it to a man who posed as an innocent purchaser for value. In time the poor Receks discovered that they had been defrauded, and the case came to my associate, and to me by way of personal attention; and I set to work full of indignation determined to get the lot back for the Receks. I tried this case, and it was my second case in a court of record. My first case had more dramatic consequences, and precedents too. I fought for the Receks with all my power, subjecting Ullman and Moore, and all the witnesses to the most merciless cross-examination that I could command out of a natural talent for that process, and my observation of the ways in which Socrates in the *Dialogues* confuted his adversaries. I won the case after several days' fight in court; and then the rascals appealed from the decree. It went directly to the Supreme Court, as the matter involved a freehold, and there I lost the case. Then I journeyed to Ore-

gon, Illinois, in the beautiful country of the Rock River, there
to see the Chief Justice, who, as it happened, had written the
opinion which beat me. I found that Judge Payne, before whom
I tried the case, had written him a letter of criticism about his
decision, and I had therefore a ready ear as I applied for a stay
order to hold the case while my petition for a rehearing was
pending. The preparation of such a petition was great labor.
It had to be printed, as the briefs had to be, and the labor involved was exacting in the extreme. My petition was denied at
last, and I had to try the case over again as the decree stood
reversed. This time I took another tack, and was compelled to
do so. I centered my fire upon Ullman, not on his confederates,
of whose guilt the Supreme Court had not been convinced.
After another struggle I secured a money decree of about
$3,000 against Ullman; and then I filed a creditor's bill, and
threw Ullman's properties into the hands of a receiver to collect the rents and hold them wherewith to pay the Receks
their judgment. The receiver, Charles L. Boyd, managed these
properties for several years, collecting the rents and accumulating a fund; and finally one day I was able to hand to the
Receks a check for their money. They came to the office humble and dumb. They had waited in perfect patience for this
day, and it had been postponed many years, four or five. The
old man mumbled something as he took the check. Great tears
rolled out of his eyes as his stiff hands, like the claws of an old
hawk, took the check. The old woman, who spoke English
better than her husband, showered her blessings upon me, and
wept as well. This was one of my typical cases. I got perhaps
$500 for this long battle. There were young men in town of
my age who were starting in railroad offices, or as clerks in the
large firms, and who were preparing to head great businesses
twenty years later. This was my labor and my lot.

In Petersburg I had played ball with Billy Caples, who was
a son of the sexton of the Presbyterian church there. One day,

much to my surprise, Mrs. Caples, grown elderly, entered my office to tell me that Billy had been killed while working as a switchman. The family had left Petersburg for Chicago several years before this, something that I had not known before. The death of Billy was peculiarly tragic: He had followed along by the side of a train on a track which curved and ascended, making ready to couple it to a car standing at the top of the curve. When the time came he found that the automatic coupler did not work. He therefore went between the cars to manipulate the links and pins by hand. Owing to the curve, the corners of the cars were brought so close together that his body was crushed almost in two, bringing death in a few minutes. After studying the law for days and briefing it to be ready for the wily and skillful lawyers of the railroad, I went into court, where I was beaten by the rule of law that a railroad is not obliged to lay its tracks in the safest manner; and that Billy Caples assumed the risk of the curve, the holes and cinders between the ties, and the upward incline of the tracks. Mrs. Caples was heartbroken. I spent my own money for the costs to take the case to the highest court in Illinois, and was defeated at every step, in spite of all the ingenious and elaborate arguments I could make to escape the deadly rules of law which tangled me. When the last ditch was reached Mrs. Caples came in to see me. Her eyes were full of querulous wonder, and even of searching criticism. She felt that the case had been lost through my lack of skill.

At this time and for years later I had been making a digest of the Illinois cases in tort, helped at last by James Boyd, a companionable man who was a member of the Press Club, and the son of the receiver Boyd who handled the Recek funds. At last this digest came to over four thousand pages, and I made a contract with a law publishing house to publish it. When I delivered the manuscript they wanted it edited all over in a way that they had thought out for themselves. The labor of this book had already cost me several years of time; and with all my other work I could not re-edit the book. And so it was never published; but it furnished me in my cases with the readiest reference to any principle of tort, and there was nothing like it in print.

In spite of these endurances and labors I wrote poetry, but I did not publish anything of moment. I had drawn away from the *Inter Ocean,* and by this time George Horton, a good poet, and an editorial writer on the *Herald* when I first came to Chicago, had gone as consul to Athens. And I did not send anything to the magazines. After a few trials in Lewistown at appearing in the pages of these periodicals I had given up the quest in disgust. They were then stuffing their covers with wheatless straw, such as sonnets on themes a thousand times treated; whereas what I wrote was fresh and original, if nothing else. Making new friends along the way, I became acquainted with the family of a former judge of one of the courts who lived at Riverside, a forest-skirted village some twenty miles from Chicago. On a Sunday I went there for dinner; and after dinner I took a walk with one of the daughters of the judge, along the banks and through the woods of the Desplaines River. I was filled with memories of Big Creek and of Alfreda and Anne; and with mysterious feelings about nature. I came back to the Thomas boardinghouse and wrote "The Desplaines Forest" which appeared in my first book. Then many times I went to the house of my associate, who lived near Wicker Park, out among the foreign scenes of Milwaukee Avenue, which was a neighborhood that filled me with dreams and delight. There was a German group there who played poker and drank beer. Having no taste for poker I spent the time talking with the womenfolk of the house, or listening to the piano played by the sister of my associate. Sometimes I recited my verses for them, in particular "Helen of Troy."

One day a lawyer, who had been a student at Knox College while I was, and had located in Chicago at about the time that I had, came in to see me, and somewhat breathlessly told me that Anne was at the boardinghouse where he lived, and wanted me to come to see her. Our parting had been friendly there at Julia's gate; but somehow I had a disinclination to see her. However, after some importunities I consented and went down to Englewood, ten miles from the business district, and there found Anne in this boardinghouse which was run by a man who had come to Chicago from a town near Lewistown. And my schoolmate was there, and his brother. After dinner Anne and I retired to a corner, where she began to tell me that she was about to marry the prohibition editor of Lewistown. He was a man then over sixty, half paralyzed, and not of immaculate habits, or appearance. Anne wanted me to advise her. Earlier in the day my college mate had told me in so many words that I ought to marry Anne. But that was farther now from my mind than ever. Anne seemed in better health than she had when I last saw her; but she looked visibly frail. And here was I with cases for Mrs. Caples and for the Receks and without an income sufficient upon which to support a wife. Anne went on to say that the editor was the best man in the world, of the highest principles, of Christian devotions, and that in many ways they were in accord. To which I replied that a marriage with him augured well, these things being true. The conversation finally petered out, and I went my way. She married the editor, and the last time I saw her she was wheeling a baby carriage on the streets of Lewistown; but it wasn't many years before she died. In many ways she had been one of the most inspiring friends of my youth.

I was ill for a time during this summer of 1895, ill from anxiety. In this state of affairs I received an invitation from my sister to visit her and Carl at Lake Chautauqua, where Carl had bought a summer cottage. And in great happiness I set forth, stopping at Niagara Falls where I fell in with a Chicago politician who was driving about with a rather gaudy woman of large physique, and her young lady friend. I had as much genuine fun in the two days I was there en route as I ever had in my life. We drove over into Canada, we dined here and there, we laughed and talked. The politician was a Catholic and very scrupulous of his marriage vows; so that he contemplated nothing further than this merrymaking; but the young woman took such a fancy to me that her friend taunted her. But I was full of caution having escaped recently from the torture of fear, and went on to Lake Chautauqua with a quiet mind.

Uncle Beth and Aunt Minerva and their son Harry, the musician, were there; and my sister entertained them all in honor of me. As a generous hostess, as a woman who loved to give delight, my sister was unexcelled by anyone. And whatever she did to me whether through consulting her own interests, or by way of accident, she was always proud of me. She never had a box party at the opera in Chicago that I was not invited, and she bestowed hospitalities upon me without end all her days. I must say this for her prefatory to any report of the curious way in which she troubled me at times, or to any criticism of the manner in which she complicated me at last. At Chautauqua I met a rollicking, companionable girl from Springfield, Ohio, who that summer had become my sister's boon companion. One night she and I went to Point Chautauqua where drink could be had, for I was temporarily troubled and needed some blackberry brandy. After the drink we sat on the stoop of the hotel waiting for the boat back. But it came in and departed as we discovered finally; and there we were fated to spend the night away from our respective abodes. Lucy was in great terror. In those days no explanation would suffice for such a disappearance; no one would believe that Lucy came back a maiden. She was in a panic; but in the midst of it a tramp boat came along which took us across the lake, and all was well. After my niece was baptized, for which I was asked to stay on as I was selected to be a godfather, I went back to Chicago.

I began early to follow a course by which I would not get into ruts. To this end I was avoiding the habit of lunching too much at the same place, or walking about town without change in the same streets. I might have applied this excellent principle to some other things, perhaps more important. But I did follow it with respect to boardinghouses. Every time I moved I was glad that my life was changed by a new environment. And now I felt that I should leave the boardinghouse of Mrs. Thomas. Several things entered into this decision besides escape from the monotony of the same street, the same house and the same people. One was that I had heard of the gay times that were going on at an apartment building in Groveland Avenue; and at Mrs. Thomas's I had no men associates except her son, who was a shambling, languid youth, who knew very little. I wanted to see some men at evening when I came home. But the critical matter was Lena. Lena's heart was absorbed in me. Her humility and her passion made me sadder than I can describe. She would sit at my feet and rest her arms on my knees into which she would bury her face. Then she would look up at me with tears in her eyes. Sometimes she would lie back on the floor of the little study and cover her eyes with her hands. I was afraid that some day I should forget my resolution to save her from herself. It was bitter winter weather now, and my room at Mrs. Thomas's, heated by a register, was just mildly warm. But at the room that I had found at the apartment building on Groveland Avenue the steam heat kept the air like summer against the winds and the snow that came out of Lake Michigan. And I had found a young and handsome landlady there who was mistress of a large apartment. Saying good-bye to Mrs. Thomas and her son and finally to Lena, whom I told I should see soon and often, I took my departure. The Yarroses were by this time living on the more interesting North Side of town.

All the while there was Stella. She had done secretarial work for me from the first days of my professional life in the Ashland Block, and after considerable coquetting on her part, and cautious dallying on mine, we had made an alliance. My fears concerning her were justified. She became another Madam Y and even worse. For, instead of taking another lover when she saw me inclined to draw away from her, she began to hint that I had taken unfair advantage of her, and to make threats. My Irish associate knew all about the affair, and saw the way Stella was acting. His opinion was that I was tangled and would have to marry her. Perhaps I had a dim idea that something would happen to relieve me of Stella when I got into new living quarters, and into livelier associations.

Chapter X

TAKING UP MY ABODE IN THE APARTMENT OF JULIA A NEW chapter in my life was opened, and another numerical heading in called for. I cannot speak too well of Julia, of her charm, her beauty, her generous nature. I knew nothing about her or her situation in life when I went to the bright room of her apartment and set down my belongings. There was a brass bed in the room whose windows faced Groveland Avenue, there was a blue velvet carpet on the floor, and some colored prints on the wall, and a mahogany chiffonier in the corner. Julia had done everything for my comfort. I felt a sense of luxury about me for the first time since I had started to rooming about in Chicago. I could lie on the bed before retiring, or stretch out before arising in the morning, and hear the wind whistle from the Lake, and see the snow pelt the windows, all secure against the storm in this summer heat of Julia's apartment. At first when I got home at night I went at once to my room, speaking to Julia if she happened to be in sight. Once in my room I sat down to study, and in more earnest than I had lately done; though at no time did I neglect to read something in philosophy, poetry or fiction, or biography which was a passion with me. Always along the way a voice said to me "hurry, hurry, don't let the time go by without doing something." At the same time I was casting my eyes every way in order to choose the right path and not the wrong one, in order to get on. In Lewistown I had read Goethe's *Dichtung und Wahrheit*, and his *Conversations with Eckermann*, and his great example had inspired me to make the best of my time. Yet this autobiography shows plainly enough that I did not always do so.

Carl's guardian in chancery lived far out on the West Side, in a small frame house, though he was prosperous enough, and his wife was rich in her own right. We called him Uncle John. He was of German blood and well versed in German literature; and when I went to dine with him we spent the evening discussing Goethe and Schiller, Jean Paul and Heine, or debating the Battle of Waterloo, and the part that Blücher took in it. Before coming to Chicago I wrote a sonnet entitled "On Reading Eckermann's Conversations with Goethe." This, too, was published in *A Book of Verses,* and I believe first appeared in the *Inter Ocean.* I showed this sonnet timidly to Uncle John, who pronounced it "glorious." He made the same comment to my sister, who respected Uncle John's opinion so much that she felt reinforced in her hope of my talent.

In the basement of the Groveland Hotel was a buffet run by Henry Hughes and his happy bartender. And here every night gathered a group of young men, who lived in apartments upstairs, to drink themselves into intoxication, to sing, tell stories and cavort. One of them was from Lewistown, who had been in Knox College when I was, and who was now practicing law in Chicago. He was a huge fellow who had been a halfback on the football team at school and he was a mighty drinker and plaquet fumbler. Nearly always I passed through the buffet when I came home at night, and took a cocktail and then went to my room. I rarely fellowed with this crowd; for I was always cautious of drink as a daily habit. They would roar at me to join them, for soon I knew them all, or before this, as some of them were lawyers whom I was meeting in the courts. They were a reckless crowd of roisterers, and in fifteen years every one of them was dead, including the great halfback. I celebrated Henry Hughes's buffet and some of its habitués in "The Church and the Hotel" written and published twenty years after this time.

One night passing down the hall of Julia's apartment I saw

her and a woman friend in the dining room having beer and cheese. Julia invited me in, remarking mildly that I seemed a distant sort of person. So I went in and talked with them and drank some beer. Her friend's name was Hattie, a very homely, but humorous woman. With this beginning I started to talk with Julia whenever I saw her. She had a fund of naughty stories, and I gathered from the Press Club and downtown a full amount of the same sort of humor. At last it came out that she had left her husband to live with a man about fifty named Jake who was financing this apartment. Jake got home at two o'clock, or later in the morning. He slept all day, but he was gone forth to the gambling hall that he ran by the time that I arrived at home at night. So that Julia and I were free to conduct ourselves as we chose, so far as any danger of Jake was concerned. Just the same I had had a glimpse of Jake's huge bulk, and supposing that like all gamblers he was expert with a pistol I was full of caution about making advances to Julia; while she was plainly enough willing to take a chance with me. Often she had delicacies in the pantry that she invited me to share with her, and our association soon became very happy and intimate. But my conduct remained impeccable.

My sister was now living at the Lexington Hotel, the most fashionable in Chicago in these days, and as before I was often with her and the niece, generally in the evenings. At the hotel she had become a close friend of Marcella, who was just out of an Eastern finishing school; and these two talked and read French together. Marcella's mother was a fat elderly woman full of braggadocio about her dead husband's late importance in Chicago life, and with intimations about the riches he had left. Marcella was an heiress! But she was also rarely beautiful, with her blue eyes, sparkling with intelligence and amorousness, her fair skin and her exquisite figure. I could have lost my heart to Marcella at once but I was afraid of her riches. I could not see how I could marry her and keep my self-respect, considering that I was making so little, and that I could not possibly support her in the style to which she was used to live. However I trifled with the idea, led on by Marcella's seductive charm. I called on her a few times, but always her mother sat in the room as a watchful chaperon. But sometimes we met in my sister's parlor where we had more freedom, meaning by that that we could talk at will of anything that occurred to us. Pretty soon on some of these visits I met Marcella's brother, a man about my own age. His mother had given me to understand that Charley was wasting his life, and she would be glad if she could put him under my influence, since I was industrious and attentive to my business. Charley spent his days at one of the athletic clubs boxing or swimming or drinking. He had literally nothing to do with his time. Finally the suggestion was made that Charley and I take an apartment in the building where I was rooming with Julia. The mother urged this course, and she offered to furnish the necessary silver, dishes, and kitchen utensils out of her things in storage. All these apartments were provided with rugs, beds and bedding. I was happy over this idea, and Marcella took to it as well. For on account of her friendship with my sister, her knowledge that I was fascinated with her, I was approaching a state where I was in a sense a familiar of the family. And as I see it now Marcella's mother was satisfied with me as a husband for Marcella and expected me to be so. The result was that Charley and I took an apartment together, furnished by his mother. We hired a negro girl to cook for us, and in our seven ample rooms set up as gorgeous bachelors, and with no greater expense to myself than I had incurred before in paying room rent and getting meals at restaurants.

I would come home at night to find Charley more or less in liquor and waiting for our cook to serve the dinner. Or else he would be upstairs calling upon two girls with whom he had got acquainted at once, and plying them with what arts he had. These two girls lived together in the most innocent and secluded way, so far as men friends were concerned. All the roisterers who had essayed to capture them were rebuffed, and the word went around that they were "lady lovers," which was then the term for Lesbians. Charley would return from seeing them with curses, and with the growl that they were "lady lovers." After dinner we sat talking until I showed that I wanted to study. Then Charley would go downtown to his club, or out on Cottage Grove Avenue looking for a girl. He never had any luck of moment, that I could see; but he was full of boasts about his wonderful conquests in the past. A few times he took me to his club to swim and to dine. I had begun with Maltravers to swim at the tanks on the North Side; and once finding how refreshing it was as an exercise and how beneficial to my nerves I was swimming here and there wherever I could, and I have kept up the habit almost daily to the present time.

About now I had my first case in the Supreme Court, for it preceded the Recek case which I have told about in connection in general with my laborious professional life when I was making so little. A man named F. W. Smith had been sent to the penitentiary upon the revival of a sentence suspended nearly ten years before at the time of his conviction by a jury for jury bribing. He was to be free during good behavior. But he fell in with some arsonites in Chicago who were renting store rooms, filling them with crockery and cheap merchandise, then setting fire to the place and collecting the insurance. As my old Irish friend, the father-in-law of my associate, had sent Smith to the penitentiary while acting as fire inspector of Chicago, using this old conviction to do so, he decided to help Smith to get out after he had been in prison several years, and after Governor Altgeld refused to pardon Smith, and after several other lawyers had failed to get Smith released. The fire inspector came to me and told me the circumstances. I said at once that the sentence was void, that it could not be lawfully pronounced after such a lapse of years during which time Smith was not held within the jurisdiction of the court by a bond and a continuance of the proceedings. My association and talks about the law with my father had given me that understanding of the regularity, or lack of it, in a case like this. The fire inspector furnished me with the necessary costs and I went over to the jail and got Smith to give me a note for $300 for my fee. He had just been brought from the penitentiary to the jail on a *habeas corpus ad testificandum*.

I briefed the case carefully and went before the Supreme Court, where, after some delays and some following of the court to its various meeting places in the state, I filed my petition and won Smith's discharge from further imprisonment. The experience was very arduous, owing to traveling back and forth; for Mount Vernon where I got the court to hear the case is several hundred miles from Chicago. Smith left me at the station in Chicago promising to come in to see me the next day and pay the note. He didn't come; in fact, he went away from Chicago and I did not see him again for months, or hear from him. I sued him on the note, and got a judgment after many months. By that time he was in Connecticut. He came back to Chicago and the word went around that he had money. So I got a *capias ad satisfaciendum*, and had him arrested. He appealed to the county court for discharge, claiming that he had nothing. The county court found that he had money and was fraudulently withholding payment, and remanded him to jail. Then appeared on the scene one of the dignitaries of the Bar Association, the man who later headed the committee in Chicago which had in charge the celebration of the centenary of Marshall's accession to the Supreme Court. He was a donkey-faced Jew, and together with his son-in-law, a criminal lawyer, they went to a judge without notice to me and got Smith released on a *habeas corpus* all behind my back. Smith fled and I never was paid a cent.

But Smith's case became a leading one in the reports on the question involved. Over and over again I was plunged into turmoil of this sort, into strife with this kind of revolting human nature. It is not a good atmosphere in which to write poetry or to write anything. The only explanation that I have ever been able to give of Smith's conduct is that he meant to cheat me thus to pay back what the fire inspector had done to him. Anyway, I have never known of more detestable ingratitude, while the amount of the fee was absurdly small.

Charley, whom I told about this case as it was in course, advised me to get a gun and kill Smith, and that I would go scot free before any jury. And in point of fact I was about to kill one of Smith's lawyers, a shyster who was drunk at the time he came to my office to persuade me to let up on Smith, telling me that my note was without consideration. I went for my pistol in my desk, but the lawyer fled, and my associate came in and stopped me from pursuing the fellow. But that is not the worst. The lawyer who defended Smith on the note filed a plea of no consideration, which of course was overruled. This lawyer was then a man of professional prominence, and later became one of the most distinguished and prosperous lawyers in Chicago. Smith was able to get all the lawyers he wanted, good and bad. This was the law business in Chicago in those days.

It was not long before Marcella and her mother were leaving for California for the cold months, and Charley had a chance to go with them on his mother's bounty. That left me with the apartment on my hands. But one of Marcella's friends, a handsome dandy from Rhode Island, who was in Chicago to escape a woman to whom he had been engaged and whom he had deserted, was brought forward by Marcella to take Charley's place and share the expense of the apartment with

me. In spite of myself and contrary to my aura and my character, I have so many times fallen in with people who did not
belong to me, and who did me no good. This was the case with
Charley, and with Roger his successor; and I have all my life
wasted myself or been wasted by such adventitious associations.
Roger was drunk a good deal, and when drunk he was weeping
about the woman he had left in the East, and who was writing
him letters about her approaching motherhood. He was fond
of me, and like Charley he waited for me to come home at
night. I was as busy as ever at the office on cases that did not
pay, and I was trying to make my evenings profitable by study.
The negro cook was discharged now, and I was back at the
restaurant again.

Carl was after me to join the Calumet Club, to which he
belonged, and where he played pool. He had nothing to do, like
Charley, until my sister forced him to study medicine for
which he had no more mental capacity than a child. My sister
was ambitious for herself in a social way, and for Carl that he
might support her position by a professional standing. And
soon Carl was in a medical college dissecting and listening to
lectures. He prevailed upon me at last to join the Calumet
Club, saying that I would meet men who had profitable law
business for me to do. In fact nearly all the richest men in
Chicago belonged to this club, men like Marshall Field, the
Pullmans and others. This was one of the most incongruous
steps I ever took. My politics and everything about me could
do nothing but repel patrician loafers and capitalists; while my
aloofness, my timidity, my pride and independence of spirit
made it impossible for me to unbend, and manipulate such men,
and win their business confidence. I knew that young men out
of the colleges were marrying heiresses in Chicago, and as young
lawyers were winning places in the law departments of the
railroads and the like. I saw some of these fortunate schemers
at the club. But I could not do anything with my club mem-

bership after I got it. I was so obscure that the rich horse
fanciers and cotillion leaders and ineffable snobs did not remember me after I was introduced to them. And the whole thing
resulted in my moving about as a shadow from the writing
room to the dining room, from there to the poolroom, sometimes in company with Carl who was proud of me and did
everything he could to advance my acquaintance. Sometimes
I did some of my correspondence from the club, for Marcella
and I were exchanging weekly letters, but that was a slight
benefit for the amount the club cost me in dues and house
accounts.

Roger did not last long in the apartment. He went back
East saying that he might marry the girl whom he had deserted, and so I was alone, as I have been much of my life.
Sometimes as I sat in study I could hear the roisterers down in
the buffet singing "Charming Kitty," but I did not join them.
And the football halfback from Lewistown did not come to
see me. I passed through the buffet, as at first, taking a cocktail
and pausing for a minute's conversation with the crowd. Clearly
a man such as I was then would not be liked by such fellows,
and if he were he would not be profited. It might have been
that a crowd to my liking and of congenial spirits might have
been at hand in this situation of my life. It was not so.

In the cold days I caught what was called la grippe, and
was very ill for several days. There was no telephone in my
apartment and I could send word to no one of my predicament.
But a window washer or waiter from the café downstairs sent
out the word that I was in bed; and one day there was a knock
on my door. I struggled out of bed to answer it, and opened
the door. It was Julia. She had brought me a tray of food, and
upbraiding me for not sending word to her, she entered and
served me. I lay in admiration of Julia's blue eyes, her fair skin,
her voluptuous figure, and her golden hair. She rattled on in
her way telling me many funny things. She smoothed down my

bed, and tidied the apartment, and then went out giving me a kiss as she departed. We were on the same floor of the building, and only two doors apart. And so Julia came in every day bringing me toast and tea and eggs, until I was able to go out. I had liked Julia all along. Her laughing badinage and her humorous off-color stories made her very companionable to me. But after this kindness during my illness I had a genuine affection for her. She was human, generous, full of a kind of magnetic good will, and thoughtfulness. But I could see that she considered it her duty to be faithful to Jake, the gambler, for whom she had left her husband.

I had days of thankless labor at the office, of disheartening disaster which sent me down to the depths. Then if I didn't go to the theater, or call upon my sister and Carl at the Lexington, I was remitted to the loneliness of the apartment. But Julia was just down the hall, and there was no one who lifted me out of the bad mood of a hard day better than Julia. A holiday came on in the midwinter, it may have been Washington's Birthday; at any rate, it was one of those days when families are gathered together, and when detached people must shift the best they can. Seldom did I drink champagne, both on account of its expense and because it disagreed with me; but toward this evening, commencing, perhaps, in the buffet with some extravagant night-hawk, I drank some champagne, and then a little more. After which in a bold state of mind I knocked at Julia's door. She answered with her finger on her lip. Jake was home, and had returned early quite drunk, and she had put him to bed. He was asleep, and so soundly that there was little danger of arousing him. I invited Julia to come to my apartment. She reflected momentarily, and stole down the hall with me to my door. I went out and got some champagne and some cake, and Julia and I started to drink and to feast. With such feelings as we had for each other we could not escape what soon happened. Julia called me a "dear boy," she revealed herself in maternal caresses and smoothing of my hair. She said that I needed a wife to take care of me, someone to get my laundry gathered up and sent out, which always accumulated into a great pile amid my many and hurried occupations. At the same time she blamed herself for what she had done, saying that it was unfair to Jake and that he would kill her if he knew about it. Still Jake was over fifty, while I was about twenty-six, and Julia about thirty-four. Along the way I had told Julia about Stella, and how she kept after me, and how my associate had recently said that Stella would kill me if I did not marry her. Julia laughed at this. She asked, "You don't believe that Stella never had a man before she had you?" I replied that Stella insisted that such was the fact. Julia tossed her head, exclaiming, "Nonsense!" Recently I had been with Stella when she was taking an abortifacient, and was up and down hour after hour drinking water and saying that she was dying. I told Julia about this. Her comment was that there was nothing to do but to get married; there was no other escape from this life of exhausting anxiety. Julia said, "Get married, be true to the wife, have some babies and be happy." That made me think of Honoria whom I sometimes saw; but I was not fanning the flames there as I might have done.

The newspapers were now full of political comment touching the money question and how it was dividing the parties. The Cleveland administration had dissatisfied everyone; and Altgeld was making ready to commit the Democratic party to free silver and a radical program. My father wrote me that he was a delegate to the National Convention which was to meet in Chicago, and in time he came along and stayed with me. I had many rooms and beds. He was now fifty, but as full of power and youth as a man twenty-five. A few gray hairs were visible amid the black curls about his brow, but he could eat and walk and play and drink, and practice law and make political speeches, and never seem to tire or to need sleep. I have never seen one of equal vitality. He was also wittier and fuller of stories than ever; and we sat to all hours when he was not out with his fellow delegates planning for the moves in the convention. Maltravers came to see him and we had a wonderful evening. But at times his eyes deepened, and his talk grew serious. He regretted that I had not had better luck, and when I told him about Stella he was visibly disturbed. My brother had made a great deal of trouble for him; first by failing as the publisher of an advertising paper. He was but fourteen when he made this venture, and my mother thought it was a stroke of precocious genius. But he had incurred debts for printing and the like; he had given notes and checks for obligations of various sorts, he had collected the advertising profits and spent them traveling about the country, once as far as Butte. My father had had to make all these losses good, and they had cost him many hundreds of dollars. Since then my father had tried to give this brother an education. First and last he sent him to Abington, to Illinois College, to Morgan Park Academy, to Notre Dame University, and I think to Northwestern University. He was later to send him to the University of Michigan. This brother had done no good at any of these schools; my impression is that he had flunked his studies in all of them. My father said in a melancholy tone: "I have spent on that boy's schooling in one year more than I ever spent on you in your whole life for everything that you had, schooling and all, and it isn't right. I don't like it, and damned if I know how it came to be, except that your mother thinks that he is a genius and more wonderful than any of the rest of you, and of course I was not very prosperous when you were home." He took from his pocket the gold watch which I had presented him on his fiftieth birthday. "Here it is," he said, "and no one but you ever did anything like it for me." All of this made me turn back to my studious days in Lewistown, to the writing I did there, to the hopes that I had cherished of becoming a poet and as a poet to influence the thought and progress of America. And here was I in this apartment badly deviled to make a living, and doing that in a business which destroyed every imaginative impulse, and took all my strength and all my time. Truly now I despised myself for Stella, for all my wasted hours; but I pitied myself too that with all my aspirations and efforts I had been so caught and tangled down, and shoed with lead, and held back as in a nightmare. I did not know that day by day I was living a life that gave me vast understanding of human nature and of the world. It is clear that I should not have had more numerous or significant facts of life brought before me in newspaper work; whereas if I had lived a cloistered life I should not have learned much besides books.

My father gave me a ticket to the convention which met in the Coliseum on 63rd Street where during the World's Fair I had often seen Buffalo Bill's Wild West Show. And there high up to one side where I had a view of the vast audience, and of the rostrum, I heard Altgeld, and David Bennett Hill, and at last Bryan. It was a spectacle never to be forgotten. It was the beginning of a changed America. Bryan's voice, so golden and winning, came clearly to my ears as he said, "You shall not press down upon the brow of labor this crown of thorns, you shall not crucify mankind upon a cross of gold." And as the vast crowd rose in ecstasy and cheered, and as the delegates marched about yelling and rejoicing for the good part of an hour I sat there thinking of what I had read in Milton, in Mill, in More, in Bacon's *New Atlantis,* in Shelley, and resolving that I would throw myself into this new cause, which concerned itself with humanity, and left behind ignored and forgotten the monotonous commonplaces of the tariff, and the quarrels of the War Between the States. A new life had come to me as well as to the Democracy. And at night at the apartment my father and I talked. Bryan would sweep the country, and it would be reclaimed from the banks and the syndicates who had robbed the people since 1861 and whose course had made it so impossible for a young man to get along in the world, save by allying himself with financial oligarchs. Andrew Jackson had come back in the person of Bryan!

That summer Maltravers was out of work and in hard straits, and even without a place to live. His family had scattered, and he was no longer able to live in the house near Humboldt Park. So I invited him to come to my apartment where there was plenty of room and to stay without pay for as long as he wanted to. Maltravers was always in love and walking on his toes; or else he was out of love and full of ribald irony. This summer he had just parted from a lady, and he was running over with cynical ballads and the like, in which women were set down as bawds and nuisances each and all. From this classification he excepted his mother to whom he was passionately devoted. By this time I had taken up the study of economics, for I was getting ready to make political speeches. I had read a good deal in economics, but now I directed my mind toward the money question, and devoured Jevons, Mill, Smith, Ricardo, and English currency reports, and much else. But at night Maltravers and I often repaired to the roof of the apartment building where we could see the stars and breathe the cool air from the Lake. There we made merry with talk, and with the improvisation of ballads serious and obscene.

The apartment building was in the Third Ward, and I set about making the acquaintance of the politicians who manned the ward. I was appointed precinct committeeman, and took part in organizing the voters. I got up political meetings. I went down to the headquarters of the National Committee, and there because of my father's prominence in the state, and his being a delegate to the convention, I was able to get two notable speakers for a huge mass meeting that I managed at the American Theatre in 31st Street. But the Irish henchmen

who controlled the ward cared nothing about what I did.
They had in mind money and offices for themselves, while I
was thinking about America's new day and what I could do
for it. I was repaid for my labors by being made an alternate
delegate to the county convention. A politician named Solon,
who was boss of the ward, disliked me and did not want to
see me rise. I wanted to address the voters of the ward, but
was prevented from doing so except at a small meeting where
not more than fifty persons were present. However, after I
had gone through the books on the money question I wrote
out a careful speech, and managed to get the state committee
to let me deliver it in Petersburg. There I had a large audience.
They all turned out to hear their "old boy" orate for free
silver. It was as impossible for me to speak well as it was for
me to waltz, or play the violin. There is a rhythm about it;
and as some people have an impediment in their ears and conse-
quently in their feet, so I had something in my mental constitution which kept me bound and would not loose my tongue.
For that matter I read this speech, and that detracted from its
interest. Then I was terrified almost to death, and everyone
could see that. There were Republicans in the audience, who
listened for a few minutes, then rose and went away. My
cousin Nell, married to a farmer near Petersburg, came in to
hear me. She was one of the keenest minds that I have ever
known, a laughing woman, full of humorous talk. After the
speech she teased me, and called attention to some of my mis-
pronunciations. Then I went out to the Masters farm. My
grandfather was not interested in "Billy" Bryan. He was going
to vote the Prohibition ticket. My uncle Will was bitterly
against free silver. The farmer's wheat would be worth nothing
if the gold standard was not maintained. Besides, Bryan was
an anarchist, Altgeld had pardoned the anarchists, and was no
better than a murderer. I went out into the fields to see a man
who was working for my grandfather, as he had done far back

in my boyhood days. I tried to convert him to Bryan. This man was a veteran of the Civil War, and he, too, said that Altgeld was an anarchist, and that the poor man could not afford to have a cheap dollar. A meeting was being held at the Shipley schoolhouse to be addressed by Tom McNeely whom I had known all my life. He was a lawyer and former congressman from Petersburg. I went to this meeting and was asked to make a talk. My uncle was there to hear what could be said in favor of a platform which advocated riot and repudiation. He sat looking at me coldly as I talked. All the distant Celtic blood, the blood perhaps of Lawrence Young, that was hidden in him changed his face before me to that of some dark Irishman from County Kerry. I went away and returned to Chicago considerably dispirited. My law associate spoke of the absurdity of free silver; Carl lamented my commitment to that cause; my sister, however, stood for Altgeld. At the Calumet Club I was looked upon with mild contempt, though I did not go there often. Bryan was in and out of Chicago all summer, and as late as early fall his election seemed very probable. Then the tide turned, but many of us did not realize it; I didn't and my father didn't.

I appeared at the polling place in my ward at six o'clock on election morning; and there I stayed all day and until four o'clock the next morning when the count was completed and the ballots sealed. At midnight an old man named Ellis, who was a Republican watcher at this polling place, went out and returned, saying that news had come that McKinley had lost his own precinct. Later that morning he dropped dead. As the Democrats had done very well in this Republican precinct where I was the captain, I felt that perhaps Bryan was elected. In this state of mind I crawled back to my apartment around the corner and fell into bed and into profound sleep at once. It was toward noon that I found myself trying to get out of the window, and gazing at the stone sidewalk three stories below. I was having a dreadful nightmare. I went forth now to learn that Bryan had been overwhelmed. The new day had been swept away by a great storm and by thick clouds. In order to solace myself I went to the West Side, where my sister had gone to live in order that Carl would be convenient to the medical school. And there all day I played with my niece Elizabeth, and tried to talk to my sister about the great disaster that had come to the country. She didn't see this.

The campaign being over, I was back to the law. Carl's fortune was about $80,000 at first, my sister was not economical, and their income of about $200 a month was always overspent. He was having a hard time to get along. He had been compelled to foreclose many mortgages, law work that I did for him with considerable profit. Though he was a parsimonious man at first, owing to his raising by a thrifty aunt in Indiana, he grew to be generous; and he was liberal with me about fees, and in this way and in all others did his best to advance my fortunes. His business, therefore, took much of my time; and also just now, or a little later, I had a great many foreclosure suits for Catholic priests who lived down in the state. These cases were sent me by a lawyer whom I had known as a schoolteacher in a town near Lewistown. I had enough to do, all told. And my associate and I were managing a railroad case, for which I wrote the briefs for the upper courts. We had to fight this case stubbornly for several years, and won it at last only to have a mortgage banker who had sent us the case come in for a part of the fee, which was small enough anyway. I resisted this demand, but the mortgage banker had the client in his grip on a loan, and I had to yield, following my law associate who gave up the struggle at the very start. My will, my enthusiasms for my convictions, my passion for ideals, plunged cruelly at every turn against spikes and granite. And the law business tortured me.

And all the while there was Stella. The campaign being over, I decided to pay court to Honoria. Her stepfather was against Bryan, but in nearly every other way we were in accord. But I craved music, I wanted to talk books. I wanted the soothing influence of a woman like Honoria. I left the office one night intending to have dinner and then go to see her. But Stella followed me to the street demanding that I go with her. She knew nothing about Honoria, but she had not seen me much, if at all, during the campaign. For of course there was Julia and the decent seclusion of my apartment. I turned about and faced Stella as she called after me. I was quite angry, for passers-by saw her and knew that she was asserting some claim to my attention. I said to Stella: "You should be ashamed of yourself. Why do you annoy me this way? I am tired of it. You go about saying that you will have your brother come up from Missouri and kill me; and you know that I never wronged you at all—never! You have taken me for a greenhorn to say that I wronged you. I know whose girl you were before you came to me." I didn't know this exactly; but at times I had seen a prominent capitalist from the North Side come out of Stella's office, and he looked at me in a furtive way that made me suspicious. By saying this to Stella I had gripped her in my power. She grew very meek, she looked down humbly. Then she said, "If you will go with me this time I'll never ask you again." I decided that I would do this, as it was now only about six o'clock. So we went to a hotel, and she parted from me in tears as I went to the North Side.

On my way I bought a large bunch of roses for Honoria. I was thinking of her beauty, her intelligence and intellectual courage, and of the remarkable family by whom she was surrounded and who had molded her mind. I had decided to let myself go, and fall in love with Honoria. Marcella had used this phrase to me. She had said, "You never let yourself go." I was conscious of myself as cold fire; but I also knew that when I allowed my heart to slip I could not thereafter control it. And as caution was one of my predominant traits I had that and my will with which to possess my course.

Bearing the roses I rang the bell at the home of Honoria. Her mother came to the door, ejaculating surprise when she saw me. "Is Honoria at home?" I asked. "Here are some roses for her." The mother's face instantly took on a grave expression. She said, "My dear, Honoria is ill almost to death with typhoid fever. She is delirious, and I can't even take her the roses. I'll just keep them. It will be many weeks before Honoria can see anyone. But you must come up when she is better." So expressing my sympathy, I turned away.

It was a cold night with a high wind blowing over the Lake, which was black and stormy to the east of me about three blocks away. I walked back to the corner, pushing my way against the wind and full of sober reflections. The wind boomed around my steps, and I felt the desolation of the night in the very depths of my being. At the corner I went to the bar of Hoffman's restaurant. I was the sole person present as I drank whisky to keep me warm, and to pluck up my heart. In one of those mystical moments which come over cities a profound silence had settled on Chicago. No one seemed to be astir. I stood there thinking, under the bright lights in the ceiling and about the bar which cast a sort of astral luminousness over the scene, almost a phosphorescence. The bartender said nothing to me; I said nothing to him. I went out and took the car for the four-mile ride to my apartment. I was wondering what I should do next. I was alone, I was lonely. I heard the wind from the Lake whine at my window. The campaign had been fought and lost. There was to be no new day for America, of the kind I dreamed. My father was in Lewistown struggling with his problems. Maltravers was settled in a far part of the city. And so I lay there thinking. Stella's sallow face came before me, as it looked in her capitulation and humility. I thought of Honoria's lustrous eyes, her sensitive beauty, and almost prayed for her recovery. Then I fell asleep.

I did not want to marry anyone. That feeling had deepened in me; yet I would have married Honoria. My admiration for her was of the most thorough sort—for her mind, her character, her convictions, her ideals. My passion for her was much less than my admiration. I had not seen her intimately enough to feel great passion for her; then her ethereal beauty did not arouse passion as yet, such as I felt for a woman about this time. This was Louise whom I met by chance in a box at a theater one night when I was playing around with a railroad lawyer. After dinner we went to the theater and to a box, since there were no seats. In this box was Louise, about twenty-six, in company with her aunt about thirty-four. So it turned out. Louise had a kind of beauty that had always fascinated me: a delicate, aquiline nose; hazel eyes, brown hair such as Zueline had, and beautiful teeth. Louise was conscious of my admiration as I stared at her during the performance. After it was over I approached her and introduced myself. The next afternoon I called upon her on the far West Side, and a mad courtship began. Nothing could have been more foolish. I knew nothing about her, I was running counter to my prejudice against marriage; yet at this stage of our association I would have married her. Louise was visibly affected by my ardent addresses, and delicately tried to make me understand that she was mine for the taking. Once in a small park on the West Side she wept as she told me that she was not in good health, that I was just starting into the practice of law, and that she could not keep house or be of any help to me. Later one day she opened the door of her bedroom and showed me a picture of a man in a silver frame. The man owned one of the skyscrapers of Chicago, and she told me that she had been his secretary until she was taken ill. I understood now, and great streams of acid coursed through my blood. I thought then that

I might as well make her mine for the passing happiness of it. I tried and she repulsed me, and I drifted away.

So it was that I went about venting and controlling my volcanic heart. Prostitutes filled me with loathing and fear, women like Louise were a torture. I didn't want to marry. All in all Julia was the best solution of my nature at the time; and she was far from perfect, for always there was Jake. What was she to do if Jake caught her? She had left her husband. With Jake turned against her she would be on the dusty way of making another alliance.

Chapter XI

IT WAS HARD FOR ME TO TAKE UP LIFE AGAIN AFTER THAT
Bryan campaign. It had been so full of wonder and hope and
excitement. Bryan himself, then slender and athletic and handsome, had left a picture on the imagination as he rode about
Chicago followed by cheering thousands as the bands played.
There was such silence now! I kept thinking of him far west
there in Nebraska gone back to the common days of daily
duty of some sort. The newspapers in Chicago were ringing
the changes upon the skill and patriotism of Mark Hanna, and
others, who had saved the nation from repudiation, dishonor
and anarchy. The morning that Bryan's defeat was announced
one paper contained a huge picture of Bryan on the front page
in which he was given staring, fanatical eyes, and the intense
face of a crusading madman. I with some others could take a
sustained spirit in the redoubtable pronunciamentos of Altgeld,
who was saying in interviews that the election had been won
by bribery and intimidation; and at that Bryan had triumphed.
He forecast that there would now be great bond issues, that the
government would pass to the control of trusts and syndicates,
and that corruption would rule. He called upon the hosts of
democracy to reform their lives, and get ready to fight again.

Down the street in Groveland Avenue lived John Barton
Payne, one of the judges of the Superior Court, a Democrat,
but against Bryan. I had become very well acquainted with this
judge first when I tried Krebs *vs.* Brandner, soon to be noted;
and later in the Recek case. My acquaintance with him by a
strange route led me to matrimony. He was a Virginian recently come to Chicago, and by a fortune in politics elevated
to the bench almost as soon as he had the necessary residence in

Illinois. There was something at once terrifying and attractive about his face and presence. His head was rather large with a full square brow, which seemed ridged, especially over his eyes where the bony prominences made hoods for his black eyes, full of piercing and satiric shrewdness. His eyes and eyebrows curved in harmony with the rhythm of a severe mouth, which dipped with sardonic firmness. From the first he had done everything that led to success in Chicago. He was a Democrat, but he fellowed with the rich Republicans at the Union League Club. Very soon he joined one of the churches, walking down the aisle in the presence of a large audience to be baptized and received into the congregation. He became noted almost at once for the manner in which he expedited business, for his way of brushing aside delays and technicalities. He sent men to the gallows with a kind of sadistic smile on his lips; and the fact that he was not for Bryan, though taking no part in the campaign, enhanced his standing with the powerful rich men of Chicago. When my father was at my apartment during the convention I took him to call upon this judge, and in the talk he remarked with judicial finality that historic Democracy would survive Altgeld and free silver. How my intimacy with the judge began and what it led to might be considered mystical if it were not true that all things must begin, and that after they do whatever they lead to is but the natural sequence of events. But why they begin, and why the sequence should be often makes us wonder, and gives life all the magic of drama.

One day on the West Side a workman was standing on a stepladder painting the wall of a brewery. The stepladder broke and threw the workman to the ground, injuring him severely. An engineer named Brandner in the brewery, hearing this fellow groan and cry out, rushed from the engine room, and then across the street to summon Dr. Krebs, whose sign was in an upstair window there. Dr. Krebs was a prudent man. He asked Brandner, who would pay for these medical services; and

Brandner said the brewery would do so; again he said that he would see that the brewery did so. Thereupon Dr. Krebs took care of the injured man. As the brewery did not pay the doctor he sued the engineer, Brandner, for his fee. And that was the case I tried before Judge Payne, then about forty years of age, and full of swift intellectual energy.

I prepared the case with great care, and felt confident that I could not lose it. When I arrived at the courtroom it was full of lawyers and clients; for it was the Short Cause Calender day when cases were set down for trial under a limitation that they would not take more than an hour to dispose of. The judge raced to the bench at last from his chambers, and looked down upon lawyers and clients with something approaching bitter contempt, as if to say "ye common crowd of curs." When the cases began to be tried he kept saying, "overruled"; "go on"; "play ball"; "don't be absurd"; "hire a lawyer if you don't know how to go on." Case after case was swept from the list, tried, dismissed, thrown out. And finally Krebs *vs.* Brandner was called. My teeth were chattering with terror, but I stood up summoning all my courage. "Is your honor ready to hear this case?" I asked idiotically, for something to say by way of getting my self-control. He turned his piercing eyes upon me and replied, "I should not have called it otherwise." But as he said this his eyes seemed to take me in. Perhaps he saw that I was different from the Polish, German, Swedish and other lawyers of alien blood who were in the courtroom; perhaps he saw something of Virginia in my face. Whatever it was his eyes twinkled with good will and in the politest tone of voice he said, "You may proceed." It did not take long to put in the testimony. And then my adversary, an older and more experienced lawyer, made his argument. By this time I saw that I was in danger, and I was indignant that the engineer should be sued for this bill. Hence with some energy and direct-ness I contended that Brandner could not be held for the default of the injured man, invoking the Statute of Frauds to that end. The judge was patience itself; but at last he said: "I'll have to beat you. Do you want to argue a motion for a new trial? I'll set it down for next Tuesday morning in chambers, Washington's Birthday. The truth is I am not clear in my decision after all." And that was done.

With my arms full of books I appeared at the appointed time; and the judge was there smiling upon me, and bidding me go on. The doctor's lawyer had also brought many books; and thus we began to contend about this bill of about $80. It was ten o'clock when we commenced; it was two o'clock when we finished. And the judge adhered to his decision. I went to the Appellate Court with the case and was defeated there. Brandner paid the bill, if the brewery did not pay it for him. But I had become acquainted with the judge, who all the while had lived in Groveland Avenue unknown to me. After this I went to his house in the evenings when I was lonely, always to find him immersed in history or biography, while his young butterfly wife welcomed me with delight, since she did not read and would be about the rooms with nothing to do. I took walks with the judge, for he was a great walker; and later I bought a bicycle and went wheeling about with him to the far South Side and through the parks. In this way we became companions if not intimates. If I had been a Republican, or if I had not been a radical, he would have made me his protégé, much perhaps to my profit in the law. As it was we kept apart, for out of my reading I came forth with ideas which he did not know how to take in or to handle. They distressed him and repelled him. He had a sagacious mind, but by no means a profound one; and his pragmatism concerned itself with money and success, and with that kind of good reputation which though it may be suspected cannot be impugned.

A man named Sam Jackson was now sharing the apartment with me. He was a Canadian with walrus mustaches, and heavy blue eyes, and a high narrow forehead. He, too, was a lawyer, but without many clients. When I told him about Krebs *vs.* Brandner he remarked that the judge would naturally beat me, that the judge went off half-cocked, and though he posed tremendously he didn't know much. Jackson's opinion was that by no stretch of principle could the engineer be lawfully called upon to pay this bill. The apartment was a very different place from what it was when Charley and Roger lived in it. We kept no cook, and my association with Julia was circumspect out of deference to Jackson, who had a certain respectable air suitable to his forty years and his English blood. He had all kinds of well-bred habits; he had a razor for every day, he took a cold bath of a morning; he had a bathrobe; and for walking forth he had a frock coat and a cane. I soon imitated him, and got these accessories of a gentleman. For a decade he had paid court to a very rich woman living in a mansion at 47th Street and Drexel Boulevard; and it was soon evident that his confessed desire to marry her was sustained not only by affection, but by ambition thus comfortably to settle his life. Our talk at night was about this woman and his hopes; or about the judge, or about the Bryan campaign, which he excoriated as the most impudent attack on property and liberty that America had ever seen. I hadn't a friend about me with whom to indulge in regrets for Bryan's defeat. I never could see that Jackson had any amorous indulgence. But he drank habitually, though rarely to excess. Sometimes when business was hopeless, and his beloved woman again told him that she would never marry him, he would drink much Scotch down in the barroom, and come up to the apartment and walk the floor, exclaiming, "oh hell, oh hell, oh hell." He read a little at times, while I was deep in some philosophy, or something in poetry that I had not come to before. Poetry was an absurd form of writing to him; while the writing of it connoted nothing but the verses in the newspapers and the failures who published in them.

Indeed, that was the judge's opinion. Both knew that I wrote verses. Though I was not publishing much now, and when I did send verses anywhere it was always under a pseudonym, I could not hide away my devotion to poetry. There can scarcely be a doubt that I should have gone forward with the art faster and better if I had been moving in a circle which understood it and loved it. As it was every step I took was against the wind.

The judge rarely escorted his wife anywhere. In truth at times he was quite short with her when I was calling. And later he was divorced from her, and married a rich woman of position. In order to go to the theater or to parties she called upon the young lawyers of her husband's acquaintance to accompany her. And one morning I met her as I was going to the train to business, and she asked me to be her beau that night to a bazaar at a mansion in Drexel Boulevard. I consented, but when I appeared at her house the judge came to the door, saying that his wife had gone on in order to arrive early, and for me to proceed and join her.

The location was near 42nd Street and Drexel Boulevard, and in a neighborhood of rich men, some millionaires. There were some houses farther south on the boulevard finer than any in Prairie Avenue; but no one living there as rich as Marshall Field. The society there was second class compared with Prairie Avenue and the Lake Shore Drive. My sister, already in the Prairie Avenue set, knew nothing of Drexel Boulevard, and when she heard about it she merely lifted her brows. Arriving at the number, I stopped to look at the row of houses before me. They were of gray stone, three stories in height, of different architecture, but all built by the same man and for sale to men who had acquired a few hundred thousands and wanted to set up in a way of life which followed, or partly imitated, the very rich. These houses looked wonderful enough to me at this first glance, there in the darkness and under the winter stars and drifting white clouds. The judge's wife had told me that many pretty girls would be present at the bazaar, and so I scanned the lighted windows of the house where it was being held, and heard the laughter of feminine voices behind its walls.

Whenever a thing has been beautiful to me it has looked far more beautiful than it really was. My eyes have been adjusting themselves all my life, bringing me amazement concerning past admirations. It was just so with these houses. They were not very large and they were not distinguished. And yet I was impressed. In this mood I entered.

There were rooms in suite crowded with young women moving about under bright chandeliers and wall lights, and amid what seemed to me rich furnishings, and upon fine Oriental rugs. It was the home of a family named Black. Soon the judge's wife saw me, and raising her hand above the heads of those who surrounded her she motioned me to join her, which I did. She then presented me to Cecile, a woman in her early twenties. She had brilliant dark eyes, dark silken hair which was combed down smoothly in an old-fashioned way. Her lips and cheeks were full of color, her teeth were regular and white and her smile full of charm and friendliness. Cecile was a Virginian, and a protégée of the judge and his wife. Her aura was blue, if I may speak in mystical terms, blue as Anne's was, as the little girl that I knew when I was eleven years old. These dark eyes and red lips and silken hair always fascinated me. For a long while I thought that I could admire no woman who did not possess them. Then Alfreda came along and Gertrude; and Stella's charm, such as she had, was of the same yellow aura. I had thus oscillated between blue and yellow. Now as I was taken about by the judge's wife and introduced to the many laughing young women whose eyes beamed with excitement and happiness, I was presented to a young woman with a yellow aura. She was outlandishly dressed, but she had a face of wonderful sunniness, her eyes twinkled and laughed, and were large and of yellow-gray color. I noted creases in her brow over which the tendrils of hair, not very carefully done, but of a golden tint, ashen and golden, strayed at will; but her nose was delicate and of faultless shape. Her blouse was purple and fastened at her throat by a diamond brooch of star shape. Her skirt was some kind of neutral gray. So she stood before me in her yellow aura, laughing with her eyes, and evidently delighted with my presence. I selected her for the evening, perhaps because she came to me more readily than any of the others. I went about with her to the booths where I bought her some trifles, and I took her to the dining room when ice cream was served.

Going home the judge's wife asked me slyly if I did not think Cecile was beautiful, and I hid my preference for the Golden Aura by saying that Cecile was the most beautiful girl in the crowd. I may have thought so; but in fact Cecile was far more beautiful than the other. Sam was up when I arrived at the apartment at about midnight. I told him of Cecile and the Golden Aura. "Yes," he remarked, "I know her, I know her father. Her father is a Sunday-school superintendent, and you'll have to behave yourself if you go to his house to see his daughter." I then began to ask Sam questions, and he answered me fully, saying that the father was a Bar Association man, a great churchman, and until recently had been very well off. The bank in which he was a stockholder had failed and he had lost heavily. But he was a highly respected and able lawyer and was still holding the position of president of one of the elevated railroads.

I had parted from the Golden Aura without asking to call upon her. But in a day or two I wrote her a note from the Calumet Club by way of maximating my importance; for the daughter of a railroad president had to be properly approached; though I might have telephoned her if I had been familiar enough with the simple ways of doing such things. I waited day after day for a reply from the Golden Aura, passing the mailboxes of the club and searching them in vain. Thinking that I had been rebuffed for placing the Golden Aura in a position where she would have to put herself upon paper, or ignore me entirely, I turned to Cecile, and getting into communication with her, somehow, I went to see her.

Cecile lived not far from the Golden Aura, but upon an ordinary street and in an apartment that showed evidences of the economic struggle. Her father was an ex-Confederate soldier, and half broken in health. Her mother was a handsome, matronly woman who took me to task mildly for some of my radical ideas. This was not the household of Honoria and her gifted mother. Cecile had a sister, older and more beautiful than herself, who was already engaged to a huge berserker German of great wealth. I could see that the family considered the judge the most wonderful man in the world, and that in one way and another he and his wife were helping this struggling family. Nevertheless, Cecile had many pretty dresses, and when I took her to the opera she looked distinguished and queenly. But in point of fact she did not have the intellectual shrewdness of the Golden Aura, something which appeared to me in those days to be a matter of genuine mind. However, their minds were not far apart in quality and strength. The judge's wife was very happy that I was paying attention to Cecile, and doubtless knew about every call I made upon her. My sister and Carl met Cecile and were struck by her beauty; and thus we were going on when one day, weeks after I had written the Golden Aura, I was at the Calumet Club when the clerk at the desk stopped me and said: "Here's a letter for you, Mr. Masters. It got put aside, for the clerk did not know you." The letter was from the Golden Aura and had been written the day she received my note weeks before, and in it she had welcomed my call at the time that I mentioned when writing her. So now I went to the telephone and talked to her, telling her what had happened, and asking to call two evenings hence. She consented and I went as Sam yelled at me to watch my step. I was full of fear and nervousness.

The heavy outer door was opened by a Swedish maid, the glass inner door was ajar for me to pass through, and I was ushered into a parlor from which I could see a suite consisting of a music room and a dining room, all nearly exactly like the interior of the Black house; but not furnished so well. There were no Oriental rugs, but velvet rugs of neutral color; there was an upright piano instead of a Steinway; there were engravings of snow scenes and the like, instead of paintings of meadows with flowers; there were chairs which had been gilded to redress their oak or mahogany material; there were couches and chairs reupholstered in mauve tapestry; and in the walls were mirrors, one of large size, but these were the same as in the Black house. The Golden Aura was dressed as indifferently as she had been at the bazaar, which made me suppose that she wanted me to like her for herself. She had a way of flashing her eyes downward when she talked, not looking directly at me; but I felt somehow that she was appraising me with keen analysis. She was an exceedingly pretty woman, especially when she gave her beautiful figure and her smiling face the proper advantage of harmonious color and shape and cut of costume. I got from her a distinct vibration of romantic emotion, but held in control by principles, and at this time I was something of a judge of such hidden things in women. She talked of church work, of distinguished people whom she knew on the West Side, where she had lived until recently; of her schooldays; and of her dearest girl friend resident in Milwaukee; and of men who had been intimate with her brother at Harvard. Her father figured in this conversation largely as she spoke of his honors in life, and his position in Chicago, though she did this by indirections which saved the revelations from the quality of outspoken boasting. While we were talking her father and mother came in from missionary meeting; and they were exactly such people as I had seen in the Presbyterian church at Lewistown. But they seemed kindly and simple, and in fact that was their character. The father was tall and dignified, and about fifty years of age, somewhat shorn of his light hair, and with a beard in which there was little if any gray. Seriousness covered him; and his eyes seemed to ask what kind of man I was who was thus commencing a courtship of his daughter. They were deepset eyes, while his mouth was thin of lip and firm. He looked absent-minded and troubled. The mother had great blue eyes and dark brown hair. She would have been beautiful except for the largeness of her mouth. It was she who laughed and talked with spirit and good will while these two stayed in the room. They soon walked out saying good night; and took their noiseless steps up the pretentious stairway of golden oak which ascended from the narrow hallway.

Thus commencing I went on swiftly enough. Sam was telling me that I should have to leave off beer and cigars, and join the church if I made an alliance there. But I told him that I should do nothing of the sort. However, the Golden Aura soon found out that I smoked and she did not like it; she learned that I sometimes took a drink and she abhorred that. Nothing came up about sex and women; but she probably suspected me of affairs. She wanted to know about my people. My trump card was my sister, whose picture and name she had seen in the society columns. That seemed to settle matters on the score of the worth of my family. But there were my principles, religious and political. I had to confess that I belonged to no church, that I had never been baptized; but I added that I thought Jesus was a great moral leader, comforting my confession to that effect by thinking of what Goethe had said of Jesus in the *Eckermann Conversations*. But my politics distressed and confounded her. She had been to the Union League Club with all the bankers and capitalists when there was rejoicing for the overthrow of Bryan and Altgeld; and she was frank enough to say that Major McKinley, whom she had met, by the grace of God had saved the country from the infamy of Bryanism. Well, this was not far from what Honoria's father had said. And why should I not hear it under religious connotations? Ah, yes! She had gone to a reception at a great house not far away, to the house of one of Marshall Field's partners, where Major McKinley was entertained; and she had taken his hand and looked into his honest and patriotic eyes! A little later when I was entertained at dinner her father looked down at his nose when my political activities in the Bryan campaign were mentioned by the Golden Aura, who didn't do so by way of censure, but in pride that I had made speeches in Chicago and at Petersburg, even though in a bad cause. When her brother heard this he snorted the most withering contempt.

I was full of amorousness for the Golden Aura, and I was impelled by amorousness, and captivated by those ways of hers which were girlish and by her remarkable beauty, when she was beautiful; and I was impressed by her piety, which I took as the equivalent of goodness, by her chastity which was fuel to my passion, by her shrewdness, her self-control, her sure-footedness; and perhaps not least of all by her deliberate thoughtfulness about every step that she took, most of which came to pass after long resistance of my granite will. Her voice had a quality of wonderful sweetness, especially when she was emotional. She knew French pretty well, and read music with something more than ordinary skill. She had read some fiction; and at college she had taken courses in history, which gave interest to her serious conversation. Altogether she had many virtues when I went over in my mind the matter of proposing to her; and when I was comparing her with Honoria. But, indeed, Honoria remained an invalid for many weeks while this courtship was proceeding with the Golden Aura.

I had many things in mind in weighing the matter of getting married. First, I had decided never to marry; but there was the unending loneliness of having no one intimately in my life. I had to do everything for myself, such as to sew on buttons and to get my laundry gathered up and sent out, which always bothered me more than it should have done. It made no matter how much I was worn down and distracted, how much I felt my talent for writing wasting away under the attritions of the city, living the hurly-burly life that I lived, I still kept my passion for poetry, and there was a hurt always in my heart that I was forced to neglect the call that I felt. I fancied myself settled with a wife with my books around me during long peaceful evenings, when I could turn to write a poem. And the Golden Aura admired my verses and was rather proud of those I showed her. Then my Irish associate in the law was growing more and more impossible and even offensive, and our clients were not increasing. Our business was hard to get, it was hard to manage and it was difficult to succeed with. I imagined that I should have no trouble in finding a place in the railroad office by grace of its president if he became my father-in-law. And with my economic state thus settled, though modestly and merely by way of a salaried position, I could write in peace at night, on holidays and during vacations. These were the dreams I dreamed. With eyes that saw intensely, but sometimes myopically, that saw beauty and goodness where they were often not present, and as frequently dangers where none existed, I contemplated marriage with the Golden Aura. But one thing that was as controlling as any was the sex matter. I had been through literal hell many times both when merely playing and when in love, and I longed inexpressibly to have one woman and to put all this anxiety, all this hunting for satisfaction out of my life forever. I was prepared to pledge the Golden Aura the strictest fidelity. But I never had any madness for her, such as I had for Zueline, for Alfreda, or even for Louise.

Very soon then I asked her to be my wife. She took the

proposal at first with utter calmness as if she was prepared for it. Then her eyes misted with tears. Her reply was that I would have to see her father; and the next day I called upon him at his old-fashioned law office in rooms that he had by then occupied perhaps for twenty-five years. He had been born in Missouri of farmer people, he had supported himself while in college for a few years in Illinois, then he had come to Chicago. It was just after the War Between the States when the city did not have two hundred thousand population. At first he went to law school from which he was later graduated, supporting himself the while by odd work. After his law course he had become the assistant of a referee in bankruptcy, and on the referee suddenly dying he had become the referee. He had saved his money along the way, and by his probity and industry he had built up a remunerative chancery practice. It was his reputation for integrity that had given him the presidency of the elevated railroad; for he was a good figure of reliability to put at the head of that ship manned by the piratical capitalists who had organized and bonded it. There was nothing in my financial condition to make him turn a deaf ear to my plea for his daughter. And at once I saw that he was not concerned with that. He wanted to know about my religious faith. I told him quite truthfully about it: that I had never joined a church. He asked me if I gambled and I told him the truth about that, which was that I didn't even care for cards. The matter of drink interested him, and I said that I had no habit of drink, but that I sometimes took a drink. That did not alarm him. It was the religious question. It was lamentable, he thought, for a home to be set up where there was no faith in God. And he regretted greatly that his daughter was not to have a husband to walk by her side in the work of the church.

There was a man in Lewistown who was the circuit judge when we first moved there. This judge had made it as hard as possible for my father to get established there; for the reason perhaps that the judge's former partners were practicing law there and were his pets. This judge had been elevated to the Supreme Bench of the state, but coming up for a second term was thrown aside because of his dubious career, it was hinted that he had accepted a bribe in the Cronin case; and at the time he was involved with a woman. I had grown up to hate this man and with reason. I never saw him that I did not think of Pope's words on Lord Bacon: "The wisest, brightest, meanest of mankind." For this judge looked like Bacon, with his great dark eyes, his large shapely head, his impressive figure. And he was a man of unusual ability. When he was denied a further seat on the Supreme Bench he opened a law office in Chicago and at once attracted a practice. In this interview with my father-in-law to-be, he asked me if I knew this judge. I replied that I did; but I did not foresee how this insidious genius would figure in my affairs.

But when I went to see the Golden Aura and get my answer I found at once that her father had interviewed this judge and had asked him about my father and my people. Her face flushed, and her lips trembled as she said that this judge had told her father that my father gambled and drank. So I was confronted with this contumelious falsehood.

There in Lewistown, which was without amusement, and in Petersburg, at the Sangamon Club, my father played poker with the lawyers, just as the judge did; and as to drink, my father drank like a man, but never to an extent that hurt his health or interfered with his business. I was inexpressibly hurt by this revelation and I told the Golden Aura that the judge had lied, that he was a well-known scoundrel and had been kicked off the Supreme Bench; and that he had always been an enemy of my father. She wanted to know why he was an enemy. I could not make it clear to her; and she confessed that she did not understand such things; that her father had no enemies, and that so far as she understood life people who lived as they should did not have enemies. Yes, I was badly hurt, and I was furiously indignant too. I could not see anything but demoniac malice in what the judge had said about my father, and I was wondering how those old Lewistown days could follow me into Chicago, in this far-off wandering of mine in which I had found a woman whom I wanted to marry.

The Golden Aura dried her eyes, and calmed herself at last. What she had told me strengthened my resolution to marry her in order to defeat the hostility of the judge, which I took as representing all the enmity through which my father had fought to success. Then growing sunny again and yielding, the Golden Aura accepted me, and we were engaged, after I had promised her to quit smoking, on no account to take drink unless I was ill, and to do my best to believe in Jesus. Nothing was said about sex. But on my own account for self-discipline and out of respect to my bonds I started this night on a course of continence which lasted all through that engagement of more than a year, in which my tortures were at times almost unendurable. For there was Julia at the apartment building who at once saw me keeping away from her, and who when the engagement was announced laughed at me and called me "the good little boy."

I told my sister what I had done, and she made ready to call upon my fiancée. I went to Maltravers with my secret, who with much difficulty concealed a smile. I took this at first to mean his contempt for matrimony. But he happened to know the father of the Golden Aura, and he was thinking, as it turned out, of the difference between my father and the lady's father. No one ever smiled at my father, but everyone smiled with him. I could see that Maltravers had doubts about the wisdom of what I had done; but he clasped my hand heartily and wished me well. Then for days I bled internally over what the judge had said. At times my wrath rose to such an extent that I was on the point of seeing my fiancée, and telling her that I could not abide by the engagement. My pride was mortally wounded; my sense of justice frightfully outraged. And there I had left her with her mind still unconvinced, and I kept hearing her voice as it said that people who lived as they should did not have enemies. It was a far cry to convince her that such people are the very ones who have the bitterest enemies. Her father's manner of life, while impeccable, was just of the sort which by its conformity and its innocuous regularity disturbed no one, not even the brigands of the elevated railroad.

In a few days the engagement was announced and teas and dinners were soon given for my fiancée, and sometimes for both of us. Her picture was printed in the papers, and her family was extolled; and at last I got publicity on the score of my father's professional and political prominence, and concerning my pioneer grandfather who knew Lincoln. My sister entertained for my fiancée; and the grand lady who was my sister's mother-in-law called in state upon her, making the Drexel Boulevard hearts flutter. My father came to town and was entertained at dinner by my relatives to-be. There he sat at table so handsome and vital, so clearly a product of the soil, with that authentic and inherited integrity which was written in his face and on his brow—there he sat where I could compare with him the narrow shoulders, the pious and ascetic face of her father. I raged to think that circumstances had put me in a position where I had been obliged to repel the false words of that lesser Lord Bacon. What was her father compared with mine? He was nothing. But these two fathers got along very well together, talking about law matters. I did not have to defend my father after this dinner. My mother-in-law to-be was swept away by his broad shoulders, his fine face, his wit and his easy and fascinating manner.

Now followed a year of submissive obedience in which I strove to twist myself into a form of growth such as my fiancée wanted me to attain. I went to church with her, and sat listening to the same drivel that I had heard in Lewistown when I was fourteen years old, and was sometimes forced to accompany my mother. My very back crawled with self-contempt as I sat there eyed as the young man who was going to marry the daughter of the Sunday-school superintendent. At times I hated myself so furiously that I wanted to run away or even to die and get out of the poisonous thicket which I had been led into by desire. What will a man not do for a woman? "All a man hath he will give for love." Yes, and for a year I was chewing gum to abate the terrible craving for a cigar. I had quit smoking, and I didn't take a drink, not even of beer. At the apartment building Julia laughed at me, for I told her one day that I had been put on my good behavior. She said: "You'll break one of these days. When you do I'm going to turn you over to Hattie. She's been without a man for a year and is as crazy as you are." Maltravers treated me sympathetically, as much as to say that he had been afflicted with every form of insanity for a woman, except the kind that now possessed me, which was perhaps no worse than some that had made a fool of him. Not the least of my agonies was going to dinners and parties in the Drexel Boulevard neighborhood. These were church people who had grown rich on running grist mills, plumbing factories, piano factories; they were managers of dry-goods stores, and proprietors of elevators and wholesale candy houses. There were no saloonkeepers, owners of breweries, no free-faring men, lovers of sport, and horsemen such as there were in Prairie Avenue and on the North Side. There were no philosophical anarchists or single-taxers, or readers of Herbert Spencer. They were all Republicans. They read *Ben Hur* and Drummond's *Ascent of Man*. These were the specimens of odious respectability, and of faint nauseating smells of both hypocrisy and self-sufficiency that I had to meet. The great nerves in my solar plexus coiled and constricted like an enraged snake, and I stood speechless with shame for myself and with revulsion for the faces before me.

However, there were reliefs from this consuming boredom. I soon met Lou, my fiancée's cousin, and Charley, Lou's husband, and Auntie, Lou's mother, and a dear old lady who was my fiancée's stepgrandmother. Lou and Charley kept an open house. Charley had fine whisky on his buffet, and a box of cigars which he offered to me until he saw that I neither drank nor smoked. The dinners they gave, simple and hospitable, were a delight to me. And it wasn't long before Lou confided her hurt heart to me. It was that she had done her best for years to create a warm relationship between her household and that of my future father-in-law; but that he had no time for anything except church. "My religion," said Lou, "teaches me that Jesus is as happy to see people having a good time and enjoying the society of each other as he is to see them preaching, kneeling and distributing tracts." These words gave me a very illuminating side light on the home into which I was entering, cast, too, by one who had known it for years, from childhood. Very soon Auntie, who was the sister of my mother-in-law to-be, expressed herself in much the same manner as Lou had done. Both Lou and Auntie gave me to understand that for years, and until they had grown tired, they had invited these relatives of theirs to dinner on feast days without ever having the compliment returned; and that they had grown tired at last of pouring themselves out without appreciation, and without return.

What should happen now but that I should meet a man named Frank Winkler at the home of my fiancée. He was a chum of my brother-in-law to-be, since he did the condemnation work of the elevated railroad, while the other had a legal clerkship in the general solicitor's office. This Frank Winkler and my Irish associate had been hired assistants in the great law office of which I have spoken, where Maltravers was also employed, and I had met Winkler not long after I came to Chicago. Then I was full of indignation for the execution of the anarchists, and also armed *cap-a-pie* with arguments in defense of Altgeld's pardon of the anarchists who went to prison on a commuted sentence. I had had several verbal encounters with Winkler in those days now six years past. He was a windy Scaramouch, full of swelling bluster and egotism, and bent on patronizing me as much as he could. In a sense my future father-in-law was his superior at the elevated railroad; and when he saw me in the parlor of the house, and knew that I was going to marry the president's daughter, he made no attempt to conceal his envious feelings. His purple face, purple from whisky, grew almost black, and his eyes stared with that kind of laughter which gives force to a sudden and malicious blow. He was fearing, doubtless, that I would supplant him with the elevated railroad, where he was making large fees, and spending them recklessly for a gourmand's table and for whisky. "Well, I'll be damned," he exclaimed. "If here ain't the anarchist. Well, congratulations." Though his fears were never realized, or ever on the point of being so, for which reason I was never in his way, this man trailed me for twenty-four years after this time and made untold trouble for me. He may have kept me out of the solicitor's office of the elevated railroad; but I have no facts to say that he did.

So it was spring again, and more than a year that I was engaged and on probation to see if the lady wanted to carry out the promise she had made. It came to just that, or else there would have been no reason for postponing the marriage. In April I went to Lewistown, taking with me my Irish associate who was eager to see that country where Lincoln had traveled the circuit and had stood on the steps of the old courthouse and addressed the people. One day we went to the cemetery, just at the edge of town; and as we were standing by the grave of a Revolutionary soldier the Presbyterian bell began to ring, then the Methodist bell, then all the other church bells, joined by the fire bell on the city hall. This did not sound like the announcement of a fire. But it was the signal of national calamity. We raced to the square to learn that war had been declared against Spain; and there was my father on a drygoods box addressing the people, and calling upon the young men to go forth and free Cuba from despotism and superstition. Something ominous entered my heart at the cemetery; now, seeing my father and hearing him say that the war might be by no means an easy one to win, and that America might be called upon to put forth her utmost strength against Spain, and especially if the latter drew allies into the contest, my heart slowed down with sickness. I had read enough in the papers to know that war was avoidable, and I resolved to have nothing to do with it. I did not know, and no one much then knew, that Henry Cabot Lodge and Theodore Roosevelt had manufactured the war and had pushed the compliant McKinley into it. Nor did many then know, as I did not, that Roosevelt, as assistant secretary of the navy, had several months before this time sent Admiral Dewey to Hong Kong, as a nearby port from whence he could shoot forth and seize the Philippines, if war was declared against Spain. America was on the point of being changed for me and for everyone, and I felt vague fears, and groped for prophecies of what would happen. I was in a changed mood when I returned to Chicago, especially as the household of my fiancée was enthusiastic about the war. All were saying that President McKinley knew what he was doing, and that every patriotic heart should trust him. I knew that he was a weak and shifty character. I had no confidence in his integrity. I believed with Altgeld that he was a man of one idea and that idea wrong. But my fiancée looked unhappily at me as I protested the war. She remarked that it was a calamity that I was against nearly everything and everybody. And what would become of me?

Now I began to see more clearly than before where I was, and how I had arrived there. From a valley one climbs the side of a mountain, but sees only part of the landscape as he goes along. On the top he can cast his eyes far and near over the whole scene. Along this year I had been brought into one situation and then another, face to face with one person and then the other, and by doing so I had seen myself and my engagement in many different lights. The war somehow raised my spirits to greater strength and clearness of vision; and with a better analysis, and one which rose over erotic considerations, I set down the anthitheses which existed between me and my fiancée. She was a Republican and I was a Democrat. How much did that political difference matter? I thought that out, saying to myself that my Democracy involved the whole human question of liberty and happiness, and that we were in disharmony on that. She believed in revealed religion and in the importance of the church. To me revealed religion was a pure superstition, and the church was nothing but a lodge where morals had petrified, and where small men maneuvered about to get business and to hide their villainies. She thought her father was the ideal man, and that mine was of doubtful character. Our bloods therefore rebelled against each other and begged not to be mixed. Her dreadful will which had used my infatuation to bend me almost to the breaking point into her ways of life filled me with aching anxieties for the future. I had been a slave for a year, and I longed for freedom. I wanted to fly to the Masters farm and there go hunting with my uncle, wearing old clothes and turned primitive again. I wanted to get drunk, and go to Julia. I was full of shame for myself, I was in fierce rebellion. And yet I could say that my fiancée was at fault for nothing. She could not help her nature any more than I could mine, and all her will exerted over my course had been with an idea that she was doing me good. Her will or mine had to yield. Mine had surrendered in this erotic season; but whose would capitulate in the future? If it was to be hers, what kind of woman would I have on my hands? What could be made of one who was so dyed in the dye of her father? And what would I be, reduced to her standards and her opinions? Well, that could not be. I was too deeply grounded in my own philosophy of life, and my will was too stern and powerful ever to be bent and kept bent. I would spring back into place, and then what would our life be?

Thinking all these things I went to see my fiancée. I began by saying that my heart was not changed at all, but that my mind was full of reasons for the breaking of this engagement. I pointed out the various disparities that existed between us. I told her that I was not good enough for her, by which I meant that I did not sympathize with the moralities which she held to be beyond question and indispensable to the good life. I mentioned that our rearing and environment had made two very different beings of us, and that I could not change myself, and that she could not change herself. I apologized for leading her into this alliance, at the same time that I said that I had gone into it with good faith. I mentioned that it was better to separate now than to get married and to have either a lifetime of disharmony or to be divorced. The first would inflict a hurt which would heal; the second would become a malignant wound which would grow upon what it fed. By this time she was in tears, looking at me with pained and accusing eyes. I felt so unhappy as I looked at her that I almost wished myself dead. And the impulse to cross the room and take her in my arms and comfort her was hardly to be resisted. In a broken voice she began to speak. Why had I not said all this before? How was it that I had changed my mind? Why did I allow these months to go by in which she had been featured day by day as my fiancée, while she was entertained everywhere amid hundreds of people? How could she face these people again? What would they say? She would be shamed to the earth. To this I urged that she say that she had broken the engagement. She replied that she would not tell a lie. It would not be herself who broke the engagement, but it would be I, if it were broken. She went to her little desk and brought forth some verses which I had written her. "How could you write such adoration, and then ever change your mind? You are really a wonderful mind, but your character is not all I could wish. With a better character your success in life is assured." She was growing angry now and getting a better control of herself. I noticed perhaps for the first time that anger widened the pupils of her eyes until they filled the whole field of the iris; and moreover that her face mantled with color like a deep inflammation, while her short upper lip looked strangely cruel to me, and the nostrils of her shapely nose widened as if to inhale more air for the flame of her indignation. Seeing her thus I was able to compose myself into a kind of resolution resembling hardness, and saying good night to her I walked to the door. She followed me to let me out with her eyes blinded with tears. I said at parting: "Think all this over carefully. I'll come soon again."

I had a good deal to do at the office these days, but at last I was about to publish a book. I had brought up with me from Lewistown many manuscripts, literally hundreds of poems. I had shown many of them to Maltravers, and he said that the sonnets and some of the lyrics were as good as anything then being done in America. So I weeded out perhaps a hundred and had Stella make a typescript of them. Maltravers showed them to Way & Williams, two young men who had started a publishing house in Chicago, financed by their families. They accepted the book when it was cut down to about sixty poems. All this was two years before this spring of 1898, and now after this delay the book was about to be published. My fiancée knew all about this and she was proud of the book, though she made me change some lines in "Helen of Troy" which expressed the mutability of love; and it was not until years later that it was published just as I wrote it. Well, if she would do this, why would I not be censored all my life at her hands in order to bring me down to the mores of the Union League Club and the church? I went to call upon her soon as I said I would do, and had dinner with the family. It was an oppressive and embarrassed occasion, during which her father and mother, who were always most kind to me, rather emphasized their good will and friendship. Her father talked about my book, saying that it would not hurt me at all to be known as a writer of verse, that Chief Justice Fuller was known as a poet while he was practicing law in Chicago. But of course the law was my real forte, there lay my success and real distinction.

After dinner we went to the drawing room where merely casual talk followed. My fiancée was sagaciously watching me, and on my part I had said everything that there was to be said. About some things and in certain situations she had a shrewdness not to be despised. So the call ended without the subject of the engagement coming up. What she had said to me had gone deeply into my mind and heart. I could not bear to be dishonorable; I hated to hurt her. I could see the force of her words that night when we parted, while she was in tears and I was in a dark mood. In the meantime I had thought of the matter from every angle. I could not rid my mind of the conviction that it was better for her to have embarrassment and a heart hurt now than to have a lifetime of unhappiness. I was certain that I could not make her happy. These considerations had nothing to do with her worth, and nothing with mine. To break the engagement was no reflection upon her, and I did not ask to be released with any idea that she was anything less than she really was, which was that of a beautiful woman with a character in which there were many virtues, too many for me. But I had no one to take advice with. I didn't want to talk with Maltravers, well as I knew him. I did go over to the West Side and lay the case before my sister. She was busy getting ready to move back to the South Side, to Calumet Avenue in the Prairie Avenue neighborhood. And she acted preoccupied. Yet she sat and heard me through, looking at me with wide eyes and relaxed lips. Then she arose, went to the piano and ran her fingers over the keys. "Well, Madeline," I urged, "have you nothing to say to this? No advice to give me?" Her reply was: "If you don't love her don't marry her. But in point of fact you do love her, and you are just going through one of those chills which follow the fevers that afflict those who are in love. This is too personal a matter for me to advise you about." This was strange talk coming from her, considering that she looked down on my fiancée and her family, and later treated her so shabbily that if I had been really happy with her I should have been infected with the poison of her attitude to some kind of inevitable alteration of my own feelings; or I should have stood in resistance to her, which would have resulted in unfriendliness toward her and that would have changed the entire complexion of the family feeling, with my wife drawn into the thorns.

It happened now that my father came to Chicago and argued a case which had been brought up from the country to be heard by Judge Payne. He lost the case and was very indignant toward the judge, as I was. But later I felt that the judge on the whole was right. Taking my father to the train for his return to Lewistown, I asked him to tell me what I should do about my engagement. He knew the lady quite well by this time. He had called her shrewd. He had no liking for her father; that is, there was no basis upon which these two could fellow together. They were both lawyers, but my father was a barrister and one of the most brilliant; while her father was an office lawyer, and one of the kind who are recruited from the ranks of diffident men of inferior physical power and nerve. My father was a man of the world; her father was a churchman—and so on to the end. My father had never said a word in dispraise of her father, but I knew very well that he had no admiration for him. He was not my father's type of man at all. My father now listened to me, and then he said: "Well, you've got to marry someone. You have seen me live with your mother now for nearly thirty years, and you know what it has been, I have never known but one happy couple, and that is my father and mother. This girl comes of a good family, she is pretty and the old man will put you into the railroad office, and you will do better. I want to see you succeed, and not go on all your life, as I have, in a catch-as-catch-can way. I'm glad you are not fitted to be a jury lawyer. You never can be one. But you know a lot more law now than I do, and you can get into a kind of practice that will make you well off. What is the matter with you now is that you have another attack of the hypo. The girl is as good as anyone, which is to say that none of 'em are any good. A man has got to have one of 'em, and to have her he has to work and support her. That's the game that Nature has laid out for us to play. No escape! Besides, it ain't going to do you any good to have it known that you went with a girl for more than a year, and then quit her; and it will come out on you. And I suppose you have been fooling with her too." "No, I haven't," I rejoined quickly, "not at all." My father did not know how egregiously chaste the lady was, or he would not have said this. "Well, no matter," he went on. "No matter if you have, and no matter if you haven't. You have been with her enough for anything to happen. You took her on the train to Chautauqua last summer to visit Madeline; and the whole thing is that you have stuck too long to back out. That's my opinion; besides which I think you have the hypo again, and that the girl will answer as well as anyone you will find. Let's get a drink."

He was feeling irritated from his defeat before Judge

Payne, and he wanted a stimulant. This talk of his was so matter-of-fact, and had such truth in it in spots, that I was suddenly quieted in my mind. I still felt like a little boy in his powerful presence. He had a sort of emphatic way of talking, as if there was no other truth than what he was saying. And I began to believe what he said. He in a sense hypnotized me. We got out and I took my first drink in more than a year. I felt relieved, and lifted over into a kind of masterfulness in which I was saying: "Suppose the lady is on the other side of everything from me, and all the rest of it? What of it? I can go along with her. And any woman would have diverse opinions from me." With these thoughts my mind soared free and almost exultant, like a man who is suddenly released from a great anxiety, and brought into a place of safety. I said good-bye to my father and went to my office. That night I called upon my fiancée. She saw at a glance that I was in a different frame of mind. She, too, knew me as temperamental and changeable and sometimes moody. Coming toward me and putting her arms around me and kissing me, my well-considered judgments vanished away.

And so the wedding day was set, and the dressmakers were called in to make the trousseau. The house now became a busy scene. Invitations were engraved and sent out. The papers announced the date. The minister was engaged, and at last I went to the clerk's office and got the license.

That afternoon I packed my suitcase at the apartment, and closed my lease on it. Sam came in finally and went about saying "oh hell, oh hell, oh hell." He was quite depressed seeing that I was getting married and that he couldn't. He, too, was invited to the wedding, but did not appear, though this afternoon he said he would be present. I never knew why he didn't come. My father and mother and brother were staying with my sister who was now installed in a mansion of some size in Calumet Avenue; and I was amid excitement on all hands. Saying good-bye to Sam, I went to the house of my bride. She was in tears. She had expected something magnificent from my sister in the way of a present. Instead my sister had sent a small tea set which had cost about $30. But on the other hand, her father and mother had presented us with a china cabinet, which was shopworn, with the brass decoration on it bent and tarnished; and my brother-in-law gave me a life insurance policy for $2,000 payable to his sister, and with the first premium paid of about $70.

Well, the time came. The rooms were full of men and women in evening dress and in silks. My sister was on hand to act as matron of honor. My wife's cousins from Keokuk were the maids of honor. There was an orchestra at the head of the stairway which at the appointed time played the *Lohengrin* march, and like a man going to the electric chair I entered the room, stared at by all these people, and took my place in the corner by the pier glass. I was as pale as death and terrified beyond measure. I was as flustered as Lord Byron was when he married Miss Millbanke, and for similar reasons. My father stood there watching me. Judge Payne was present, but not his wife. Maltravers in a doeskin cutaway, and with an artist's collar and a large flowing black tie, fastened glittering and smiling eyes upon me. And pretty soon the orchestra began to play the march. My heart beat very fast now. And then the bridal party entered. My father-in-law, looking very grave and more ascetic than ever, walked in in great dignity with his daughter on his arm. She was more beautiful than I had ever seen her. Her cheeks were flushed, her eyes were smiling, she was perfectly self-possessed, a kind of spiritual sunshine radiated all about her. Then the minister began the rigmarole of the ritual. When he said, "Whom God hath joined together let no man put asunder," my mother called out in a loud voice "Amen," which shocked the assemblage so that everyone felt everyone else thrill. I stood there stunned as though by the fangs of a cobra. It was supposed that she was some kind of Free Methodist, and the company overlooked this ebullition of religious ecstasy. But in truth my mother with her clairvoyant eye saw that her son was making a pact of probable disaster; she did not approve of my bride or her people; and her satiric spirit rose up recklessly to strike this discordant note amid the festivities.

The next morning we started on a wedding journey through the East and back home by way of Canada. Ah, yes, what happy days men and women spend when they run away together in lawless amorousness! A wedding trip is intended by nature to be an occasion of feasting and loving, of laughter and free faring, of romance expressing itself to the full, of happiness completely realized. But this wedding journey was anything but that. Ten years later, not to say twenty years later, I could have managed everything much better. But what distressed my bride were nameless little things that I could not possibly have foreseen. She watched my expenditures until I was almost exasperated; she wept when I paid more for a steak than she thought I should have done. I was trying to give her happiness, but I didn't do it. Almost everything I did displeased her. At Philadelphia I left her in the room to dress while I went downstairs to order breakfast. Being fatigued I went into the bar and took a whisky, disguising my breath with cloves. She came down and seeing what I had ordered for breakfast fell into silent tears for my extravagance—for a steak that cost a dollar! On this wedding journey wine was in keeping with these festal days. But she was a total abstainer, and there was no wine. All the while she was in terror of becoming pregnant and there was no genuine peace in any hour that we spent. At Marblehead I was frightfully sunburned on my shins while carelessly sitting in the July sun after coming from the ocean. I was laid up at a hotel in Boston for ten days in great pain, and even in danger. And so it was as we went sightseeing, and traveling back to Chicago.

Arrived there, we went to her father's house for the night, and the next day to take my sister's house for a few weeks while she was in the East. Then my wife's father and mother urged us to take the third floor of their house, which was unused. They were as generous and kind as people could be. We installed our cabinets, silver and rugs in these three large rooms, and I sat at the great windows of the front room looking out into Drexel Boulevard, and trying to think along the path that had brought me to this prison, and what it meant, and what the future would be. I was sure that a new life had begun. I would not be alone as formerly. I could settle down to long evenings of study. I should have to work harder than ever at the law; but now every night I went home to someone who was waiting for me, and the little things of domestic management, like my laundry, need worry me no more.

Chapter XII

I REMEMBER WITH WHAT AMBITION I ROSE NOW AND HURRIED off downtown to business. I was as full of power and energy as it was possible for a young man to be. I had not given up the hope of writing, but rather I expected to write along the way, consoling myself with Walter Scott's example, who wrote under a pseudonym while he was a lawyer and a sheriff. But if I should have very good luck and make a competence, then I would devote myself exclusively to writing. Thus I planned; and always I have been able to map out a course with great clearness and plausibility. The fluid stuff of life has a way, however, of escaping the mold of a plan.

My father-in-law's household ran like clockwork, just as my grandmother's did, but with nothing like the same charm. It was more mechanical. Breakfast was at a little before eight, dinner at 6:30; and bedtime not later than 10:30. And it was a peaceful household too. The son was dutiful and deferential to his parents; there was a daughter who in some ways was more beautiful than my wife. This sister-in-law was as proud and happy as possible over my being in the family. She was just out of Smith College, and was about to enter the University of Chicago. The father and mother were devoted to each other without being tender exactly. For it was clear that the father was an inhibited nature. He did not like to be kissed when he departed for business of a morning. His wife had to chase and capture him as he was going out the door.

I could have lost my heart to this sister-in-law, if I had had the least encouragement. Something in nature says that when a man has accomplished his course with one woman he shall have another. He has enough procreative spores for many women. And what shall be done with them? Shall they come to naught? Nature says not. But at the same time, the nature of human life throned higher than mere biological power issues a different decree, and punishes remorselessly for its violation. Thus a man is caught between these contradictories; and life has them at every turn, of one sort and another, with the result that the truth dodges about and man must guess and consult a pragmatic safety. They have a certain peace who see down a straight path, who see only one thing and not many things and many paths. The Pyrrhonists meet with difficulties; and I was one.

In these days of my thirtieth year the wings of a thousand angels of idealism flashed before my eyes, and I had faith in the triumph of the good and the beautiful. They had the inherent power, and truth had it, too, to rise above evil and ugliness, and falsehood. They were watched and sustained, if not by God, then by Matthew Arnold's Power of Righteousness. I had been a constant reader of Arnold's essays, though not so much of his poetry. Beauty in women was one manifestation of the divine influences that controlled the world, and as mystical as they were. At the same time I had never been able to see anything wrong in erotic indulgence. On that subject I was as emancipated as an animal; while beauty in women had filled my heart with mystical adorations since I was six years old. There is an apostrophe to woman in Poe's "The Poetic Principle," where he rhapsodizes on the grace of her step, the luster of her eye, the melody of her voice, her soft laughter and the angelic rustling of her robes. That sort of lush romanticism was not mine. I saw my divinities through the poetry of Shelley, clothed in woven wind, and innocently walking before me in their immaculate nudeness, willing to yield their loveliness in obedience to unashamed passion. My eyes glowed when I saw bowed lips, large eyes filled with clouded wonder, or bright with luminous emotion, especially eyes that were far apart like Hera's. I could revel in Keats's sonnets where he sings of accomplished waists and for myself, the evidence of virginally rounded breasts and delicate ankles filled me with ecstasy. White teeth, shapely noses, were my passion; and laughing amorousness that pranked and withheld its bestowal for the most aesthetic conditions carried me away. All through my poems to the present day there are lines which sing the beauty of women; but often writers in America pass along without being perceived in their essential selves. Once I was introduced as a poet of passion by a scholarly woman when I was lecturing at Mount Holyoke College. I have been mentioned enough as a poet who was immersed in sex, but little, if at all, in this higher role of a poet who expressed the ideal phases of the erotic impulses. I have deceived the public and critics, too, who have not been able to identify me, and who have failed to classify me as a priest of the Uranian as well as of the Dionaean Venus.

Nothing then came of this flicker of passion for my sister-in-law. Though aware of what I could feel for her, I kept to my path with scrupulous faith. One evening I brought home copies of my *A Book of Verses* which was available the very day that Way & Williams made an assignment for the benefit of their creditors. They never published it. The whole edition bound and unbound was turned over to Stone & Kimball who refused to publish it. So I went there at last and got as many copies as I wanted. Some of these I sent to the press, some I gave away. Eventually I got the whole edition and carted it to my basement. The reviews were creditable enough. Dr. Simonds, the head of the English department at Knox College, praised the poems, as much as I could have wished for, in a college periodical. The night I brought the book home my father-in-law retired to his study and read it studiously; and my wife looked it through with pride. It had been brought out in gray boards with a white label and red lettering, a book of 207 pages printed on excellent heavy paper. The last poem in the book was entitled "Farewell Muses," and the last stanza of this poem is the following:

> But all spent sheaves
> My muse retrieves,
>   She fashions and weaves
>   With wheatless straw.
> Whilst ye were thieves
> Of my days and eves—
> So my bosom heaves
>   For Themis the law.

This book contained several sonnets which were admired by Madison Cawein, with whom I was soon in correspondence, and by Lord Bryce. "Farewell Muses" was written in the measure of one of Chaucer's virelays. Then there was "Helen of Troy," which a professor of the University of Chicago, a writer of books on American literature, persists in admiring to this day. I mention these things for what they are worth by way of characterizing this my first book. The first stanza of "Helen of Troy" reads:

> This is the vase of love
> Whose feet would ever rove
>   In fragrant ways;
> Whose hopes forever seek
> Bright eyes, the vermeiled cheek
>   And cloudless days.

That is not the way I wrote it in those days of rapt fascination for Gertrude at the World's Fair. It then read:

> This is the vase of love
> Whose feet would ever rove
>   O'er land and sea;
> Whose hopes forever seek
> Bright eyes, the vermeiled cheek
>   And ways made free.

To my wife's mind the poem as thus written suggested free love, and I changed the lines in it to satisfy her scruples. Some of my friends were furious when they saw what I had done. I was not only mutilating my expressions to please the prejudices of my wife, but I was now upon a course of life where I was submerging and choking in my breast what was most vital and determined to live, and doing it for nothing but a living. I could see no way by which I could make any money whatever by writing, especially by poetry. The art was then all in control of formalists in the East, and was at a very low ebb, with Hovey and Carman coming to the front. In Chicago Moody had not yet arisen, and neither in the physical atmosphere of Chicago nor in the spirits of men who were struggling there was there the slightest encouragement of this art which is a far severer mistress than the law. In these circumstances was I caught after years of reading in the poetry of the world, and after the practice of the art to the best of my gifts, with the limitations which this autobiography already reports.

In less than a month after we were married my wife was pregnant. This condition, which filled her with terror and anxiety, thinking of the state of my finances, was another thing that I had to think of as I toiled at the law office. Her eyes at times shone with a kind of mystical pain and wonder. All her precautions had failed, and all the bungling attempts to avert the issue of nature were without avail. She had to have the child. Now my father-in-law went forward to get me a place in the law department of the elevated railroad; but he was unable to do so. I never knew exactly how much influence he had with the officials; but certainly he did not have enough to get me placed. And now there happened one of those things that have marked my life. I have rarely been helped by people on the upper levels of life, but always by those on the lower levels.

I knew a race track tout and gambler, a man whom I had

met during the World's Fair at the gambling halls where I went
sometimes with my Irish associate, or with my father to watch
the roulette games and to see the gamblers, and as it turned out
to gain a knowledge of every phase of life. One day this Fitz
came to me bringing a client. The case had to be tried in
Michigan, and I went over and tried and won it, coming back
very happy on the boat with my rejoicing client, and with a
fee of $600 in my pocket, which I shared with my associate;
for just now he was in a hard way and I wanted to repay him
for his many benefactions to me and because it was a way to
salve his wounded state. Look! Fitz the gambler had helped
me more than my father-in-law, the railroad president.

Thus the days went by with the law, and the evenings with
study, for soon after the Battle of Manila Bay imperialism
raised its head on American soil; and I started to study to fight
this hated thing. On Sunday I went to church, and called with
my wife about the neighborhood, where I did not meet one
congenial soul. Honoria had recovered, but naturally she was
utterly out of my sphere, as were all my friends of the boardinghouse days. I was alone with my wife and her people. Matrimony did not please me, yet I was toiling with all my strength
to pay the bills that had doubled by reason of taking a wife.

On Thanksgiving Day we had a reunion of the Masters
family at Lewistown. My sister and Carl were there with their
two little daughters, for by this time Emma Louise had entered
the world, and my sister was on the way of giving birth to her
son, Buddie, whose fate will be told later. My dear old grandfather and grandmother, one eighty-six and the other eighty-
four, journeyed over from the farm by train to attend this
reunion dinner. And with my father and mother and my
brother there was a large table. My grandparents took lovingly
to my wife, admiring her for her religious devotion, for the
piety of her father, for the rearing that she had had in a Christian household. They told stories, they laughed and talked with

the same old spirit of vitality, wholly unchanged. My wife liked them better than she did my father and mother. Indeed, on this occasion she was not very happy, both as the result of her condition and because she saw at every turn things in my life or in my relatives which displeased her.

The Philippine venture filled me with furious championship for America as a republic setting an example to the world by keeping out of the tangles of commercial exploitation and militarism. I determined to master the history that went to the making of the Constitution and our republican system, and plunged myself into Montesquieu, More, Plato, Aristotle, and into histories like those of Gibbon, Motley, Macaulay, to give my understanding a sense of history and of general background. I read almost untold books to this end, and began to write articles for the Chicago *Chronicle*, of which Horatio W. Seymour was the editor. He became my friend on the strength of these bitter philippics against McKinley and the men who were steering our country into colonialism. I published an article on John Marshall, who was then being much celebrated since he had expounded the implied powers of the Constitution and thus paved the way for America to seize the Philippines or a part of China if it chose to do so. This article on John Marshall made a considerable stir in Chicago, and raised my name as a protester against all that was being done by Republicans. I was also praised and censured all over the country in papers and in law journals. There was then on foot a movement to celebrate the centenary of Marshall's accession to the chief justiceship; and the asinine pharisee who had beaten me out of my fee in the Smith case had fastened himself upon this nation-wide movement as its leading sponsor in Chicago. He attacked me almost personally in the columns of the *Chronicle* for my Marshall article. My father-in-law was deeply grieved. He didn't approve of my article, for he revered Marshall as a lawyer as much as he worshiped Jesus as a god; and then the pharisee was his friend, living just up Drexel Boulevard. Sometimes he called on my father-in-law, to find me with the family sitting on the steps of the porch. Without making the slightest impression on my father-in-law I had told him what the pharisee had done to me. He acted as if I must be mistaken about the facts. But the pharisee cultivated my father-in-law, and had done so for years, with oleaginous arts, by way of saving his own character from being understood. He put himself by the side of my father-in-law in Bar Association movements, as the phasmidae will lie by dry sticks to be taken for a stick.

One day in the spring after I was married my father-in-law called me to his room. He had been complaining of an ulcerated tooth, but when I saw him that morning I was alarmed at his appearance. His face was frightfully swollen, and was malignant looking with its ugly inflammation. He wanted me to take hold of some of his cases which needed immediate attention. He was afraid that he would be confined several days, as he was. And so I started to serve him in his need. He did not want to entrust his son, a graduate of the Harvard Law School, with this business. A surgeon came and lanced the gum, but in doing so cut a salivary duct, which began to leak on his cheek. When he finally got back to business he had to wear a bandage around his head and cheek to absorb the constant effusion of saliva. He was a proud man and hated this ridiculous appearance. And he was now a very troubled man. His health was gone permanently, and he was in the midst of a thousand anxieties. Having lost his bank stock in the failure of the bank, which happened before my marriage, he was now assessed double its amount to pay the debts of the bank. Soon he was let out as president of the railroad, and his law business began to be less, while he was not so able as formerly to take care of it. There was also a mortgage on the residence, as I found out when I was in the family, and the interest on that had to be met. While business property that he owned on the West Side did not rent advantageously, and his Minnesota farm yielded but little. After a lifetime of toil and thrift disaster was taking him. I was paying all that I could for the rooms on the third floor; and it gives me happiness to say that both he and my mother-in-law in return were as generous and kind toward me as people could be; and they were proud of me into the bargain, despite their regrets that I did not belong to the church and the Republican party.

These were the circumstances which attended the birth of my son Hardin, named for my father after I had won my wife to doing so, who did not like to have it done. He was a sound and, I thought, a handsome baby; but when my mother came to Chicago to see him she turned the coverlet aside and glancing at him remarked, "I know who he looks like." He did then resemble his grandfather on his mother's side, and my mother, though religious herself, had no great admiration for my father-in-law. To her he was something of a "stick," as he was to my sister. One of my vivid memories is the sickly attempt of my mother to dance with him when she came to visit us after I was married. My wife loved dancing and had attended balls over the objection of her father. She was playing the piano on this occasion, while my mother and my father-in-law went through the awkward proceeding of footing it in the parlor. He had done this in spite of his prejudices, and to show that he was a good fellow after all.

With one thing and another my life thus lived grew unpleasant. I wanted to be by myself. And then changes were taking place in the family regime. My sister-in-law had fallen in love with a young Irishman, a Catholic, the son of a Democratic officeholder. I was her confidant during this experience. At the same time her people wanted her to marry the son of a millionaire manufacturer, who lived in Drexel Boulevard, in a great stone mansion. She didn't like him, and he behaved himself toward her, face to face and in notes, with a caddishness which betokened his bloodless character.

The young Irishman was ardent and chivalrous. But the opposition to him was finally successful, at about the time that she was graduated from the University of Chicago. I was talking now of taking an apartment in the Tudor Building near 42nd Street and Ellis Avenue; I was bored to death with my life with my wife's people. Then the family decided to move back to the West Side where my father-in-law had commenced life, and where all his reliable associations had been built up in the Union Park Church. As in all such cases it was a vain dream. But he tried it out, and I moved to the Tudor. That winter he became tubercular. It started in the cut and jaw which had been infected, and he was off to California for his health, while I was helping to take care of his business. I had enough at the law to do now, though it was not very profitable, while my relations with the Irish associate grew daily more unpleasant. For that matter he had good reason to complain of me. He could see plainly enough that I did not respect his mind; while he felt that he was not enough honored at my wedding, after his munificent gift to me, and that was true. I hate ingratitude and have always striven to avoid it. But I have been required to give it many times where I could not give my friendship and admiration, and that makes a case of badly mixed emotions.

At the Tudor we had two chambers, and an entrance that was wide and was really a room, a dining room and a kitchen. All the rooms except one chamber and the living room were dark as a cellar. But I bought some jute rugs which quickly grew faded and frazzled, and with some old furniture which my mother-in-law gave us we furnished the flat. I was happy to be alone. Lou and Charley had presented me with a writing table, a very stable and good study lamp with two burners, some library scissors and a paper knife—all these for wedding presents. I put the table at the end of the entrance hall and got ready to write in the evenings after the hard days at the office. Having written a play called *Benedict Arnold* in those days at Mrs. Thomas's boardinghouse I decided to write another drama, and to use for material the imperial attempt of Maximilian in Mexico by way of speaking my mind on the Philippine conflict. I bought books of history and biography and mastered the material. Then I set to work. My custom was to drink coffee with dinner in order to spur my falling spirits. For I was all day in the law office and I came home nearly spent. Thus I would write till midnight, while my wife slept, and the maid who was also a nurse kept the baby quiet. I would fall into bed utterly exhausted. When morning came I could hardly get out of bed for fatigue. I had to crawl to the bathroom, and there fall into a tub of ice water, in order to come to for the day's work in the law office. This habit of the cold bath, which I had learned from Sam, kept me in good health as much as anything I have ever practiced by way of hygiene; and I have kept it up all my life.

In this way *Maximilian* was written in 1900. By this time, as I remember it, Maltravers had published some city poems through Richard G. Badger, of Boston, who was the first publisher of Edwin Arlington Robinson about 1897. Badger brought out my *Maximilian* rather handsomely in 1902, and I sent it to actors without receiving so much as an acknowledgment. It sold a few hundred copies. Now that it is out of print and is largely forgotten, I can revive a sort of memory for it by quoting from the reviews of the time. A reviewer in the Boston *Transcript* wrote: "the drama contains numerous forcible, quotable passages, many of them being poetry of a quality rarely found in the drama of the present day."

I did not know William Marion Reedy at this time, yet I sent him a review copy. He said in the *Mirror:* "There are fine, and even splendid passages in the play. He has caught the color of the event, in particular, with remarkable fidelity. He has produced a piece of dramatic writing that is worthy of the warmest praise, and it may as easily be made into an acting play as Mr. Phillips's *Francesca da Rimini* or *Ulysses*." The Chicago *Record Herald* and the Chicago *American* praised it, as did some reviewer in the *National Magazine* of Boston. At this time William Vaughn Moody was a notable name in Chicago. He had brought out his *Poems* in 1901, and was protesting in noble and eloquent verse against our adventure into imperialism. I did not know him and never knew him. But when a mutual friend told me in those days of my isolation and struggling obscurity that Moody greatly admired *Maximilian*, my heart was thrilled.

From the Tudor, where we lived something more than a year, we moved to a larger and lighter apartment a half block north in Ellis Avenue. The rent was more too; but I was growing a little more prosperous by this time. While I was yet living at the house of my relatives in Drexel Boulevard a new minister had come to my wife's church. He was about my age, and as he had no more religion in fact than I had we became fast friends and habitual companions on walks. He was quite scholarly, a graduate of Brown University, and had taken a course somewhere in Europe. He came frequently in the evenings to see me; for he was unhappily married to a woman twenty-five years older than himself, an alliance that he had entered into when he was in his twenties, and the woman as his teacher of elocution had ingratiated herself into his gratitude and into what he supposed was his heart, when he was green and ignorant of human nature. We read Ibsen's plays, all of them, and mostly together, as well as many books of philosophy and poetry. He did not always admire what I wrote; but he was sympathetic with my ideas and enthusiasms.

I must say that my little boy Hardin gave me great happiness. He had many cunning ways, and he was a handsome child with very blue eyes and golden hair. On the back porch of the

Ellis Avenue apartment he was wont to stand and watch for me in the evenings as I came along a part of 43rd Street where there were no buildings to obscure my approach. He would jump up and down and shout, and when I entered he ran to my arms. I had lavished my affection upon my sister's children; now I had this boy of my own. Yet my heart was unsatisfied. I was not unhappy, but I was heavily worked and my life seemed scrappy and unmanageable. And my wife was not happy. She tried to make herself over into what she fancied I wanted her to be, but it tore her to do so. At night I was likely to be silent or absorbed, and if she displeased me I was sometimes guilty of sharp words toward her. Then the next day I would bring her flowers; and later when I became more prosperous I gave her rings or jewels on occasion by way of peace offerings. Thus she was in tears both for my offenses and for my contrition for them.

I had a third cousin downstate who had considerable wealth. I had seen him once, when he was attending the University of Michigan, as he passed through Chicago. He was a fellow student of my brother Tom at this institution, from which Tom had decamped, without finishing any course, to be married. This was shortly after my marriage. This third cousin had the dark eyes and the physiognomy of the Masters folk, and also its tendency in his own branch of the family to lung trouble. I knew about his wife Isabel, but did not know her, and never saw her until the time of which I am now about to speak. One evening when I came home my wife told me that Isabel had telephoned and was coming the next afternoon to call. She was visiting in Chicago in the family of a lawyer whom I knew. So I left off business at the office and got home while Isabel was paying her call upon my wife. There was no particular reason for this call. My wife, then about twenty-six, was older than she. I had known her husband but slightly. In fact, his father and my father were not friends. Still here was

Isabel. She had eyes as blue as the color of small woodland violets, her nose was shapely and a little aquiline like Louise's, there was an exquisite pallor in her face tinted with an auroreal faintness. She was slender and graceful and rather tall, but not too tall. Her voice was musical. Her aura was blue like that of Anne and Cecile.

She looked at me in a way that made me think that she saw in me a resemblance to her dead husband; and indeed, there was one. And I looked at her fascinated with her beauty, and thinking that her defeated honeymoon had left her with a sting which troubled her flesh and her imagination. She was very polite to my wife, asking her to come down to the country to visit her, and then turning to me, she hoped that I would have time to come along. She was living back home with her father in this her widowhood which had lasted now a year or more. That was all and she went her way.

In a few days I received a note from her addressed to me to my office, written from her home down in the state. In it she thanked me for my kindness to her, but in fact I had done nothing for her. She sent vague remembrances to my wife, all in an exquisite handwriting. I began to reflect upon these evidences of a flirtation. She had gone to a finishing school, she was well bred enough to know better than to address me at my office. The letter should have been to my wife, and not to me anyway. However, I answered the latter, and she answered me; and soon we were in a steady correspondence; for I had gone on dreaming about her as she looked that afternoon; and these letters of hers faintly scented with lilac or some kind of exciting odor, and the tantalizing obscurity of many of her words, and the compliments that she paid me yet with such guarded words, set my imagination afire. Besides, a particular piece of enchanting music was then running in my ears, something I had recently heard at the theater. Music and beauty in women have always mixed themselves mysteriously in my psyche. Chopin and Schubert have acted as adjutants to these passions of mine. Thus Isabel and music enthralled me. Finally I wrote asking to come to see her, and she replied immediately inviting me to arrive on a certain day on a certain train. Her village was not far from Lewistown. All this she did knowing the circumstances of her position in her mother's home, of which I was soon apprised. It was clear that she meant to take a hazardous chance, and to get through with it by a quick consummation.

She met me at the train in a phaeton, and we drove into the country past some of her father's farms. For he was a banker, too, and very well off. Besides, she had inherited a large fortune from my cousin. As we rode along I felt under a sort of restraining hypnosis. I touched her hand delicately, once I encircled her with my arms and kissed her on the cheek. She smiled and said nothing. The cold fire of my nature was burning. The strange diffidence which so many times before entered my heart to slow down its beat which was but recently so hot and so fast, and to moderate its desire, took me with a kind of psychical impotence. All the while the air was cold, for it was fall, and I kept thinking of facing her father and mother. Once she pointed out to me a farmhouse which was unoccupied, she said. It was one of her father's. We might have gone there. But between fear and a sense of absurdity for this wild trip, and with thoughts of what might happen of discourtesy to me at her house I was as helpless and lax as if under an anesthetic. I asked her what her father and mother thought of my coming; she replied that they were very happy about it, that they liked all their relatives. But I was not a relative of theirs, I was the third cousin of Isabel's dead husband.

After this stupid ride we returned to the village and drove into the yard which surrounded her father's very good and rather large house. He came to the horse's head, and took it by the bits as he was introduced to me. He received me with great courtesy. But when I entered the house and faced Isabel's mother there was a very different reception. She stared and glared at me with indignant angry eyes which seemed to say, "You seducer, how do you dare to come here in this impudent way?"

At dinner she did not appear. Isabel said that her mother was ill with a cold. So at table there were Isabel, myself and her father, who was as courteous to me as I could have wished. After dinner we repaired to the living room where there was a bright fire in the grate. Isabel's father handed me a cigar and we smoked together, and talked about American imperialism, which he refused to call that. It was a matter of America doing its duty in a predestined and unforeseen contingency. He was a Republican and wanted the honor of the flag upheld over the wretched Tagalogs who were assailing it. At nine o'clock he rose and said good night, and went upstairs. Isabel and I looked at each other, then we drew closer to the fire and began to hold hands and talk.

There might have been a consummation in a few minutes, but the perils were great; and my congenital caution held me back. Besides, I felt that Isabel had thought out some better plan which would be later revealed. And now suddenly there was a great thumping on the floor of the room just over us, as if a shoe were being pounded on it. "What is that?" I asked Isabel. "Nothing," she replied calmly. Then there was louder thumping. "That is your mother pounding on the floor," I said. "Oh no," Isabel assured me. Then the mother's voice called to Isabel, "Put out the light and come to bed." I stood up now saying, "I'm going to the hotel." "No, no, no," pleaded Isabel. "That will never do. Having come to the house you must stay. The people here know that you are here. What will they say if you go to the hotel?" She went hurriedly for a candle, and conducting me to the foot of the stairs looked at me with wide eyes as she held the candle before her face. Her color was heightened by the excitement. Altogether she was more beautiful than ever. She directed me to the first second door down the hall, and kissing her gently I ascended the stairs, entered a bedroom where the furnishings were of the guest chamber kind, and went to bed. But I left my door ajar, with the idea that if the house grew quiet and Isabel wanted to come to me she could enter noiselessly. I stayed awake an hour waiting for her. Then I fell into profound sleep.

The next morning at breakfast the mother appeared. I talked about the family, about my wife and boy, about my grandfather and grandmother, who were the great-uncle and great-aunt of Isabel's late husband, all with the idea of making the nature of my visit one of family interest. I got through fairly well, so much so that Isabel's mother became quite cordial. Then I went to the village store with Isabel where she marketed for luncheon. I could catch no train for Lewistown until about two in the afternoon. On the way Isabel and I talked with great seriousness. She protested that I did not really love her, that it was only an infatuation, and she raised the matter of my duty as a husband to any further step in the path that we were now on. She did this freely, however; for she confessed that she had been drawn to me in a way that she did not understand. She said: "I passed your open door a hundred times last night. Then I went to my room and asked God to help me, I tried to get a message to Lucian that I needed his care and love." Lucian was her dead husband's name. There were tears in her eyes as she said all this. After luncheon she took me to the train and we parted with vague words and vaguer feelings. But Isabel was sad of face, and doubtless I was too. Arrived in Lewistown my mother with her clairvoyant eyes read my thoughts. She knew I had not come from Chicago, but from the south somewhere. And what was I up to? A woman, of course! And she scolded me. This business, which cost some money, and three days' time, and abstraction from my business, was not worth a pinch of snuff.

Once back in Chicago I was more under the spell of Isabel
than ever. My passion sublimated itself. I wrote verses to her
addressed to Héloïse and signed Abélard. She replied, "I understand." Pretty soon I had a letter from her saying that she would
arrive in Chicago on a certain train, and asking me to meet
her. My heart burned with assurance now that our defeated
passion would be realized. But when she stepped from the car
her aunt and uncle were with her, something that she had concealed from me in her letter. Thus she manufactured evidence
of my reckless devotion to her, and of her coldness toward it.
For in the hearing of these relatives of hers she declined all my
invitations to dinner, to the theater, and even to tea. We separated when we got to the Loop district and I never saw her
again. But still not with stupidity but with that will which
forged ahead always expecting to overcome all obstacles I
wrote her to meet me somewhere. She replied that she now
understood my lecherous attentions and to desist from them.
Ah, yes, the long search across the desert, the thirst, the
mirages!

Yet I never seriously neglected my business, and fortunately
I kept up my studies. But I was vastly lonely. I heard about
writers in Chicago who were producing books, I heard of literary societies here and there. The University of Chicago was
full of activities, but I did not know how to get acquainted
with Moody and the others there. Somehow I did not have
time to find these men.

Near at hand were two young men, both poets, who were
running a little press and bringing out their own books, and
some of other writers. I made bold enough to call on them,
but they did not like my verses. Through them I met a young
artist, a woman of great beauty whose mother was a charming
lady in middle life. They lived in an apartment on Lake Park
Avenue. And sometimes in the evenings when I was in the
pangs of intellectual starvation I called upon them. They moved

to New York very soon after our friendship began, where I saw them when my trips to New York started to be a frequent matter of law business.

All the while there was my sister, and on occasion our boys were brought together, both now about three years old. She hoped to have them educated together and to grow up into friends for life. Carl had traded a house which he got on a foreclosure for five acres of woodland in Lake Forest, on which he built a pretty cottage, and a barn where he kept a horse for a station wagon. Lake Forest was the most elite suburb of Chicago, thirty miles away, inhabited in the village and in the nearby environs by rich businessmen, and by families old for that country. When the trains came in at evening the station wagons and carriages would be thick by the platform, many in charge of coachmen ready to drive the proud millionaires to their secluded homes in the woods, or by the Lake, or into the country. Thus my sister had entered this community, and was a member with Carl of the Ontwentsia Club, where golf was played, and the men contested at pony polo, and where there was much drinking, and ogling and social rivalry. Carl's mother had by now given him an allowance, and with the remnant of his $80,000 he had bought a house in Prairie Avenue, on which he spent considerable money to refinish the rooms in mahogany, and to build a spacious dining room. In a word, my sister was in society, and she was pictured and mentioned accordingly in the press. She rarely came to our apartment, but her invitations to me and my wife to come to her mansion for the evening or for dinner were almost daily. This was a form of patronization, and in fact she patronized my wife habitually, with the result that the feeling between us was not happy at times, and occasionally resulted in refusals on my part to obey a telephone summons to come to her house for the evening or for dinner. Yet if I did not do this I was not likely to see much of her. However I was devoted to her children, and often saw them as I dropped off the car on my way home farther south.

Somehow Carl had been licensed to practice medicine, and he had an office in his Prairie Avenue residence; but no one trusted him as a physician; and between being out at night to the opera or to dinner, between the dissipations of the Lake Forest set and his enforced idleness, while his expenses mounted for nurses and governesses for his children, for dresses for his wife, for giving dinners, for the thousand things that came upon him in this mode of life, he was visibly harassed and degenerating. He was naturally prudent about money, and when his income vanished and he was pressed to get more, and couldn't do it, he grew reckless about his habits, and my sister began to complain of conduct which she had herself influenced. His fortune was enough for her to have lived well, though simply. In that case she might have gone on with painting or sculpture, both of which she had affected since her course at Knox College. But in these days of bearing children and of figuring in society all those dreams were put aside. On my part, I was more and more mentioned in the press for something I had written in verse or prose.

The law business had grown very poor, and my relations with my Irish associate were often strained; and he was by no means prosperous. One day the streetcar union sent representatives to see me asking me to act for them as counsel in an arbitration of hours and wages which had been agreed upon with the board already selected. I was known through the *Chronicle* articles, and otherwise as something of an economist, and as a lawyer interested in public questions, of labor and the like. The fee was quite alluring, considering that I was struggling now to support my wife and boy. At the time my associate was doing nothing. I did not want him with me in this matter, but my sense of gratitude forbade me from keeping him out of it. Nor did I need his help, for he knew nothing about the questions involved. However, I invited him to assist me and to share the fee. I went to work then and gathered up a vast amount of statistics on wages, cost of living and hours of work in other cities for like service of conductors, drivers, motormen and all that; we appeared and I began to introduce this evidence. At once I could see that my associate was writhing with some kind of green poison. He took a violent dislike to one of the arbitrators, and insulted him in these hearings day after day. The arbitrator mentioned was a sort of touch-me-not connected with the University of Chicago. He was plainly a toady to wealth and a kind of sycophant. But for all that he was polite enough to both of us, and the success of our cause depended upon keeping his good will, and that of the other members of the board. Finally my associate made himself so obnoxious that all members of the board made no concealment of the fact that they regarded him as a fool, as well as an insolent fellow. When the time came for the board to take the matter under advisement, and to confer with the lawyers of the railroads and the employees in order to solve the details of the award, they refused to allow my associate to be present. I was asked to come to a room in Kinsley's Restaurant, but not to bring him. I should have told him this; yet it was possible to have had this meeting, then for the board to have made its award publicly, and for my associate to have supposed that it had come about without this private conference. But I was also asked not to tell him about the luncheon at the room in Kinsley's. So I went. We were watched by some of the men; and my associate suddenly knocked at the door of the dining room, and when it was opened, there he stood with flashing eyes and trembling from head to foot. He then accused the board of tricky conduct, and mentioned me as a young man who had been duped. The board told him to go away, and he left in great wrath, and went about telling the men what was going on and that they were being robbed. There was nearly a riot. All the while everything was as it should have been. We had agreed on the wages and hours that the men asked for, and the award when announced made the men happy. Still this Irishman had won them as the more reliable and trustworthy lawyer as between himself and me. And to shorten this recital he took the union over as his clients, and handsomely furthered his political fortunes through them.

Naturally I was now done with him, for he had sown suspicion of me among the streetcar employees, who believed that I was about ready to betray them, and that I had been prevented from doing so by his loyal alertness.

My office at the time was in the Ashland Block and on the same floor with the suite occupied by Altgeld in his last days. I first knew Altgeld in 1892 when he was campaigning, and came to Lewistown to see my father about the political conditions in that part of the state. In Chicago I had seen Altgeld a few times, and I had heard him speak when he ran for mayor in 1899, and on other occasions. In the Ashland Block I encountered him often in the hallway. I had a very pleasant association with him about 1901 when we were chosen to draw the articles and by-laws of a new Bar Association. All the time I was full of radical activities, and Altgeld looked upon me as a young man after his own heart. By this time, the spring of 1903, Altgeld was dead; and his late firm had been reorganized with a criminal lawyer at its head, who was well known in Chicago, and as much feared and disliked as Altgeld himself. This criminal lawyer had known me since 1898 when I was instrumental through Judge Payne in having him appointed attorney for the receiver of a bankrupt building and loan association. When the time came for us to settle our fees, this criminal lawyer resented my demands and grabbed the larger share of the money, though I had done most of the work. He posed as an altruist and as a friend of the oppressed, but I doubted him. He was not in good odor in Chicago, and that made me fearful about listening to his proposal to join his firm. However, the man had charm, he had plausibility, and he lavished praise upon me for the way I had conducted the case for the streetcar men. Now he proposed that I join his firm, as in fact he had done in 1898. He offered me what I thought was a fair percentage of the partnership earnings. His firm was busy and quite prosperous at this time.

And here was I so anxious about the future that I had no peace. There was a chance now to be at ease on the score of money, and to have some opportunity for poetry. Perhaps in a few years I could lay up enough to retire and write poetry.

I was known over Chicago and in Illinois by this time as the author of the constitutional articles and political essays published in the *Chronicle,* and in Tom Watson's *Jeffersonian Magazine;* and also as the author of a pamphlet entitled "The Constitution and Our Insular Possessions," which had made the conservative lawyers of Chicago indignant at me. Thus my life had moved in such a way that I was unwelcome among the lawyers who were doing a large business, and there was no place for me to go but to the radicals. That suited me well enough. But though I was by this time a lawyer of ingenuity and force, I was going on year after year, never making any alliances of moment, never taken up by anyone, never invited to join any large office or to enter any settled partnership. I saw slow tortoises at the law, men of my own age, advancing to fortunes. I was now turned thirty-four years of age; how much longer could I go on in the casual way of chance business and not come to disaster in days of less strength? I did not approve of what the corporations were doing, or what they required their lawyers to do at times. Yet I thought I could work for one as a lawyer and retain my integrity. I meant to do that, I think I could have done it; but I never had the chance to work for one at all. They didn't want me. On the strength of my political writing I thought the Democratic party might take me up for something. I tried to go to the Illinois legislature; but when I consulted the reform leaders, those who were talking about purging the legislature of corruption, I found that these pretenders wanted men more complaisant than I was, and I was turned away here. Therefore all the doors had been closed along the way; and I was married, with a son, and had to make good somehow. I had desperate hours when my bank balance was down, when there was no fee coming in, and when the bills piled on my desk. And all the while my heart was on poetry and the literary life.

My father-in-law did not like the criminal lawyer mentioned. He thought he was an atheist and an anarchist, and a disturber. He doubted his sincerity and his honesty of mind. He thought he was an immoral fellow. It ground him to see me associated with him. But what was to be done? At last he counseled me to accept the offered partnership, and to keep my character intact, and to watch my professional integrity, as I had always done. He said that if I did this I would stand with the community for just what I was, and that perhaps this association would not hurt me. And so I formed this partnership, and was given the running of the office. This was April, 1903. My wife disliked the criminal lawyer intensely, and feared him as well; but she was too happy over the prospect of a settled income to make any objection to this partnership.

Chapter XIII

NOW I HAD VERY CONGENIAL ASSOCIATIONS. FRANK WILSON, afterward a judge of the Appellate Court of Illinois and later of the Supreme Court, was one of my partners, and we were excellent friends. As for the head of the firm, he had amiable qualities. His drawl and his sleepy ways, his humorous turns of speech, his twisted ironies made him a pleasant man to be with. He seemed an old-fashioned soul, easy and lounging and full of generosities. As a matter of fact, he was penurious, grasping, and shrewd. According to some of the descriptions of Lincoln, those who speak of Lincoln's cunning and his acting ability, I think he was more like Lincoln than anyone I have ever known. But it is only fair to say that he gave me free hand to run the office according to my judgment, and that for some years he kept his partnership contract with me to the letter.

But how I worked! My labors in the law before this time were as nothing to what they became from the day of this partnership. Often night after night until ten o'clock, or midnight, I prepared for the next day, or dictated to a secretary. This hot summer of 1903 I was in court almost every day defending the rights of strikers against the injunction which the Kellogg Switchboard and Supply Company had obtained against them; and taking appeals from the decisions of a petty tyrant named Holdom, who as the chancellor was giving great delight by his decisions to the membership of the Union League Club. Finally I took the whole question to the state Supreme Court in a brief of about 350 pages in which every point was argued with Mill, Spencer, Adam Smith and the liberal decisions of England and New York for authority. It was the first case of "government by injunction" to be presented in that forum. And I was defeated.

I had will cases and many cases involving constitutional questions, and those in which the validity of laws was contested, and difficult injury cases; and every kind of case except criminal cases. Even as to these I wrote many briefs. In fact, I had one secretary taking dictation nearly all day long, day after day and month after month. This was during the time when Moody was climbing Parnassus in Greece with Ridgely Torrence, and when Robinson was writing and publishing *Captain Craig.* Yes, I was making more money than I ever had made; I was making it to have leisure for poetry! What a mirage through which to be laboring to the perfect good!

When *Spoon River Anthology* was published ten years after this time I was mentioned by affrighted souls as a criminal lawyer. The whole truth is that I sat with my Irish associate in one or two murder cases, taking no part except that of making notes of the testimony. And in this new partnership I tried one assault case at the instance of the Hearst newspapers, for which our firm was general counsel in Chicago. For the rest I was concerned with civil business, which, other things being equal, is no more ethical than criminal business. Yet there is one more criminal case to report.

Before that I must tell of the John Turner case. He was an Englishman who was known as a philosophical anarchist, that is, an anarchist who philosophized, but did not throw bombs. He had come to America to lecture on Tolstoy, on the martyrs of 1887, that is, the men hanged in Chicago for the Haymarket bomb throwing, on the single tax and other things. When President McKinley was assassinated Congress was stirred to pass a law excluding anarchists advocating the overthrow of government, of the government of the United States or of any government, from entering the United States; and also excluding those who preached the abolition of government. Turner had been grabbed in New York and ordered deported. It was after one of his harmless lectures. The Free Speech League of New York wanted our firm to manage this case, as to its constitutionality, in the Supreme Court; and so I set to work to write the brief. I threw my best self into the task, drawing upon all my piled-up learning which had come out of the days of 1900 and the writing of *Maximilian*. The brief was sold in New York as a brochure on free speech. We went to Washington where many members of the league had come to hear a masterly argument from the head of our firm on the great question at issue. It was plain that the court didn't like the case. The term "anarchy," even "philosophical anarchy," did not reverberate pleasantly in that room where once Webster had cried for "liberty and union." I was greatly heckled by members of the court, and asked to define philosophical anarchy by Judge Harlan, who smiled with sympathy, and yet with a kind of condescension upon me. I talked over an hour. Then the great lawyer arose amid hushed expectation. He proceeded very well for fifteen minutes; then his wings wobbled, and in five minutes more he came down. He made a very bad talk. The members of the league trailed out of the room disgusted. And in a few days the court ruled the exclusion law to be constitutional.

Well, there is one more criminal case to report here. Carl was trying to practice medicine, and he had fallen in with a palpable quack as a partner. This quack wore side whiskers, and Carl grew some too. I did not know what he was up to; but one day a woman I knew came to my office and showed me a circular advertising contraceptive articles, which she had received through the mails from him. She was friendly to me and had come to give me this warning. At once I sent for Carl and showed him the statutes on the subject. He laughed and said that doctors were doing this. But very soon one day when I was attending to a thousand things in the office, when at the very moment I was dictating a difficult contract, my sister called me on the telephone, saying that she was with Carl at the Federal Building, and to come at once. I dropped my work and went there, only to find that she and Carl had signed a bond for him to answer the meeting of the Federal Grand Jury, and had gone home. So I went to see the Federal inspector who had procured Carl's arrest.

He was a staring, narrow-faced man with a brisk manner of authority. I told him that Carl's wife was my sister, that there were three beautiful children whom I wanted to protect against scandal. And considering that Carl had been tricked, that they had set a decoy and had induced him to send a circular to this decoy, no one was hurt, and the law was not in truth violated. The inspector said that the law was the law; that if the officers of the law depended upon evidence of its violation to be given them by women to whom the circulars were sent on request and for actual information, there would be few convictions. He said that the country was full of sexual immorality, and that the way to stop it was to have the women understand that they could not indulge themselves without taking the risks of nature. In short, I could do nothing with this violent fool. But what our office did manage to do through the district attorney's benevolent attitude was to have Carl indicted under a fictitious name. Then he was tried in chambers and fined $500, and there was not a word about it in the press —until some years later.

These were years of hard living; for besides my professional work I was in studies of one sort and another. Now and then I would brush up my Greek and read the New Testament in the original language, and sometimes a little of Homer. But every spring I read Homer in some translation. In 1904 I published my *Chronicle* articles together with some never published before in a book entitled *The New Star Chamber and Other Essays;* and in 1905 I brought out a book of verse under the pseudonym Dexter Wallace, verse that I had written against the Philippine conquest, and other lawless ventures. The review of these books gratified me exceedingly. In 1904 I took my wife for a long trip through the West, and in 1906 to Europe. I organized and was president of the Jefferson Club of Chicago where we gave banquets to Bryan and other celebrities, and thus tried to keep the fires of Democracy burning in those dark days of constant defeat for the Democratic party. I first became acquainted with Bryan when my father entertained him in Lewistown in 1899, when I happened to be there. On the European trip my wife and I called on him and his wife in London at the Cecil; and he invited us to change our tickets and return with him and his party by way of Gibraltar, and not from Liverpool, as I had planned. I accepted this invitation and sailed on the *Princess Irene* from Genoa. He and his party boarded the boat at Gibraltar. But on the way I saw little of him, as he was in his cabin composing the speech which he delivered at Madison Square Garden on landing in America.

Bad news came to me as our mail was delivered to us at Fire Island. Lou's husband, Charley, had been killed in August in a railroad accident, and I was hurt as badly as I have ever been in my life. For he was a devoted friend, and his continued life would have meant much to me. He had built a cottage near Elk Lake in Michigan, where I had visited him one summer, and where we had had happy times fishing together and roaming that beautiful country. Earlier than this he had taken me to Grand Haven where he was born and raised. There we had a magical day going up the Grand River in a launch, and a wonderful evening at the Pines, a resort hotel on Spring Lake, which empties into the Grand River near Grand Haven. This country took my heart so completely that I never got the sorcery of it out of my blood. Sometimes I sent my wife and children there for the summer vacation, when they did not go to Twin Lakes in lower Michigan or to Harbor Point, or to Ogonquit, Maine. I was keeping up life insurance, I was under heavy living expenses. I was not pursuing the life of a contemplating poet, but the life of a drudging lawyer. I had got into this while doing my best to free myself for what I believed was the exercise of my gifts. I wanted to write, but I had to live. I tried to flee loneliness and took a wife. Nothing came easy to me, I had no luck except after great labor. My head was always bowed in the attitude of attack. No one came and discovered me. All my friendships were accidental, and many of them were of a sort that should not have been made. They were of the kind against which Confucius gives warning: inferior people who in adversity cannot be leaned upon, and who in happy days merely take time and give little. A good deal of this was my own fault; and some of it grew out of the mere chances of life. One must have someone in his life; and all human disaster comes from the weakness or perfidy of those who are in one's life. That's the story always.

One day when the newspapers were investigating the records and files of the clerk's office of the Federal Court with reference to the conduct of one of its judges and other officers the bond that Carl and my sister had signed was discovered. The whole scandal came out. A facsimile of the bond was published by the Chicago newspapers. It was a rich morsel for their editors, some of whose wives envied and disliked Carl's mother, and regarded my sister's social aspirations as invidious. Carl gasped like an animal caught by the dogs in a thicket; and my sister took a mortal wound which bled as she faced the matter with as much courage as she could summon. But there was no escaping the fact that her position was badly damaged. From this time on Carl dragged about lonely and avoided by the adulterers and roués and tosspots with whom he had been friends at the Calumet Club and in Lake Forest. He sought me out in his desperate unhappiness, and I did my best to sustain him, telling him that he had really done nothing, and that in a civilized society he could not have come to this disaster, in this way.

My father-in-law was going back and forth to California, and finally he was about well. Also he had won back his law practice by persistence, and was in a fair way to be comfortably well off. One Sunday he came to our apartment for dinner, he and his wife. He was then about sixty, but he was a changed man from what he had been when I first knew him. No longer did he hold the conservative opinions in politics with which he was infatuated in those days when I lived at his house. A mild radicalism had taken hold of him. He thought the corporations needed checking, that great wealth should be curbed, that corruption had raised up Bryan to fight it, and that Bryan, whom he once suspected of every vagary and villainy, had great virtues after all. As to religion, he had passed out of his old orthodoxy: Jesus was a great man, not a god; the future life was doubtful. All along his son was wont to say, "You're ruining Papa." I don't know how much I influenced his thinking. But I did so to some extent, I am sure. Thus we talked that Sunday. And I praised him for the fight he had made to repair his fortune, and to get his health back, saying that I had never seen greater courage and will. He said: "Yes, the doctor says I am well again; all the evidences of tuberculosis have gone away. And I am in a case now which will make me well off again. Then I am going to see life and have a good time." All his years he had stuck to his law office season in and out, rarely taking more than two or three days' rest at a time. When he left I walked to the corner with him. A cold fog had come out of the Lake, such as pierces to the bones the flesh of Chicago denizens. I said, "You should get off to California at once." He replied that he would be gone in three weeks, as soon as he could settle the case he was then handling. So I parted from him at the corner. The next day he was in the hospital with flu, and getting infected again with tuberculosis, was dead in two months. It was March and just a little before my daughter Madeline was born.

And now for Carl, the Faun; he could not fight it out. He had nothing to do, he could get nothing to do. His life was to arise in the morning full of sleep and fatigue, and saunter downtown to find someone to be with. He drank too much, and he fell into shabby adulteries which alarmed my sister. She became afraid of him, and contemplated a divorce. To this end she went with her children to Springfield, to consult my father who was living there by now. My brother Tom had come back from Ann Arbor with a wife, both of whom my father helped until Tom was admitted to the bar. Then he went into partnership with my father in Lewistown when he was in a prosperous and easy practice, which automatically kept itself going. Tom had a high temper and a dreadful tongue, and did not get along with the lawyers and the clients whom my father had learned to live with peacefully because of his equable temper and his winning manners. Hence the move from Lewistown to Springfield came about in a sense after the Lewistown field ceased to produce as it once had.

My sister was in Springfield on this mission for a number of weeks, while Carl was roaming about Chicago an utterly lonely and resourceless spirit. A part of the time he slept in his home, and a part at his mother's home. By day he was motoring into the country, seeking the bubble happiness, or lounging about town. Somewhere he contracted typhoid, and after some days of hastening about with a fever, which he did not suspect, he had to take to bed. My sister came back to town to watch over him at the hospital, and in his extremity she submitted to a transfusion to save him. Meanwhile I was in the trial of a long case which ran steadily for thirty days. At night, though I was spent from the day's work, I went to the hospital to be with my sister, often staying with her until midnight. My wife was soon to give birth to our daughter Madeline and she was in terror lest I should go through a transfusion for Carl. Always when I left the apartment after dinner she made me promise not to do this. Nothing availed. Carl had exsanguinations, and to give him blood was like pouring water in a sieve. He had been delirious for days; but as the cold air of death blew on him he seemed to come to himself. He opened his eyes in a sudden consciousness, and telling my sister that he loved her he began to gasp for breath, and was gone. He was of those baffled millions who seem never to have a chance in life, their natures being considered. But he was so hustled about in bewilderment, and so forgotten when he died, that I feel impelled to make this record of him, and to say that his heart was good, and that his penitence was pathetic. He was devoted to me, and with his exit and that of my father-in-law and Charley I was hard hit. But by this time I knew William Marion Reedy.

I had to defend a libel suit in Hannibal, Missouri, and needing a local lawyer to assist me I went to see Reedy, of whom I had first known through Maltravers. By this time I had contributed a poem or two to Reedy's *Mirror*. Reedy recommended Chester Crum, an old-time lawyer of St. Louis who dated back to the War Between the States and had been a close friend of General Grant's. I saw Reedy both going to Hannibal and returning from there on my way to Chicago. Reedy in his youth had been a slight man, his bones were small. Now at about forty-four he was of huge corpulency, but nevertheless of nimble step. His face and head were massive; his brow low but full and ridged above his eyes. His eyes were the arresting feature of his face. They were large dark mirrorlike eyes, which laughed and twinkled, which became severe and ironical by turns. His mouth was large and expansive, from which came the orotund eloquence of his fluent talk. We became friends at once. At this time Reedy's *Mirror* was famous in St. Louis and Chicago. It was especially read and pondered by single-taxers, and by those who learned to follow Reedy in political and literary judgments. In the next thirteen years Reedy was more and more a national figure.

Periods in one's life just close, and oftentimes quite suddenly. There were other things to happen now to mark a changed day with me. I had more or less taken part in politics since 1896, and very definitely since 1900. Out of this had come essays and poems, and some public speeches, though I never learned to be a speaker. As the first president of the Jefferson Club of Chicago I had been very active, and had met many of the leading politicians of the country like Tom Johnson, and others who were entertained by the club. We gave many banquets to Bryan from 1905 on; one in particular when he returned from his trip around the world; and one in the spring of 1908 on the occasion of Jefferson's birthday. This was held in the Auditorium in order to accommodate the great crowd. Bryan was still athletic and radical. He had not become theological and dour. He fascinated the banqueters that night, as well as a crowd of Republicans who stood at the back of the room. On this occasion I gave a breakfast in his honor at my apartment, and to show how the old enthusiasms were falling away from him I may mention that driving downtown after the breakfast in company with my partner, Bryan asked him if he was going to support him this time. His reply was that he would do so if he was promised the patronage of Illinois. Bryan's jaws snapped shut, and there was a painful silence. We were in a fight in Illinois with the remnants of the renegades who had wrecked the party in 1896, and I was taking the lead to secure a faithful Bryan delegation to the National Convention. To this end one day I went to Peoria to confer with Bryan. After disposing of callers Bryan took me to the bathroom while he shaved, and when I told him about the battle in Chicago and asked the advice of his generalship, he turned his face covered with lather toward me quickly and said: "Masters, you and your committee do what you think best. I am so tired that I wish something would hit me so hard that I couldn't get up."

It happened as he wished that campaign. His speeches were more compact and better ordered than ever, but he pulled against a stream that would not let him ascend. In the middle of the summer, after he was nominated and I could do nothing more, I resigned the presidency of the Jefferson Club, and went back to Aeschylus, Sophocles and Euripides, and to my poetical studies with a sense of vast relief. Other changes ensued. My sister, greatly crippled by the disasters that had befallen her, decided to go to Paris and there live and educate her children. Elizabeth was now fourteen; Emma Louise, eleven; Buddie, nine. They were beautiful and vital young creatures. The girls grieved for their father, but they were not aware of the whole tragedy that had come to their mother, which had stripped her of friends, if such people can be called friends, and had left her to contend with a social Chicago that had turned its thumbs down. Her mother-in-law, once powerful, was getting old now, and her strength was relaxed. I went with my sister and the children to New York and saw them off on the boat. It was several years before I saw them again.

Suddenly now my clergyman friend announced his resignation from his pulpit in Chicago to take a church in the West. It was several years later that I found out why he did this. He had given enough dissatisfaction among the old orthodox crowd to account for this step. His intimate association with me did not help him with these old bitter roots. But in truth he had been carrying on an affair with a young married woman, a member of his church; and he had tried to be divorced from the old woman who was his wife in order to marry his beloved. Failing in that he had kept up his attentions to her, and finally she committed suicide, leaving a husband and two little children. The matter had been hushed by the church; but the clergyman was forced to resign. In a curious way I heard the whole story first from an intimate friend of the woman, then from one of the church deacons. He himself had never given me an intimation of what was going on. Then silence fell upon our communications which had once been so full and frequent. He did not write me for years, not until he placed in my hands the matter of his divorce from the old woman, so that he could marry someone he had found in his new home.

And then one day as I was having luncheon in the restaurant of the Ashland Block Maltravers rushed in suddenly upon me, and thrusting his hand to me quickly said, "Well, good-bye, Lee." When I asked him where he was going he replied that he was leaving Chicago for good for the Far West, for Oregon first. I was stunned. For three years before this summer he had lived on a farm near Lewistown supporting himself and his wife by writing descriptive articles of nature, of hunting and fishing. He had this summer managed the campaign of a county candidate, having left the farm. And now he was leaving not to return. He stood momentarily as we talked of our friendship of nearly twenty years, then in his characteristic manner of stoical acting he hurried away.

In a few days I was on my way to the Thousand Islands for a brief vacation, and was reading *Sister Carrie*. That book gave me a sense of a refreshing realism, and honesty that meant something. I did what I have not often done: I wrote a letter of congratulation to Dreiser, and he soon replied in gratitude. Thus our acquaintance began.

All my life I have endured loneliness; and now with all these changes come to pass I felt desolate enough. As a boy on the Masters farm the silence of the prairie had seemed to me to be the silence of my own heart. And in the stillness of evenings when the sun set beyond the farthest farmhouses I walked about the pasture where I flew kites with something choking in my breast, with a longing that I could not understand. When I found Shelley and read such lines as "I thirst for the music

that is divine" I saw that eternity and the mystery about life
beckon sensitive souls to realms that lie below life's horizon.
At last I understood that my passion for beauty in women, and
my attempts to realize myself through erotic love, were just
futile searches to fill the void in my heart. And what a void
it was! Study did not fill it, my children did not fill it, nor
business. Sometimes in the rapture of writing I found the balance level with creative forces. But how rarely that was. I
had inherited great vitality from both my father and my
mother, and great nervous energy from both as well. As a child
I used to disturb my grandmother with my never-ending rest-
lessness, and that had grown upon me. It kept me hastening and
seeking, stung with vague desire and full of impatience, especially as I saw my life going on, while I had done nothing, while
indeed I had crushed down what was most insistent in me just
for the sake of a living. I was making money at the law, but
I was not getting rich. Far ahead was that dream of a country
place where I would have horses and cattle and dogs, and where
in a study and with my books I could write poems. And all the
while material for creative work was accumulating so fast within me that I was on the point of bursting. I had seen and lived
so much, and read and thought so much. What was to be done
with it? In 1907 it occurred to me that I might make enough
money on a play to retire upon. So I wrote *Althea* and had it
printed in order to circulate it quickly among several producers
at once. A paper in Chicago got a copy of it somehow and
heralded me in a sensational article. Nothing else came of that.
Then I tried again, writing *The Trifler* which was founded on
my experience with Isabel; and several others, all printed and
sent about in the same way. I got no nibble anywhere, save
for *The Trifler*, which Harrison Grey Fiske liked and tried to
get Mrs. Fiske to produce. She considered the matter for nearly
a year, then turned aside to play *Salvation Nell*. Fiske wrote
that the adultery theme of *The Trifler* filled Mrs. Fiske with

apprehensions for the play's success, and it was an unpleasant theme to her. So this door was closed.

I thought at times of writing a novel. In 1906 just before going to Europe I went to Petersburg to say good-bye to my grandmother who was then ninety. My grandfather died in 1904, aged ninety-two. On this farewell visit my father joined me. Driving into Petersburg after we had seen Grandmother I told my father that I was going to write a novel someday, which would be my only book. I said that the law was more and more engrossing my strength, and that I should do well to write one book. He wanted to know what it would be about. I told him that my life in Chicago had shown me that the country lawyer and the city lawyer were essentially the same; that the country banker and the city banker had the same nature; and so on down through the list of tradespeople, preachers, sensualists, and all kinds of human beings. That was the germ of *Spoon River Anthology* written eight years after this time. Well, suppose I wrote a novel, that would be only to get leisure to write poetry. And why not practice law for that leisure? My case was not like Walter Scott's, whose forte was writing novels, and who having relieved himself of his lawyership by successful novels, was then ready to go on with his proper career. But then there were Lamb and Trollope and others, who kept at grinding tasks and at literary creation too. And there was Wordsworth who lived on little. And why did I not take a few thousand dollars and go to the woods or the prairies, and, forsaking the world, give myself entirely to poetry? Well, I wasn't that kind of poet; and there were my children and my family obligations, while I faced an income of no moment whatever through the writing of verse. My sister was not a Dorothy Wordsworth. She was proud enough of me, but her influence was not inspiring. Her own aspirations made her respect mere distinction, wealth, and the reverence of less fortunate people. It would be wonderful if I became a famous figure, but that was for me to attend to. She was generous in her way with hospitality and with holiday gifts and the like. Nothing else was called for from her, for my earnings were enough to pay all my expenses. And for that matter she was not rich enough to give me an income even if that had occurred to her, and if I had been willing to accept it, which I should not have been.

If I needed anything I needed wise eyes to see what I was and to guide me. And yet I am not sure that that would have been of much good to me. I knew that I wanted time to write. I had lived in Chicago a good deal as Milton lived, fighting for liberty and justice. Perhaps I had as much time as he had to write; but I never had an easy income and never a patron. But there were vacations. I did the wise thing of resting myself after each strenuous year by going to the country for a month. Why didn't I write poems on those vacations? Did Keats have more time than I had? I suspect that he did not. But he had far more inspiring friends, and far richer cultural influences about him than I had. And I did write some poems on those vacations and at odd times in town. But always with the feelings of a thief that I was taking time that belonged to a full concentration on my business. And what I wrote reflected my prison, my unhappiness. I could not give my full power to these poems. My imagination would not come to a complete burning of the flame, fed by abundant oil, and undisturbed by chance winds at the open window. These words are in no sense an apologia. I am merely setting down my circumstances, and without sparing myself. I was the chief influence in my own career. Americans do not come to a possession of their gifts as early as English writers do, and I was an American, and circumstanced with the most characteristic conditions of American life.

Finally, there was my wife. She read with admiration almost everything I wrote, and gave me encouraging words.

I think she would have submitted to any kind of life that I wanted to live. If I had said that we were going to the country where I could be free to write, I believe she would have consented without a murmur, though her happiness was club work and taking a part in the social affairs of the far South Side. I was seeing now that my teacher at the high school spoke truth when she wrote me that the law and literature were oil and water. I did not believe her at first, but day by day I realized the force of her words of warning, when she advised me to make a choice and to abide by it.

Somehow little by little I got the feeling that my wife in spite of her almost meek compliance was enervating me and cutting off my hair, and putting out my eyes. Chance remarks from my clergyman friend to the effect that she had an inflexible will and an unwearied purpose caused me to wonder if I was not being biologically used and enslaved. My sister sometimes begged me not to sink into complete domesticity, and especially to walk by her side in social ways. When Dreiser came to my house in 1913 he remarked laughingly that my wife had things in her that I did not suspect, and that would one day possibly surprise me. That's all he said. What he meant will be made clear later. On the whole my spiritual atmosphere seemed desiccated; I did not like my home, though I did everything I could to make it happy and even beautiful. Yet I was living in an Avalon of good health and a sort of equanimity of mind. An uninspired existence of unvarying monotony pulled me down into a kind of indifference. Discouragement preceded this false content. When I rose from it it was like a man resisting an anesthetic. Then I would sink back to the landscape that had hypnotized me with its reiterate features, and I would ask why change? I was surprised one day when my sister told me that one of her relatives had said that I was a weak man. Could that be possible? Perhaps it was, and all my driving energy and will were nothing more than the struggles of a man who can't accomplish anything, and just for lack of strength to do so.

I wasn't married long before I had evidence in plenty that my wife and I were not mated, which I had surmised when I tried to break the engagement to her. It was not her fault that she was not my mate; it was not mine that I was not hers. It was the fault of the social system that made her shamed and terrified when contemplating an abandonment of marriage. If in that day one could have changed one's mind about a marriage, and not have suffered a kind of ignomity, she would have released me, and the future would have been better for both of us. She was no more to blame for our marriage than I was; she was not to blame for that passionate pride that was hers so deftly hidden under her quiet and colorless exterior, that pride that later rose up with all the power of a Medea to avenge its wounds. She had inherited that pride; and I had inherited a kind of tenderness which never inflicted a wound without taking one myself far more painful, without experiencing a remorse that was half neurotic. That night I should have walked away resolutely and never returned. If I had done so I should have saved years of suffering for both of us; while on her part she would have been unhappy for a few weeks or months at most. Partings between lovers are tragic mostly where there has been an erotic consummation; and there was none between us. Of course her life would have been influenced for some time by this experience, but it might have been that she would have turned to the tame Robin who had long wanted to marry her, and with the riches which he afterward acquired, and his conventional nature, she might have been happy, living in an assured state of respectability and wealth. She had put this man aside for my more virile self, my more promising career; and she had thereby forsaken the path that her guardian genius intended for her. So to sum up this matter, our virtues did not combine into the creation of a

third level of life, which might be called a marriage; while our
faults wounded each other at every turn and kept us more and
more apart. And that is not to say that we were desperately
unhappy, though often at first she was in tears. These dried
at last, and she changed her ideas about many things. She learned
to like a cocktail at dinner, and to see no harm in taking one;
and she more and more admired my father who was always
at our home on his frequent trips to Chicago; for he was devoted to my son, his namesake. My mother rarely came to see
me; my brother never came. I had evidence that she strove to
adjust herself to me, that she tried to keep house, something
she could never do. But being like her father, a kind of spiritual dust collected about her. In spite of her sunny nature, her
dutiful ways, as it seemed, her nature lacked magnetism, that
quality that made my grandmother's home so delightful, that
quality that makes a hut or a cottage a place of irresistible
charm.

My law partnership lasted for eight years, from 1903 to
1911. But for three years of this time it was a dying thing. I
had put every pound of my energy into making its success. I
worked unceasingly, and for that matter with the selfish motive
of accumulating enough to retire upon and devote myself to
literature. By 1908 I saw that my plan so clearly visioned at
first and so industriously pursued all these years had come to
little. I had saved $5,000 by 1905, which I put into stock of the
Bank of America, organized by an ex-judge of the Circuit
Court, who pursued the illegal plan of borrowing money with
which to pay for his stock of $250,000, and then of withdraw-
ing the money to pay back the loan as soon as the state auditor
had counted the money, licensed the bank to open, and had departed. My partner bought $25,000 in stock and paid for it
with borrowed money in like manner. I paid for my stock in
cash and lost it. My partner hurried about and paid for his
when the bank was about to be placed in the hands of a re-

ceiver after running three months. The ex-judge was caught, and could not pay for his. He was sent to the penitentiary.

I had saved some other money and bought mining stock with it. The mine failed and I lost that. I had a few thousands saved in addition; these I had invested in a new abstract company, and in some other things. That was all, after these years of labor. And by 1908 our business had fallen off. My partner took to the lecture platform, speaking for the liquor interests against impending prohibition. He was much away, and naturally did not turn his fees as a lecturer into the law office treasury. At the same time he was doing little of the work of the office; and my own burdens were heavier in consequence. I remonstrated with him repeatedly, but to no avail. He was the business producer and therefore was in a position of authority. I brought in one case which yielded a fee of $10,-000, and several others of smaller amounts; and during the last three years of this partnership I had a great deal of business from the office of Carl and Abraham Meyer, of which Alfred Austrian was a member; and thus we went on despite our disorganized firm. At that time Frank Wilson was in the early thirties and had hardly got hold of himself as a lawyer. But above all my partner went West to defend men charged with assassinating a governor. He was gone from Chicago for twenty-six months. He returned at last a sick man, having had an operation for mastoiditis. He had turned into the firm treasury $14,000 of his $50,000 fee. The rest he had spent in doctors' bills and in living expenses. He was broke when he landed in Chicago. The first thing he did on arriving was to beg off on the payment of what he owed the firm. My share was $9,000. I told him that I would not press it; but that he would have to pay it sometime. The matter may be ended here by saying that he never paid it. Meanwhile he had received his share of the proceeds, sent him every month by our bookkeeper. We had paid the heavy rent of a large suite, we had supported ourselves, and there was $1,000 in the bank which my partner immediately drew upon for pressing expenses.

At the time that I entered the firm I was confronted with the request of allowing the name of a young Jew to be made a part of the firm name, and to appear on our stationery. This man had been recently convicted of jury bribing, for the benefit of the surface railroads, of which a prominent lawyer, an old friend of my partner's, was the general solicitor; and the young Jew who was shielding the general solicitor from prosecution for the jury bribing in question was receiving from him, or the surface railroads as the more likely case, an honorarium of $150 a month. All this I learned after I was installed in the firm. I refused to allow the Jew's name to appear in the firm name or on the stationery. I said that his name could appear possibly when the scandal concerning his conviction had subsided. My partner, who at first urged the propriety of carrying the Jew openly as a partner, finally said I was right and sided with me; and his name was withheld. I liked this young Jew very much. He was a generous fellow, and with everything else an excellent claim agent; for that was what he was in our organization. But the bad days of the firm and the loss of his share of the fee in the western case filled him with plans of reprisal. Soon it was discovered that he had been settling cases and failing to turn in the money; that he had been getting extra money secretly in the settlement of cases. My partner was furious about this, and threw the young Jew incontinently into the street. The firm was then reorganized by taking in a lawyer who had been trying cases for the railroads. But the energy was gone from the business. And my enthusiasm and interest were gone too.

It was now that I committed the spiritual error of falling into indifference, and even casual attention to business. I had done my best and all this was the result. I was as far from a competence as ever. I had sacrificed my ambition to write to this heavy labor and had reaped scarcely anything for doing so. Many of my old friends were gone, politics was out of my life, the drudgery of the law business was wearing me down every day—and in consequence I began to look for happiness. I was in the late thirties, and full of vitality, of energy that was not exhausted, with emotional power that knew no ends. Life was rapidly going by. Should I allow it to do so, and have only what I had had, and what I was having, and would have in this course of life? Was there nothing else until I should arrive at sixty and get a cut on the cheek like my father-in-law and then die after sacrificing all my powers to a marriage that did not satisfy my heart? Was I all the years to be to go downtown to the office on the Illinois Central, after nerving myself for the day by exercise and the cold bath; and then at night return home spent and fit for nothing but reading, and to sit in the quiet room where my wife read, following the books that I became interested in? What was I getting out of life for this endless bowing of my back? There were the children, to be sure, and I resolved to see them through if it killed me. Often I went out in the morning thinking, This is the day that I'll drop dead. I really expected that I should do so. But there was that insurance, and what little money I had saved by this time.

Altogether just now I was in a half-torpid state of life. My plan to make a fortune sufficient to retire for literary work had not materialized, and I had spent six years in attempting its success. Now to find that the law business was declining in my hands added another edge to my disappointment. And every day I was going back and forth on the train to my office; and every day I was at work on whatever there was to do, winning cases that I half expected to win, and losing cases that seemed impossible to lose. This was the state of my life when I was in the Public Library one day and suddenly on looking up from my book saw Marcella at another table. Her face radiated a smiling salutation. We had not seen each other for years. She had married and been divorced. She had been abroad and in California. Her mother was now dead, and Charley was about town, almost an old man before his time, used up from late hours and dissipation and idleness. I went over to Marcella, and she said, "Why don't you come to see me?" "Where do you live?" I asked. She told me that she had an apartment in a North Side hotel, and she invited me to come to see her the next night. Though a rather conventional woman, she extended this invitation as a matter of course. Somehow the word was about that I had married into an inharmonious family. And Marcella did not like my wife and had never called upon her.

So here was Marcella, as beautiful as she had been more than ten years before when I called upon her shyly at the Lexington Hotel. Here she was, a divorcee, matured in the experiences of life, and as it seemed ready for a romance with me. No longer the chaperonage of her mother; no longer tame conversation about trivial things! There could be something real now. There could be romance now. And why not? With this idea in my mind I accepted Marcella's invitation, and left her working over books at a library table as she smiled upon me as I said good day. A new day of profound experience was opening for me. I did not know it, and could not have known it.

Chapter XIV

THE NEXT NIGHT PROMPT TO THE HOUR I WAS AT MARCELLA'S apartment. She was alone, and seemed to be living alone. Marcella was then about thirty-five or so, and had retained the bright beauty of her complexion and the blue brilliancy of her eyes. Her hair was still spun gold, and she was dressed in taste, as always. We talked about the old times, about my sister and her children in Paris, about Carl, his wild brief life and his tragic death; about books, about her own studies, for she was taking a course in medicine preparatory to becoming a physician. Marcella looked at me with twinkling eyes of interrogation as if to ask how life was faring with me, and if marriage was a success with me. She made no inquiry about my wife or my children. It grew to be ten o'clock, and of a sudden the door at the end of the hall opened, and Marcella said, "That's Deirdre." And Deirdre came along the hallway and entered the room lugging a heavy suitcase. She had just returned from Detroit. I suspect at this distance that she had been there on a love jaunt with the man whose mistress she had been, and that this was their farewell assignation. But I did not know that, not even later, though the reader will see the facts which justify me in this supposition. I knew Deirdre by sight, and had even been introduced to her five years or so before this time at my sister's house in Prairie Avenue, where she was teaching music to my sister's two daughters. I had not seen her in the meantime. Deirdre was a teacher in the elements of music. And so now Deirdre and I spoke to each other, and she sat down to rest a moment. But as it turned out she stayed in the room until I left and with Marcella came to the door to say good night to me. She sat there as Marcella and I talked, but without joining in the conversation, except with an occasional monosyllable. She was an extremely interesting woman to look at. Her brow was conical, her hair sandy running to reddishness, her nose prominent and strong, her mouth delicate and shapely; her face as a whole foxlike. Her form was slender, she was taller than Marcella. Her aura was of mixed coloring, some blue, some red, some green—but no yellow. But her eyes were hazel hued; and she sat there for the most part looking down. I thought she was a little shy in my presence. But at any rate her eyes looked down; and there was a sort of vaticinating mist on them and before them, as of a demon that is dreaming. She was obviously concentrated about something, or remembering the hours just past with her lover, or imagining hours to be with me.

We planned a dinner all together as I left that night: I was to bring up a man friend implicitly to pair with Deirdre, for I was Marcella's friend primarily and by preference. This man friend was younger than I and not then married. We stopped in the buffet of the apartment building and had some drinks with the result that we were both keyed for adventure when we faced Marcella and Deirdre. As the four of us started for the restaurant Marcella and I preceded Deirdre and her partner down the hall which was long, so long that the entrance door was out of view to one in the living room at the front. I knew that Deirdre and her escort were somewhere in the front room, but standing where they could not see Marcella and me; and in a sudden frolicsome spirit I put my arm about Marcella. She repulsed me furiously, with sudden feline anger and with violent words heard by Deirdre, who immediately stepped into view. I was frightfully embarrassed, and suddenly in a revulsion of aversion for Marcella who had so needlessly publicized my innocent approach. Resolving at that minute that I was done with her I stood nevertheless until Deirdre and her escort came to us, not betraying my feelings at all. In a second I

could see that Marcella repented her foolish outburst. By way
of deceiving her and to make the dinner happy I passed over
the incident with as good humor as I could command. But I
was done with Marcella. I reflected upon the waste of time and
money for this dinner, and how I might have been with Marie
or Grace, or many others with less expense, and with no
affected gestures of virtue to mar the Dionysiac hour. One
always pays for these ladies of studious technique. The young
man and Deirdre faced each other mildly. He cared nothing
for her, and she was plainly indifferent to him.

In two or three days after this Deirdre appeared at my
office asking advice about a small bill that was owing her for
teaching music. I perceived that she was using this matter to
conceal her tactics in seeking me out. She was shrewd enough
to know that I would never enter the apartment again to see
Marcella. Divining her, I asked her to luncheon that day, and
she accepted. Just a little before this my daughter Marcia had
been born, and my wife was nursing the child and was not
quite well, and had been in fatigue and nerves for months.

I had not had a sudden admiration for Deirdre; in fact, I
liked Marcella so much better by comparison that Deirdre had
not entered my imagination at all. But now that I faced her at
a secluded table at luncheon and saw that she was a probable
conquest I began to study her face, and to follow her conversation carefully by way of fathoming her mind. She had some
thinking powers, she was rather well informed in the drama,
Shaw and the Dublin school who were then engrossing the
public. She mentioned various North Side women of prominence with whom she had association in her work, or with
whom she was on terms of friendship by reason of contacts in
social settlement interests. She expressed some radical ideas;
and we had not met many times before I knew about her childhood and rearing. Her mother had been a follower of the
Claflin sisters, and through this mother she had been raised

in the faith of free love. But the mother had died when Deirdre was in her early twenties, and her father having married again Deirdre was driven from home; and taking her little sister, she had come to Chicago. That sister had died in Deirdre's arms of meningitis; her father had died, and she was thus alone. All this I soon heard from Deirdre.

It was a sorrowful tale in all, and spun forth by Deirdre for the purpose of winning pity. One of the sagas of the time of Lief the Fortunate warns men against the tears of a whore. Her friendship with Marcella and her life with her in the apartment were characteristic of her general policy, which was to be as close to the rich and patrician people of Chicago as possible, choosing these, like Marcella, who had fallen out of conventional circles because of a divorce, or who had left them behind for parlor socialism or mauve radicalism. At this luncheon Deirdre was faultlessly dressed, but with great simplicity. I noticed her shoes which were handmade, and her dress which was of fine material and fashionably cut. It turned out that the rich women whom she knew gave her these things. They were misfits, or they had been worn a little and cast aside. Thus by the little that Deirdre made and by the gifts that she received she was managing to live.

I hadn't the slightest idea of becoming involved with Deirdre. At the luncheon she seemed easy enough to take and to leave in one of those lighthearted adulteries that do no harm, and involve nothing but a technical breach of conjugal fidelity, which not being known are as innocuous as a walk or a talk. If I had foreseen what I was being drawn into, and indeed what I was walking into, I should not have seen Deirdre after this luncheon. I did not conceive much of a passion for her, certainly no fascination for her. All of that was to come, and Deirdre played her hand with wonderful cunning and farsightedness. It was clear finally that, having learned from Marcella about my married life and possibly how I had come to get married, she intended to bring about a divorce and marry me.

Spring came on and we took walks through the park. When Marcella was absent we went to the apartment; but Deirdre fled my grasp with the skill of Daphne. She began to unfold to me. Her mind seemed more wonderful day by day; and she plied me with compliments about my natural ways, my radical ideas, though of these she professed to be afraid. I had sought reality all my life, which in truth is the most expensive thing in the world; and seeking it now through Deirdre I was to pay. At first I took it for granted that she had had a lover before me; but as she fought me away I began to think that perhaps she was the old maid, which she looked at times to be. She was about thirty-three at this time, and I was forty. June came and Marcella, who probably knew nothing of this affair which was maturing, went away for the summer. That left the apartment to me and Deirdre, and I was there nearly every day, somewhat neglecting my business. But the office had degenerated, and I could not help its state. Nothing seemed to matter. An affair with Deirdre came in as a cure for all my ills, and as proper payment to the genius of misfortune that had descended upon my industry and my concentration of mind. As for my wife, I never intended that any harm should come to her for this free faring. I had made up my mind that women in general expect that lighthearted adulteries are carried on behind their backs and that they do not care so long as they do not know about them, so long as their own favored positions as wives are not affected. What they rise up against is adulterous love. I had no more idea of falling in love with Deirdre than I had of killing her when we laughed and talked in our walks by the Lake.

Ah, but Deirdre played her hand skillfully. We went on until I was half mad about her, and still she eluded me. One day I told her that I was through. This was after three months of struggle. When I said this she wept bitterly and began to talk of her desolate state: she had no mother, no father, no sister. And here was I who could be a brother, a friend to her, and wouldn't do it. I was acting just like all bounders, and she was disappointed in me. That meant of course that she was looking forward to marriage with me; and that if she capitulated to me she meant to marry me; for she loved me with all her heart—that is what she said. Truly speaking, I ignored the hook; but on the other hand, I was tired of the chase. So I said: "Very well. I'll be your friend, whatever that means. I am not ever again going to press you about this." I took her out to dinner; we had wine and talked. Then I went home vastly relieved that it was over.

The next morning I had a note from Deirdre saying that she had gone to the country until Thursday; but then she wanted to see me very much indeed. She had underscored those words. Thursday came and I was trying a case. I forgot all about Deirdre. Friday morning she telephoned me. I went to the apartment and contracted madness in her kiss. The next day I had a letter from her saying that she had gone to Michigan with Rachel, her chum, and would be gone some weeks. What, so cold, so indifferent after this nuptial consummation? There was nothing to do but to follow her, and I did so. She was at a summer camp with Rachel, and I had to take a room in the little hotel in the nearby village. She kept Rachel by her side constantly, and we had no privacy together at all. We three lay on the warm sand by the Lake at night looking up at the moonless sky full of stars, and listening to the wash of the waves. That was all. Finally I had to return to Chicago completely defeated. I afterward put this trip into the poem published in *Songs and Satires*, "In Michigan," but with many imaginative variations.

Deirdre came back at last, and the path was at once smoother and seemed to be permanently free from obstacles. In

the meanwhile my wife and children were away for the summer. They returned in August when I bought a house for about
$12,000 and presented it to my wife, asking that she hold it in
trust for the little daughters as well as for herself. Having this
done, I felt freer to play. And Deirdre and I played to the
full. Marcella came back, and the apartment was no longer
ours at will. We had to wait until Marcella was to be gone for
the evening, or for the afternoon. It made no difference at
what hour Deirdre could see me I was there, putting aside
every other engagement, business or what not. I was completely
enthralled. The protagonist of Tennyson's "Maud" was not
more tortured with erotomania than I. Deirdre had a friend
who lived in St. Paul, and she said that it was best that she
allow him to come to see her, as it was a good blind. And he
came two or three times during the course of our affair. Then
one day when I telephoned the apartment Marcella unexpect-
edly answered and told me that I might reach Deirdre at the
office of a certain man whom I knew of but had never met.
She said this with an informative inflection, with something
of a mock in her voice as if to say, "Don't be a fool." This man
was one of the Lake Forest snobs who had married a rich wife.
After this Deirdre told me that she had been his mistress, but
that they had parted just before the time of my first call upon
Marcella. She had a wonderful whopper to dole to me, which
was that this man was engaged to the rich woman at the time
that Deirdre herself met him; and that he offered to break his
engagement and marry Deirdre. This story was a part and par-
cel of the whole texture of Deirdre's nature as it was gradually
unfolding. Above everything, above her tendency to flash
strange fictions before my eyes, to indulge in mysterious
silences, and to drape herself in clouds and mists, I could see
that she was subtle and designing beyond any woman that I
had ever known. All the while she talked frankly to me about
her movements every day, and wrote me a note every day,

even when I had seen her. She even told me that she had spent the evening at her apartment with her former lover, but that I should believe her when she said that it was all innocent. In the state of mind that I was in I did not know whether to believe her or not; but in my mind there was a residue of distrust of her which settled down into something acrid, and permanently sickened me. From this day forth my reason told me to be done with her; my passion and even my heart would not let me leave her.

In the fall I had the benefit of a temporary antidote to the daily poison I was taking, and for a day I was repossessed of my real self. For I was now like Antony in his obsession for Cleopatra:

> His soul lived in her body, as 'twere born
> A part of her, and whithersoever she went
> There followed he. And all their life together
> Was what it was, a rapture justified
> By its essential honey of realest blossoms,
> In spite of anguished shame.

This autumn of 1909 my grandmother celebrated her ninety-fifth birthday anniversary; and in the state of mind I was in on account of Deirdre it seemed to me that there would be healing in communing with this venerable woman who dated back to my childhood with infinite memories of happiness and peace. So I journeyed down to Petersburg, leaving Deirdre to her former lover, if he chose to see her, or to her friend of St. Paul, who occasionally came to Chicago and took her about to the theater and to dinner.

When I arrived at the farmhouse my uncle and aunt cautioned me against a sudden entering of the room where my grandmother was lying in bed. She had suffered a sort of paralysis of her legs about four years before and had been confined ever since. They said they would enter the room softly and tell her that I was there, and thus prepare her for my entrance. They did this and came back and ushered me in. She looked at me with a tenderness that went right through my heart— looked at me from under those eyelids that always drooped with soft contemplation, and now kept a meditative steadiness as they etched me out of the half-lights of the room. She beckoned to me to approach her, and when I did so she put her arms about me, and called me a "dear man," and a good son to come to see her, "to come to see your old granny" were her words. My aunt and uncle then withdrew from the room and Grandmother began to talk.

Her property was being managed by Henry Houghton, a neighbor about the age of my uncle, and a lifelong friend of both. And everything had been well managed. Her cattle had sold off profitably. She told me of recent events in the neighborhood: Flora Kincaid had died in childbirth; Nellie Tate had moved to Nebraska, and so on. Then she began to talk of my father. He had tried to set aside the will of Grandfather by a suit in chancery which alleged undue influence on the part of my uncle. After many bitter interviews, after great expense to my uncle, the case had been settled. My father received about $2,000 more than he would have received under the will. Grandmother's face took on the dignity of some old queen as she talked about this regrettable affair. "I don't like what your poppie did," she said. "Your grandpa was a just man. He took everything into consideration. He made that will as carefully as a man could make a will. And everybody should have abided by it. He had Branson, the best lawyer in Petersburg, draw the will. And the truth is it couldn't be broken by the court. Your poppie found that out when he got right down to it, and so he settled the case. Willie paid out thousands to lawyers; and there is bitterness now, and I suppose forever. It's bad business. I don't like what your poppie did. He hasn't been around much since this thing happened."

And so she went on with perfect memory and reason talking of many things both those of recent years and of the last few months, and those of the long ago. She even mentioned her old grandmother Rebecca Wasson, and the days at Whitehall and Murrayville; and she talked of Andrew Jackson, Old Hickory she called him, who was president when she was fourteen to twenty-two years of age, and whose death occurred when she was thirty-five. She had a peculiar affection for the Warrior of the Hermitage, for she, too, was from the Nashville country, and had brought over from her girlhood days the magical admiration which permeated the country for the hero of New Orleans.

I sat there listening to her as she talked and talked. I was thinking of Deirdre. I wanted to talk to her about Deirdre, but I knew what she would say. She would have reproved me, she would have characterized Deirdre out of that matter-of-fact morality through which she had all questions of the good and the bad life settled. And only to think that they resembled each other in certain physical aspects! Both were slender, both had conical foreheads, both had spiritual reserves and powers that seemed alike to me then. But how different they were from each other as characters!

Finally I rose to go. Grandmother encircled me again with her arms, and I passed to the door. Pausing there a moment I looked at her. She had turned her face to the window, and was looking out, and was apparently unconscious of the fact that I was taking a last look at her. The leaves were drifting from the great maple tree near the window; and she seemed to be watching them. I never saw her again. The following January she died. So I left the room and joined my aunt and uncle in the old living room where I had sat with my grandfather and grandmother in those days of more than thirty years before.

I had telegraphed to Deirdre when I arrived in Petersburg. Now I was anxious to get to Petersburg to telegraph her that I was on my way back to Chicago. She had been in my mind all the time, so much so that I could not enjoy anything, or anyone. When I arrived in Chicago I went at once to see her, and we walked through Lincoln Park. She was in a laughing, a light mood, the more so probably for seeing the somber reflections that possessed me. She knew that I was sinking deeper and deeper into her power.

My wife became apprised of the affair and threatened to expose Deirdre. That would have ruined Deirdre; for her living depended upon a good name. She was teaching children; as an adulteress she would have been without pupils at once. Now the idea of marriage emerged concretely. I had to do something to save myself. If my wife and children were at stake in this exigency, so was I at stake. I was so tortured that I felt I should have to have peace or die. I could cure myself by marrying Deirdre, and whether I stayed married to her or not, to be cured was the all-important matter. I asked my wife to release me, she refused saying to me that Deirdre really amounted to nothing, and in large she was right in saying this. I intended to go on practicing law and observe all my obligations the same as before. When my wife would not release me Deirdre proposed that we run away together. I refused to do so. I said that I would never leave my little daughters, come what might. And then Deirdre prepared to strike.

A year had now elapsed since we had entered upon this insane business and she was making ready to spend the summer with a woman friend in northern Wisconsin. This woman was the wife of a Chicago judge and in Chicago society. Deirdre told me that she knew all about our affair and had no word of criticism for us. Before Deirdre went north we took a trip to Michigan on the night boat and stayed all the next day in the woods by the St. Joe River. We had a stateroom returning; and I said farewell to Deirdre at the station quite calmed after our erotic hours. I turned away thinking that at last I was cured. But in two weeks I was afire again. And after a long, hard journey in which I took the wrong train and landed in Minnesota instead of Wisconsin, I joined Deirdre at a hotel; and there after a day and a night I felt in control of myself again. Deirdre wept bitterly on this occasion, and I was in a state of mind almost satiric as I stood on the dock as her boat sailed back to the island where her friend had her summer home; certainly I was in a kind of contempt for myself for being so bewitched about this woman who looked so red-nosed and commonplace as she stood waving me farewell.

We had come to a definite impasse: I wouldn't run away with Deirdre, for I saw that ruin followed in the wake of such a step. She wanted me to go to another city with her, and there practice law. I foresaw the great difficulties of establishing myself again, in a strange place with scandal following my steps. I had seen men try that. There was one in particular in my part of Chicago, who had had a brilliant career as a lawyer in a Western city, and had come down to inconspicuous days in Chicago as a writer of briefs for a railroad. He had run away and married the woman. Always there were my little daughters. I would not leave them, unless I could be divorced and with a legal re-establishment for myself in which my income would suffer as little as possible. I proposed to Deirdre that if she would go on with me as before I would finance her. That she would not do. Solutions were thus reduced to running away or marriage. I said to her: "If we part you will soon have a lover. If love means anything, if it be not pure idiocy, what insanity to break this love of ours, and then for you to take another lover in a few months." To this she was silent; being pressed she said she wouldn't take another lover. What foolishness all around! In fact a dull, rubber god guided my steps. Marriage with Deirdre would have been ruin. That is my judgment twenty-five years after those days. I see her now as a cold, uncanny, farsighted mind, with a sort of congenital nymphomania. We never would have lived in harmony. For after a time I should have taken her in hand, and if she had resisted my control I should have left her.

With all these considerations, and facing these obstacles, I resolved to master myself. I began to draw on the antibodies that I had built up at eleven years of age with Zueline. Arrived back in Chicago from Wisconsin I bought tickets and took my wife on a long trip through Canada to Vancouver and Victoria and then down to San Francisco and back. I determined that I would conquer myself, I could stand no more of this torture and degradation of spirit. If Nature had no pity in laying this terrible hand upon me for her own blind biological purposes I would have no remorse in fighting Nature with Nature. I would use my mind and my will to exorcise this demon that had entered into me. All along with Deirdre I had endured the agony of fears and desires that gave me nausea in the seat of the solar plexus, and had caused the great nerves of that center to writhe and constrict like entangled snakes. This was physically true to an extent that I can scarcely describe the feeling. When she was in Wisconsin, when I was separated from her for a few days in town, this sensation of sinking, this aching and this rising of a pulsing despair, a grief without words all up and around my heart until my breath seemed to be going out of me could be allayed in a minute by seeing her. Now in Victoria, so far from her, it had no medicine but my will to put it away, nothing but my sense of the ridiculous, my capacity to laugh, nothing but talks with a man there in Victoria who knew every pang that I had, having been through this madness several times himself. But what were those doubts and fears when I was but a few minutes away from Deirdre compared with those I had there by the far Pacific? How was she solacing that amorous heart of hers, into whose arms had she fallen? When I was near her I could see her, or if I could not see her I could telephone her. Now the distance between us was like the unscalable walls of hell, and I went to bed to toss half the night; I rose in the morning in great weariness to follow one more futile day with the English crowd that commenced at eleven with Scotch and drank all day.

Through all this my wife feasted and went about with new-found friends; and on a few occasions we sailed around the harbor with a young man and his bride, who was talkative and witty and made me laugh in spite of myself. In the months past when I was descending into this enchantment I read *Liber Amoris*, and apprised myself of the ignominious slavery into which Hazlitt slipped with his serving wench; I read de Musset's *Confession d'un Enfant du Siècle*, and followed his torture at the hands of George Sand; and just then Sudermann's *Das hohe Lied* was sweeping the country and I read that trying to nerve myself to play the part of von Prell to Deirdre's Lilly. Now I could not read. My mind was like the weight of a scale when it is at the far end of the beam: I was tipped out of myself in an imagination and a desire that stretched back two thousand miles to Deirdre and to lost delight, and would have overcome all circumstances, whereas they could not be overcome at all. I built up antibodies to my spiritual infection by dwelling upon every fault of Deirdre that I could think of: her deceptions, her sinister secretiveness, her whoppers, her probable infidelities, her sharp words at times which indicated that she thought she had me mastered and could drive me about at will, whereas no one could do that, and she never did. I dwelt upon the unfavorable phases of her physical being: her eyes which looked as if she might sometimes have exophthalmic goiter, and really protruded; her mouth which slacked at times into the semblance of sullen sensualism, her strong nose easily made into an ugly prominence by satiric exaggeration. And here was my wife with a really beautiful nose, with a shapely figure which put to shame the slender flanks and legs of Deirdre, with a disposition that had no witch moods, no eyes filmed with demon dreams. I had a picture of Deirdre with me and I showed it to a man friend. "Yes," he said, "she looks like I thought she would." He went on to say that Deirdre was a dangerous, false woman, such as he had dealt with in his mad days, now happily over, since he wondered now how he escaped with his life and his reason. We went over the points together that were involved: True, I wanted no one but Deirdre but I could not have her without complete ruin. On her part, if she told the truth she wanted no one but me, but she would not have me longer except in marriage. The man said this was absurd. She would immediately take another lover, and why not continue with me? Yes, why not? "Why," said my friend, "she started from the first to break up your marriage, and now that she cannot do it, she wants to quit. That's her love; that's the love of all such women. She will run away with you, but if you did that she would have you completely in her power. Your business would be ruined, your place lost, and you would have her and nothing else. And she is so cold-blooded that she would then cheat on you or run away from you." He was putting the iron of hate in my heart for all this complication, so absurd and so crucifying. Meanwhile I was waiting for a letter from Deirdre, day by day I waited, with my solar plexus twisting and aching, with my breast full of distress. Finally one day I got a letter. It was very long, written in her cultivated handwriting, and full of feeling, full of sorrow. It expressed regret for any pain she had ever given me, it begged me to believe in her lasting love, to take heart from her fond wishes for my plans in life; it begged me to respect and cherish my gifts and to make the most of them; it was full of her best self, and that was perhaps the only self of her that there was. Her other selves may have been the creation of my imagination, my jealous dreads. She had sent this letter from Indiana where she was rallying from a nervous attack which threatened to be a neurasthenia. I showed the letter to my friend. He said:

"She's smart as hell. She can write too. I never saw more beautiful handwriting." All this brought back madness again.

I had been troubled with insomnia all summer; this letter aggravated that maddening horror. As I look back on my own case I wonder that something of serious physical ill did not befall me. But nothing did; on the contrary, I was strong and well all through this enervating business, save on days when depression was more than any organization could stand.

When I got back to Chicago something happened almost at once to strengthen my will. Marcella's brother Charley came to my office full of wrath. He went on to say angrily that if I wanted to run around with a whore like Deirdre that was my business, but he would not permit his sister to be dragged into the affair. "What are you talking about, Charley?" I asked in great surprise. "You know damn well what I am talking about. You and that bitch plotted to have Marcella picked as the woman in the case if there was a scandal." "Why, Charley, that is the most absurd thing that ever entered your head. And I won't allow you to say such things to me. If you have come here to talk in that absurd manner you can go. I won't listen to you." "That's what I say," he persisted. "Well, it's a lie, there's nothing to it at all. What do you mean?" "Look here," he flamed, "what about that time Deirdre took Marcella's trunk with her initials on it when you two went to Detroit? What do you say to that?" "I say that I never heard of it till this minute. I say that I had no more to do with it than you had." Charley's face was red with wrath. He could not help but trust me, yet he wanted to revenge himself on someone. He turned hurriedly and left the room.

So it was clear now that Deirdre and Marcella were no longer friends and I had no idea where Deirdre would live when she returned from Indiana. Meanwhile after all this tensity of will to put Deirdre utterly out of mind, my spiritual muscles relaxed. And under the influence of days that I could not wholly master I was much depressed. The neighborhood of the house that I had presented to my wife filled me with frightful nostalgia. A bell on a church a block or so away tinkled with the pathos of far-off things on Sunday mornings, as the orthodox people of my street walked solemnly to prayer. Somewhere near a piano gave forth the deathly sweetness of Ethelbert Nevin's music. It was autumn and the leaves from the lonely poplar trees along the street were falling, and ticking strange loneliness as they touched the earth. I could not read, I could not write. At the office I took up heavy tasks which had no interest for me. And every night when I came home, which was by no means always, my wife was sitting on the porch waiting for me, and smiling in weariless friendliness upon me. She had triumphed over Deirdre.

And one night her smiles were more than usually bright as I got to the porch where she was waiting for me. Deirdre had been to see her that afternoon. Deirdre had knelt in penitence at her feet. Deirdre had been sent by the society woman, who entertained Deirdre in Wisconsin—sent, to assure my wife that the romance was over, and that she would see me no more—sent to say that she had loved me and had sinned, but would sin no more. All this had been done behind my back. At that moment I was full of raging indignation. My blood curdled. Instantly I saw my predicament: Deirdre was lost to me, my wife was not reformed, and could not be reformed. I was alone again. Yet I smiled, then I laughed, as proud indifference entered my heart. I told my wife to dress and we would go out for dinner; and down we went to Rector's where we had champagne and the best dinner that I could buy; after which, instead of going home, we went to a hotel and took one of the most expensive suites available.

The next morning early Deirdre tried to reach me on the telephone. My telephone girl never connected my desk without first saying who wanted to talk to me. When she told me I replied that I was out. All that day Deirdre telephoned, and at every call she got the word that I was out.

Then came a long letter from Deirdre explaining her course: It was either to make peace with my wife or be ruined. Already there was talk about town, and my wife had threatened her with exposure everywhere which would deprive her of every pupil and bring her to beggary. What was she to do? We could not marry, I would not run away with her, to continue our liaison was ruin for her. My law studies, my natural cast of mind made me see both sides of everything; and as I perceived that Deirdre's words had truth in them, I was penitent. I took up the telephone to talk to her; then I dropped it and did not call her. Finally I learned somehow where she was living. It was in an ordinary boardinghouse. And like the man who returns to the scene of his crime I went there one mad night and was received into her room. But the charm was gone. That was the end; except for the long convalescence through which I passed. All that winter I wandered about Chicago avoiding the restaurants where Deirdre and I had feasted in our happy days. I made friends with a hard Englishman who knew literature pretty well, especially erotic literature, and we exchanged ribaldries, and I showed him my abandoned ballades, as we prowled these iron nights.

It was three years before I extirpated Deirdre's poison from my blood, extirpated it as immediate sickness and agony; for the rest, does one ever get well of a poisoning? Rarely has a sensitive man had a love affair like this without great disaster; and literature is full of their descriptions. They are egregious errors judged by any prudent standard of life. They may, however, be rich schoolings for the mind and heart.

Deirdre struggled along after we ended our relationship. She made a brave fight as she attached herself by her uncanny maneuvering to society women in Chicago, and took trips with them to Norway and the Continent. But in her poverty and

with her handicaps she never overcame the consequences of this
eighteen months of checkered ecstasy. She married a few years
after we separated. Her husband turned upon her bitterly after
a few years, and they were divorced. Later she committed
suicide.

But what did Deirdre and adulterous love do to me? What
besides the time she took from my business, what besides the
distraction she brought upon me from my home and my path,
what besides the money I spent on her, and the vast vitality
that I gave to my devotion to her? Aye, too if I had been mated
to my wife she would have destroyed that emotional concentration on a spouse which is the bond of marriage, and the
strength of its happy continuance. These are the fruits of
adulterous love. But on the other hand, I learned through
Deirdre the secrets and the agonies of all the world's lovers,
of all the Antonys, the Abélards, the Troiluses. My emotional
powers were enormously deepened by Deirdre. I was enabled
through her to reread every word of Shakespeare's plays of
passion under a light which reflected up and out of the printed
page every meaning, and even more than he was able to set
down. Taking up Brandes's work on Shakespeare, I saw into
Shakespeare's heart; I had explanations for Shakespeare's silence
after the London days. I could not have written "Tomorrow Is
My Birthday" if I had not had the experience with Deirdre;
nor could I have written many other poems without this
severe schooling in what was practically erotomania. For the
rest, I was badly injured. Nothing can be more suicidal to the
spirit than to fight fire with fire, to destroy beauty with acid
and knives, to do terrible surgeries to the heart when it is most
tender, to take poison as an antidote to poison, to get back
self-mastery by coarsening one's nature, by dulling one's
sensitivity, by increasing one's resistance and spiritual muscle
by the heavy food of obscene and satirical associations, by

drabby contacts in which memories of ecstasies can be mocked until their beauty can no longer be recalled to mind.

Once I had made up my mind to be done with Deirdre my will, strong by nature and disciplined for years, came to my assistance. I left her completely alone after that casual visit I paid to her room. Meanwhile Deirdre wanted to be friends, not friends who saw each other, or telephoned each other; though we might meet here and there, we might telephone if there was occasion for it. I would have nothing to do with such temporizing with a bad malady. And one day I was phoned by the woman who ran the music school of which Deirdre was one of the teachers. This woman wanted me to come to see her. I refused, but consented that she might call at my office. She came and began to tell me of Deirdre's agitated state of mind. That morning Deirdre had started to teach and had collapsed, had fainted at the piano. This woman asked me, "Why can't you be a friend to Deirdre?" "What is that?" I returned. "What is being a friend? What can I do? You know the story?" She nodded to this. "That being the case you must see that complete cessation of all communication, complete silence is the only way. I am a busy man, with many things on my mind. I can give no more time to Deirdre."

The Englishman whom I mentioned earlier in the chapter ran a literary column in a musical weekly, which carried the advertisements of singers, pianists, piano dealers and music schools. In this column he published literary comments and sometimes a poem. For ten years this man had been publishing favorable word of such poems as I allowed to see the light, and he had admired my *Maximilian*. Now in the fall after my rupture with Deirdre, in November it was, he published my "Helen of Troy," which had first seen type in the Sunday *Times* of Memphis, Tennessee, in September, 1893, by grace of Howard Hawthorne McGee, an editorial writer on that paper. Now my English friend wanted to resurrect it from *A*

Book of Verses, where it was securely entombed, and publish it in his column in the musical weekly. He did so. Then in a few days he called at my office and told me that the head of the music school where Deirdre taught had called upon the publisher and protested against anything of mine published in the weekly. Further, she said that she would withdraw her large advertisement of the school from the weekly if I was again admitted to its columns. After telling me this my English friend said that hereafter he could not even mention my name, and that he had been so instructed by the owner of the periodical.

So it was that the cords of the Lilliputians shot around my steps, and tangled them. I was in Chicago where there was no literary page worth mentioning, where there were no literary interests of moment; and this little tube into the outer world from my tomb, this musical weekly, was taken from me. Even though it was worth nothing but for its sustaining influence, nothing by way of giving standing to my name, I needed spiritual support in these hard days. I had to trudge along with my two little books in the years 1910 and 1911, *Songs and Sonnets,* and *Songs and Sonnets Second Series,* books that were reviewed in the Boston *Transcript,* in the Boston *Herald* side by side with *The Town Down the River,* in the *Dial,* in Reedy's *Mirror* as poetry beyond average merit; but in the Chicago *News* I was reminded that I wrote of love which, quickly attaining its desire, has no beauty left, and revenges itself with a sneer.

Was it wonderful all in all that in these days I solaced myself with Grace, Adele, Marie and Virginia? I had to do this, or I had to turn monk or Hindu, and seek Nirvana by crushing out my restless vitality.

Chapter XV

NOW WITH DEIRDRE OUT OF MY LIFE I HAD TO STRUGGLE TO make it a going concern again. I was desperately lonely. I believe that autumn of 1910 was one of the hardest periods of my life, if not the hardest of all. Naturally my home life was disorganized. Yet my wife had triumphed and was apparently happy; at least she was no longer in any anxiety. For myself I had settled down to business as hard as I could, and the office was far from what it had been in its prosperous days. At first I had the ambition to make the law an instrument for political and social reforms. I no longer had any faith in that. Every liberal program in Chicago had failed ignominiously. Municipal ownership of the streetcar lines had gone to ruin as an issue. A new charter had been granted them; and that reform was swallowed by the victorious capitalists who owned the lines. All these reverses, my own included, gave me a revaluation of life, and filled me with a skepticism about a new day of justice in American politics; and many other things caused me to look forward to a career for myself in which I would accept the country as it was, and interpret it as I saw it. At the same time I meant now to make some money. My partnership had failed to yield the competence that I hoped for it. I was tired of this partnership now. My senior partner was lecturing, and I was toiling away to clear up the receivership of the bank of America.

Just now a plan was on foot to sell a piece of ground in State Street which belonged to the Stone estate; and my sister and her children had an interest in this property as the widow and heirs of Carl. It was to be sold for $500,000 and the money divided. There were questions to be settled, and already I had

begun a study of the will made by Carl's father in 1877. I
spent weeks in the law library working out these difficult
problems, and continued to study this will for two years after
this.

Ultimately there was a considerable fee for me in this
litigation; and I saw that I did not have to depend upon my
partnership for a living business. Just now my senior partner
was making ready to go west to take part in a criminal case.
I knew he would be gone for months, if not for a year or two.
I told him that he was rusty on the law, that he was going into
a strange forum, and that he would be handicapped. I did not
foresee the disaster that came to him. It was no use now to
urge him to stick to business in Chicago. Several years before
this business had poured into our office, and we could have
become rich on it. But he neglected the most important cases;
and the result was that they ceased to come to us. Saying that
I would not stay and run the office while he was in the West,
as I had done when he was away before, I picked up my bust
of Jefferson, my books and pictures, and moved to the Marquette Building. I had been in the Ashland Block for eighteen
years; and I wanted to go to a finer building where the tenants
were of a better class of lawyers. So this chapter of my life
ended suddenly in the spring of 1911.

Far back in the Lewistown days when I was reading Plato
and Shelley my father called me a "daydreamer"; now after
eighteen years of the law, what was I? Scientists can bombard
the fruit fly with X rays and alter its germ plasm until its off-
spring turn up with white eyes instead of red, and with smaller
wings. Cyclopean eyes can be created in frogs by chemicals,
and the development of frogs arrested by chemicals until their
mature specimens are no larger than bees. The law had been
an X ray to me, and many kinds of chemicals; the law, and my
contacts with so many varieties of people. And now imagine
a human being with one great eye in the center of his forehead

with which he saw everything with realistic clearness; but suppose him in retention of his two normal eyes, which in their normality saw beauty where it was not, and truth where it had never been. That was I who saw through people with penetration, who could weigh arguments and facts judicially, but who with dreaming eyes looked down paths without seeing the tangles all in all, Pyrrhonist as I was about life and success. For I was reading science all the time. De Vries and others, books on botany and biology; and I saw but one story, which was that Nature pours forth creatures and lets them live or perish, according to chance. All through my poems there run the two strains of realism and mysticism. I wrote with my cyclopean eye many of the portraits of Spoon River, and with my dreaming eyes I wrote "The Star" and "The Loom."

Just before the State Street property was sold one of the trustees of the estate, a brother of Carl's, made complaint to me that my sister was spending too much money in Paris. I knew nothing of her life beyond what I learned from her letters to me. Often she mentioned titled persons whom she knew, with whom she traveled to Rome, or to the sea resorts; and she wrote me that her daughters were in school in Paris and spoke French as well as natives; and that Buddie, her son, was in school at Ferney. The trustee was sending her a good allowance, to which the grand lady, her mother-in-law, heartily agreed; and I can truthfully say that I never saw a more generous family than that into which my sister had married, or one that had greater family loyalty. There was a truly Jewish quality to it; and later I half suspected that the grand lady had some Jewish blood. However, my sister always needed money, and could never get enough for her expenses. I could say nothing to the trustee's protests, for in fact there was a question whether my sister under the will of the founder of the fortune was entitled to any income whatever. On the other hand, as the will provided that the widow, the grand lady, should have an income according to the judgment of the trustees sufficient for the support of herself and children, and as she had taken all of the income of the estate since 1877, save what she doled to her children, to Carl at times, the question was whether the trustees, one of whom was the grand lady herself and the other the son mentioned, should not account to the heirs for something like $200,000. My sister was eager that this accounting should be enforced; for the reduction of her income, the question raised against her manner of life put her in fighting spirit.

Hence when the $500,000 was paid for the State Street property, and was on deposit with a trust company ready for distribution the crafty plan of the trustee and his lawyer came forth, which was that no money was to be paid anyone until the trustees were absolved from that $200,000 default. I was in a furious mood over this, for nothing had been so much as hinted of such a thing before. The matter of my sister's income had passed off; and there had never been anything but talk of the trustees' malversation. However, I faced a resolute lawyer acting for the trustee, and probably for the grand lady, also a trustee; while without their consent I could not get the share belonging to my sister and her children without embarking upon a suit which would have taken months.

The grand lady had a daughter whose husband was indignant about the disposition of the income of the estate. But when it came to the scratch his wife would not do the undaughterly thing of attacking the integrity of her mother; and a son in Boston took the same position; whereas the other son, the trustee, was against such a proceeding for the greater reason that his own pocketbook was menaced. My sister, only a relative by marriage, could not stand against this opposition. So that the trustees were given a clear acquittance, and the $500,-000 was distributed.

But I had weeks of torture and anxiety over this tangle. Then I became guardian for Emma Louise and for Buddie of

their share of this money. I put it in bank and tried my best
to invest it. I looked over vast lists of mortgages, since the law
forbade my investing it in anything but mortgages, and approved bonds, and I could find nothing that I considered safe.
For that matter I could not make investments for myself, try
as hard as I would. I made an $8,000 fee in this matter, and
could find no place to invest it. It remained in the bank and
poorer days coming on I spent it for living expenses. Why
didn't I buy a country place and write poetry? Well, it was not
enough to retire on; and then the city gave me daily interests.
Much as I had always loved the country, there was a good deal
of Chaucer in me. I was interested all the while in people.

My father, after a contest of his father's will, had about
$8,000 ahead, and he bought a farm of forty acres near Sauga-
tuck, Michigan. He had gone fishing with me and Charley
Shippey before this time and had become infatuated with the
Michigan country. He ran up a flag on his front yard with the
device "Masters Farm," and though he was now sixty-one he
was as young as ever and could pitch hay or chop wood with
undiminished vigor. He expected to make money out of his
eighty bearing cherry trees, and out of his hundreds of peach
trees; but he soon found that the market men in Chicago
reaped all the profit in them. His reward consisted, mostly, in
looking at Lake Michigan which bordered his frontage, and in
swimming in its waters, and in loafing at the country store
near at hand, where he became friends with the owner and the
farmers about.

In these days I used to go to see him and my mother who
was displeased with the purchase of the farm, and fretted herself almost into sickness over the futile work of raising fruit
which brought no money returns. In town, besides taking
walks with various companions, I kept up daily swimming at
the Illinois Athletic Club, which prospered my nerves. Indeed
except for swimming during those exhausting days following

the collapse of my affair with Deirdre, I should scarcely have kept my health and strength.

The son who was trustee of the Stone estate died, and the great lady died, and the estate was ready for division. Meanwhile my sister had remarried in Paris. Her new husband was a composite of Rosmersholm and Tesman and Cagliostro, and a very strange man; but with a certain charm. He had been born in Denmark and was a full-blooded Dane; but he had been graduated from Harvard, and had worked in the wheatfields in the Dakotas and the West, much as Hamsun did, and almost at the same time. He was known in the drawing rooms of London and Paris, and my sister, who loved oratory and urbane manners just as my mother did, was carried away by his conversation and his public addresses on international questions. The wedding was reported in the Chicago newspapers just as if the parties to it were of the nobility; and very soon they were in Chicago to attend the division of the estate.

I was still the guardian of my sister's children, and my position soon became trying beyond words. I had come to the conclusion after my long study of the will of 1877 that my sister had no legal interest in the estate; yet naturally I wanted her to have one, but as a guardian of infants I could not consent that she take one. Carl having died before the period of distribution of his father's estate, the question of her dower was greatly embarrassed. Quarrels among the heirs about this and the other matter impended every day; and soon the large law firm of which Judge Payne, of the Groveland Avenue days, was the head loomed as the lawyers who would take this piece of business away from me. I knew every word of the will and all the law connected with all its clauses from those two years' study, and I could not bear to lose this business, seeing that my sister and her children were interested in the estate. I was always able to plan the campaign of a lawsuit, to play chess with it, so to speak; but to checkmate shrewd fellows in business matters puzzled me greatly, and I might as well confess that my talents never lay in that direction. So what to do now? In the first place I had to resign my guardianship, which I did and turned over the uninvested money with bank interest to my successor. And then one day after there had been much talk about filing a chancery bill to dissolve the trust under the will of 1877, and to vest the title in the heirs, my sister's children and the rest, a meeting of all the lawyers and heirs was called in the office of Judge Payne; and there the judge, looking sardonic and acting pontifically, presided, and posed as of old. It was known that I had studied the will and knew more about it and the law of it than anyone. Judge Payne, a lawyerlike mind but not a well-read lawyer, certainly not a profound one, led off by asking who would file the bill to divest the title to this large Chicago property; also, what would the fee be? I spoke up at once and said that I would do it for $1,000. That was my way to act quickly and to take a stand that could not be undercut. The judge remarked, "That's dirt cheap." And so I got the job and finished it. Not one of those ivory-headed people of splendid flesh ever offered me a dollar more. I got a check from each of them at the conclusion of the business for $250. But my sister scarcely understood that I could not fight for her; and her children never understood why I had resigned my guardianship, and what I had done to protect their interests. While the Great Dane, thinking that I had done everything to prevent him from getting his hands on a fortune, became my enemy. However, he and my sister were soon back in London and Paris with about $40,000 which an ingenious lawyer named Albert Kales, representing my sister in the suit, had managed to get for her by adroit metaphysics in the law, in which he was an adept.

With one thing and another I had in bank now $12,000, which I tried in vain to invest. I looked over Wabash Avenue property and refused to put my money there, and wisely. I didn't look at North Side property. If I had foreseen the development of North Michigan Avenue, which came as the result of the new bridge over the river in that thoroughfare, that $12,000 would have made me very well off. Houses on the cross streets in the neighborhood of the Drake Hotel, when it was built, could have been bought for five to seven thousand dollars. They became worth many times that much when business began to advance toward Chicago Avenue. I tried to be wise in business, I was diligent in it, I strained to see what was the best part of Chicago in which to invest my money. I couldn't see. All I did was to refuse to buy property in South Wabash Avenue, where I certainly should have lost my money. That much I foresaw.

In that desperate spring of 1911 when I had no congenial companions, but only men of the world friends at the club where I swam, where I walked about at night, and went about at times by day trying to find a friend, I joined the Chicago Literary Club composed of solemn, erudite lawyers, and amateur writers. It was just a poor makeshift for my famishing heart. The meetings were preceded by a dinner where a member, a judge he was, drank much Scotch and consumed large steaks. Afterward he sat stuffed and somnolent as someone read a paper on the Mendelian law or something else equally technical. Tagore came to one of our dinners, and stood by a table with his hands folded in front of him, and spoke, in a scarcely audible voice, of poetry, looking about him with diffident eyes. He meant nothing to me at the time. I was asked to read a paper before the club, and with a half-heart composed one on Browning and Tennyson. It was one of the feeblest efforts of my whole life. All in all the club palled on me; I began to miss meetings, and finally ceased to attend.

Ah, yes, in the Fine Arts Building there was Angela. I had known her as a girl of thirteen as she looked in the apartment building where my sister first lived. She was then heralded as a child prodigy on the piano; and I took her once to the White City Club, presided over by Mrs. Holden, who was then writing a column for the *Chronicle,* called "A String of Amber Beads." Here Opie Read and others told stories; and amateur poets read their poems, and local singers, and those recruited from the theaters, sang. By this time Angela was thirty; she had been married and divorced and married again. She had been put on a conspicuous musical program, and being seized with stage fright, had failed. That was followed by a nervous collapse; and when she was well again she took to teaching. Her career as an artist had failed. Straying about, perhaps at some time when I was in the Fine Arts Building attending a meeting of the Literary Club, I saw Angela's name on the directory of the building. I knocked at her door one day. She opened and greeted me with enthusiastic delight. She had grown voluptuous, she showed the effects of drink, her eyes were wise and weary. Her first remark to me was: "You are suffering! Yes, I know."

She then proceeded to tell me that she had been deserted by a lover, to tell me at once all about her life, about her marriage, her adulteries, her heartbreaks one after another. I did not give her my confidence; but she saw that I was in a mood to philander, and perhaps with her. But when I thought of the girl of thirteen with pigtails down her back, and then looked at this embittered woman, schooled in treachery and bitten with skepticism of love and truth, I drew away.

Before the days of Deirdre I had fared happily with some lawyer friends at the Bismarck Gardens, and elsewhere. Those were occasions of great, free delight. We drank sparkling Burgundy, and fed on steaks, and listened to the music.

Those old friends had drifted away. Some had taken wives and settled their lives. I tried vainly to bring some of them together again with me, thus to revive past delight. Every attempt to re-create my life, to find the path again, failed me.

I had utter loneliness, and boredom, walking, and swimming, and attending to my law business. With everything else, I had evidence that Deirdre had taken another lover. What was there in life but self-interest, passion, and falsehood?

For some time now I had been hearing from Reedy three or four times a week. Sometimes he printed a poem of mine. I had seen with my own eyes the tireless work of Bryan to keep the Democratic party from disintegrating under the machinations of the East, which was striving to turn its career back to the days of Tilden and especially of Cleveland. I wanted Bryan to have a third trial at the presidency. Finally when Woodrow Wilson was nominated Reedy wrote me that he did not know much about him, and he wanted me to write something about him for the *Mirror*. I knew nothing about Wilson, save that he had been a college president and was governor of New Jersey. Neither of these things spoke very much to me for his democracy. So to write this article I bought Wilson's *History of the American People* and read the six volumes through. His faint praise and sometimes condemnation of Jefferson, and his preference for Hamilton, settled Wilson for me. I turned from his work convinced that Wilson was another Alton Brooks Parker, that he was not a Democrat. And I so wrote Reedy, who published my letter without disclosing the identity of the writer, and with damnatory remarks of his own. Later than this Bryan came through Chicago and asked me to call upon him at the University Club. When he asked me how I liked Wilson I replied that he would not do, and told him what I had learned by reading Wilson's work. Bryan then said that if I were a Presbyterian I would understand that a man can have a change of heart. "Not at fifty-six," I retorted. But moreover I was thinking that a Presbyterian change of heart was merely a matter of changing coats. Having resolved to have no more to do with politics and to stick by poetry and literature, I took no part in this campaign.

It would be ridiculous to test a man's moral character by his fidelity to the cause of free silver, the Democratic creed of 1896 and 1900; but there was everything involved in those campaigns of Americanism and Democracy as against European domination and Toryism. In 1896 Wilson opposed Bryan; in 1900 when the real question was whether America would adhere to its principles as a republic he did nothing for the Democratic party. Then the years went on until Bryan failed entirely, though keeping the devoted adherence of more than six million voters. True to his puerile ideas of the Christian life, he came forward and delivered his wand of leadership and his following to the Anglophile Wilson who by this time was trying to make the country believe that he was something of a radical and had a plan for a new freedom. He didn't have democratic convictions, and he had no plan of any moment. His real character came forth when he made appointments to office. He put House and Page in positions of great authority and these two led us into the World War and ruined America for years to come, while the Bryan who had made him and given him all his power was thrust aside as a visionary, as a man from Nebraska without solid worth. He put the gold Democrat, McReynolds, on the Supreme Court Bench, a perfect reactionary. So at last the gold Democrats showed with terrible results what they were in their essential beings, and what they meant to America as Americans.

When Wilson was elected Bryan wrote me from Florida, and wanted me to start the necessary campaign to be appointed judge of the Circuit Court of Appeals in Chicago. In talking with Judge Kenesaw M. Landis, who was a walking companion of mine at the time, I took to this idea. Landis said that I could write opinions with one hand and poetry with the other, and would have the time to do so. Besides, we agreed about many economic questions, while the court above him as then constituted reversed him more than he relished. Hence in time I secured the endorsement of all the Supreme Court judges of Illinois as well as those of the lower courts; and finally I had the support of the Democratic Congressional delegation of Illinois. Later Senator Kenyon, at Landis's instance, came to my aid. In the Wilson cabinet I had the aid of Secretary William B. Wilson as well as Bryan. It looked like a formidable array of adjutants. Bryan took up the matter with President Wilson in a conversation or two. I must say that if I had been a Republican, and the President a Republican, considering what I had done in politics and what I had written to bring on what Wilson was calling the New Freedom my appointment would have been a matter of course. In fact, I should have been pursued to take the place. The end of the story can be better told a little later. I embarked upon this ambition just to care for my family obligations and yet to have time for literature. But in truth I was repeating the course I had followed when joining the Calumet Club. I didn't belong on the bench, not in those days, at least.

My life at home was now one of splendid neutrality, except that I had great happiness with the little girls. My attachment to the elder of the two was almost mystical. Her strange gray eyes filled at times with meditation and dreams fascinated my imagination; and then perhaps her elusive ways helped to lead me on after her. At times I thought she was closer to me than anyone in the world; then Marcia's dark Masters eyes and her more artistic nature, as it seemed, made her an object of more passionate interest. But at times I felt that neither one gave me the love that I gave them. I also divined that they cared more for their mother than they did for me. My mother, who visited us rather frequently in these days, sat with observing eyes on my family scene. Later she told me that these daughters and my son, for that matter, were being won away from me by my wife. I didn't see it then. And my opinion now is that my wife was doing what women will do in the face of domestic catastrophies: that they will build up with the children support and sympathy for themselves. Sometimes Madeline would break forth into some expression that thrilled my heart. One time I was in Milwaukee on business when she was not more than seven years old. When I returned I found her in bed with a serious throat infection. She was very ill and blood was coming from her mouth. She sat up with all the serious authority of Cromwell's daughter, and said, "You are the father of me, and you know how to take care of me." Her mother had been nursing her without a doctor. So I took everything in hand with a doctor and a nurse and brought her back to health.

Aye, but these illnesses and the operations for tonsils and adenoids, and the hospital expenses for my son who was run over while riding a bicycle contrary to my injunctions, but by the secret permission of his maternal grandmother! This cost me a cool $1,000. The money went as fast as I could earn it, what with these things and for maids and groceries, and for office rent and taxes and coal bills, and insurance premiums. One day a month I had my secretary, Jacob Prassel, drawing checks which I signed at the end of the day, depleting a bank account that had been filled during the past thirty days. Then I had furnished the house with Gorevan rugs, with some pictures, some nice pieces of mahogany; and I was adding to my library all the time, until I had many hundreds of books, all ranged on either side of the mantel in the living room. My Hindu hymns and Oriental books I kept in my bedroom upstairs; and a great lot of the classics in the Bohn edition in a case in the entrance hall. For the rest, I did not spend money on myself. My suits were very inexpensive, I had but one club, the one where I swam, I did not drink to speak of, I did not gamble, I had no expensive vices, if vices at all.

Jacob Prassel was a German youth who had been a clerk in our office in the Ashland Block. He came to the Marquette Building and asked to become my secretary, and I was glad to have him. He was intelligent, and he was the fastest and best stenographer and typist I had ever had, perhaps except Stella. But he was a useful aid in many ways. He had an agreeable manner and could receive people graciously, or with a bland way say to them that I was out, and thus bow them away and save me time. He knew how to interview witnesses and to take affidavits, and he knew the run of the courts. It was his way to sit in the outer office reading either law or some serious book, and there to guard my door. One day he stepped in my private office smiling all over his face, as he generally smiled when making announcements. But now he radiated expectation. I thought some wonderful client had come. Jake said, "A gentleman here named Dreiser to see you." "Who is he, Jake, do you know?" "Very tall and well dressed." So I said "Show him in," and in walked Theodore Dreiser!

He was wearing a heavy coat with fur collar, and looked distinguished. His eyes were full of friendliness and a kind of merriment. I noticed his buck teeth, which were very white and well cared for, and I studied his long fingers when he took off his gloves. He had come to get the names of lawyers, editors and businessmen who knew Yerkes, who ten years before this had been the streetcar magnate in Chicago, and had been ousted from his power by an indignant people. Dreiser went on to say that he was going to write a novel around Yerkes, that he had looked into the careers of twenty American capitalists and that Yerkes was the most interesting of all of them. So I gave Dreiser the leads he wanted; and after a brief call he went his way. However, we lunched together later and I saw a good deal of him during the several weeks he was in Chicago this time. One time we walked to 22nd Street on Michigan Avenue and back while he told me the plot of a contemplated novel which he intended to call *The Bulwark*. It all sounded as if he had known my father-in-law, considering what he said about the central character of the book he was meditating. The good man who loved God and kept his commandments, and for a time prospered and then went into disaster, had been selected by Dreiser for ironic portrayal. On another walk he outlined to me a philosophical work that he was about to write. His mind was seething with ideas and plans, and I was astonished at its strength and fertility. In fact, I was not long in seeing that he was much greater than his books. If Dreiser could write as he talks he would be one of the most humorous of men, for one thing; for another, he would not be the prolix and confused handler of words that he is. In conversation he can tell a tale or draw a character quickly and to the point. In fact his odd staccato way of talking, his elisions disposed of by saying "Don't you know," his chuckles and laughter as he proceeds add immensely to the vividness of what he says. But all the while one is impressed with the power of his mind, and with the vast understanding that he has of people, of cities, of the game of life. I have never seen anyone who knew as much of these things as Dreiser does; while, on the other hand, I perceived at once that he didn't know much about literature, though more than he is sometimes credited with knowing. We had delightful talks together.

He was back in Chicago in 1914 when I took him to Oakford, Illinois, to stay overnight at the home of John Armstrong, the son of Jack who had been defended by Lincoln for murder. This was the case in which the position of the moon figured, and in which Lincoln used an almanac. John was a fiddler and a famous storyteller. Besides, he was wonderfully hospitable; and his wife Caroline provided a table of great variety and abundance. John had been my father's boyhood friend. They had been separated more or less during my father's residence in Lewistown. Since 1906 they had been chums and hunting companions. Dreiser sat by the base-burner in John's little house in Oakford, folding and unfolding his handkerchief, and laughing quietly to himself as John told neighborhood tales and played the fiddle. He was as much fun to watch as John himself, as he sat there clothed in the exhaustless patience which stands him in such stead in gathering facts and writing. On such occasions, and others, too, for that matter, Dreiser seems tenderly affectionate, with a kind of pliant humanism; but then he may suddenly break forth with a sort of gargoyle ferocity; and he can be the most boorish, the most unfeeling of men, just as on this occasion when he got off the train at Springfield where we took a train for Oakford he treated my father, who was there with me to meet him, with unexplainable discourtesy. My father would have given him much to interest him if he had known how to get it. I had talked much to Dreiser about my father, about his stories out of the soil, and his great knowledge of that part of Illinois. Dreiser may have wanted to show me that he cared nothing about such things and less for my father; but I was surprised that he was not arrested by my father's appearance, since he had the distinguished face and figure of Edwin Booth. Other people have told me of Dreiser's bad manners with them. One man in particular confided to me that Dreiser came to see him when his mother was lying dead and Dreiser acted a sort of godlike unconcern about it, as much as to say that under the aspect of eternity the death of a mother was the death of an ant. This stuffing of Spinoza into a tin cup lacks logic, as it lacks heart. Dreiser's *Sister Carrie* and *Jennie Gerhardt* show the marks of loving care; on the other hand, some of his other stories betray the fact that money and lust figure in his psyche, and that when he dramatizes ruthless capitalists and women hunters he does so out of his own wish fulfillments. To be fair, however, we must agree with Goethe, "You are like that spirit which you comprehend," and to comprehend it you must be like it.

While my efforts to be a Federal judge were in process I came to New York and saw Dreiser again, and under very happy circumstances. I had come from Washington where I had seen Bryan, who was surprised that the appointment had not been made. I saw the attorney general, who was frank enough to say that no man over fifty would get the place, and that an applicant in Illinois who was sixty had no chance whatever. I set forth to see some congressmen and strengthened my fences by lunching with Champ Clark. I wanted to call on President Wilson, but Bryan dissuaded me. All the while I was unable to get the support of one of the Illinois senators, and I suspect I failed because my sister had always treated him with humorous patronization, as well as his wife who affected society in Chicago. And I could not pin down Governor Dunne, who skipped about with pretensions and professions which did not square with what I knew was going on. At last for some reason I wanted to see and to copy some of the letters of recommendation which I had sent the attorney general in a bound portfolio. Judge Cartwright, the chief justice of the Supreme Court of Illinois, who had beat me in the Recek case and in many others, who was a Civil War veteran and a Republican of marvelous blackness, who differed from me on the laws and lack of laws that gave or didn't give protection to the poor; Judge Cartwright who on occasion had sat out of temper when I argued cases before him, and had almost told me to desist from further argument, had written for me the most commendatory letter that I had gathered up from any source whatever. He had written President Wilson of me: "He is learned in the law and skilled in its practice and of good repute among all men." His letter consisted of about four lines.

For some reason, then, I wrote the attorney general that I would like to have the portfolio for a few days and would return it soon; and in the next mail I received it together with a letter from the attorney general's office expressing regret that I had withdrawn my candidacy for the judgeship.

Then quickly a man was appointed who was about fifty-five, and I was out and freed to write *Spoon River*. Another plan to finance myself for the leisure of literature had gone dwindling and vanished. All my life I have overestimated my strength. I thought I could write opinions as a judge and write poems too; but likely I could not have done so. Certainly it would have been out of key for a Federal judge to have written some of the *Spoon River* pieces.

Chapter XVI

THE WINTER OF 1914 CAME AND MY BANK ACCOUNT WAS
again low. I had lost the Kellan will case after vast labor, and
Jake could not understand why the jury beat me. In this state
of affairs Elizabeth Maloney, the president of the Waitresses'
Union, walked into my office. Thousands of women had gone
on a strike, a bill had been filed to prohibit them from picketing. They were charged with conspiracy to injure the business
of hotels and restaurants. I took the case at a satisfactory fee.

There was in Chicago a hotel and restaurant keepers' association concerned with making war upon the employees of
restaurants and hotels, especially when they grew insubordinate. This association had a large treasury created by the
contributions of members; it had lawyers retained by the
year; it had a system by which information was passed to
members concerning union labor, and by which a discharged
employee could not get work except by grace of the last
employer. If the waitresses were in a conspiracy against the
particular restaurant which filed the bill, this restaurant was
in a conspiracy with the hotels and restaurants against the waitresses. So, charging such a conspiracy on their part I filed a
cross bill. I brought into evidence the by-laws and orders of
the association and showed what they did to dominate labor.
After a long trial the court, consisting of three judges sitting
en banc, dismissed both charges of conspiracy, but directed a
decree so Delphic that neither I nor the lawyers for the association knew what it meant; while the press ridiculed the decree
as much as an observance of the proprieties permitted. Then
followed months of hearings on contempt charges, made every
now and then.

But while I was in the actual battle, at a time in the court-room when there was a recess, a tall man came to me with a copy of the *Mirror* which contained a poem of mine, express-ing admiration for it. He made himself known to me as Carl Sandburg, a reporter on the *Day Book,* an odd little daily. And he wanted some news about the injunction case I was in.

He was taller than ordinary, and with a martial bearing. His voice was deep and drowsy, the smile on his large loose mouth with its fleshly lips, broad and ingratiating. He wore steel-rimmed spectacles through which his gray-yellow eyes stared or grew luminous with sudden interest. He looked much like Larson, the Swedish cobbler of Lewistown, in whose shop I used to loaf years before. It was evident enough that Sand-burg was Swedish.

At once Sandburg began to call at my office for items about the injunction case; and we always had time for words on general subjects and upon poetry in particular. One day he brought for me to see a little sheaf of prose poems, or aphorisms might be the better word, which from its binding and type I took to be the production of Elbert Hubbard's press of East Aurora, New York. It was dated probably 1904; but at any rate I read it through with interest. Down in Lewistown two of the students under Mary Fisher had fallen into a style of gnomic utterance which was poetry in substance and prose in form; and these pieces of Sandburg were something of that character. In 1903 he had written "Milville" in such lines as these:

> Down in southern New Jersey they make glass
> By day and by night the fires burn on in Milville and bid
> the sand let in the light.

This observation cannot be called poetical, nor is it in any way important; and so it was with some other pieces in this sheaf. But there was a refreshing realism in them just the same. He was not following the poetical idiom, the stock imagery and the often-repeated subject matter of the prominent poets then writing. He was off on an entirely new trail. I was prepared by Ossian, Henley, and some of Goethe's poems like "Prometheus" and constant reading of the Old Testament for a disregard of rhyme and meter and for any new rhythm that a poet brought forth from his diaphragm. When Whitman died I wrote and published a poem on him, which was included in *A Book of Verses;* and I had read Whitman all those years constantly; and after him the free verse poems of Matthew Arnold, and the Greek Anthology, which whether it be translated in prose or given a verse form is still poetry. There was nothing novel therefore about Sandburg's experiments in the same direction, save when his subject was prose and his form also. What had enthralled me with Whitman from my days with Anne in Lewistown was his conception of America as the field of a new art and music in which the people would be celebrated instead of kings; and the liberty of Jefferson should be sung until it permeated the entire popular heart. I looked forward through Whitman to a republic in which equality and fraternity should bind all hearts with a culture of that profound nature which enabled an Athenian audience to sit in the Theater of Bacchus and follow with appreciative delight a tragedy by Sophocles. In that America Whitman would be the Hesiod and someone yet to arise the Homer. In the paper I read before the Fulton County Scientific Association in those far days this idea was advanced. History does not repeat itself in this way, whatever young dreamers may dream, as I dreamed.

In October of 1912 Harriet Monroe had started her *Poetry: a Magazine of Verse,* and Reedy had written me, "Yes, a magazine of verse." So far as I knew about it I thought the magazine an efflorescence of that group in Chicago which had founded the Little Room where dilettanti practiced a haughty exclusiveness, and where the lions were Henry Fuller, Hamlin Garland and some of the literary set of the University of Chicago. I had cast my fortunes with the Press Club crowd; and having done that I did not become acquainted with Henry Fuller until *Spoon River Anthology* was written; while a writer like Hobart C. Chatfield-Taylor was so much ridiculed by the men at the Press Club that I did not want to meet him. Chatfield-Taylor was one of those in authority at *Poetry*. Since 1900, at least, there had been in Chicago a circle which included the members of the Little Room, novelists like Hamlin Garland, Chatfield-Taylor, and Ottile Lilienkrantz, and poets like Harriet Monroe herself, who more or less were allied with the snobbish publishing house of Stone & Kimball. Though I saw copies of *Poetry* at times as I bought it at the newsstand, I had no interest in it, and looked upon it with indifference as one of the habitual manifestations of Chicago's amateur spirit. I may have seen Sandburg's "Chicago" when it appeared in early 1914; but later when I familiarized myself with it I looked upon it as a mere piece of interesting extravagance. I felt that he did not know Chicago, except as a city of packing plants, and criminals, and dirty alleys. It was faithful enough as a picture from the standpoint from which he had set his camera. But it was clear that Sandburg did not know Chicago as a city which had always cultivated music and the drama; he did not know it as a town of lawyers, of notable characters, of society figures, of reproductions of New York and New England culture. All the more was it strange that Chatfield-Taylor gave his vote to the prize to Sandburg for this poem. A few years before this Moody had stirred admiration with his formal odes, and one had to wonder what was going on and in what direction Chicago letters would run, if they ran at all. It was the width of the zenith and the nadir between Moody's Chicago of the "casual tongue" and Sandburg's Chicago as "hog-butcher of the world." Yet now Moody was dead, and from a thousand sources new feeling and expression were pouring into Chicago.

In a word, it was the really glorious year of 1914 that was making all America happy. After the Tory days of Taft, after the puerile imperialism of McKinley and Roosevelt, after a long domination by the trusts, after twenty years of Republican rule Woodrow Wilson was president and laws for the realization of the New Freedom were coming from a Congress that did not adjourn, but kept steadily at the task of reclaiming the country. The ideas of Ibsen, of Shaw, of the Irish Theatre, of advancing science, of a re-arisen liberty were blossoming everywhere, and nowhere more than in Chicago, where vitality and youth, almost abandoned in its assertion of freedom and delight, streamed along Michigan Avenue carrying the new books under their arms, or congregated at Bohemian restaurants to talk poetry and the drama. All this came to my eyes as though I had been confined in darkness and had suddenly come into the sunlight. Kenwood Avenue with its tinkling church bell, my law office and my study at home were not all of Chicago. I became cognizant of the Little Theatre of Maurice Browne, of various theatrical ventures, of new Latin Quarter restaurants; and in the midst of this I was in court daily for the waitresses, which was an emotional experience that revived all my slumbering humanism, and gave me eyes for a thousand new phases of life and for appreciation of the new life of Chicago, which was growing more beautiful as it had become more interesting.

About the 20th of May my mother came to visit us, and we had many long talks. She was the most fascinating of minds when she was in her best mood. She was wonderfully humorous, she was acute of perception, her mind flashed with divinations, she looked through doors and walls with those clairvoyant eyes, all this beyond nearly anyone that I have known. In our talks now we went over the whole past of Lewistown and Petersburg, bringing up characters and events that had passed from my mind. We traced these persons to their final fates, to the positions in life that they were then in. We had many sessions at this recalling of old days, and along the way I was reinvested with myself in those incarnations that had long since surrendered their sheaths to the changes of the years.

The psychological experience of this was truly wonderful. Finally on the morning she was leaving for Springfield we had a last and a rather sobering talk. It was Sunday, too, and after putting her on the train at 53rd Street I walked back home full of strange pensiveness. The little church bell was ringing, but spring was in the air. I went to my room and immediately wrote "The Hill," and two or three of the portraits of *Spoon River Anthology*. Almost at once the idea came to me: why not make this book the book I had thought about in 1906, in which I should draw the macrocosm by portraying the microcosm? Why not put side by side the stories of two characters interlocked in fate, thus giving both misunderstood souls a chance to be justly weighed? I proceeded to do this, drawing upon a fund of stories which had been accumulating for twenty years in the country and in the practice of law in Chicago. The first installment of *Spoon River Anthology* was published in Reedy's *Mirror*, May 29, 1914, and under the pseudonym of Webster Ford. My own family, Jake Prassel, Sandburg, and a little later the editors of *Poetry* were the only ones who knew I was the author. I wrote on Saturday afternoons when my office was closed, on Sundays at home, and on holidays, on the trains, at restaurants, all in the midst of the case for the waitresses. On Monday I would come to the office with a sheaf of poems, often as many as ten. Jake Prassel would smile from ear to ear as he took them and typed them for me. He was a first and ardent admirer of the work.

Then generally Sandburg would call to see what I had done; and he was uniformly and generously full of praise, as well as wonder that I could carry on the heavy work of my law practice as it then was and write these poems in such abundance. But for many years I had practiced concentration. I learned it by reading books that I did not like, but which I thought I should read; I learned it through the exercise of will, which fastened my mind upon the task in hand whatever it was. I could write, and turn to answer the telephone to talk about a case, and turn back and finish the poem.

Sandburg generally had poems to show me. He carried them in his pocket, written on rough scratch paper, sometimes they were typed, sometimes they were yet in his handwriting. Some of them had beautiful imagery, or a kind of rough tenderness. Most of them were shocking, forthright with a sudden turn of rude realism. Whitman wrote of wharves and busmen, of ships and farms, of harlots and mothers, of old men and of bright-eyed youths—all with a kind of Homeric dignity. Sandburg was celebrating bricklayers enjoying a chew of tobacco, wops selling bananas, Jews gathering up old iron and rags, grimy windows in Halstead Street, butchershops, deserted brickyards, and the gustatory delight of ham and eggs; and the weeds, sunflowers, cornfields, crows and sunsets and sunrises of the country about his suburban home. As I walked and went around with him I saw that there had come into being a Chicago of which I had had but faint intimations. The town had studios where there were painters and sculptors, it had the precursors of the flappers, and here and there men and women were living together in freedom, just as they did in Paris. This year of 1914 was miraculous, not only in Chicago but over America. But right through history one can see that these joyous periods come into being only to be quickly wiped out, and generally by war.

Summer came on and there was a pause in the waitresses' case. I took my family to Spring Lake, renting a part of a house with a great yard and many trees. Here I sat and wrote *Spoon*

River Anthology. Reedy had gone to England, leaving the *Mirror* in charge of Louis Lamb, a strange eccentrique, who wrote mystical poems and sent me abracadabra letters in many colored pencils adorned with illustrations. Every week to the extent of four to ten poems the *Spoon River Anthology* appeared in the *Mirror,* as the country began to ask, Who is Webster Ford? But there in my retreat by this charming lake, with the summer breezes blowing over me from the dunes two miles away by the fresh water of Lake Michigan, there all absorbed in this writing, and unable to set down the poems as fast as they came to me, there evil hid at my very elbow. There was a ravine between me and the place and house next north, and a broken wire fence on the line which separated the two lots of land; and in that house abode Frank Winkler, as I found out later; who as the fast friend of my brother-in-law, who as one who was married the same day that I was, who had been attached to the elevated railroad, of which my father-in-law was the president, who, in brief, depended upon these casual and unimportant things as the basis for a neighborly relationship. He bored me excessively with his blatant egotism; his gluttony and his drinking repelled me, his loquacity, in which he poured out his familiarity with history, tired me; for he was far from being an illuminated mind. In politics he was a gold Democrat and had opposed every movement which had brought on this new day of 1914. At heart he despised everything I believed in, and his envy was green and evident.

Whenever he saw me under the tree he crossed over the ravine to talk to me and to try to learn what I was doing. Finally I retreated to the house to write whenever I saw him on his porch waiting for me to take my place under the oak tree. But Frank Winkler was not the worst malice in the offing. The worst was the World War, which in the beginning of the summer had the brawling character of men more or less pleasantly drunk. It required the assassination of the Archduke Francis Ferdinand, and his wife, to throw the whole of Europe into a vast embroglio of guns and gas and knives. In truth Frank Winkler did not bring disaster at this time; while the World War destroyed the era out of which *Spoon River* came.

The little boat which plied the lake so happily arrived at noon every day with the Chicago papers. I was under the oak tree writing when it tied up one day at the dock and I got the Chicago papers and read that Europe had gone to war. The same feeling entered my heart that I had experienced in Lewistown by the grave of the Revolutionary soldier when the church bells rang joyously for the advent of war upon Spain. I never dreamed that America would be drawn into this strife; but somehow I felt ominously. It passed away and I went on writing, scarcely reading the news of Germany's advances upon France. I had to return to Chicago on business, and there in the Metropole Hotel I went on writing *Spoon River Anthology*, writing such pieces for example as "Mrs. Kessler," and walking over that part of Chicago which was reminiscent of Madam Y, Uncle Henry and Clarice. Long since was he dead and his boardinghouse further reduced from its lowly place of twenty years before.

For years before 1914, long before *Poetry* was founded, long before the fury of free verse in America, Reedy had been printing the prose poems of Turgenev and the French schools. These attracted me both for their moving simplicity and because they turned from the stock themes of poetry: Helen of Troy, the Trojan War, the mythology of the Greeks. They concerned themselves with everyday things and people, with familiar tragedies and joys in the present world. They were far away from everything American except Whitman and Stephen Crane and Horace Traubel, and even from Emily Dickinson who was not greatly known in 1914, though I was then familiar with some of her poems, and admired them with-

out reservation. In my own case, my long poetical studies, the
reading of Homer, the Greek tragic writers, Shakespeare and
all the English poets made me expert in various stops and
sounds; and after long practice with established forms I took
to a kind of free verse which was free as iambic pentameter is
free, where the lack of rhyme and the changing cæsuras, and
the varying meter give scope for emotion and music. In such
senses as these no verse is more formal than epitaphs like "Russell Kincaid," "Robert Fulton Tanner," "Thomas Trevelyn"
and many others, whose curious names I devised by recombin-
ing names I found in lists of signers of the constitution of
Illinois and in other places.

In the early fall I returned to Chicago and to the waitresses'
case which had grown tangled as the result of the decree which
no one understood. It had passed out of the hands of the judge
who believed that picketing was lawful, and out of the hands
of the judge who didn't know whether it was lawful or not,
into the hands of the Baptist member of the *banc* who was
ruling in contempt cases that picketing was punishable by fine
and imprisonment. And so I was before this judge day after
day, as the funds of the union lessened, defending women
charged with contempt of court. All the while the case was
progressing toward a stage where the decree was to be modified
and clarified in terms which expressly forbade all picketing
and every act which was done pursuant to the terrible conspiracy which these waitresses had entered into to injure the
business of restaurant and hotel keepers! My ingenious work,
which had first baffled the opposing lawyers and the Baptist
judge, was to be for nothing, and with all this time spent by
me on this cause I was to go forth with scant compensation.
But as a relief from these depressing things there was Chicago,
which was as yet unaffected by the war; and there were a
hundred new places for me to go to find forgetfulness of

fruitless toil. And there was the writing of *Spoon River Anthology*.

We had many happy gatherings at the *Poetry* office where I made friends with Harriet Monroe, Eunice Tietjens, Helen Hoyt, Alice Corbin Henderson, and where I saw the frequent visiting poets from New York and elsewhere who had come hastening west to see what it was that had struck Chicago. Along the way John Masefield made his appearance, and came to my house one afternoon in company with Mrs. William Vaughn Moody at whose house in Groveland Avenue he was staying. This house of Mrs. Moody's was not far from the apartment building where I had lived in the days of Julia. Many of the visiting celebrities took lodging with Mrs. Moody in preference to a hotel. This was true of William Butler Yeats, whom I had seen more than a decade before when he was in Chicago to lecture before the Twentieth Century Club, an unctuous and pretentious group to which I belonged when I was groping for my way and made many detours by mistake. Ridgely Torrence was also at Mrs. Moody's, and in that first autumn after *Spoon River Anthology* appeared in book form he and I took long walks together and became famous companions for a time. As a man from Ohio and an excellent poet we had much in common. Then Padraic Colum and his wife Molly were at Mrs. Moody's too, and Vachel Lindsay, perhaps more frequently than the others; and on one occasion Percy Mac-Kaye; but that was while I had pneumonia, and I did not meet him until later.

John Masefield was a sad-looking man, and a quiet man. He said little. That day at my house John Cowper Powys was there, and Powys tried in vain to engage Masefield in conversation. He never understood why Masefield acted so elusive, and I have no explanation of it. I never had more than an introductory acquaintance with Yeats. Much later than this he attended a sort of buffet supper at a club in North Michigan Avenue where Harriet Monroe, Sandburg, the *Poetry* assistant editors, and some others from New York were present. Yeats made a speech and Sandburg and I read some of our latest poems, and they were pretty audacious, as I remember it. Yeats looked amused.

Frequently we made up luncheon parties in an impromptu way while sitting about the office of *Poetry*. Nearly always some poet from afar was present. It was Sassoon, it was Ficke, it was Gibson, or Willard Wattles, or Wallace Stevens. They came so numerously to Chicago that I can't remember all of them. Whatever the group we often went to the Victor in Grand Avenue near the *Poetry* office and there had Italian food and red wine. Sara Teasdale was never in these parties when I was present; and in fact I didn't know her very well until we both lived in New York. These were happy affairs, and Harriet Monroe generally presided. All of this was immensely delightful to me, for I had been so many years tucked under tangled circumstances and in solitude. These new friends revived my spirits enormously; and in particular the friendship of Harriet Monroe, Eunice Tietjens and Alice Corbin Henderson contributed very much to the interest and the happiness of the new day which had come to me.

Harriet Monroe and her associate editors could not help but feel regretful to learn that my *Spoon River Anthology* was being published in a St. Louis periodical. It was in a sense unfitting that a Chicago production should have its appearance anywhere but in *Poetry*. But while I knew Harriet Monroe's "Columbian Ode," and was familiar with her name from reading her art articles in the *Tribune*, she knew nothing about me until *Spoon River* loomed. She had never heard of *A Book of Verses*, of *Maximilian*, of *The New Star Chamber and Other Essays*, of my prose plays, nearly all of which were printed before 1912. She did not notify me of the founding of *Poetry*, or ask me to contribute to it. But all these years I was close to

Reedy, and was publishing verses occasionally in the *Mirror*. It was therefore a matter of previous relationship that cast the *Spoon River* into the lap of Reedy. Moreover, *Poetry* was a small publication issued monthly. It could not have published *Spoon River Anthology* under two years, and then every issue would have had to be given to it. In Reedy's *Mirror*, published weekly, and devoting sometimes a page to the poems, it ran through in about six months. I could see that Harriet Monroe and Alice Corbin Henderson felt hit by the St. Louis debut of the work. Nor did *Poetry* give it the first magazine recognition. That was done by *Current Opinion* of which Edward J. Wheeler, president of the Poetry Society of America, was the editor. These little misadventures are annoying to sensitive spirits at the time; but now it can make no difference to anyone who was first to show appreciation of *Spoon River*. Long years after this H. L. Mencken told me that he tried to get some of the pieces from Reedy for the *Smart Set* of which he was editor, and that Reedy would not surrender them. I knew nothing of this until he told me; but manifestly it would not have been fitting if the poems had been scattered here and there along the months that they were being produced.

Harriet Monroe had a wonderful background in Chicago, and her spiritual roots were deep in its historic soil. Her father was a prominent lawyer who had been counselor for many of the men who became notable and rich. She knew all the leading men and women of Chicago, and was always at the most exclusive functions when she wished to be. There never was a woman of more sterling character, of more tolerant mind, of greater devotion to poetry and the arts. She knew pictures very well, and leaned toward Chinese art with intimate understanding of its beauty. As a poet she had made a record before these days. Her "Columbian Ode" may be classed with Lowell's and with Taylor's, even if not all in all so distinguished. Trained as a formal poet and living in an environment of conservative opinion, it required an enlightened and plastic mind to accommodate itself to a new art. She was at once the friend and admirer of Sandburg's work; and despite the circumstances I have related, calculated to cool her attitude toward me, she was my friend from the start. She herself adopted the new mode in such poems as "The Hotel" and many others; and much later than this time she wrote "Winds of Texas," a very fine example of free rhythms. She was skilled in the technique of verse; and she knew that poetry is thought and feeling, imagery and music rather than rhyme and meter. All the while she stood editorially for fresh creation, and the rising of new schools kept her criticism busy. Amy Lowell, of course, came to Chicago to see what was going on and to prevent anything going wrong. But Harriet Monroe handled her with tact, and for my part I think she gave her more commendation than she deserved. I did not concur in many of her judgments, but that need not concern us here, since it is not at issue.

Amy Lowell's descent upon Chicago was comparable to that of an Italian diva. She was at once given great publicity; and a poem, so called, which she had then just written on the theme of herself taking a bath gave the press just what it wanted in the way of colorful sensation. I rather shrank from meeting her; but Harriet Monroe said that it would be discourteous if I did not pay my compliments to her by calling. So I went to her suite in the Congress Hotel, where she was enthroned in state attended by a companion-secretary. She offered me a Corona cigar, and smoked two of these huge rollers of nicotine while I smoked one. We talked very pleasantly until I made some comment on a literary judgment that she had recently published; whereupon she stuck up her finger with authority and exclaimed, "Your reasons, sir?" Not wishing to get into a debate with her I glided away from the invited dialectic. But all the while I was fascinated with her eyes. They were large and blue and luminous. I have never seen more beautiful eyes, or eyes that bespoke the light that was back of them with more effulgent power. When she was preparing her *Tendencies in Modern American Poetry* she wrote me for a sketch of my life. I dictated one to Jake Prassel and sent it on to her. She included it in her book, together with inferences of her own, which my words did not justify. One was that my mother was probably a schoolteacher who had come to Illinois from New Hampshire to find prosperity in a new country. My mother was furious about this, and talked of taking Miss Lowell to task. If she had done so, New England would have met New England. In this book she did not include Lindsay, which hurt him cruelly. Her excuse for ignoring him was that Lindsay was only popularizing what I was doing, and what Sandburg was doing. That judgment was wide of the truth; but even at that Lindsay might have been mentioned as a popularizer of remarkable note. For me she had great praise then and thereafter. However, she thought that I was obsessed with sex, and wrote too much about it, and in the spirit of Strindberg besides. And that is hardly a judgment that was justified; and in fact it has passed, proving its unsoundness.

Eunice Tietjens, Alice Corbin Henderson, Agnes Lee, and Helen Hoyt all did remarkable work in these days. Eunice Tietjens had great strength, great power of visual depiction. Alice Corbin Henderson wrote some brief poems of haunting subtlety of music, and Helen Hoyt by her outspoken ideas, as well as by her radicalism in form, gave me delight and amusement, in the same way that I laughed with Sandburg and not at him. Agnes Lee was a thoughtful poet of sweet music. There was also Marjorie Allen Seiffert, who was a cultivated musician and knew how to give music to words. In fact poets, especially among the women in Chicago, sprang up all around like woodland violets in April. But also mushrooms made their appearance. The heady wine of this new interest in poetry started the half-educated, the half-formed to take their pens and their paper. There arose what might be called the School of the Half-Wits. One of these from New York was present at the Yeats dinner to which I have referred, and with the brass of his ambition got on the program where he read some lines that made Yeats look weary and wondering, and convulsed me to the core of my being. Reedy was writing me that he believed that every person in America was a poet and that he was expecting to get a sheaf of sonnets from Bryan or Woodrow Wilson.

It was in the January, 1913, number of *Poetry* that Lindsay published "General William Booth Enters Heaven," and so he had a name before I began to run *Spoon River Anthology* in Reedy's *Mirror,* and before Sandburg published "Chicago" and shocked the country. Lindsay was a little disposed to assume the role of the man who had arrived, and who looked with friendly interest on those who were arriving, and who, bless you, would surely have all the attention, entertainment, applause and acceptance that had come to him. This attitude infuriated Sandburg, who was no more taken with Lindsay's apostolic manner than I was. But in my case Lindsay's mother and mine were very good friends in Springfield; and long before I met Lindsay my mother told me of the good words that Lindsay was sowing generously everywhere in Springfield and downstate about *Spoon River Anthology.* Lindsay was ten years my junior, and I had but met him face to face when I saw that he knew little about human nature, except what his intuition taught him, and that his experiences in life were limited. His chastity and his abstention from wine or any drink amused me. At the Victor he drank water, and any visiting poetess of amatory designs might play around him as much as possible, he remained the Red Cross Knight, paying court to her as he would to the Virgin Mary. All this made him extremely gullible. On one occasion he gave a woman editor $200, which he had just received as a prize, in order to help her out of financial difficulty. She didn't deserve it, and on his part it was done with the same erotic impulse which moves the youth to hang a May basket on the door of his adored girl and then run away. The woman in question was reputed to be a Lesbian, and she took this money with sadistic smiles.

My memory is that I met Lindsay first in Springfield when I was visiting my father and mother. He brought about an invitation to both of us for dinner at the home of two handsome young women, who had known him always and had no more romantic feeling for him than they had for the middle-aged Sunday-school superintendent of their church. They called him by his given name, and treated him like a relative. After this I saw Lindsay in Chicago frequently, often at the *Poetry* office, sometimes at Mrs. Moody's house. Indoors he wore a black alpaca coat and looked like a pastor. For that matter Lindsay had no distinguishing feature. His eyes were yellowish gray and without any particular illumination such as one nearly always finds in persons whose brains are afire. His mouth was large, with the upper lip overlapping. His nose was large and fleshy. His forehead ran back. The shape of his head was that of a zero tipped back. His hair was sandy to brown in color. He looked like a Poor Pierrot. His conversation was commonplace, with chuckles, which meant nothing, interrupting its flow. He gave vent to remarks which were past understanding, for his mysticism often pressed him for expression; and if he sometimes adumbrated in verse these strange visions of his, he never did it when talking. One time when I was at luncheon with him he turned to me with sudden earnestness with the question, "What is a cat?" I had to think for a minute to see that he wanted my explanation in a cosmic way of the cat nature in a cat body. Why was this? But with everything else Lindsay was a heart of the greatest generosity and fairness, and a poet unique in American annals. I think he is America's greatest lyric poet, because his only rival, Poe, had less poetical ideas and a more limited gamut. His very last books contained lyrics of ethereal beauty, differing from his early work in both theme and melody, and full of the delicate melancholy of a dying soul.

In 1926 I saw him in New York and proposed him for membership to the Players. He was a little opposed because he had read some poems in the lounging room in a booming voice which might have disturbed members reading and writing. However, he was elected, and wrote me that he was prouder of it than anything in his life. I never saw him again, though he was about New York in the fall of 1931. My *Lincoln: The Man* offended him greatly. But by this time whatever critical or historical faculties he had ever had had been wasted by sorrow and disappointment. He was unable to weather the storm past fifty-two years of age.

Returning from Spring Lake I had to go on with the case of the waitresses with redoubled energy. And I was pouring out the *Spoon River* pieces from a reservoir that seemed exhaustless. My wife was begging me to end it, because she was anxious to see me announced as the author, and to have the work appear in a book. Except for the circumstances which followed the *Spoon River Anthology* would have been a larger book at the very first, and a much larger book in its definite edition.

In the November 20th number of the *Mirror* Reedy announced me as the author of *Spoon River Anthology* in a long article written with all the facility and the eloquence that he could so richly command when his mind and heart were stirred. I read it with a strange happiness, but with a kind of terror, a kind of sickness, such as one might feel who has died and for a moment is permitted to look down upon the body that he has abandoned. For *Spoon River Anthology* had taken out of me much that was in me. I was now running to exhaustion physically and did not know it. The waitresses' case was taking my days, my finances were low, and I was full of anxiety. The flashing of Reedy's article to New York brought on a kind of publicity which made my former anonymous life impossible, and the light in which I had to stand added to my nervousness. Besides I had to meet many people, and I was going about town to the *Poetry* office and elsewhere by way of diversion and for the recuperation of my depleted vitality. I had created hundreds of characters and exploited many tragedies. At this last stretch the flame had become so intense that it could not be seen, and I wrote with such ease that I did not realize the sapping of my life forces that was going on. I had no auditory or visual experiences which were not the effect of actuality; but I did feel somehow by these months of exploring the souls of the dead, by this half-sacrilegious revelation of their secrets, that I had convoked about my head swarms of powers and beings who were watching me and protesting, and yet inspiring me to go on. I do not mean by this that I believed I was haunted. I only mean I had that sensation, as one in a lonely eyrie room might suddenly feel that someone was in the next room spying upon him Often after writing, during which I became unconscious of the passing time and would suddenly realize that it was twilight, I would experience a sensation of lightness of body, as though I were about to float to the ceiling or could drift out the window without falling. Then I would rush out of the room and catch up one of the children to get hold of reality again; or I would descend for a beer and a sandwich. These nights I was playing on the victrola the Fifth Symphony of Beethoven, out of which came the poem "Isaiah Beethoven" in *Spoon River Anthology*. Truly I was in a hypersensitive state of clairvoyance and clairaudience, just as I was later when I wrote "The Star." That poem came from one of those moods which music or a woman frequently brought to me with all the power of a supernatural possession. This woman, one of the poetesses of the *Poetry* office who was strangely drawn to me as I was to her, had no beauty, and in fact she was so odd-looking that I wrote "Ship Shoe Lovey" using her as a model. Nevertheless, she entered into my being like some delicious drug; and as she was afraid and I was afraid, we kept away from each other. I had no romance during these years, and none until five years later.

One can see the state of mind I had come to by consulting the files of Reedy's *Mirror*. In the number of December 25th appeared "Joseph Dickson," "Harlan Sewall" and "Alfred Moir," with others which were, however, in the first realistic key. In the January 1st number appeared "Russell Kincaid," "Aaron Hatfield," "Isaiah Beethoven." In the January 15th number I epitaphed myself under the pseudonym "Webster Ford" which I had used for the work. That was the last. And I was about ready to be laid away and given a stone with these verses. For with the waitresses' case and this writing I was exhausted and did not know it. I went about as usual, but as though in a dream.

One day toward the latter part of January I was before the Baptist judge making an argument in answer to a new set of lawyers, who had moved to modify the decree in such express words that there could be no doubt that picketing was forbidden. I stood the greater part of the day fencing with the judge, and answering interruptions by these new lawyers, both of whom had spent much time in fighting labor unions, and doing the law work for employees in this kind of a proceeding. All the while I felt that I scarcely knew where I was. The inner core of things became the exterior of things, and nothing seemed real. Yet I went on. At the end of the day I tried to restore myself with a swim at the club. I had dinner with a client that evening, and went to the theater, arriving home at two in the morning in the bitter cold and dampness of a Chicago night. The next morning I awoke and stretching myself in bed felt as usual, but on arising I soon became so weak that I had to lie down. The next morning, which was Monday,

I expected to go to the office. I was unable to do so. A doctor came to see me, but could find nothing wrong with me. If he had been skillful he would have put me to bed to rest for a week, and that would have saved me the illness, I am sure, which came on in ten days.

In the meantime I was about the house, walking to and fro, fuming, smoking and sometimes taking a drink of whisky. The doctor told me that I could eat what I chose, and go out if I wanted to. But I didn't go out, though I ate imprudently. I should have been in bed all the time resting. One day I ran a fever. The next day I had none. Then I had a bad rhinitis, but that passed. I was sitting by the grate fire in my room a good deal of the time reading Dante in Italian. For the rest, I was moving restlessly about the house. One morning after ten days of this confinement had passed, and while I was reading Dante by the fire, I was struck with a chill as with the suddenness of a stroke of paralysis. It was middle January, 1915. Jumping up, I went to the dresser and took my temperature. It was 101. I undressed and went to bed. The doctor came in the afternoon and looked me over with casual eyes. He didn't know what was the matter with me, and after saying that I would be all right soon, he was about to go away, when I said, "Don't I need a nurse, doctor?" He replied, "Oh, well, it won't hurt; I'll send one to you." That evening at seven Jane, the nurse, came; a diminutive pretty woman she was. She took command of the room at once; and that night I was traveling through Spain, and heading toward the Isles of the Blest.

Chapter XVII

WHAT A SICK MAN I WAS THAT NIGHT, SICK AND RESTLESS!
Jane brought a cot into the room, and bundling herself in thick
blankets, since they kept the window up, slept by my side. It
was about 17 degrees below zero outdoors, with great banks
of wonderful white snow piled along the curbs. By day the
sunlight of this fine winter weather reflected from the snow
filled my room with glaring radiance, and cast dancing daggers
of flame on the ceiling. The next morning a solemn rawhead-
and-bloodybones entered the room softly. I knew him as the
doctor who a little before this had heard some one in his house,
and taking his Winchester had waited at the head of the stairs
until a figure crept up the landing. Then he fired, and without
a sound the burglar sank to the floor. The papers made much
of this event. He took a drop of blood from my ear; and the
report came back that I had 30,000 white cells to the cubic
millimeter of blood. In spite of the fact that these long months
of writing and practicing law had drained me almost to death,
there was still good resistance in me.

I did not know how much I had in bank. I knew it was not
much, and fearing that I might be in bed for some days or
weeks I took thought of my finances. I told my wife to see her
brother and borrow $200. He was a money lender, and she
could pledge the credit of the house, which she owned. She
didn't do this. But when my brother Tom came, as he did with
my father in about three days, for they expected me to die
knowing that I had pneumonia, my brother at the intimation of
finances offered grandly to furnish my wife with $200 a week
while I was sick. By this time he was in practical possession of
my father's law practice, and my father, his work finished,

was enjoying life with John Armstrong, the fiddler, at Oakford with whom he hunted and played. Tom did not come into the room to see me; but my father did. He stood for some minutes looking at me with his hands clasped in front of him. He might have been saying to himself, "I saw this fellow born in Kansas forty-five years ago. Now I am seventy and as young as ever, and he is ending." He told me that he was going hunting the next week with John Armstrong. I said that I would be up about then and would join them by way of a vacation. I did not then know that I had pneumonia, and I expected to be out of bed soon. My mother did not come to see me; and as for Tom's magnificent offer, nothing more was heard of it. As the next resort, therefore, my wife borrowed $200 from her brother.

With these things arranged Jane settled down to a stern fight to save my life. She reminded me of a terrier tackling a large and vicious rat. She had all the meticulous and commanding manner of the efficient nurse, and a little more than that, all hidden in her small body and her modest way of talking. Something happened at once between her and my wife. By the time her service was ended they detested each other cordially. But no sooner had Jane entered the room than I trusted her and felt myself in capable hands. She ran her hand over my brow saying with a little laugh, "You're not so sick." She was somewhat comely, but nothing to get excited about; and she didn't seem so comely when she was in one of her authoritative moments. She started to rule the sickroom with rigorous regulations. The first day she was in charge of me she locked the door, and my wife did not enter the room once that I know of until I had passed the crisis. She permitted no one but the doctor to come in, and my father, who was present but a few moments. Every night Jane smoothed down the bed and gave me codeine, or whatever she was directed to give me; then she would let down her hair, go into the bathroom to disrobe, and emerging in her nightdress she would tuck herself under the heavy blankets to protect herself against the open window. If I spoke, however softly, during the night she was up and at my side. Jane was greatly beloved by my children to whom this sickness of mine was an exciting event which had brought her into the house, as well as Grandfather from Springfield, and many people inquiring at the door about my condition.

The Macmillan Company was bringing out *Spoon River Anthology*, and the proofs came while I was delirious. Sandburg came down one evening and being forbidden by Jane to see me stayed long enough to help my wife with the evening dishes. My niece Elizabeth was about to be married in London, and I was announced as the godfather who would give the bride away. But there I was; and it depended upon Jane, my vitality and Fate whether I would get up to read the proofs of *Spoon River Anthology*, and to go about as before.

I knew where I was part of the time, I talked to Jane rationally enough. But then I would drift away. I had a form of schizophrenia, for there seemed to be two of me: one who was sick and in danger, one who was not sick and whom nothing could hurt. The words ran through my mind quite definitely, "That fellow there is in a bad way, and will probably die; but as for me I am safe." Later toward the last I heard at times the sound of a bugle blowing "thin and clear" from a height far off, as if from Elfland. Then I heard symphonic music, more beautiful than I had ever heard any orchestra play, and of a richer, more sublime sort. Then the bugle would blow. Finally I saw a black disk like a victrola record. Above it was suspended, as if it had touched and ascended from the disk, a phosphorescent tongue of light. That was the last I knew until I felt myself swinging up and down on a vast warm tide of ocean water. Nothing could have been more delightful than that rhythmical movement of those giant swells and falls. It was a gray light that I awoke in at last. It was eight o'clock in the morning on a Wednesday just a week to the hour since I had been struck by the chill. There stood Jane shaking the thermometer. When she saw that I was in possession of my mind she said triumphantly, "You're well." The fever had left me and she went to the kitchen to prepare some oyster soup. Coming back she had to feed me. I could not lift a hand.

In a few days visitors were admitted to see me. Harriet Monroe came to congratulate me on my recovery. Her small, durable physique had weathered an attack of pneumonia, and I believe more than one. She knew what peril there was in this cruel invasion of the pneumococci. She sat looking at me as she corrected the proofs of *Spoon River Anthology*. Ay, but I had had pleurisy too, which left me with a corneous nodule on the pleural wall. It scratched wickedly and in a way to drive me frantic with nervousness, and my side had to be bound with surgeon's plaster. And that right lung of mine! It felt like tough cowhide, impervious and dead, through which air would not pass. So I lay there for three weeks. Jane made me get up one day; but when I tried to stand on my feet my knees started to buckle, and it was days yet before I could walk to the big chair and half recline and half sit in it to rest me from the bed. Finally I got out to take a walk with my wife. She seemed strangely silent at my side. The weather was still cold, and I had agoraphobia, and dumb tears oozed from my eyes. My wife wanted me in the interest of economy to discharge Jane; but I felt that I could not get along without her for a while yet. And so she stayed on. While I was yet in bed I had diverted Jane with stories and bits of humorous verse. She laughed uproariously at these half-hysterical sallies of mine. And I laughed, too, with as much heartiness as I ever did in my life. I laughed because I was getting well; and then there was the mood that shouted to retreating Death the challenge of humor.

My wife renewed her requests that I let Jane go. But she

had grown to be such an agreeable companion, and she knew so well how to do what I could not do for myself that I could not bear to part with her. I was attached to Jane, as was natural. She had served me with great skill and fidelity, she had saved my life. That summer when I was writing fifty more pieces for the definitive edition of *Spoon River Anthology* I drew Jane in the epitaph on "Paul McNeely." But at last Jane had to go. The expense of keeping her was too much. And I could manage without her. As she left the children wept bitterly, and Jane wept, and I took her hand full of grateful emotion. She went to visit her people in Danville, and after some weeks returned with a box of candy which she had made for the children. My wife received it coldly, and Jane turned away full of hard resentment. To this day I don't know why my wife disliked Jane so intensely. She hadn't the least reason to be jealous.

The May days came and I was not myself yet. I would arise feeling rested and powerful. An hour at the office made me so weak that I had to lie down, even though I had done nothing but read letters. And my finances were growing exigent. If I took a drink of whisky for a pickup it made my lung feel more leathery than before. I got no stimulation from it. Finally I decided to go to French Lick which I had visited several times before. This great hotel of Pluto water was run by Tom Taggart, known as the gambler, and much berated by Bryan. What he did was to furnish rooms where guests could play roulette and chuck-a-luck, as they are played in the Kursaalen of Europe. In addition he had horses to ride, a golf course on which to play. The food was excellent, the service admirable, and he himself was the most genial host I ever knew. He stood in the lobby smiling and talking with guests and making inquiries if your room was satisfactory, or if there was anything he could do to add to the delight of your visit. The country about the hotel is hilly, and I tried some climbing, but my breath was short, and my heart beat too fast at times. Yet I walked, for the spring flowers were out, and the birds were singing. At other times I sat in my room reading *Spoon River* in book form, and wondering about this creation which had come from me and now seemed to have no relation to me. I was in a pensive and faraway mood, and in a way still going through a schizophrenia.

In the midst of this season of convalescence I received a telegram from my sister, who had fled from Europe, and was in Chicago waiting for me to return to file a bill for divorce for her from the Great Dane. She asked me to come to Chicago at once, that it was important. So I went. She was staying at the Chicago Beach Hotel, near where I lived, and I went to see her. I found the weather raw in Chicago, whereas it had been mild in French Lick. My back wrinkled into nervous premonitions of another chill, such as I had suffered when pneumonia struck me. If I hadn't been assured that I could scarcely have pneumonia so soon again after the thorough infection through which I had passed, I should have been in terror; in fact, I was not fully convinced that I might not have a relapse. Yet with my overcoat buttoned up around my neck I sat in Jackson Park with my sister and listened to her shocking relation of what she had endured. She was going into further details when I grew very faint, and told her that I could stand no more. It is enough to say that a large amount of her fortune had been dissipated by the Dane, she had lost $14,000 worth of jewelry, and her boy, then two years old, was at stake. I refused to take her case on the ground of professional impropriety in doing so. But I took her to Alfred Austrian, who didn't handle divorce suits. But when I told him that I would do all the work but the trial of the case, which his skill and energy would be requisitioned to fight the warlike Dane, he consented generously to act, saying that he would do anything for me that he could. He had his office look into the law, and I made a brief. We met then to confer and agreed that my sister would have to live in Illinois for a year before she could file her bill. She was greatly disappointed with this news, as she wanted to return to Europe. I advised her to get a small house and read; or to renew her study of sculpture at the Art Institute. I wanted her near me where she could see my children frequently, and where I could call upon her in the evenings without too much exertion; for I was saving myself these days. Instead of doing this she went to the North Side, to a hotel where the society reporter of the *Tribune* lived, an old friend of hers. And from there she went to Lake Forest, where she cleaned and painted her summer house, which had long been unoccupied; and buying a car began to amuse herself with entertaining the society reporter and some others. As she was thus thirty miles away from me I saw her but a few times that summer, and always then I went to her. She and my wife were on less cordial terms than ever.

Yes, and how I was troubled by finances now! The expenses of my illness, including Jane and the doctor, had not been very great; but the bills for living went on, and I was making nothing. Also there was that loan of $200, and my wife's brother wanted his money and asked me for it. With all this I was tortured with my lung; and I was in that sensitive state where one imagines that no one cares for him. I was lonelier than ever. Sandburg was not so cordial as formerly. I was tottering one day on Michigan Avenue when I met him. He stopped with jealous fury in his eyes. He had read about the London wedding of my niece, and what right had a man born to the manner of Illinois to have a niece married to an English lieutenant under all those fashionable circumstances, with myself announced as the uncle who would have given away the bride except for his illness? Besides all this, the daily publicity about *Spoon River Anthology* filled me with nervous diffidence. I dodged about in order not to be seen; I went to little restaurants in order not to meet people whom I knew. I sat in my office waiting for law business, troubled beyond measure about money. Clients did not come in, but people from New York and over the country called to see me as the man who wrote *Spoon River*, and to ask without end how I happened to write it, and where I got the idea.

Before Reedy announced me as the author he came to Chicago to urge me to reveal myself. We talked all afternoon about it, with my wife begging me to do so, while I pleaded that my law business would be ruined if I were known so generally as a poet. Reedy replied that it was no difference if my law business were ruined, that I could make a living writing; and besides, why after these long years of obscure labor deny myself the full fruit of this success? One had to die, one had to incur disaster, no matter what one did. I might have died of pneumonia, but I had lived to see *Spoon River* published. I was asked to look at life and my own life not under the casual aspect of the law business, and making a living, but under the broader view of an opening career which could not be abandoned, and which was more important than the law business, come what might. Finally I turned to both of them and said, "I know what I am talking about. But you two may take the responsibility." In these days now back in the office I could see at once that clients did not come to me. I heard that the report was about that I had closed my office, that I was in New York, that I had gone to England. But, on the other hand, suppose I did get clients again, what should I do with these surging themes that rolled up in my mind, with the material that I had which I had not yet touched? Should it be killed and buried?

One day Henry Fuller came to my house to see me, accompanied by the representative of a New York weekly. This was my first meeting with Fuller. The agent thus introduced by Fuller wanted to engage me to write a column a week, using

Spoon River material for prose portraits. These periodicals are always watching for new men, for new sensations. Here I had created a new form, and this agent, a literary man himself, and his periodical naturally were willing to have me reduce my style to the popular demands of a million circulation weekly. If I had done this my material would thus have been used up, and I should have had nothing but a little money. And at the end of it the periodical would have discarded me. I refused at once, much to the surprise, and even the indignation, of the agent. That door of money was closed. I did not then fully know, as I knew later, that these periodicals do not want the best work, and that they will not buy from the best writers, except where those writers can by possibility lower themselves to the taste of the plebeian readers whom they cultivate. In this case, as I was a novelty at the time, I was acceptable, especially if I would use prose, and write so that the populace could understand me.

One May day of weary wondering as to what I should do a short powerful man was brought into my private office by Jake Prassel. He was a St. Louis lawyer with a Chicago client. He had come to ask me to try a great case that could be easily won, and there was a large fee in it. The client was Helen Lee, who was the niece of Thomas Bermingham, lately deceased, a paper dealer who had left several hundred thousand dollars. The story was that Helen Lee's mother, who was Bermingham's sister, lay dying of cancer. She was anxious about the future of Helen Lee, then but ten years old. She offered to let Bermingham, her brother, have Helen as his daughter to raise in the Catholic faith, provided that Bermingham would legally adopt Helen and make a will leaving her his fortune. This Bermingham promised to do. There were two witnesses to the promise. Helen's mother had died. Helen had taken her place in Bermingham's home, and had lived with him as his daughter until her recent marriage to Owen Lee. Bermingham's wife had died. He didn't make the will, he never adopted Helen by formal proceeding in court. One day while saying to a friend that the next day he was going to court to adopt Helen he fell dead. Just a few weeks before this he had married again; and the new wife had been appointed administratrix, and as such was in possession of the money and securities of the estate. This was the case.

I had never had a case like this; I wasn't familiar with the law of such a case. The St. Louis lawyer told me that he had fifty witnesses whose statements he had taken, and that the case, as he outlined it, could be fully substantiated. I did not feel well enough to read these statements; nor was it necessary before I knew whether the law was on our side. The St. Louis lawyer had a brief which he drew forth and showed me. I glanced through it, seeing at once that he did not know how to make a brief. He was very insistent that I should take the case and try it, and finally I told him to leave his brief with me and I would look it through. He went away saying he would be back the next morning.

In the meantime I could not bring myself to read the brief. I had had so many cases that required enormous labor, and even skill, as in the recent case for the waitresses. Was I always to have these desperate causes, and few of easy money? The St. Louis lawyer returned the next morning promptly and was manifestly disappointed that I had not read his brief. He went away saying that he would be back the next morning; and true to his word he appeared. I had not yet read his brief. Whenever I looked at a lawbook I became so fatigued and nervous that I had to lie down. The St. Louis lawyer showed impatience now; and I promised that I would be ready to talk the law with him the next day. Then I scanned the brief. He had cited one case that was in point and well considered, a New York case it was. I saw that there was a chance to win for Helen Lee; and I told the St. Louis lawyer so when he came for my answer. So I signed a contract to try the case; and as soon as I could summon strength I made a brief of the law, finding many more cases than the St. Louis lawyer had found, and many on important points which were involved closer to the facts of our case.

But truly I was a tottering man. I saw that I would have to get life in me in order to fight the irascible and contentious lawyer who represented Bermingham's widow. My nephew Buddie had come to Chicago following his mother; and with him and my son Hardin I went to St. Joe, Michigan, to play golf for two weeks. These youths, now sixteen, were as full of life and frolic as two young police dogs, and they took their part as guardians and companions admirably. I returned in better strength, and the case was set to begin on July 7th before Judge MacDonald, an excellent lawyer and a fine gentleman. Also, as it turned out, he knew the law of a case like this thoroughly, so that I didn't have to argue points about the Statute of Frauds, and the like.

The morning the case was to start I met the brother of my adversary. These two were not friends, owing to a quarrel about their father's estate. This brother told me that his brother was very disagreeable in court, but that he was a coward; and if I hit him at once and hit him hard he would lie easy to my hand. The first thing that morning my adversary in stating the facts to the chancellor remarked that the case was blackmail; whereupon I hit him with some retort as hard as I could, and true to the prophecy he wilted. For twenty-two days we took evidence before a jury. At night I came home exhausted and went to bed to twitch for hours before I could sleep. It went over town that I was trying this case. Sandburg and Harriet Monroe came in to see me box with the ill-tempered man, who fought without weariness as he went to his knees. The judge was with me from beginning to end. My adversary made feeble references to me as the author of the atrocious

Spoon River Anthology, and the judge smiled. I won the jury, and the judge set the motion for a new trial for a speedy hearing. Meantime I was getting letters from New York to come east and let the people see me. I think I had a letter from Dreiser to this effect. At any rate when the motion for a new trial was overruled, and the decree entered giving Helen Lee all the property, I went to New York, and to a hotel on Washington Square.

Soon I saw Edward C. Marsh, of the Macmillan Company, who wanted another book of verse as soon as I could assemble it. But he said: "The critics are sharpening their pencils. They won't let you repeat the success of *Spoon River* if they can help it." I remembered then what Goethe said by quoting some witty Frenchman, which was "If a clever man has once attracted attention of the public by any work of merit, everyone does his best to prevent his ever doing the like again." Marsh's words did not alarm me; for I was resolved to put forth the best work that I could, and to let time deal with it; and I felt confidence in that course of events which rarely allows good work to be lost. This summer and fall, however, I was occupied in writing an epilogue to *Spoon River,* and in adding to the pieces portraits which I had not drawn, but was meditating when circumstances forced me to close the pages of the book as it was first printed. But I was willing to accede to Marsh's request for a new book; though it is bad policy for a writer to hurry himself, and just as bad for a publisher to spur a writer forward even if it is done to reap the interest of the public while it is keen and fresh.

During my month in New York at this time I did not do any writing. I was having too much entertainment, I was meeting too many interesting people to withdraw for composition. And I needed the rest of all this happiness and diversion which poured around me so generously. Dreiser was most cordial, even brotherly. His sister, a kindly woman, had an apartment in 11th Street, west of Sixth Avenue, to which I was invited to come for a room. But I preferred the hotel which was near to Dreiser's house at 165 West 10th Street. I learned, not then but later, that Dreiser had somehow got proof sheets of *Spoon River* and had given them to John Cowper Powys; and he had used them as the basis of his lecture on me which was contemporaneous with Reedy's thundering announcement in the *Mirror*. But I did not meet Powys on this visit to New York, and not until that fall in Chicago.

I was interviewed and pictured and entertained at gay suppers in Greenwich Village, which was then at the height of its Bohemian glory and vitality. But the largest and most rollicking party that I was honored with was given by Dreiser, where artists and writers from over town were present. There in his rooms in West 10th Street under the light of many candles, with some kind of decoration of flowers, we came together in the most gay and cordial manner. Dreiser walked the floors laughing and joshing. His immense humor fairly boiled over. His teeth stuck out, his face was red from health and excitement. His eye turned up with added bubbling of spirits, as he folded his handkerchief and poured forth thunder-lizard words. Altogether he was the most waggish, quizzical serio-comical, grotesque, whimsical character I had ever seen. He kept the company in roars of laughter. He seemed to know everyone present intimately, both men and women, and he addressed them as he walked back and forth in the first piece of banter or chaffing that came into his mind. The party centered around my reading from *Spoon River;* and at last, with my lung hurting me and my breath short from diffidence and excitement, I took my place under a lamp and read, as those pretty women and interesting men were grouped about me. Dreiser sat very still, making no comment, but looking with concentration as he folded his handkerchief. I wrote a poem entitled "Theodore Dreiser," which was published in *The Great*

Valley in 1916; and I may say here that *Songs and Satires,* my first book after *Spoon River,* was also published in 1916 as well as the definitive edition of *Spoon River.*

During the month that I was in New York I saw Dreiser almost every day. Sometimes we walked together, sometimes we ate together; but nearly every night I was at his house. One night a large party of us, Dreiser included, took a bus ride far uptown. I saw that I was expected to choose some girl from this fascinating collection of pretty women. But my psyche seemed to be dwelling in infinity, I was far off, and it was with an effort that I was bringing myself back to earth. I had wandered to some galactic sphere so distant and alien to human life and its creative passion that I was returning only by slow degrees. Taking count of men whose confidences I have had I have known many who regretted rosebuds that they failed to pick, but few who regretted those they had added to the bouquet of life's experience. Here were these pretty women all about me, all in a mood of lighthearted sportiveness, all interested in me as the new man of the hour, and I was moving among them in a trance. I was taken for a cold man, for a sexless man, for a woman hater, and all the while I was just an ill man.

On this bus ride quite suddenly as I was looking at the scene on Fifth Avenue I thought of the scheme by which I might use the material for what later became *Domesday Book.* Back in Lewistown when Will and Reese and I spent our evenings in my father's law office talking logic and philosophy, the idea of a story came to me which I wrote at the time, but never published. The manuscript of it on newspaper copy paper is still among my papers. I imagined a group of four or five young men similarly engaged as we were in discussion and study. One of them, a skeptic and misanthrope, committed suicide. The others came into the room and looked at the tragic scene. When they took in hand to report what they saw they differed from one another in many details, some important, some trivial, just as I had seen witnesses do in the cases that I saw my father try. They also gave varying and contradictory analyses of the suicide's character, and even of his physical appearance. I have observed that few people can remember the color of the eyes of their friends and acquaintances, something that I always take note of with particular care. That story which came back to me on this bus ride after that long lapse of twenty-five years or more was the germ of *Domesday Book.* And I mention this here to say that I wrote that story before I ever read a line of Browning's *Ring and the Book,* and perhaps before I ever heard of it, to which *Domesday Book* has been likened.

On this trip to New York I brought with me the script of Sandburg's *Chicago Poems* to find a publisher for him. I submitted the book to two different publishers who declined it. For if I was assailed for *Spoon River* Sandburg was beaten with cudgels at first. Edward J. Wheeler called him a horse fiddle. And thus he may have been given a part of the rotten eggs that were intended for me, and which could not always be cast at me because of the popularity of *Spoon River.* Some critics using that timeworn weapon of killing a writer off by saying that he merely follows in the footsteps of another writer called Sandburg's work an imitation of mine. There never was anything falser. He had written but one poem at that time, or near that time, which was a character picture. That one called "Chick Lorimer" was as different from my work as the great difference between our inner and outer eyes could make it. For the rest, his subjects and his rhythms, his visualizations and his vocabulary had no resemblance to mine. The state of poetical criticism was at a low level at this time, for America was coming out of the slumber into which it had been sunk by the various Knickerbocker schools, which represented American poetry after the death of Whitman. As poetry is a living expression of life it cannot be judged by erudite schoolmen who are prone to measure whatever is done by the masters of the past.

In Illinois I was fiercely attacked, almost personally impugned, by a scholarly professor of influence named Sherman, who later getting into Greenwich Village, so to speak, swallowed *An American Tragedy* and called it good. I am truly puzzled by such men. They have read nearly everything and know the history of literature; yet having eyes they see not. One would think that the criticism of Goethe would bring them to reflection and cautious words. "I honor both the rhythm and rhyme by which poetry becomes poetry," he wrote in his autobiography; "but what is really deeply and fundamentally effective, what is truly educative and inspiring is what remains of the poet when he is translated into prose. What is left is the pure essence, which beauties of form may strive to simulate when absent, and when present only serve to conceal." Goethe is here speaking of prose translations of poetry, but his words well describe what is done in free verse when it is excellent.

I could fill a page with the names that I was called, and put beside them the high praises that were given me, but I shall merely refer in passing to H. L. Mencken, who was a friendly critic of the new movement; and to an unnamed poetaster, my friend of many years by then. *Spoon River* smote him with madness almost. He wrote letters for publication to Reedy's *Mirror* in which he mocked *Spoon River* with all the contempt at his command. He wrote me letters of the same tenor; until finally we parted company and I did not hear from him for twenty years.

After a month's holiday in New York I returned to my law office in Chicago. The first letter I opened was from my sister, who censured me severely for deserting her in her day of trouble. The Great Dane had come to Chicago and won her back to his arms; and she blamed me for that surrender on her part. I had not come to Lake Forest to see her, and thus in her loneliness she had taken up again with the only life that offered itself! I had been occupied twenty-two days with the Bermingham case; I had gone to New York to rest and to enjoy something of the acclaim that I was·receiving there. Meanwhile there was nothing for her to do but to remain patient until the year elapsed which would establish her residence. She had abandoned the campaign, and rejected the counsel of Alfred Austrian and myself, and had flown to England and France. I passed off her hard words with an hour's irritation, then I turned to my problems.

Living expenses had to be met, and there was not much law business. The Bermingham case was in the limbo of the Appellate Court. In a few days I met Austrian, and asked him why he did not send me any more business. His law office was congested with cases, and it was the custom of himself and his partners to send clients that they could not serve to me and to others. To my question he said, "I heard you were living in New York writing poetry." "No," I protested quickly, "I am going right on with the law, with the same equipment as formerly, and ready for anything good." Then I told him of my sister's reconciliation with her husband, and asked him to send in a bill for his fee. "I have no fee," he said. "I did that for you." As I had no fee either, the matter was thus ended. But how I wished then, how I have wished all my life that my sister had had a more understanding interest of me and a closer sympathy with my problems. That would have made a difference in my life, I am sure.

During the fall Chicago was a storm center of poetry and the *Poetry* office was almost daily entertaining some celebrity from afar. I met most of these people. Mrs. Moody was housing them from time to time, and I was there frequently to talk with Mrs. Moody, who as a student of literature and as the widow of William Vaughn Moody, and by that fact in intimate possession of the secrets of his genius, was a most companionable person. However, she was a Christian Scientist and gently took me to task for my "sex obsession" as she termed it, and for my materialistic tendencies. That she misjudged me will be clear enough when all these pages are written. I had no sex obsession, I was merely on the search for beauty.

In my library I had Stedman's *American Anthology,* and I had read it studiously, as I supposed. But when she mentioned Edwin Arlington Robinson the name meant nothing to me. I could not remember that I had read one of his poems. She thought that both of us practiced a Crabbe-like realism and were spiritually akin. At that time Robinson was very little known. He had published little or no verse for some years before 1915-1916, but like myself had given himself to prose plays. He, as I learned later, was ambitious to be a playwright; while I wanted to make money on which to write poetry. I longed to escape the life of a pack horse, and I had entered a partnership that I did not relish to do that, and then had written these plays which did not violate my principles of truly portraying life, but did not get produced either, and thus did nothing to emancipate me. When Torrence came to Chicago and was at Mrs. Moody's he also told me of Robinson, for he and Moody and Percy MacKaye had known each other at Harvard. So I had to confess to Torrence that I knew nothing of Robinson. On the other hand, I was familiar with Moody's poetry, which was in the great tradition and made the formal lyrics and sonnets of that time, and the neutral coloring of Robinson's brief verses, inconspicuous by comparison.

One day a tall, rather bent man with frizzed black hair, with the manner of a traveling scholastic, was ushered in by Jake Prassel. It was John Cowper Powys, one of the most extraordinary minds that I know, a genius in every sense of the word. He had a way of jiggling when he was excited, of kowtowing so to speak, of laughing with wide mouth, and thus exposing a great row of Piltdown teeth. His eyes were blue and penetrating but a little simian; his forehead above his eyes was ridged, and not very high. His head was small and compact and shapely. His manner reminded me of the friendly countrymen I had seen about my grandfather's farm, as he rubbed his hands, and laughed and exclaimed "my word," and entered into everything I said with joyous sympathy, with deferential agreement. We became friends at once. His understanding of me, his generous appreciation of what I had done won my heart naturally; while our differences of opinion were not of a sort to create any dissension. It was at this time, I believe, that he gave a lecture on *Spoon River,* at Maurice Browne's Little Theatre, which was filled with Chicago people to hear what the Cambridge scholar had to say about me. I sat in a box behind the curtains and was not known, until the lecture was over, to have been in the audience. He went on saying that I was the reincarnation of Chaucer. I am unable to tell how terrified I was as I heard him. I fairly shook with excitement. For here I was: Suppose I was some kind of a reborn Chaucer, how was I ever to sustain that role which had been thrust upon me? How with my law business, my expenses, my shattered health which a thousand emotions and themes bore down with crushing force?

The next spring I published *Songs and Satires.* It had a few pieces in it which I took from *A Book of Verses,* but most of it was new. It contained "So We Grew Together," "The Loop," "The City," "In the Cage," "In Michigan," "The Sign," "Simon Surnamed Peter," "The Idiot," "The Star," "Silence." But some of the critics had sharpened their pencils for it, as Marsh had predicted. They wanted more *Spoon River,* they turned in contempt from "Helen of Troy." If I had gone on in the *Spoon River* manner they would likely have said that I had but one set of strings; in fact, when I published *The*

New Spoon River in 1924 these same spirits lamented that it was a fall-off from the Anthology, and that one book of the kind was enough. However, I was pretty indifferent to what they said; for in many critical quarters it was well received. It had a decent sale and I was too occupied with writing, with using my long-gathered material, to stop to listen to men who had nothing to tell me that was of use to me. I can truthfully say that I have never resented criticism that I thought was honestly intended. No one has said severer things of me than H. L. Mencken, but I respected his judgment and integrity. But criticism which came out of obvious malice, or which was stupid or personal, I have treated with unforgiving contempt.

In the spring of this year of 1916 Chicago was full of stir, literary and other. America was becoming infected with the war mania, and we were drifting toward war. Bryan had left President Wilson's cabinet on account of the discrimination which he made in favor of England's invasion of our sovereign rights, and against the acts of Germany striking back against a blockade which was starving her. If we had then had an Andrew Jackson or possibly a Grover Cleveland as president, both England and Germany would have been told to lay off our neutral shipping, or accept the gage of war. In that case neither would have gone to war with us. Both would have mended their bad ways. But America was being run by House and Page. As the time for conventions drew near some Democrats were saying that Wilson had kept us out of war, while the Republicans were demanding preparedness and Hughes was exclaiming "America first and America efficient." The Republican convention was held in Chicago; and Mrs. Corinne Roosevelt Robinson, being present to watch in a sisterly way over the political chances of her brother Theodore Roosevelt, came to my house one night with a party. She became fascinated at once with my little daughters who were then lovely beyond comparison.

In the summer I took a cottage on Spring Lake, on the same lawn with The Pines, where Charley Shippey and I had feasted after that memorable day of fishing up the Grand River. Adlai Ewing was the father-in-law of the owner of this cottage, who also owned the master house on the same lawn. The whole was called Belle Point, a rise of ground which looked south on the lake to Spring Lake Village and across an estuary of water to the grounds and new brick mansion of a rich advertising man with a new wife. His divorce was stirring the scandal tongues of the inhabitants about. Ewing was a cousin of the late vice-president, Adlai Stevenson, and as an old friend of my father's became a delightful companion as we sat about his huge fireplace on cool evenings, or upon the lawn under the moons of June and July. His daughter Lucy was a woman of exquisite taste and manner of life; and prepared our cottage for occupancy with every care. It was simply furnished with summer chairs and lounges; but the kitchen was a delight for its conveniences, and the beds and blankets, and the bath, everything that anyone could desire. Between swimming and riding in the fine launches which Lucy had at her disposal, both a racing launch and a large launch which accommodated thirty people, I started to write *The Great Valley*. I wanted to interpret and memorialize Illinois and the country which had given so many distinguished men to America. It will be many years, if ever, before those poems and those of *Toward the Gulf*, written the next year, receive the attention which a people of self-conscious culture give to such portraits and epics of a land.

In the midst of this happiness of both play and creative work I received a telegram from my sister to come to Chicago. She had left the Great Dane again, and wanted to file a divorce suit. Her idea was that a residence assumed in Illinois before had not been interrupted by her absence in Europe. I meant to have nothing to do with this case. Besides, it was summer vacation and I was writing a book. And I did not answer her telegram. Pretty soon she appeared at Spring Lake with Buddie, and took rooms at The Pines. My wife was furious, and Lucy took a dislike to her at once; and so there I was without tranquillity to remember anything. However, it was a delight to see Hardin and Buddie swim and play tennis together. They were both excellent swimmers, and they dove off the pier into deep water and swam far out under the glittering sunlight that poured from those clear skies. I portrayed these two youths in "Canticle of the Race" published in *Toward the Gulf*.

Finally my son and Buddie snapped each other like two dogs at play, and Lucy more and more manifested her lack of welcome to my sister, as my wife did, even though she was housed in The Pines and formed no part of our immediate group on Belle Point, save as someone hovering near. As for myself, I felt disturbed; though I have been able to write amid the storm of Chicago, the consciousness of someone near me who is sending vibrations of a disturbing character paralyzes my thinking. As the result of everything my sister took her departure for Chicago, and there summoning my brother from Springfield to manage her contemplated divorce she settled down for a fight. And the Great Dane fought. The case dragged along making great expense for her. Then again she returned to the arms of the Great Dane, leaving my brother and a Chicago associate to mourn the loss of rich expectations. Sometimes I feel that my sister was cursed by fate. I have grieved enough that her heart was never satisfied, that she wandered over the world seeking happiness, and never found it, but was always in a sense lonely and misplaced.

In the fall of 1916 *The Great Valley* was published. On my soul I wish that the poems about the Illinois country were better, saving such as "The Mourner's Bench" which is in this volume, as well as "Slip Shoe Lovey," "The Garden," "The Tavern," "Susie," "The Church and the Hotel," "I Shall Never

See You Again," "Malachy Degan" and some others. One afternoon at the home of Mary Aldis I read to the group "Steam
Shovel Cut" which appeared in this volume. I think they were
greatly repelled by it. Also in this volume are "The Apology of
Demetrius" which I wrote one day at Belle Point while Buddie
and my sister were there; and "Desolate Scythia" and "The
Search" as a companion piece of the "The Death of Launce-
lot," which H. L. Mencken accepted for *Smart Set* some time
before this. As early as this Mencken and I exchanged a few
letters. His communications were humorous and waggish with
a vital abandon. Dreiser had already told me much about
Mencken: about his vitality, his erudition, his courage, his
forthrightness. But I did not meet Mencken until about 1924.

Well then, back to Chicago and the law office with the
summer over once again. My books were making money, but
the days of settlement were long delayed by the terms of the
contracts. Law business daily proved that a name in poetry
frightens clients away. But the Bermingham decree seemed a
sure source of money if ever the Appellate Court got through
with it and I was borrowing money on the strength of it for
living expenses. I spent weeks on the brief in that case, which
came to two hundred pages or more and contained every decision in the English tongue that bore upon the issues. And one
day the Appellate Court adjudged that the decree of Judge
MacDonald was erroneous, that the widow of Bermingham
was entitled to a dower interest in the estate, despite Bermingham's contract to give all his property by will to Helen Lee.
Still the court held that except for that dower interest Helen
Lee was rightly entitled to a daughter's share. In point of fact,
I had offered at the time the decree was entered to let it express
a dower interest for the widow. This was indignantly spurned
by the pugnacious lawyer who represented her. Now the Appellate Court had given it to her; but she and her lawyer were
angry, and started to go to the Supreme Court. But that court

shut its door, and coming back to the trial court a decree was entered in accordance with the directions of the Appellate Court. From this the tireless lawyer of the widow took an appeal, though what could the Appellate Court do but dismiss the appeal, since it was obviously frivolous and taken for delay, for spite? However, there was no way to prevent this appeal, since the widow was willing to give the huge appeal bond of $200,000. She did so and several months of delay loomed before me.

At this juncture of affairs the St. Louis lawyer came to Chicago full of wrath. I don't know how to negotiate, I never did know the arts of negotiation. I should have sat in my office and waited for the law to take its course. I was so disagreeably affected by the opposing lawyer that I could not have gone to his office and proposed an armistice, hardly to save my life. But the St. Louis lawyer was of a different spirit. He was as tough as a ditch digger. He had no pride, he had no reluctance about walking into the office of this lawyer and saying: "What will you do now? Why fight any more? Let's get the money." The St. Louis lawyer hated this man so bitterly that they almost came to blows during the trial. Yet now he walked over to the man's office to see him; and after some parleying the terms were agreed upon. Helen Lee got $200,000 in cash and first-class stocks and bonds. And I got a fee of $27,000.

In 1904 at Elk Lake I had met Murray, who approached me through Thoreau and Emerson. He was of that sort who have little time to read, who have not had much schooling, but who choose the best things by way of self-culture, and thus improve themselves as the years go on. Murray had a court reporter's office in the Ashland Block, and for years I gave him a great deal of business. He did the reporting in the Bermingham case, and before I had pneumonia and after we were walking companions in the Indiana Dunes, where on Sundays even in the bitterest weather we climbed the hills and traversed the valleys of that beautiful spot. He became a good *fidus Achates*, a convenient man for me to have around me, and a sounding board for my ideas in our talks. He was married to a Catholic woman and had four children being raised in that faith against his will. Such dissension had come over this religious question that he left home and came to me with his troubles, and I prepared to act for him as his solicitor in a divorce proceeding. I knew his wife slightly, and upon being requested to do so she came to my office and expressed her willingness to let Murray go free upon the payment of moderate alimony for the support of herself and the two daughters, who were about twelve or so. All this done Murray had no home; but the third floor of my house was unused and I offered it to him. He was profoundly grateful, for by this time he knew my daughters, and my son, whom he had met when we all went together to the dunes. Thus he installed himself in my house, paying to my wife about $10 a week for that whole floor with a bath. As time went on he became one of the family almost. Often he sat at table with us, and often took breakfast before he went out into the cold. My little daughters were quite devoted to him, calling him uncle. And as neither of them had ever been demonstrative toward me, or very reciprocal of my caresses, I felt at times that they cared more for him than for me. He was more of a novelty than I, and then he played and talked with them more frequently than I did. I was absorbed in my studies and writing.

Now with the Bermingham case settled I paid the bank what I owed it, $5,000, and deciding that I needed a rest, and particularly a relief from the bitter February weather of Chicago, I went to New Orleans with Murray as companion. In less than a week my wife and daughters followed me, and we went about the city for about two weeks while I lectured at Tulane University, and my wife paid visits to some relatives who lived there.

On my return to Chicago I found a letter from Theodore Roosevelt asking me to locate him through his sister, Mrs. Robinson, when I was next in New York, and to lunch or dine with him, as it might be convenient for me. The letter was extremely cordial, and he had fine words to say of *Spoon River*. All this was so much in contrast with Bryan. I had spent hundreds of dollars to keep the Jefferson Club alive, largely for Bryan's sake; I had made myself disliked in Chicago for my fidelity to his cause; yet from Bryan I had nothing but a telephone call one day in which he said, "I hear that you have written a book." He laughed in a jocular way, which meant that I was perhaps pretty naughty and a little dangerous. And here was Roosevelt, whom I had scored in *The New Star Chamber* and whose political principles I had trampled in *Spoon River*, who sought me out with such hearty good will.

And just now I was going to New York to attend a reception given for me, and Reedy was going along. So I wrote Roosevelt that we would have breakfast with him, mentioning that Reedy was with me. I had seen Roosevelt once before. It was in 1900 when he made a political address at Electric Park in Chicago, and a dodge-under and dodge-around address it was. The audience was composed almost entirely of Union Labor men. He made a very poor impression upon me as he read his speech and scowled his resolute resistance to license and disorder at his listeners. Bryan, who later spoke from the same platform extemporaneously, and with such easy charm, made Roosevelt seem a crude amateur by comparison, and even a dubious character.

But now as Roosevelt came from the elevator at his hotel prompt to the very minute of eight-thirty, and as he extended a warm hand to Reedy, whom he knew before this, and grasped my hand cordially when we were introduced, I began to see what it was in his personality that made him beloved and popular, and even made people who knew him forget his atrocious principles, his dangerous bellowing for war, his rhetoric about the strenuous life, his admonitions to hit the line and hit it hard, his counsels to speak softly but to carry a big stick. We sat at a table where the talk went on at an amazing pace until one o'clock, while his secretary appeared at the door every now and then to remind him that he had a certain appointment. Roosevelt waved him off and went on. He talked Celtic poetry, and bass fishing; he talked free verse and lion hunting; he talked wildflowers and biology and evolution and geology and history, and the American wars. I said very little, though Reedy took a fair part in this freshet of discourse. Roosevelt was particularly interested in my reasons for excoriating the Philippine conquest. I told him frankly that I considered the cause as bad as a cause could be, and that a Republic had no place in such business. As we parted he asked me to come to Oyster Bay sometime where we would have more leisure. There were "five hundred things," he said, that he wanted to discuss with me.

By the time I was back in Chicago the United States had declared war on Germany, and the Chicago of 1914, and just before, and the America of that period were saying their last lines of a happy day which had promised to be happier. They were just making their ironic exit from the stage of history. And I decided to buy a country place and to have apple trees and bees, flowers and vegetables, and to work in the open air and to have tranquillity for writing. If there was forever to be war, first the Spanish-American War, which changed the form of our government, and now war upon Germany, which would solidify that change, I wanted to get to the hills. It didn't look much now as though I should ever have an estate such as Walter Scott's Abbotsford, which had teased my fancy always to live as he did. But I could get a country place, and I set about to do so. I went out to the Rock River country and motored about with Judge Baum looking at farms. I found sixty acres which I liked. But the owner wanted more for it than I could pay. It was unimproved and a house had to be built. I preferred to stay in Illinois; but not finding anything around the Rock River I returned to Chicago to get a new start toward some other locality.

Chapter XVIII

SERIOUS TROUBLE IS NOW BEGINNING. I HAD THAT NICE PURSE of $27,000; rather, I had over $20,000 when my debts were all paid. To the reader it must be clear that I was now free to leave the law, to go to the country and to settle down to the literary life in earnest. However, let the crowding events of my life which followed be studied to see if this was possible, or belonged to my life's pattern. All Chicago knew that I had made this money, and I was besieged by the usual life insurance and real estate agents, and the usual mountebanks who had great investment schemes to lay before me. But in the Marquette Building was Frank Winkler, who all these eighteen years since I was married had in a sense kept track of me. There is something very curious about this. On my part I had practically nothing to do with him. I laughed at his history and his economics when he talked, and corrected him on points of law when we happened to discuss law cases. After I came to the Marquette Building he frequently motored me home, since we lived in the same part of Chicago; and though he bored me, and though I knew that he was consumed with envy of me, still we had these contacts. When I first moved into the Marquette Building he called upon me at once and looked my law library over with a sneer, saying that he had ten times as many books, to which I retorted that he hadn't read them. He professed to like *Spoon River,* but he observed that men who sought publicity made him laugh. No one craved notability more than he. When he traveled to London he fed his silly vanity by having his picture taken with a wig seated on the wool sack to show how he would look as an English judge; and he blowed about his great lawyership in helping to hang the anarchists; and how he had driven an adulteress into suicide by showing her up, by which he referred to one of the great scandal cases of Chicago. In these days in the Marquette Building I encountered him every day, conscious all the while that he was secretly unfriendly to me under his uniform bearing of geniality, and yet more or less submitting to the chance association of a few minutes' talk as we passed, and sometimes having a drink with him at the bar of the building. He was a whisky drinker, and one of daily and almost unlimited draughts. His wife and mine pretended to be friends, and once I was induced to go to Winkler's house for dinner; and once he came to mine. Beyond this and what I have told there was nothing more to our association. But now I come to something else by way of fate threads.

I had not been long in the Marquette Building when the news came that my former law partner had pleaded his clients guilty in that case in the West; and fast following this was the word that he himself was in trouble. And pretty soon the papers announced that he had been indicted for jury bribing. Reedy now wrote me that this lawyer had been watched in that first case in the west, with the result that his tactics were studied, and having been followed up in the later case, he had been grabbed. In the meanwhile letters came to me from him saying that he was in a terrible plight, that the authorities had given him assurances, but that he feared they would not keep them. I suspected at the time what I afterward was sure of from all the facts, namely, that he had pleaded his client guilty in order to escape prosecution himself, and that the authorities, having got all that out of him, had turned upon him. Finally came a letter from him to the effect that the worst had happened, that he had been indicted, and that he needed the help of all his friends. In point of fact I was done with him, and with the whole experience with him in which I toiled to make a competence, and failed largely because he failed. Still I did what I have often done: I went against my feelings in order to discipline myself into a way of complete fairness. In the meanwhile I wanted nothing to do with his case, I did not want my name mentioned with his.

At this juncture of affairs things sometimes looked suspicious around my law office. He was sending me letters, asking for help, by a circuitous method and under disguised handwriting; for every move he made was watched. One day two men came to see me asking me to incorporate an agricultural association for them. I hadn't passed ten words with them before I suspected that they were detectives who wanted to get at my mail and pick off a letter from this lawyer to me. I took this piece of business, and they paid me well for it, and then disappeared. The Chicago address that they gave was false.

Then this lawyer wanted money, he was completely broke. I went to the receiver of the Bank of America and got $1,000 and sent it to him. I got this money with great difficulty, because the receiver said that he wanted to pay no more out to lawyers until the estate of the bank was completely settled. I dug it out of the receiver, telling him of this lawyer's plight; and of course it was my labor that made this money. He had never lifted his hand with reference to the legal work of this receivership. Then he wanted something else.

He wanted depositions taken in Chicago to prove his reputation there for integrity as a lawyer by which to repel the idea that he was a lawyer who would bribe a jury. So I took this on for him, all the while cursing myself that our association of years before entailed this consequence upon me; all the while of the opinion that he was guilty; all the while struggling and wrestling with the circumstances that would not let me be done with him. I hired a stenographer and went about gathering up character witnesses. I brought these witnesses to my law office where they testified. They were the judges of the state courts, nearly every judge in Chicago; they were Edward

F. Dunne, once mayor of Chicago and later governor of Illinois; and Carter Harrison, many times mayor of Chicago, and many citizens prominent in politics, in civic reforms, in education, and even in theology. These depositions made a large volume when bound and shipped to him for use in the court. Many of these witnesses told me that they would testify out of compliment to me. However that may be, I failed on only one man. Judge Kenesaw M. Landis met my request with a storm of indignation. His remark was that I wanted to use his office to bolster up this lawyer, and that he wouldn't allow it to be used. He went on to say that he would do anything he could for me, but nothing for this lawyer, that they had caught him at last and he was glad of it. The depositions cleared him, so he wrote me. When he returned to Chicago *Spoon River* was the sensation of the hour and he proceeded to ask me for six copies at wholesale rates. He came around me, never suspecting that I was not friendly to him. In fact, later in *Songs and Satires* (1916) I published "On a Bust" which he saw; then he understood my feeling. In many ways he was obtuse, and even in the trial of a case unalert. It never occurred to him until I told him in so many words that I would not forgive that debt of $9,000.

So much for the distaff that made the threads of 1917 and later. When I got up from that attack of pneumonia I found my law office gone to ruins. My brother-in-law had one of the rooms. He had done nothing to hold my fences in place, and in fact he was incapable of doing anything. The suite was expensive. So I moved to the Portland Block; and there I was when I was seeing the Bermingham case through the Appellate Court, and when I settled it and began to look for a farm.

The reason that I did not go at once to Spring Lake to buy a farm was that I wanted to be in Illinois, and the land in that part of Michigan was sandy, though very wonderful soil for grapes, apples and peaches. I could not think of a piece of land

around Spring Lake that was large enough and placed as I
wanted it. Hence I did not think of the Spring Lake country,
much as I loved it, while looking about for a farm or country
place. But one day I saw an advertisement of a Spring Lake
place for sale. I answered the advertisement and the owner
called to see me. I did not know him at all, and did not know
his name before. He went on to describe the place that he had
for sale; and I saw at once that it was the place that Frank
Winkler had occupied in 1914, and during succeeding summers. So I asked the owner what relation Frank Winkler had
to the place. The owner explained that Winkler had made a
contract to buy it, and had undertaken to pay rent as interest
on the purchase price; but that he had not paid the rent for
several years. He went on to say that Winkler evidently intended to occupy the place this year, for he had had a man
put in a garden two weeks before this time. However, Winkler
owed $1,000 rent, and the contract could be forfeited. Indeed,
he was now trying to sell the place in order to get rid of
Winkler. I told the owner that I would have nothing to do
with the place until Winkler was out of the way, and any
possible interest that he had in it canceled. The owner would
have to bring me a writing that Winkler didn't want the
place, or couldn't buy it; and also a cancellation of all his equity
in the property whatever it was over his own signature. The
owner then posted off to see Winkler. He returned shortly
saying that Winkler was drunk, as usual, and laughed derisively when he was asked to pay the purchase price and take
the place, if he wanted it. "Why," roared Winkler, "you damn
well know I haven't got a cent. I couldn't buy it at half the
price you want for it." Then the owner asked him if he could
pay the $1,000 back rent if he was allowed to occupy the place
for the ensuing summer of 1917. And Winkler replied that he
could not do that. Then the owner said that he wanted to can-
cel the contract, as he had a prospective purchaser who wanted

everything as to the title cleared. Winkler now grew curious. He asked the owner who wanted to buy it. The owner refused to tell him; and Winkler canceled the contract. The owner brought the cancellation back to me and laid it on my desk as proof that everything was now ready for a deed. And so I bought the place, after going to Spring Lake and walking over the twelve acres which it contained, and looking through the old house and sheds on it.

In a few days I was sojourning at Arbutus Banks, a summer hotel about a half a mile from my place, and walking from there to rake leaves and clean up the grounds. I raked five years' accumulation of leaves, I cut and burned brush, I made a flower garden and a vegetable garden, I trimmed apple trees, and cut away alder bushes and piled dead branches for burning, and cleared my 1,000 feet of water front. This is the country of Hollanders and some Swedes. I found an old man named John Weringa to help me. We worked together the livelong day, and he told me all about the people of the neighborhood for years back. One of his stories I put in the poem "Sweet Clover," published in *Toward the Gulf*. Truly these were happy days. There was much rain and the spring was late; but also there was glorious sunshine, and the birds sang to the echo in my orchard. Could I not have bees as Virgil and Horace had them? John would attend to that for me. Already I had an incubator and was raising some chickens. At night tired to the bone with labor, I fell asleep at nine o'clock. I was up at five and off to the place at six to meet John and go to work again. I was hastening, for I wanted to get the place habitable for the writing of a book. Pretty soon Winkler's daughter came to remove what furniture they had from the house. She was very distant and angry looking. In the meantime I had a contractor making the house over. I built a beautiful outside chimney with two large fireplaces, one in the living room downstairs, the other in my study upstairs. I laid hardwood floors, and put in a hot and cold water system, and built an icehouse, and a fine concrete pier into the lake. I dug a cellar in which the 500-gallon tank for the water system was installed. All this cost me about $3,000. And then, naturally, a man who could buy a summer place could buy war bonds; so to have peace I bought $3,000 worth of bonds. I had to have some kind of car to get in and out from the village which was two miles away, Grand Haven being five miles away. So I bought a car which had been run 200 miles for $600. Its retail price was $1,000. And thus by July the children were out of school, the house was finished, and they all joined me, and we sat in the dining room which I had made over looking through a long mullioned window through pine trees into the water of the lake.

I set to work to write *Toward the Gulf,* taking my exercise by working in the flower and vegetable garden. My son did not care much for this kind of work, and did it only when he could not avoid my insistence that he build up his physique by this open-air employment. He was well enough, but inclined to be weak in his chest like his maternal grandfather, and his uncle. I became so infatuated with my flower garden that I could not stay away from it. I was still retiring early and rising early, sometimes by four o'clock. I would get up to look at the poppies, the calendulas, the zinnias, which danced in the white dawn, and seemed to thrill as the golden sun came up behind the sand hill at the rear of my acres. My daughter Madeline, as mystical and beautiful as a dryad, would sometimes hear me as I arose, and would follow me to the flower garden. One time when I was looking at my flowers as the sun came up I heard a twig snap behind me, and looking about saw her with her tangled golden hair as the sun smit it, and with her eyes still heavy from sleep. Hence the poem "In the Garden at the Dawn Hour," in *Toward the Gulf.* Ay, but these were beautiful days before the mists came! Lucy and her father called on us; and there were rides again in her launches, and there were rides every day on the little steamer which plied the lake delivering groceries and taking people to the village and Grand Haven. And there were walks and some parties, and long hours in that orchard as the Bartlett pears became ripe. Such orioles and robins and thrushes here! They made everything of sunshine and balmy winds that song could make of them. And there were moonlit nights, particularly when the pear trees were a sea of snowy blossoms, and the fireflies rode the night zephyrs. That orchard is pictured in my poem "The Lost Orchard," published in *Godbey* nearly twenty years after I lost it.

But insects were breeding and getting ready to fly and sting. Frank Winkler rented a house on the lake and proceeded to circulate the story that I had cheated him out of his beloved place. His wife and daughter and two sons were busy paladins in the sowing of this slander. I was absorbed in my book, and at first did not know about this. I went to my study at nine; at one I descended to the dining room with my eyes turned in, and my energies sapped until food and a ride restored them. One day one of my daughters ran in to tell me that the captain of the little boat, whenever he approached my pier, or stopped at it, called out "Winkler's Pier." This captain was telling everywhere over the lake that I had cheated Winkler out of the place, and that Winkler had vowed that he would get even with me, if it took him fifty years to do so. I heard this now from many quarters, from the contractor who rebuilt my house, and who was in a way the principal citizen on the lake, and others. To these I told the whole circumstances of the purchase. Winkler owed everybody in the village and for years back, and his word did not count against me finally; but he had certain partisans, and in a country place where envy easily sprouts, and gossip is the main amusement, his enmity made things unpleasant for my children. My wife was rather friendly with Mrs. Winkler, and made allowance for Frank on the score of his old friendship for her father and brother. However, Winkler only stayed a few weeks. Something happened, and he went fifty miles away and got another summer place. I was too busy to pay much attention to what he did anyway. For I was having land plowed to set out another orchard, and getting the sand hill ready for a vineyard, and as busy as possible with my book.

No, Winkler was not the worst June bug, or cockroach, or stinging worm. In a dream one drifts along and suddenly encounters a lion, or what not. I had drifted down to Spring Lake utterly oblivious of any evil that lurked about it. One of my first discoveries was that Cecile, whom I met the night that I met my wife, was living two or three places up the lake. Long since she had married and had two children. Her children and mine had met and were beginning to play together, but not harmoniously for long. Thus after twenty years Cecile and I completed the circuit and met again. She was very mild toward my wife. It was her way to drive in occasionally when she was going to the village, and just say good morning, and then go her way. She didn't call or pay visits to our place; and as my wife did not like the golden-haired new wife of the rich man up the lake, nor the wife of the contractor and her set, she was much by herself. But all this was nothing to what grew up across the lake. There in state lived the wife of the Berserker, the sister of Cecile, whom I never saw until this summer.

One day I went to the village and found her in company with my son, who introduced me. She was a wonderfully beautiful woman, but she had the bad breeding to ask me to call, and to sit under her apple trees and talk with her and her husband. She had not yet called upon my wife, and to make an end, she never called upon her. My son, not regardful of the proprieties in such cases, kept teasing me to cross the lake to see this lady, saying that she admired *Spoon River* greatly, and wanted to talk with me. I told him that I would not go, and why I would not go. All the while in a way I knew that he was sometimes running the lady's car for her, or her launch, or was at her house for luncheon or dinner. The lady had two daughters, one of whom was about the age of my son, and these two had guests from Chicago, young people, and they played tennis and swam together, so that the lady's place was fascinating enough. But I had a tennis court and a pier, and a car, and work to be done in the orchard; and I wanted my boy to keep to his own place, at least not to be away from his own place all the time.

After a morning of writing I would descend wanting to go to the village for the mail or to take the air. I would find my son gone with the car. He was across the lake at the lady's place. My little girls would be there too. Sometimes they would be home for supper, sometimes not until eight o'clock or so. I remonstrated about this, asking my wife to co-operate with me in keeping the children home. She saw no harm in what they were doing and said so emphatically enough. Finally I locked the car up. Then the lady sent her launch across the lake and took the children to her place. I did everything but get a whip to keep my children home. But while I was writing they could easily steal away, especially since they had the encouragement of their mother to do so. Between writing and working in the orchard and the garden, between resting and trying to get happiness out of my place, I was helpless to run about corralling those children. And my characteristic indifference about what I can't help came along to let matters drift, especially when I did not feel energetic enough to fight.

We had a colored cook, a wise humorous woman she was too, and the best companion in the world for talk that appraised character and took account of the ways of the world. She was alert to what was going on, and thought that the children should stay at home. One day she said to me, "That woman is stealing your children, doctor, that's what she's doing." Over there, too, was the son of an ex-congressman from Michigan, about the age of my son, and not a desirable companion for him. Boys of this age were wild to go to the war. Buddie by this time had run away and joined the British Army. And this Michigan youth, being of Dutch descent, was under neighborhood surveillance, even as the German people about were. His crafty father had put him in a military school to get ready for war, thus to quiet patriotic suspicion. Like my son, he was about eighteen, and would soon be of an age to enter the army. My son was getting the war fever, and I was most anxious that he should stick to his school and let the war go.

Besides all this, the Berserker was a native German who had never been naturalized. The report went about the lake that he had a wireless on his roof by which he was communicating with German spies. The time came when his boats were commandeered, and his automobiles, and he was forbidden to appear on the piers at the village or at Grand Haven. In a word, he was practically interned. As the war went on the very air became surcharged with hate, with intangible poison. I could breathe it and smell it as plainly as I could detect the approaching fogs from Lake Michigan. I knew that we were surrounded by perils at every hand. For myself, *Spoon River* was anything but an assurance of my blind patriotism; my radical life and ideas were easy to use to intrepret my guarded speech into a secret sympathy with Germany. All the while I did not want France crushed, because of what France had done for us in the Revolution; but on the other hand, I thought England was using us, and I was bitterly against that. I was in deadly fear every day that the Berserker would be arrested, and that my son would be found at his place and perhaps taken into custody too. I strove in vain to keep him home. Thus my flower garden, my orchard, all that I had done to make this place beautiful, all my labor to buy it as a haven, as a retreat for creative work, fell to this visitation of serpents of fire that flew about my head, and at last poisoned every moment. Granted that I was hypersensitive, that I was over-cautious, that I saw perils that did not exist, I was entitled to have been catered to after all that I had done to make others happy. And as always I was nothing but a pack horse. Still for another month I went on, for I loved this country with all my heart and the summer was so golden, so beautiful! The white clouds soared high in perfectly blue skies, the breezes swept over my porch with cool refreshment in the afternoons; and at night they blew through the orchard where I was wont to walk. I took the family one day in the steamer *May Graham* far up the Grand River, that little boat which once traveled up and down the St. Joe River when I was there with Opie Read and his family sixteen years before this.

Those wastes of whispering rushes along the flat shores, the wide swift river, the farms and farmhouses along the way in that poppy air which made them manifest, as though seen through a magic glass, all this gave me great delight. My father came to see us, and some guests from Chicago. But altogether by September I was weary of the insects and the flying ser-pents. Circumstances of other days closed in on me like hostile spirits that have waited for the opportune moment of retribu-tive consequence. These were the spawn of my own nature in part, and in part the mere forces of life and circumstances, over which I had no control. Once Powys said to me that my nature had a way of evoking devils about me; and perhaps it is true. If so, the reader can judge of that. Rightly or otherwise I felt that my place was ruined. One day, it was September 13th, something unusually exasperating happened, and I packed to leave, and to abandon my orchard and my house, and to turn over to the family the car, the garden, letting the enchantress across the lake do as she would. A sturdier spirit, perhaps, would have sent the family back to Chicago. Somehow I could have gone on with the negro cook. But my book was written, I was tired and I wanted a change. I started across the porch followed by the cook who begged me not to leave. But I went, acting as I have always acted, suddenly and without turning back after my patience has been exhausted.

I had in my satchel the script of *Toward the Gulf*. There were 46 poems in the book, nearly all written that summer. Among them were "The Lake Boats," "Cities of the Plain," "Johnny Appleseed," "The Loom," "The Landscape," "The Grand River Marshes," "Front the Ages with a Smile," "The World Saver," "Dear Old Dick" and "My Light with Yours," which has been taken as a love poem, but which was in fact inspired by my daughter Madeline. Also in this book were "Christmas at Indian Point," "Widow La Rue," "The End of the Search," and "Botanical Gardens," in which prophetically enough were these lines:

> As we sat in silence
> And coming night, what seemed the sinking moon,
> Amid the yellow sedges by the lake
> Began to twinkle, as a fire were blown—
> And it was fire, the garden was afire,
> As it were the world had flamed with war.

I returned to Chicago to find everything changed, my friends occupied with the war or gone to France. The *Poetry* office was not what it had been. Studios of happy assemblage were silent. I must mention one woman who had been the charming center of a studio where I used to go. The word came to me that she had gone to France, and had become a nun, enduring then the initiate of scrubbing floors upon her knees. The world had become insane, and Chicago was insane. This is what I found in a few hours after leaving the wind-swept hill of my lawn, and the stars between the oak trees that overlooked my roof at Spring Lake. As it turned out I had left them for good. I was traveling toward the writing of *Domesday Book,* and into a life of war days and suffering out of which it was to be born. My steps were taking me toward days of unbelievable happiness, which were to end in disappointment, rising with a command to me to assert my will and strength again and to climb another hill.

* * * * *

This is by no means the end of the story. It is the end of the volume except for a canter, an epilogue. All the years after 1917—to—to when?—remain to be told; years in which I produced and published a book a year, sometimes two books, out of what I had lived and was living. Leaving Spring Lake that fall of 1917 I was again in Chicago, where the war was roaring. And immediately the Fates begin to spin and to weave. I went wandering and roaming troubled by the distressing days of war. I was in New York, Boston, New England, and Grand Rapids. Much later in 1921 I was in Egypt, riding a camel over the sand about the pyramids of Gizeh. From Egypt I went to Athens and saw its wonders; and then to Rome. I was led to this by what happened to me in 1919. One night I wandered out of the iron-dark air of Chicago into a ballroom. And there was Pamela! She led me into meadows of larks, into gardens of robbins, into happiness beyond anything I had ever known in my life. I was sure that she was the long-looked-for woman, and I tried every honorable means to free myself to marry her. When I couldn't, I took this trip to Egypt. When I got back to America, Winkler and that lawyer for whom I had gathered depositions and to whom I sent money when he was broke came upon me like footpads from an alley and smashed down my plans. They crawled like pythons across my garden mashing down its blossoms. Chicago grew impossible as a place of residence for me. By the time I left I had lived there more than thirty years. I should have lived there always, except for the circumstances and their consequences which came upon me. All that I had accumulated, my farm in Michigan, was lost in the settlement of my affairs. I lost everything except my health and my concentration of mind. I kept on writing poetry and publishing it. My father grew old and died, and my mother as well. My sister died and my brother, both in consequence of their own natures, their own dealing with life and life with them. The thirteen years that I have lived in New York City have been the most peaceful of my life, and the most productive. Here I am in a hotel room. All I have to do is to close my eyes and I can look at the Mason County Hills and see my kite high among the clouds!

Epilogue

HERE THEN IS THE STORY TO THIS POINT TOLD AS TRUTHFULLY as I can tell it. Yet it is a story that has a thousand angles, and is capable of being told from a point of observation which would have included other details. Looked at through my mystical eyes, its pattern seems inevitable; looked at with my realistic eyes, the pattern is the result of things that happened, and that is all. There arises the question, however, what made things happen in the way they did?

> So schaff ich am sausenden Webstuhl der Zeit
> Und wirke der Gottheit lebendiges kleid.

Perhaps these lines from *Faust* explicate the mystery; perhaps Hegel laid his hands upon the secret in his philosophizations about history. For myself, I cannot rid my mind of the colorations which my imagination throws upon human life and the earth scene; indeed, my thinking seems to be lighted along the dark corridors of thought by the circling and the holding aloft of the flashlight of imagination. Some secrets seem thereby revealed; but often that light has blinded me to pitfalls right beneath my feet.

And this brings me to say that I have lived in the imagination. Perhaps this is the deepest secret of my nature, namely, that imagination has been the controlling influence of my life; and that I have not lived among facts of economics, among buildings of brick and mortar, among the concrete matters of worldly success. I feel that I twisted my genius, my nature when I went into the law, and set my will to master the law, and did master it. If anyone would appreciate what I did, and how I had at least two personalities, let him consider the youth who wrote the poems that went into *A Book of Verses,* and then look at that very youth entering the iron ways of that Hittite city called Chicago, and who at once started to fight with thieves and dullards in the justice courts, in the police courts, and in the little better courts of record of that time of 1892-1893. Yes, having been pushed into the law by Fate I resolved to be a learned lawyer, and I became one. The reports of the Supreme Court of Illinois show my varied activities in that court over a period of many years. I met the hard, shrewd, money-grabbing corporation and business lawyers on their own ground, and fought them toe to toe. Some of these now are millionaires, all are patriots, nearly all are pharisees. As I would not have traded places with them then, much less would I do so now.

That delusion I had of being two persons when I was sinking away with pneumonia is not all delusion. Whatever my luck has been, and often it has been bad, I have always somehow been conscious of a good daemon, a brother god, who would guide me along according to the fortunate direction that went forth at the time of my birth. It may have been the adoration of my grandmother, the attention that was paid me from the first at school, the position that was given me at Knox College, that gave me the feeling, the illusion that I was born to something fortunate and distinguished, come what might. Much that I have lived did not belong to me, was not in character with myself as the grandson of Squire Davis Masters; yet my stronger self has lived through these lower levels and gone ahead. I have felt that after all distractions, all detours I would return to the full possession of myself. But in ways of daily living and associating with human beings I have been two persons: first that person who has been annoyed, fatigued, even degraded by inferior human contacts, by experiences, amorous and other, alive with contaminations—I have been this person, at the same time that I was that other person existing aloof and untouched by demoralizations.

My strength and my weakness have been that I have lived in the imagination. When I was eighteen or nineteen, and was reading with Will there in Lewistown he often remarked that my words were freighted with similes; and I have always seen back of a tree or a hill something that was immaterial. For which reason the books of Swedenborg have held my interest from my reading days to the present time. As a boy on the Masters farm my grandmother kept a paper knight, an embossed figure it was, in her bureau drawer. I am unable to describe the emotion that this simple object gave me, of the thrilling association of fancy which it stirred in me. The horizon in those days made me ache; the depth of the skies entered into me with a kind of rapturous torture as I lay in the Masters pasture and watched the buzzards wheel in that hot sky of thunderheads. Then I had strange visions singing "Babylon is Falling," in marching around the farmhouse with a broomstick for a gun. Nearly all boys do these things, but not all boys do them with the rapt imagination that I did. I have shadowed forth what I saw and felt in my poems "They'd Never Know Me Know" and in "Worlds Back of Worlds," and many others. While in "Botanical Gardens," "The Loom" and "The Star" I have given some evidence of the mystical eyes with which I have looked upon the world. I was teased by the light that never was on sea or land, and by the pathos of distance in my boyhood, long before I knew a word of Wordsworth or Nietzsche.

In the first diary that I ever kept, dating from my fifteenth year, I see no trace of myself as I am today, or of myself as I grew to be along the way. I should say, perhaps, no trace of any of my selves, for I am not one person, but many. Here is a record of a ball game in which I played pitcher, for in these days at Lewistown I made my mark as a ballplayer. There is also here journalizing about my roller-skating, and the weather, and of events at home, our guests and entertainments. And one entry about the death of a young girl, the granddaughter of Colonel Ross. This is headed with some lines of Tennyson's, "Break, Break, Break." Also a report of a Sunday-school experience when the lesson was about Paul and Silas. To quote from this: "I told her [the Sunday-school teacher] that if we had some miracles like that performed in these days that more would believe." However, with years and study I came to the definite conclusion that the Bible should be thrown away, and utterly eliminated from human interest, except as literature, so far as it is literature, and that Hellas should take control of America. In spite of New England theology America started under the influence of Hellas. Thomas Jefferson's was the great mind and vision that tried to commit America to the beauty and the rationalism of Hellas. Two summers ago after reading H. L. Mencken's excellent *Treatise on Right and Wrong*, I read Aristotle's *Ethics* for the first time; and it revived my conviction that what America needs is the magnanimous man, not the man of charity of St. Paul. In a word I think that Christianity has falsified and enervated the world, America included. It has bred the hypocrite, who was a far less prevalent character in pagan days. I think I can say this with as much justification in reason as I could say that a great pestilence and a vast slaughter in war were disasters to the world. To my mind there is hardly an utterance of Jesus that is sound and true, while his mind and his character are inferior to those of Socrates, Confucius, Aristotle and Plato.

Returning to my diaries, here is the beginning of that self of me who at nineteen read Spencer, Huxley and Hume, and contemplated turning metaphysician, between hours when the art of poetry or the short story captured my aspirations. I was determined to lay my hand upon the actual facts of Jesus and the miracles, as my notes prove later when at Knox College I read the New Testament in Greek and filled voluminous pages with notes concerning the witnesses of the miracles and who they were, and whether the Gospel reporter in question was present when the prodigy was brought off.

Then there is the next diary, or commonplace book, filled with quotations from Shakespeare, Swinburne, Byron; and with verses of my own, romantic and satirical. Its latter part is taken up with notes of my studies when I was twenty, which was a busy year. I was then reading Thackeray, Scott, Blackstone's *Commentaries*, Taine's *English Literature*, Shelley, Milton, Chaucer, Spenser and *Faust* in poetry. In history I read Herodotus, and made notes, some of which went into the sonnet "Nitocris," contained in *A Book of Verses*. This year I read Montaigne, Addison, Bacon and Macaulay's essays. Ah, yes, and here is a book I kept at Knox College which contains my translation of the first book of the *Iliad*.

All this shows, no doubt, that part of me which has never been at rest, but was always moving, and indeed moving toward a visioned end. That part of me has not been obliterated by any distraction, or disaster, or by discouraging days. Many men would have been broken completely by those years of mine between 1919 and 1929; but I went on writing books. Many men would have been sunk to their eyes by that spiritual mud through which I walked from 1900 to 1915; but I kept my nose up where I could breathe, and trudged onward. Why was I not obliterated?

Well, to answer that is to delineate in part the reasons why my life has made the pattern that it has. I came into the world endowed with exhaustless, continuous energy, which passed to me from my grandmother Masters, who may have derived it from that Lawrence Young who deserted Margaret Wasson. But another matter is as important, and that is my mental composition which made me feel moral responsibility for my time and what I did with it from my first days. This phase of my nature is written in these first diaries. It is that sense of conscience which made Milton live his life as if under the eye of a Great Taskmaster. I think this phase of me came from my grandfather, Squire Davis Masters; for in spite of the words of tribute to my father on the occasion of his funeral, my deepest conviction is that when I am my best self I am that old gentleman of Virginia stock reincarnated.

I can separate the pattern of my life into beginning figures. All through my boyhood there are the pastoral scenes of the Masters farm; the Shipley schoolhouse on the hill; the Mason County Hills, the Houghton woods, the farmhouses which dotted the prairie, dipping for miles toward the Sangamon River; the still sunsets when the fire of the sun dazzled from distant windows; the call of quail, and the cry of the meadow larks flying amid the light of afternoon which concealed them —and here arose my own longings and griefs for something that seemed far off in life when I should be mature; but that something was more distant than that—it is distant now, and will ever be so.

But amid these pastoral scenes in which I see my grandmother crossing the road to gather strawberries, or sitting in her living room reading or mending, or lying upon the couch we called Aunt Mary's, to rest from her work; in which I also see my grandfather about his little duties, or sitting under his maple trees, or at Atterberry when he had bade me good-bye as I was going back to Lewistown—amid all this arises the figure of Mary Fisher. She marks the beginning of a definite period in my life. I wish to this day that she had seen promise in me. The fact that she loaned me books when I was fifteen, that for years she wrote me letters, does not show that she had any confidence in my gifts. However, she would have needed a wonderful clairvoyance to have seen anything in me; for when I knew her in school I was willful, and negligent of the school course, and mischievous and rebellious, and as far from finding myself as possible; and in truth I was existing in a mimesis which took on the color of the perfectly drab environment of Lewistown. About 1912, while I was still living down the poison of Deirdre, I called on Mary Fisher in St. Louis, and told her what I had been through. She was then a woman of fifty-four, and boasting of her virginity. She was immeasurably shocked at my recital of the Deirdre affair, which I gave her for a theme for a novel, saying that no American had ever written a love story, deep, full, analytical, free and shameless. She told me that such a novel was as far beyond her as the theme of *King Lear*. And so it was.

However, Mary Fisher first directed my energy toward books, toward culture. What would have happened to me if I had gone on from Grimm's *Fairy Tales* by myself, following my own undirected bent, I don't know. For all that I feel that Mary Fisher did not like me, or trust me, or believe in me. I know that *Spoon River Anthology* distressed and displeased her. So it did my mother.

I don't put Anne in as marking a period in my life, but rather as an influence which carried me along in the path of self-culture in which I had started through Mary Fisher some years before I met Anne. And I do not see that she had any bearing upon my emotional development. But Chicago definitely marks a period in my life. That city carried me out of overintrospection, it brought me face to face with people, it got me into a life of action, and thereby helped to aid my intellectual digestion; it cured me of the pathos of the country, and by doing that it started me toward that ruggedness of physical health which was naturally mine as the son of my father, and which I have kept more or less, despite nerves, from that day to this.

The agrarian movement under Bryan started me toward a third period, a third pattern in my life. All my studies, Shelleyan and Platonic, philosophical and scientific, became living flame in 1896. But it was not until 1898 and 1900 that another whorl of my growth appeared. When I saw imperialism take the Republic I drew my sword for a fight. It was then that I took to vast studies again, determined to rout this anachronism, and to do it with such learning that I could not be gainsaid. It was then that I read Gibbon's *Decline and Fall,* and Buckle's and Hallam's histories, and Winwood Reade, and Karl Marx, and Plato over again, and Adam Smith, besides the works of Jefferson, Madison, and Elliott's *Debates,* and works on the Constitution, and constitutional law. These extended studies, not tabulated in full here by any means, went immediately into the *Chronicle* articles; but they laid the foundation for many things in *Spoon River Anthology,* for *Domesday Book,* and for many poems of people. Little as they seemed to bear upon the art of poetry, they had their use at last and their influence for what turned out to be my real medium.

I should say that Deirdre marked a period in my life, and very definitely. She did not cure me of the woman hope, rather she laid it into an enchanted sleep, that alone from which it was destined to be aroused. Pamela, whose story is not recorded in these pages, seemed the magic princess who would put life into the silent, becalmed room of the Sleeping Palace, was for a time successful. What Deirdre did was to give me understanding. With all her faults, which intercrossed with my faults, I think of her now with full regard for her problems. Sometimes I think that she did the best she could, the best anyone could do circumstanced as she was. I think of myself as a man dominated by a towering will and a selfish passion. And yet there remains my suffering and hers; there remains the salient fact that human beings caught in such circumstances are weak and unequal to the burdens that are put upon them.

Lovers who pass from our lives are more pathetic than the dead, for departed lovers are those who are buried alive. They are somewhere yet in the world, reminding us of hopes that failed, of dreams that were misled. They are extinct worlds revolving in darkness somewhere, felt but unseen; felt as worlds that lost the flame of life while life was appearing upon them, and struggling to flower; felt as worlds that were needlessly doomed to destruction. Then the time comes when they are blown as mere ashes into infinite spaces. It is so with Deirdre. The reader can well imagine what Deirdre would say about me. Her argument is implicit in these words of mine. I think she hated me at the last. But she might ask who I was that I was entitled to happiness, to her continued possession. I ask that too, and answer it by saying that I was not entitled to either. Yet at this distance from her and those days with her I still wonder about the fate of the human heart that can burn with such longings and such dreams and still have no power either in itself or in the circumstances of life to realize them.

I have written this autobiography with an eye to the truth. But what is truth? There are levels of truth, lower and higher, and every higher level contradicts and shames the lower levels. I have rewritten this epilogue more than once, and with the purpose of achieving the exacter truth. I wrote a paragraph for it to the effect that erotic love is like wine, and the intoxication of both is similar, attended with the same exaltation and reaction. That is truth, but a higher truth is that love is the warmth of wine that flames through the heart with vital power, and brings no relapse to self-contempt, to aching regret. I wrote that a man like myself will go through disillusionment again and again, and then will enter the enchantment again and again, just as he will be duped again and again by wine. It is true, because such a heart will search until it finds; and then if it never finds it should be philosophized and filled with magnanimous understanding. I wrote, having in mind erotic love, that women serve the Aphrodite Pandemos, and not the Aphrodite Urania. That is not true, for even in sexual love they serve Urania; and certainly they can serve Urania between such natures as Pericles and Aspasia, and Robert and Elizabeth Browning. I wrote that women inspire imagination in men, but lack it in themselves, having in mind the instances where women will turn away when a man thinks he needs them, his need being a perpetuation of the fuel which feeds his ecstasy. In such cases they may be better realists than men, and what seems their lack of imagination may be their realism, or their maternal wisdom acting for themselves and for the man. Women as imagination, as the Muse, received my tribute in "Ulysses," a poem which was published in the book entitled *The Open Sea* in 1921.

Did Shakespeare know the facts of life? I think he did; but Tolstoy seems to me to be right when he says that Shakespeare did not know them any better than several other creative minds. In *Romeo and Juliet, Troilus and Cressida, Antony and Cleopatra,* and in the *Sonnets* Shakespeare committed himself to some of the ironies that I have touched upon above. But he also showed himself as a lover flaming beyond almost all lovers of the world. After my years of study and reflection Shakespeare seems as close to me at times as someone in actual life. I feel him as the intensest flame that ever rose in England, or perhaps in the world. It seems to me that he was cruelly hurt, for why did he leave London and go back to the country and abandon twenty of his great plays to the chances of oblivion as they kicked about in badly printed quartos, and in manuscript in the green rooms? Something had entered his heart to make it indifferent. He is second to Homer and Aeschylus as a poet; but as a soul afire, which burned down to the anonymous dust of Stratford after about 1611, he is the high phenomenon of the world.

Further confessing, I do not find in Shakespeare, in Goethe, in Byron, in Browning, in Keats the same attitude toward passional love that I have felt almost from boyhood. Perhaps Shelley is nearest to me. I expressed it with all the power and

imagination I had in my poem "Tomorrow Is My Birthday";
but I did not fully cover the case. Perhaps I can add other
defining words now. In Shakespeare one finds ecstatic madness;
in Goethe, manly tenderness; in Byron in his best moods, a
masculine adoration and sweetness; in Browning, a worship
of woman, a willingness to suffer when rejected by her; Keats,
dying in youth, remained the dreamer who was lulled to sleep
on the cold hillside by La Belle Dame Sans Merci, as the vision
of pale kings and princes with starved lips passed before him.
But I return to Goethe and his summation of this transcendent
matter as he did it in the last chorus of *Faust*. There he cele-
brates the eternal womanly, and love as the all-uplifting and
all-redeeming power on earth and in heaven; and to man it is
revealed in its purest and most perfect form through woman.
Goethe declares here that in the transitory life of earth love
is only a symbol of its diviner being, and that the possibilities
of love, which earth can never fulfill, become realities in a
higher life which follows, and that the spirit which woman
interprets to us here still draws us upward. So here is expressed
all that I have felt of love, both as a giver of life and as a forecast of a higher sphere, as a delusion, a satiety and a deathless
force.

I dwell upon this subject because I feel that a good deal of
my secret is contained in it, and I would be glad if I could
fully express it. For myself I divine the operation of the cosmic
mind in the love of men and women, and hence I have identified a beloved woman with the mysteries of creative beauty,
with influences and magnetisms, with summons from afar. So
identifying her I have placed all the women in whom I was
deeply interested in a rôle that flesh and blood cannot often
fulfill—but to consider myself as well, what did I do to fulfill
a vision? I dreamed what Shelley dreamed when writing
"Epipsychidion," and perhaps at times I awoke in a heart what
Shelley awoke in the heart of Emilia Viviani, to whom that

ecstatic poem was addressed. She had said to him, "The soul of him who loves launches itself out of the created, and creates in the infinite a world for itself alone, how different from this obscure and fearful den." These words Shelley took for the text of his poem. They show that she understood, and, understanding, she and Shelley grasped the secret together. Having stood thus together on the sunlit peak of youth and great divination, it cannot have been amiss for his own heart that he descended into the valley and then disappeared into the sea.

If it be an English trait not to make friends quickly then I am indeed English blood, for I have liked few men instantly, and then afterward with constancy. I have had many men of the world friendships which answered well enough for all the strains that were put upon them. But I have had the high fortune to have such men as Powys and Reedy, Dr. Alexander Burke and Abraham Meyer, and H. L. Mencken for friends. Such excellent and gifted women as Harriet Monroe, Eunice Tietjens, Agnes Freer, though for many years I have seen little of them, still go in their own orbits with something of a sustaining magnetism in my life.

Perhaps I might have had more intimate friends, except for peculiarities of my own nature: first, a caution that scrutinizes; second, a taste in human beings that is easily offended, and once offended does not right itself easily; third, eyes that do not always see at first what people are, with the result that some attracted to me drift away when not received; fourth, eyes that see at once, then lose that vision through contact, and then resume it in disappointment. As a lawyer I had few intimate friends; those who were my equals differed from me in politics and in philosophies of life. One man in particular with whom I was in sympathy in many things turned out to be a costly reckoning when depended upon. I could not ally myself with the Bar Associations, since I detested the uses to which such organizations were put for the making and the interpreting of the laws. As a writer I have made few fellowships; I have belonged to no cliques, no groups, and have lacked therefore the hailing and the maneuvering which their members give each other. I have played a lone hand as a lawyer and a writer, sometimes seen and appraised by a man like John Cowper Powys. But nearly always my double personality works. I keep back a part of myself, an inner self which is aloof and in a protecting and watchful mood from those who seem by my democratic ways and my confidences to be in such intimacy with me that everything of my personality is in their possession.

At this day my life is as different and distant from my life in the Spoon River country as the scene of New York and New England is different and distant from Lewistown and Petersburg. There are several literary men in New York who know all about that Illinois territory between the Spoon River, the Illinois River and the Mississippi River, and uniformly they hate it, even as their judgments against it agree. I do not feel so strongly as that about it. The prairies are in my blood for all time, and are closer to my heart than the most beautiful part of the Maine coast, or the hills of Columbia County or the mountains of Vermont, all so much more beautiful than anything in Illinois. But no less I feel that no poet in English or American history ever had a harder life than mine was in the beginning at Lewistown, or among a people whose flesh and whose vibrations were better calculated to poison, to pervert, and even to kill a sensitive nature. Still I don't know just what Burns had to endure in this way. But certainly he had a beautiful country about him, he had a store of native balladry to nourish him, and he had great friends near at hand.

I can see in my mind's eyes the people who used to go about the streets of Lewistown on Saturdays, coming from the Spoon River bottoms: men with sore eyes from syphilis, blinking the light; men with guns or slings in their pockets, carrying whips, and fouling the sidewalks with tobacco spit; women dressed in faded calicoes twisted about their shapeless bodies. Saturdays were days of horror for me, and for my mother who dreamed to the last of upper Vermont and of Marlboro amid the mountains in New Hampshire. These creatures at Lewistown howled in their insane cups, they fought with knives and guns and knucks. The streets stank. The shopkeepers stood in their doorways eyeing chances of trade; they walked back and forth behind their counters serving the malodorous riffraff that came from the bottoms. It was not so in Petersburg, where the stores were better, where one could see old ladies like my grandmother dressed in black silk and with hands gloved with black knitted mitts at the handsome counters of Braham's store making purchases.

People ask me over and over where the town of Spoon River is located. As there is no such town, I have to answer that there is only a river. And what a river! What a small stream winding its way through flatlands, amid hills that only distance lifts into any beauty, through jungles of weeds and thickets and melancholy cottonwoods. It goes by little towns as ugly and lonely as the tin-roofed hamlets of Kansas. Yet this is the town, or one of the towns, and this is the river and the country from which I extracted whatever beauty there is in that part of *Spoon River Anthology* which relates to a village depiction, and is not concerned with a world view. I did somehow thread my way through the vile and even dangerous streets of Lewistown, terrified but unhurt, save as the scenes affected my outlook—I did thread my way through those streets to the peace of Will Winter's study, and the hill under the oak trees where Will and I sat reading Sophocles; I did escape with Anne to the woodlands of Big Creek where she read the Elizabethan dramatists to me. I had fortune, after all. Figuratively speaking, it was my brother the god who brought it to me, whom I celebrated in "The Loom" and in "Botanical Gardens." This very year he has returned to me.

Finally I did get away to Chicago, and to other spheres. If I have not reached Paradise, I did escape Hell. I have had much happiness, days at a stretch of happiness, and even months. I cannot say with Goethe that I have not had three weeks of genuine happiness in my whole life. For the moment I can't find where he said this, if he said it. But it is not my case. Writing this book has been like being resurrected from the dead, and being compelled to live my life all over again; to go through all the absurdities, the follies, the shames, the defeats and misdirections, and mistakes of adolescence, and the trials and failures and errors of early maturity, and the checkered experiences of later years. I would not live over those things again, I would not live down judgments that I formed, which I thought were right at the time, about books and men. My own case makes me wish there was a law to prevent men of thirty or less from passing judgment on works of literature. They really have not lived enough or thought enough to know what they are talking about. I would not live over again the sacrifices I made to write poetry, the shames I endured for it, the soul humiliations and sufferings I experienced which gave me power and understanding to write it. That were as foolish as returning to the stage of the zygote.

My boy Hilary is on the way, now seven as I write, seemingly endowed with my energy. He is spending this summer of 1935 with me in New York City, going about to all the places of wonder, the Bronx Zoo, the museums, the parks; and riding on the subways and the elevated, and taking boats to Coney Island, and watching the ships from the Battery. His happiness knows no bounds as mine does not to watch him. He says to his mother, "Oh, boy, mom, isn't it wonderful all the glory that's ahead of me." That's the way the future looks to him. I wish I could guide him through the woods, and even help him through woods that I never passed through myself, for his way is bound to be different from mine.

If he could take his present energy and combine it with what I know now for the enjoyment of life, and the mastery of whatever vocation or art he undertakes! If he could only use all his powers, and not just a part of them, as human beings always do, as I have always done. I feel even now that I have just tapped what is within me, and if I had had a more fortunate start in life I might have gone much farther in poetry. At that I am meditating some kind of a summation of my characters, my more than six hundred characters, in the *Spoon Rivers* which will top off, as it will surpass anything that I have done.

But above everything poetry has been the passion of my life to which philosophy and science and history have been but handmaidens. From the days when I heard the songs of Burns sung in the grammar school, when I was fifteen and sixteen, I have thrilled to harmonious words and tried to write them myself. Recently I published a poem entitled "Development," in a Greek letter magazine edited by my friend Oswald Hering. There I told my story as it relates to Homer, contrasting it with that of Browning who was reading Homer in Greek at an age when I was reading him in Pope's rhymed translation. What poetry is is set forth in Aristotle's *Poetics;* what it is in its purest form is shown in the works of Aeschylus, in Homer, in the Greeks in a word. There is the poetry of fancy and of the imagination, and the poetry that lulls and lifts, and soothes with music and pictures. But the greatest poetry is that which founds itself upon the truth which is the beautiful, and the beautiful which is the truth. It is the poetry which proves the laws of the spirit of man, and how they work to punish and to repay and always work, and how even in love, but misdirected love, the heart must pay; and how in sacrifice and good intentions gone wrong punishment comes—but how in love in the heart in defeat and in sorrow there is reward. This is the poetry to which I have devoted myself, and which I have tried to write, using all my powers at their heightened energies to write, and putting aside success in money or in any other way to write. And somehow every time I have tried to make money I have been punished. If it has been to no great result, still there is the trial I have made. Having given practically everything in life to the art of poetry, having, I regret to say, made some hearts suffer for my devotion, I should be a disconsolate man if I had totally failed. As it is I regret that I have not done better; I regret that my passion for the good has at times betrayed my hand into words that were too severe. Reedy said to me one time that he wished that the edges of *Spoon River* were not in places so sharp. He said that because he did not want to see me miswrite myself. A man can scarcely have more than one such a friend in his lifetime; but in this year of *Invisible Landscapes* my brother, the god, has returned to me after a long absence. How shall I tell about it fittingly?

As many times as I have read Homer, I did not until about two years ago become aware of the fact, in any sense to remember it, that Homer once speaks of himself. It is in line 557 in the Twelfth Book of the *Iliad*. "And hard were it for me, as though I were a god, to tell the tale of all these things." What shall I now say and where shall I begin? In the fall of 1934 and the winter and spring of 1935 I was resting in one of those valleys of thought and reflection that come after climbing hills, and before the next hill is attempted. Everything in one's spiritual life is the counterpart of the external world: it is plains and valleys and hills; it is clouds and mists over the hills, and stars hidden and trying to emerge; it is a star that shines suddenly over the hill and proves that eternal fire is not affected by the darkness of earth. There I was as still as a rock and likely to be mistaken for one. If I wore sandals they hid the cloven hoof. That star was mirrored in a pool near where I sat; but in that pool were the hermit crab, and the snail was in salt sleep. I saw them. I knew them to be the curious and distorted forms of my own nature. I know as well as anyone that there is a devil in me which turns that cyclopean eye of mine upon what I have revered and tried to cherish and keep, when it has fled me and left me to go on alone; and after gazing upon it has poured skepticism upon it. I know all that, and the fault has cost me many pangs. I know that life and delight come through giving, and through the inevitable receiving that is the creation of the gift; and that there are only hate and pain in withholding and in being withheld. I am the mad Frederick whom I pictured in a poem called "The Star" published in *Songs and Satires* in 1916, who saw the star imaged in a pool and cried to have not the image but the star itself, confessing that the star would not be escaped, but had to be served. It was the god that saw mad Frederick, who had slipped down from a remote height and hid himself amid a clump of trees to watch the madmen of the world, and to see what mad Frederick would do when he entered the wood and sat by the pool to watch figures helpless and sleepless, laughing and crying and dying, and saying to themselves that they should be content, and saying to themselves that they would fly and get out of the wood, having searched to this pass, having drunk poisoned water, having fallen with weariness, or gone mad at last. The mood and the philosophy of that poem had gone out of me since 1916. But here again was the hill, and the pool, and the star above the hill trying to emerge, and there was to be a recurrence in part of that vision, but upon a higher level.

These pages are evidence of my love of nature. In the three summers that I spent, two in upper New York, one in Connecticut, amid hills, mountains, rocky headlands, and where old houses and windmills were touched by the low-flying cloud, or bathed in silent sunshine, my boyhood moods came back to me, the city fell away from me. The city is facts, is hard reality, is lifeless stone. The country is the haunt of something universal and deathless and infinite which broods upon the earth and reflects itself in it. In communion with nature we can wrest from the gods ideas identifying life with eternity, and death which stalks the city with images of horror, of the swift hearse, of the quick business of disposing of the body—all this floats away as meaningless phantasms, as a kind of unterrifying Walpurgis Night in the presence of the hills. I was in a way of mind to take up Confucius again and to worship the earth, and to believe with him that the only civilization is one of the feelings, and that justice and happiness are worth more than the understanding and the taming of nature. And I saw with Vivekenanda that there is no other God to seek but that one which is present in all beings, and in nature. Out of this renascence of feeling and thinking I wrote the poem "Prometheus," "The Ninth Symphony of Beethoven and the King Cobra," published in *The Serpent in the Wilderness* in 1933, as well as the poems published in the volume entitled *Invisible Landscapes* in 1935; yet many of the poems in the latter volume remained hidden away as I sat in the valley wearing sandals which hid the cloven hoof. Suddenly the clouds lifted, the star came forth, and I arose and climbed the hill before me carrying my poems.

On top of the hill I sat down again, and in a moment that star came to my side, but it wasn't a star, it was Selene, and I was not Endymion, but the goat-footed Pan with horns and a puck nose, with nothing but a shepherd's flute, yet loving music as much as Apollo himself. And yet it was not Selene, it was my brother the god, that old daemon, metamorphosed in a goddess and moved by contemplation of me looking like a rock there in the valley, and with my cloven hoof in the sandals, to come to me. In China one figure rises to pre-eminence of worship. It is Kuanyin P'usa, the goddess of mercy. Her image is in every shrine. Other images face the east or south—she alone faces the north always and everywhere, contemplating the distresses of men. She is often in Taoist temples as well as in Buddhist temples, thus to identify her influence with what is the beginning of heaven and earth, without a name, and what is the mother of all things. She was originally a male saint and became a woman saint, just as Kuan Yin did, another goddess of mercy, best known to Europeans of the Bodhisattwa. Look how the eternal-womanly emerges to the heightened imagination everywhere: to Faust as Marguerite, to Christians as Mary of Nazareth, to the Chinese as Kuanyin P'usa, who was the daughter of a rich man of rank and renounced her wealth and her ease to endure every pain and torment, to descend into hell in order that she might return to console mankind.

So now with me the nature of that old, watchful, almost cruel Panlike daemon of mine was changed into a nature of understanding and devotion to nature, of love and forgiveness, and became a kind of mediatrix between powers that punish, and myself undergoing punishment there in the valley, and there climbing the hill. Over and over through those poems light played selecting them, selecting and rejecting. It was like the movement of swift, white hands, swift with intuition, white with suffering. That book came from that hill and that star that mocked mad Frederick, and reappeared as bright as Selene on Mount Latmus.

Index

Prairie State Books

1988

Mr. Dooley in Peace and in War
Finley Peter Dunne

Life in Prairie Land
Eliza W. Farnham

Carl Sandburg
Harry Golden

The Sangamon
Edgar Lee Masters

American Years
Harold Sinclair

The Jungle
Upton Sinclair

1989

Twenty Years at Hull-House
Jane Addams

They Broke the Prairie
Earnest Elmo Calkins

The Illinois
James Gray

The Valley of Shadows: Sangamon Sketches
Francis Grierson

The Precipice
Elia W. Peattie

1990

Across Spoon River
Edgar Lee Masters

The Rivers of Eros
Cyrus Colter

Summer on the Lakes, in 1843
Margaret Fuller

The Lemon Jelly Cake
Madeline Babcock Smith

Black Hawk: An Autobiography
Edited by Donald Jackson